AN UNWRITTEN FUTURE

Princeton Studies in International History and Politics

For a full list of titles in the series, go to https://press.princeton.edu/series/princeton-studies-in-international-history-and-politics

An Unwritten Future: Realism and Uncertainty in World Politics, Jonathan Kirshner

Human Rights for Pragmatists: Social Power in Modern Times, Jack L. Snyder

Seeking the Bomb: Strategies of Nuclear Proliferation, Vipin Narang

The Spectre of War: International Communism and the Origins of World War II, Jonathan Haslam

Active Defense: China's Military Strategy since 1949, M. Taylor Fravel

Strategic Instincts: The Adaptive Advantages of Cognitive Biases in International Politics, Dominic D. P. Johnson

Divided Armies: Inequality and Battlefield Performance in Modern War, Jason Lyall

Active Defense: China's Military Strategy since 1949, M. Taylor Fravel

After Victory: Institutions, Strategic Restraint, and the Rebuilding of Order after Major Wars, New Edition, G. John Ikenberry

Cult of the Irrelevant: The Waning Influence of Social Science on National Security, Michael C. Desch

Secret Wars: Covert Conflict in International Politics, Austin Carson

Who Fights for Reputation: The Psychology of Leaders in International Conflict, Keren Yarhi-Milo

Aftershocks: Great Powers and Domestic Reforms in the Twentieth Century, Seva Gunitsky

Why Wilson Matters: The Origin of American Liberal Internationalism and Its Crisis Today, Tony Smith

Powerplay: The Origins of the American Alliance System in Asia, Victor D. Cha

Economic Interdependence and War, Dale C. Copeland

An Unwritten Future

REALISM AND UNCERTAINTY IN WORLD POLITICS

Jonathan Kirshner

PRINCETON UNIVERSITY PRESS
PRINCETON & OXFORD

Published by Princeton University Press
41 William Street, Princeton, New Jersey 08540
6 Oxford Street, Woodstock, Oxfordshire OX20 1TR

press.princeton.edu

ISBN 978-0-691-16677-3
ISBN (e-book) 978-0-691-23312-3

Library of Congress Control Number: 2022938559

British Library Cataloging-in-Publication Data is available

Editorial: Bridget Flannery-McCoy and Alena Chekanov
Production Editorial: Karen Carter
Jacket/Cover Design: Lauren Michelle Smith
Production: Erin Suydam
Publicity: Kate Hensley and Kathryn Stevens

Jacket/Cover Credit: Classic image / Alamy Stock Photo

This book has been composed in Miller

Printed on acid-free paper. ∞

Printed in the United States of America

10 9 8 7 6 5 4 3 2 1

To Max and Anna, for living it, and to
Peter and Matt, for making it possible

CONTENTS

ILLUSTRATIONS

PREFACE

IT IS A common lament for authors to describe their books as longer in the making than they had anticipated. That is the case with this book as well, in the narrow sense. But it is also, I have come to realize, accurate in a much broader way. The approach to the study of world politics elaborated in the pages that follow is quite different from the one that I would have embraced in earlier stages of my professional career. In retrospect, three brief, unrelated episodes, each innocuous in their moment but which I have always recalled vividly, mark the intellectual journey that has brought me to this point. One, surely long forgotten by others but a source of some personal embarrassment, occurred during a small dinner with a visiting speaker in my first years as a professor. Bantering over current affairs, I explained that the problem under consideration would ultimately be resolved by the compelling power of market forces. "Really?" my most senior colleague immediately chimed in, "I had no idea you were so naive."

I was mortified—though I stuck to my guns. With an uncommonly strong background in economics for a specialist in international politics, I well understood both the irresistibility and implications of relentless economic pressures. I didn't budge over dinner, but my perspective would soon change, and dramatically. Coincidentally—and quite by chance, stimulated by one lucky thing that led to another—at about the same time I embarked on a close study of the writings of John Maynard Keynes. Quickly I was a convert—not to what would conventionally become known as Keynesianism but to wisdom I found in those original texts. I now saw not simply (still formidable) market power but also market failures, especially at the macroeconomic level, as well as a much broader vision of economics as a social science than I had previously been exposed to. In his brilliant memorial for Alfred Marshall, his great teacher, Keynes explained that a master economist must be parts "mathematician, historian, statesman, philosopher," who "must study the present in light of the past for the purposes of the future."

Embracing Keynes, then, I still recognized and respected the considerable power of market forces, but the implications of those pressures I now understood to be considerably less straightforward than I once thought—and they were filtered through crucial social and political complexities. (And that dinner would have been different.) More generally, although the

Keynesian revolution had profound implications for understanding economics, increasingly I saw parallels to the application of those lessons for International Relations theory. Keynes, it should be stressed, was neither a Realist nor an IR theorist—he was a liberal civilizationalist and instinctively a pacifist, if one with a sharp, savvy, and unblinking eye for the dangerous currents and consequences of power politics. But the example of Keynes's approach to economics increasingly informed my study of world politics, with its emphasis on uncertainty, unknowns and unknowables, the indeterminacy of systemic pressures, the importance of history, and his red-line distinction between studies of the social world, which must deal with the motivations of its subjects, and the natural sciences, which do not.

The second moment occurred some years before my unhappy dinner. In graduate school, I was fortunate to take a seminar from one of the scholars who helped invent the subfield of international political economy—the politics of economic relations—something that was not much studied in the United States in the 1950s and 1960s, for reasons that a story he commonly shared makes obvious. "I would give these talks about the political underpinnings of economic affairs, and was invariably besieged by critics castigating me for embracing a Marxist perspective," my professor recalled. "But I was a philosophy major in college," he continued, "and I was pretty sure I wasn't a Marxist." In recent years, I have had a parallel experience, giving talks about realism and international relations that were often received with furrowed brows and the protestation "that doesn't sound very realist to me." Well, I'd been studying international relations for a few decades, and I was pretty confident that I was a realist. In some ways this book is a longer answer to that challenge.

Finally, there was an encounter that occurred quite early in my undergraduate years. International politics was already an intellectual passion of mine (that was why I chose this particular college), and naturally I attended a gathering of students and professors for a largely social event highlighted by comments from distinguished faculty members in the discipline, designed to welcome and encourage prospective majors. Several of those who participated would become valued mentors (I call on their advice still today). But the most memorable speaker that evening was an idiosyncratic senior scholar of considerable repute but with whom I was not familiar. He tended to glance at the ceiling when he spoke, as if referring to notes that had been taped there, and offered comments along the lines of "to study international relations is to suffer." As he explained, you return to study a phenomenon, again, and again, and again, each time realizing that you now see it in a different way—and that the clear, confident conclusions drawn previously had invariably slipped from your command with each new visit.

This seemed like an odd way to recruit students, I thought at the time. And more to the point, I didn't buy it. To the contrary, I was confident that the world could be readily understood, and that dedicated study would yield, in the words of another scholar whose work I admired enormously, an "asymptotic convergence towards the truth." I still revere that scholar, who was, justly, something of legend among my cohort of emerging professionals. But decades later I find myself peeking up at the ceiling much more often than I would have thought.

AN UNWRITTEN FUTURE

Introduction and Overview

THE PURPOSE OF this book is to elucidate an approach to the study of world politics—Classical Realism—and to demonstrate why that paradigm is a productive and valuable one, and one that is urgently needed for describing, explaining, and understanding events in world politics. Classical Realism is a minority perspective in contemporary International Relations (IR) theory. The realist community, to the extent that it exists, is overwhelmingly dominated by the influence of structuralism, that is, by an approach that models states as identical units distinguished only by their relative capabilities. Since the 1980s, this school of realist thought has become so predominant that both champions and critics of realism routinely conflate the two (realism and structural realism). Much of the larger field of IR is in the thrall of a similarly abstract bargaining model of politics, a paradigm rooted in the building blocks of individualism, materialism, and exceedingly narrow assumptions regarding the rationality of actors—a perspective so extreme (and ruinously unproductive) that it is best described as hyper-rationality. Structural realism and hyper-rationalism perform poorly when applied to the real world, due to basic errors that are hardwired into the core of their analytical apparatus. Each purports to (and boasts of) a more "scientific" approach to the study of world politics, superseding previous, allegedly less rigorous perspectives, such as classical realism.[1] But structural realism and hyper-rationalism, grasping for an illusion of scientific precision evident in style but empty in substance, have failed. This book seeks to reclaim realism, and rearticulate classical realism as a worthwhile and even vital point of departure for the study of world politics.

In clarifying what this book is, it is also important to make clear what this book is not. It is not, it should be stressed, a comprehensive overview of theories of or approaches to IR, or even for that matter an exhaustive survey of the subgenres and specialized schools of thought within realism itself. Nor, beyond its essential, motivating confrontations with structural realism and hyper-rationalism, is this book participating in "paradigm wars," or insistent that to be a good student of world politics, it is necessary to be a realist or a classical realist. The goal of reclaiming realism, and illustrating what it is, and why it is a productive and informative approach to understanding and explaining world politics, need not step on the toes of most other perspectives. Certainly realist approaches are commonly and understandably contrasted with liberal perspectives, which generally take as points of departure greater emphases on individual interests and material incentives, stress problem solving over irresolvable political clashes, and tend to place less emphasis on the urgency of the consequences of anarchy and the barriers to mutually beneficial cooperation. A realist tends to flip each of those cards over—nevertheless, a confrontation with liberalism is not on the agenda here.

This essential attribute is worth repeating. This book is not, remotely, an overview of IR theory. It is the articulation and application of one approach to understanding and explaining world politics, with an emphasis on how that approach contrasts with its two principal intellectual adversaries, varieties of structural realism and hyper-rationalism. Thus readers will not find in these pages a deep engagement with liberalism or with other contrasting (or presumably contrasting) perspectives. This is purposeful. The almost ritual rehearsal of clashes between realism and liberalism—the nadir of which was the academic "paradigm wars" of the 1990s—has been as ubiquitous in IR theory as it has been unproductive. *Paradigms* are inescapable. *Paradigm wars* are largely vacuous, as the differences between them are rooted in distinct philosophical dispositions and underlying, non-falsifiable grounding assumptions that cannot be definitively adjudicated and settled. Classical Realism has no real productive "argument" with liberalism to engage—they are different (but in many instances overlapping) ways of seeing the world, and theories derived from these contrasting traditions will commonly, but not necessarily, lead to contrasting explanations (and often, but again not necessarily, contrasting policy prescriptions).

Similarly, this book does not take a deep dive (or even much of a shallow one) into constructivism, or dwell on the all-too-common (and largely presumed) contrast between realism and constructivism. At the time of its emergence some realists recoiled, like Dracula from the sunlight, from the very notion of constructivism, because many of its early contributions seemed to suggest that some international conflicts might be transcended by processes of learning and socialization. But there is nothing inherently pacific or hopeful or ameliorative in the abstract about the consequences of, say, distinctions rooted in identity affiliations, notions that only make sense from a constructivist perspective (as group identities are socially constructed) and which can be drivers of fierce and intractable violent conflict. Fascism, to take a related example, is readily understood from a constructivist perspective but is invisible to structural realism and essentially incomprehensible to hyper-rationalism. Constructivism is indeed incompatible with *structural* realism. And, with its emphasis on the social-historical-cultural context of what actors want, it also exposes the limitations and poverty of much hyper-rationalist work, which insouciantly assumes away fundamental political questions in favor of doing some math at the margins. Nevertheless, constructivism is not inherently incompatible with classical realism. In fact, classical realism draws on one of constructivism's fundamental points of departure: that what individuals, groups, and states want (beyond some minimal achievement of food, shelter, and physical security) is not uniform across actors but shaped the perceived lessons of history and the social-cultural environment in which behavior takes place.[2]

Distinguishing Classical Realism

Not surprisingly, classical realism and structural realism share some basic underlying assumptions. They both, after all, self-identify as realist. In fact, the thinkers who, in the middle of the twentieth century, developed the approach now called classical realism simply thought of themselves as realists, full stop (just as Mozart and his contemporaries never thought of themselves as writing "classical" music). In IR the moniker only became common decades later, as structural realists sought to distinguish what they were doing from their intellectual predecessors (which is also why the term "neo-realism," implying a new, updated version of realism, is a synonym for structural realism). Adding the modifier "classical" to the seminal contributions of the past also helped suggest a sheen of modernity to the neo-realist project, which, as a rhetorical device, further gestured at the notion of scientific progress.

Nevertheless, the common roots of both incarnations are clear. Any realist perspective takes as its point of departure the consequences of anarchy—that is, in world politics there is no ultimate authority to adjudicate disputes, and in particular, there is no guarantee that the behavior of others will be restrained. Autonomous political units (typically but not necessarily states) must look out for their own survival—because no one else will. And the stakes could not be higher, as human history is littered, from the ancient past to the present day, with countless episodes of horrifying barbarism. This in turn means that states must be alert to the power and military capabilities of others, since the distribution of power will inform the nature of the threats and challenges that all states face. Note that realism is not distinguished by these assumptions—most approaches to IR theory embrace the anarchy fable—it is distinguished by the emphasis that it places on anarchy and its consequences.

Structural realism stops there: with states, dwelling in anarchy, as "like units" differentiated only by their relative capabilities. The analysis is thus limited to the effects of systemic forces generated by the interaction of states, that is, from the distribution of power and changes to relative capabilities. Classical realism includes much more than that. It considers both power and purpose—and insists that world politics can only be understood by attending to both. From this follow a number of basic divergences from structural realism. The first is that history matters. From a classical perspective, you cannot understand how states will behave without knowing what received lessons loom large in their historical memories. In contrast, "like units" dwelling in anarchy (and hyper-rationalists at the bargaining table) act as if they have no past—they see only what is placed in front of them (like that guy in the movie *Memento*)[3] and make their calculations accordingly. Another basic classical realist divergence from both neo-realism and hyper-rationalism is its assumption that states dwell not simply in an environment of anarchy but also of uncertainty—they do not know what will happen next. This is not because the intentions of others are opaque (though they often are), or because the world is probabilistic, but because actors do not know exactly how the world works—in many instances they do not even know for certain what their own reactions will be to events three steps down the road, and only find out when they get there.[4] A world of uncertainty is also a world of contingency—one thing leads to another, in ways that cannot be predicted. Relatedly, classical realism also diverges sharply from structural realism with the view that politics matters. That is, states, and especially great powers, are not simply subject to the forces generated by the structure of the international system; their behavior—that is, the choices they make—in turn shapes the incentive structures of the international system. Structural realism focuses on the imperatives imposed by the need for security; classical realism emphasizes the fact that states, and especially great powers, can choose from a menu of distinct policy postures and dispositions (each of which would plausibly ensure security), and that those choices will in turn shape the choices made by others.

Finally, and crucially, classical realism parts company with purportedly scientific approaches to world politics with the observation that even if such efforts were successful, they typically yield abstractions of little practical value. Because in international relations, the important accomplishment is not to be able to make an informed estimate about the likely behavior of an average state in a typical moment—it is almost invariably about understanding the potential reaction of a particular state at a critical and novel juncture. Given that states can safely and plausibly respond to external stimuli in a number of different ways, otherwise similarly situated states will respond to them differently, because they will have different preferences, and also make varied guesses of their own about what will happen next, and why. The paths chosen will not be obvious in the abstract. The craft of classical realism requires dirty hands.

Critics of classical realism dismiss this approach as "unscientific." This is, at best, empty rhetoric and at worst an invitation (and often a command) to bark up the wrong analytical trees. Structural realism is perhaps analytically pristine; hyper-rationalism rigorous in appearance. But what do they tell us? As *An Unwritten Future* will make abundantly clear, about world politics structural realism tells us very little—and nothing we did not already understand; the bargaining model is fatally undermined by its misguided core assumptions.[5] At the end of the day, with British philosopher Carveth Read, classical realism holds that "it is a mistake to aim at an unattainable precision. It is better to be vaguely right than exactly wrong."[6] Furthermore, chasing the implicit holy grail of exactly right, for the social sciences, will prove to be a snipe hunt. Social relations are slippery, and causes and effects of social phenomena invariably change over time, complexities that are compounded by the fact that events will lend themselves to a multiplicity of interpretations.[7]

This is not nihilism—to the contrary, it is analytical modesty, and an attentiveness to the discipline required to distinguish what, as students of world politics, we can and cannot hope to achieve. Understanding international relations is harder than many would have us believe. But the challenge is a vital one—lives are literally at stake in getting these questions right. In that spirit, the aspiration of this book is to articulate classical realism, to clarify the basic tenets of the perspective, to demonstrate its practical utility, and to present and illustrate in practice the analytical tools that it draws on. Beyond its mission to reclaim realism, however, and to illuminate the strengths (and weaknesses) of the approach, this book is not evangelical—everybody need not be a realist—in fact, that would surely be a bad thing. But all students of world politics will be better equipped with an understanding of the classical realist disposition, and the ways in which it describes, explains, understands, and anticipates events in world politics.

The Richness, Utility, and Relevance of Classical Realism

Chapter 1 lays the groundwork for what follows by distilling the foundations and core principles of classical realism from the contributions of some of its most accomplished thinkers. It begins with a close engagement with Thucydides, and his book *The Peloponnesian War*, a history of the epochal conflict between the Greek city-states Athens and Sparta late in the fifth century BCE. This immediately raises an important question—why? What could possibly be relevant for analysts of contemporary world politics from an account of an ancient conflict provided by an exiled participant—and one who would not have recognized the very concepts of international relations theory in general or realism in particular? In a word, everything. Put another way (and this is a mental game worth playing), if I was only allowed to assign one book to students of international relations, it would be *The Peloponnesian War*, which is resplendent with compelling and timeless insights into political behavior, and from which can be derived a host of lessons that are foundational for classical realism. The discussion that follows elucidates ten of those lessons, the most important and enduring of which are an alertness to the fragility of civilized order and the danger of great power hubris. (Both of these are invisible to structural realism; the latter of course is incompatible with hyper-rationalism.)

A serious engagement with Thucydides is also rewarding and requisite because his work has been enormously influential across the long history of realist thought, contributing insights that will be central for many of the episodes and analyses engaged throughout the course of this book. In addition, an attentive engagement with *The Peloponnesian War* is obligatory for all students of world politics, because shallow readings of this grand work are all too common, with Thucydides invoked simplistically, superficially, and erroneously to lend gravitas to otherwise featherweight arguments. But pulling a few selected passages from Thucydides is akin to that old joke about a day tour of Paris, in which, without breaking stride, the guide makes a sweeping gesture of the hand to announce, "And that is the Louvre Museum."

This first chapter also reviews the insights of a number of realist thinkers, ancient and modern, with an emphasis on the contributions of a handful of figures who, in the middle of the twentieth century, saw themselves as purposefully and explicitly establishing a realist approach to the analysis of world politics. Prominent among this cohort are Hans Morgenthau and Raymond Aron (Morgenthau's *Scientific Man vs. Power Politics* [1946] is perhaps the representative work of this perspective), and the foundations of contemporary classical realism can be derived from the writings of these and other scholars from that era.

Chapter 2 makes the case for reclaiming realism at the theoretical level, by challenging the internal logic of the approaches that avow to have superseded it. Each of them draws, formatively, on appeals to and transplantations of economic theory. Structural realism derives its basic inspiration from a market scarcity analogy in general and oligopoly theory in particular; hyper-rationalism embraces in whole cloth the core assumption of Rational Expectations Theory, regarding the ways in which actors receive and process information.[8] A closer look at each of these theories, however, illustrates that these approaches do not offer a scientific step forward but an unproductive step back. In particular, an attentive examination reveals that structural realism is based on a fundamental misreading of oligopoly theory, which not only fails to support the few basic conclusions that structural realism would draw from it but in fact is suggestive of outcomes to the contrary of those conclusions. As for Rational Expectations, it turns out that the theory is deeply flawed and empirically dubious, and, although perhaps plausibly productive for addressing a modest subset of particular economic questions, it is nevertheless inherently and irretrievably inappropriate for addressing questions of war and peace.

Establishing these points is important—but doing so involves getting under the hood and taking a close look at these engines of inquiry. Although not mathematical, such examinations can get quite specialized, detailed, and technical, and general readers with less interest in academic debates (or those who need little convincing of the points on offer) can safely skip to the last part of the discussion in this theoretical inquest, "The Craft of Classical Realism," without losing the thread of the central arguments of the book. This last section situates the practical application of classical realism in the general landscape of IR theory, as fundamentally informed by a proper understanding of the implications of the economic analogies reached for by others. In sum, and stated most plainly, one big reason for a renaissance of classical realism is that its would-be successors don't make sense. Not only do they misguidedly aspire to a certain type of scientific practice, they also get the science wrong.

Having made the case for the merits of classical realism in theory, *An Unwritten Future* then turns to illustrating its utility in practice, by applying the approach to two of the great puzzles in twentieth-century international politics: Why did Britain appease Nazi Germany, placing itself within a hair's breadth of brutal subjugation, and why did the United States ruinously and unnecessarily sink so much of its blood, treasure, and reputation into what was an obviously misguided adventure in Vietnam? In the first puzzle, two explanations are closely associated with a structural realist perspective. Both suggest that the enigmatic behavior is well explained exclusively by logics of power politics: buck-passing and buying time. The former attributes the sluggish pace of British rearmament to a strategy designed to force their ally France to bear more of the burden of countering Germany and spend more on defense (little matter that the French nevertheless did not do so). The latter holds that Prime Minister Neville Chamberlain, the principal and dedicated architect of British appeasement, was no fool; rather, he was cleverly buying time to confront Hitler when the country would be in a better position to do so. But the evidence does not support the contention that Britain, although certainly eager for France to do more, was motivated primarily, or even much at all, by buck-passing. And Chamberlain was perhaps no fool, but he was a supercilious prig who willfully and fundamentally misread Hitler. He wasn't buying time—the evidence shows plainly that he was bending over backward, indeed executing a series of Olympics-worthy reverse handsprings, in a tireless and fruitless effort to make the German Fuhrer happy enough that he might lose his taste for war. Ultimately it is not possible to understand the behavior of Britain (and European powers more generally) without appealing to two variables forbidden by structural approaches: history and ideology. The relevant history is World War I—no understanding of the behavior of Britain and France, among others, in the interwar years is possible without accounting for the influence of that trauma on those societies. And no explanation of appeasement can fail to acknowledge the important role of ideology in shaping that strategy—in particular, the fact that most of the elites directing British foreign policy in the 1930s were comfortable with the notion of a fascist Germany dominating the continent.

The Vietnam War is another seminal experience that illustrates how classical realism outperforms its structural cousins. The standard structuralist-rationalist explanations for such episodes generally fall under the rubric of "power cycle theory," which locates the source of distress for dominant states in naturally occurring shifts to the balance of power, which make the status quo more difficult for them to maintain and create vexing challenges at the eroding frontiers of their influence. Classical realism reaches for different variables in explaining these costly catastrophes. In parsing these contrasting perspectives, and illustrating again distinctions between structural and classical realism (and the necessity for the latter), it is illuminating to take a close look at the finest articulation of power cycle theory, Robert Gilpin's *War and Change in World Politics*. One of the landmarks of twentieth-century realist analysis, *War and Change* is nevertheless distinguished by a tension between its structural and classical elements—a tension that Gilpin acknowledges but fails to resolve. As a dynamic structural theory, the book attributes the relative decline of dominant states to a number of factors, central among which is a (plausibly postulated) tendency for the costs of maintaining the status quo to rise. But Vietnam did not demonstrate the atrophy of American power at the frontiers of its reach—it showed the pathologies that come with *too much* power. Thucydides would have had little trouble identifying the root cause of America's follies in South East Asia (and decades later, in its ill-advised war of conquest against Iraq). It did not come from the dispassionate calculation of costs and benefits at the margin—it was the arrogance of hubris.

Having made the case, in theory and practice, for the utility of classical realism, *An Unwritten Future* then pivots to a studied consideration of the problems with, and the limitations of, realist approaches in general and classical realism in particular. Typically, this sort of stock-taking is an afterthought, taken defensively or as a late inoculation against anticipated criticism. But we pause here to interrogate realism, because, having made big claims in the first part of the book, it is necessary to cast a critical and jaundiced eye at the reflection in the mirror. This was, notably, the approach taken by E. H. Carr in his seminal *The Twenty Years' Crisis*, which, having first castigated intellectual opponents and then established "the realist critique," immediately turned to a bracing consideration of "the limitations of realism" not quite midway through the volume. For classical realism, doubt is not an afterthought—it is an essential part of the enterprise. Exploring the limits of realism at this juncture also fits well because many of the questions raised there speak to issues that reemerge in the investigations that follow. Tugging at the frayed edges of the concept of the National Interest, which is central to any realist analysis, introduces questions that are reprised in the subsequent discussion of how economic factors can shape the nature and trajectory of that interest—something often assumed to be fixed and inviolable. Wrestling with the often vexing relationship between "is" and "ought"—that is, between detached analysis and policy advocacy—is a challenge for most scholars in the social sciences whose work touches on issues with real-world relevance. This conundrum resurfaces as one of the many problems with John Mearsheimer's theory of "offensive realism," which frankly conflates the two—an unpardonable analytical sin. And probing the limits of that ubiquitous realist watchword, prudence, implicates challenges associated with power vacuums and the fate of the American Order that are considered in this book's final pages.

Chapter 5 considers political economy. It is the discussion that already-on-board realists will be most likely to skip over—and the one that they can perhaps least afford to. Although there have been notable exceptions, realist analysis throughout history has had a tendency to be tone-deaf to questions of political economy, a failing that was especially common during the Cold War, the peculiar circumstances of which were permissive of such selective attention. But the Cold War is long gone. Economic relations between the Soviet Union and the United States didn't much matter—the same cannot be said of the United States and China in the twenty-first century. And the point is a general one: it is simply not possible to understand world politics without an alertness to and facility with economic issues. Any attempt to understand the origins of World War II, for example, must include a consideration of the consequences of the Great Depression; in the twenty-first century, it would be naive to overlook the extent to which China's role in the world economy has transformative political implications. The discussion in these passages offers a general guide to realist political economy, tracing its distinct dispositions, assumptions, and expectations. And once again structural realism comes up short in addressing these questions, as it leans on apparently abstract generalizations that were in fact derived from the idiosyncratic Cold War experience.[9] Classical realist political economy also highlights an often crucial variable again invisible to structuralism (and generally overlooked by rationalist approaches that stress individualism and materialism): how the social economy—that is, the assessments of groups within societies of the fairness, opportunity, and prospects on offer—can influence the ability of a state to adroitly pursue its international interests.

Chapter 6 is similar in purpose and design to chapter 3. It looks at an important question in international politics—the consequences of the rise of China as a great power in the twenty-first century—and contrasts problematic structural arguments with more nuanced classical insights. Two influential approaches to this question, Mearsheimer's theory of offensive realism and Graham Allison's notion of a "Thucydides Trap," are fundamentally flawed, with basic problems that again expose the limits of structuralism. Mearsheimer's argument is plainly deterministic.[10] For this alone the theory of offensive realism ought to be ushered quickly to the door, but its problems run even deeper than that—as will be elaborated, the argument is logically incoherent, even on its own terms. As for the "Thucydides Trap," it is based not simply on a regrettably shallow reading of *The Peloponnesian War* but on one that is routinely wrong about basic aspects of the book—and thus, not surprisingly, misguided in the conclusions it would draw from that work. This chapter also includes a consideration of the experience of interwar Japan, which offers a virtual laboratory for illustrating the distinct strengths of a classical perspective. An episode of enormous significance and consequence, the discussion will illustrate why analyses that withhold the deployment of classical tools—the role of historical legacies, uncertainty, contingency, contestation, and exogenous shocks (that is, most notably, structural realist approaches)—will fail to comprehend what happened, and in turn fail to grasp the lessons to be learned. It is simply not possible, for example, to understand the behavior of interwar Japan on the world stage without attentiveness to the profound pressures and challenges that defined its social economy in those decades. And the twists, turns, and pitched debates about its grand strategy from the 1920s into the 1930s plainly reveal that multiple trajectories for its international behavior were possible, and that those prospects were shaped by politics, international and domestic. All of these factors (and the case of interwar Japan generally) are of great relevance for understanding world politics a century later, in particular with regard to the rise of China—about which a classical realist approach must be pessimistic. Classical realism expects emerging powers to be ambitious, and arrogant (a disposition that is typically not in short supply among the satisfied guardians of the status quo as well), suggesting a clash not just of interests but also of temperaments that will make disputes, which will inevitably arise, more difficult to smoothly resolve.

An Unwritten Future concludes with a return to first principles: to anarchy and its consequences, and to the necessity of attending to both power and purpose, in the context of uncertainty and contingency, in order to understand world politics. Anarchy here is considered in its broader, more Thucydidean conception, which includes a sensitivity to the fragility of civilization and its implications. This underscores again the influence of a country's social cohesion, which in turn weighs heavily on its prospects and conduct. Illustrating this is a final historical excursus, to France in the 1930s, a society characterized by radical polarization and an embrace of unreason—and described by Raymond Aron, an eyewitness, as a country defined by little more than its vehement internal divisions.[11] This discussion is not a detour but a destination, one that illuminates how societies—even apparent great powers—can rot from within, and that this, even more than the external threat environment, can determine the prospects for their survival. A fearsome-looking, muscle-bound fighter might prove to have a glass jaw, and fetishizing the physique (apparent power) risks overlooking less visible but ultimately decisive vulnerabilities (social cohesion). Thus better understanding interwar France matters as an important case in its own right, but it is also illustrative. It showcases enduring classical conceptions through which both the establishment of and, especially, the unraveling of the American-led post–World War II international order can be seen more clearly. As with European powers after World War I, it is simply not possible to understand the United States as an actor in world politics in the 2020s without reference to formative trauma that inform its purpose in that moment: hollowing trends in its social economy (greatly exacerbated by the global financial crisis of 2008 and its aftermath) and the bitter experience of losing two long overseas wars. Efforts to describe, explain, understand, and anticipate American behavior without reference to those two phenomena may be precise and parsimonious. But they will come up empty.

Classical realism suggests a different path forward. It is, perhaps, a bit gloomy in its expectations. But fortunately, the future is unwritten.

CHAPTER ONE

What Is Classical Realism?

THUCYDIDES AND HIS DESCENDANTS

REALISM IS NOT a "theory"—it is a point of departure, a philosophical disposition, an approach associated with a constellation of theories that derive from a set of commonly shared assumptions.[1] As such, a variety of contrasting, even competing theories can be developed following this tradition.[2] Thus although any particular theory informed by realism can be evaluated for its deductive logic and empirical consistency, "Realism," like any philosophical disposition, cannot be "proven wrong." But although realists will often disagree with one another on aspects of both theory and the practical implications of those theories, they do derive their theories and root their expectations by drawing on the same set of analytical building blocks.

This chapter introduces and defines Classical Realism, establishing its core principles and general themes. It briefly reviews the contributions of a number of classical realists, both ancient and modern, to derive and explore the essential elements of the paradigm. To be clear, however, this engagement with past masters is not intended to be exhaustive or comprehensive, or to parse their contributions in close Talmudic study, nor to suggest their infallibility or uniform nature—and certainly not to genuflect before them. Rather, I revisit these standards as inspirations that indicate a shared (or at least largely overlapping) set of assumptions and principles that collectively constitute the essence of Classical Realism.

Realist analysis of world politics begins with an emphasis on the consequences of anarchy. Observing anarchy (the absence of an ultimate authority to adjudicate disputes) is not distinct to realism—placing the ominous consequences of anarchy as the fundamental point of departure for understanding international relations is. Realists need not insist that war is imminent, or even likely, but they believe that states must condition their behavior to acknowledge war as a real possibility. And it is not simply the prospect of "war" that states must understand as a possibility—in anarchy, there are no assurances that the behavior of others will be restrained. Conquest, savagery, subjugation, and even annihilation are possibilities, and have been, and remain, features of human relations since time immemorial. Once again, it is not that behaviors will necessarily be unconstrained, it is that they *may* be unconstrained, and there are simply no guarantees that the worst might not occur.

Given this foundational point of departure, states (or any set of groups dwelling in anarchy) must be attentive to the balance of power (that is, to the potential capabilities of others), to the distribution of those capabilities across states, and, most crucially, to changes to the balance of power over time, which is a primal engine of conflict. States must also attend to the intentions of others (an enormous problem as such intentions, especially projecting into the future, can never be known with certainty), as behavior in world politics is a function of both power and purpose. Power may be the ultimate arbiter of disputes between states, but purpose—what states want—will define the nature and intensity of the disputes between them.[3]

The mere existence of anarchy does not necessarily imply horrors—many groups that dwell in anarchy get along just fine, and enjoy warm relations with each other, even for indefinite periods of time. And as the weakest state is, by orders of magnitude, more secure and robust than the most capable individual, anarchy between states need not be the wretched horror that Thomas Hobbes imagined what might have been the "state of nature" between men—in his famous phrase: "solitary, poor, nasty, brutish, and short."[4] Nevertheless, although we may not be on the edge of the abyss, Realism is especially sensitive to the notion that the ground can crumble beneath our feet with surprising suddenness. Civilization, however apparently robust, is fragile. As John Maynard Keynes wrote of his content, confident cohort in the heady years of peace and prosperity before the then-unimaginable catastrophe that was the Great War, "we were not aware that civilisation was a thin and precarious crust." Rather, he compared his youthful contemporaries to "graceful water-spiders," dancing along the surface, guided by a "thin rationalism skipping on the crust of the lava."[5] It is the portion of realism to stare glumly at the volcano (even those that might appear dormant), in grim anticipation of the worst.

Part of this wariness is dispositional. Realism tends to have a pessimistic view of humanity. Moreover, the perspective is also pessimistic regarding the prospects of human improvement. Stressing continuity over change in the nature of the beast, and thus in the character of politics, Realism is unimpressed with the notion that humans today are better, smarter, or wiser than those of the distant (or recent) past—man has been, and remains, a potentially very dangerous animal who, especially when pressed, can descend into barbarism. Classical Realists in particular also tend to model their actors as ambitious (given the opportunity to have more, they will pursue it, as opposed to reaching a plateau of satiated satisfaction) and motivated not simply by material interests but by fear, status, and notions of honor.

These last three influences on the nature of interest complicate matters mightily. Fear means that even though actors have material goals, they will temper their pursuit of such goals in the shadow of (inescapably subjective) notions of perceived insecurity. And even absent such concerns, human motivations are not reducible to material benefits: people also seek status, comparing their station not simply to satisfy endogenous desires but in reference to what others have, and they crave respect. Notions of "honor" sound anachronistic—or perhaps vaguely Klingon—but they profoundly shape behavior. Many if not most people, for example (even controlling for health and safety concerns), would not choose to work in the sex trade industry, even if it meant a considerable increase in salary. Honor simply means that people value the esteem of (some) others, and thus, once adequately fed and safely sheltered, will pursue their material interests in the context of the normative structure of the group with which they identify.[6]

Individuals are the ultimate actors in world politics; therefore assumptions about human behavior are inherent to (and consequential for) any paradigm, even if they remain implicit. And so the assumptions enumerated above matter. Nevertheless, another foundation of realist analysis is to locate the unit of analysis as the group, not the individual, and to place an emphasis on political goals as an important factor in motivating behavior. (In contrast, for example, liberalism typically focuses on the individual pursuing personal material gain as its point of departure.) Realism models humans as identifying with groups, and making foundational (if malleable over time) distinctions between those inside and outside the group. Political conflict in anarchy takes place between these groups, not between individuals, with the measure of success or failure calculated by these competing collectivities. This is why Realism tends to place great emphasis on the group interest, or the "National Interest," which is not preordained and can shift over time but, crucially, is distinct from the summation of the individual interests of the members of the group and is not invariably reducible to economic gain. Thus the National Interest is distinct, but it is contestable, with conceptions of the National Interest inescapably informed by interpretations of the perceived lessons of historical experiences. It is impossible to know what states want without knowing where they have been.

The presence of distinct groups, each placing a higher value on their own needs, interests, and desires than those of other groups, in the context of anarchy, leads Realism to expect international politics to be characterized by inevitable conflicts of interest. Disputes between states are not simply the result of misunderstandings or failures to achieve mutually beneficial cooperation (although those pathologies can certainly occur) but are largely and simply manifestations of those clashing interests. This conclusion does not mitigate the enormous significance of the Security Dilemma. Indeed, the articulation of the security dilemma—that measures taken by one state to increase its own security (even by a state without any aggressive intentions) can make other states feel less secure, and that factors which influence the intensity of the security dilemma are important determinants of when mutual insecurities or conflicts of interest will spill over into war—is the most significant contribution ever produced by IR theory.[7] Nevertheless, Realism expects international conflict between states to be inevitable, even among those—perhaps especially among those—which (like most great powers, most of the time) are not motivated by fears that their survival is at stake. World politics is characterized by active, varied political contestation between actors with opposing interests.

An additional consequence of this, and still another core attribute of Realism, is that politics never ends. The clash of interests is endless, and resolving one clash (say, through a decisive war that leads to a clear victor and vanquished) will soon enough be followed by a new set of contestations. (A classic example of this is the short trip from the end of World War II, the epochal struggle against fascism that surely settled matters definitively as far as German and Japanese ambition was concerned, to the dawn of the Cold War, but the phenomenon is a general one.) There is no end zone in world politics—one political dispute will be followed by another, and implacable foes in one round will at times find they share interests in a latter, and vice versa. (Athens and Sparta, mortal rivals during the Peloponnesian War, had not long before been allies during the Persian wars.) From this perspective, disputes in world politics are less problems to be solved than relations to be managed.

One reason for this is that the power, and thus consequentially the purpose and ambition of actors in the international system, is constantly in flux, and so new challenges, previously latent or unanticipated, are constantly bubbling to the surface. More generally, Classical Realism in particular is attentive to dynamics, the expectation that the balance of power will inevitably change over time, and assumes that states' ambitions tend to grow in tandem with their capabilities. Realism in general also aspires to assess these changes with a certain analytical dispassion, emphasizing the realities of power and claiming to see the world as it is (a descriptive enterprise—one does not blame a volcano for erupting or a lion for eating a zebra), rather than as one might wish it to be. This is easier said than done—lions rarely read and write philosophical tracts—and raises vexing normative issues that will be addressed in chapter 4. But although most would agree on some easy calls (genocide is bad), realist analysis tends to be very wary of making moral evaluations about the behavior of states, and, in particular, in assessing disputes between them, is extremely cautious about labeling one right and the other wrong. With Jean Renoir in *The Rules of the Game*, realists share the view that "the awful thing about life is this: everyone has their reasons."[8]

Finally, Classical Realism is characterized by its analytical modesty—a profound awareness of what students of world politics do not know, and cannot know. Classical Realism emphasizes uncertainty and contingency in recognizing the wide and unpredictable range of the possible. In economics, the global financial crisis of 2007–8 rekindled debates about the distinction between risk and uncertainty (in the former, the underlying probability distribution is knowable, in the latter it is not). The failure of macroeconomic models based on assumptions of "rational expectations" has led to renewed interest in articulations of uncertainty associated with Keynes and, notably, two prominent anti-Keynesians as well, Frank Knight and Friedrich von Hayek.[9] (As discussed in chapter 2, the failure of rational expectations theory in economics presents an irretrievable blow to many theories of IR, such as those derived from the influential bargaining model, that embrace a fatally flawed interpretation of how to define rationality.)

Classical Realism has always embraced uncertainty. As I will discuss presently, this, and many other of the core tenets introduced above, can be traced all the way back to Thucydides, who, despite crafting his narrative to foreshadow events that he wished to emphasize, nevertheless repeatedly illustrates how, but for unpredictable developments, important events in his *History* could have turned out differently. International

Relations takes place in the context of uncertainty; to choose war (even when wise) is to plunge headlong into radical uncertainty. For these reasons, although Classical Realism models its actors as rational—that is, they have a good sense of what they want, can order their preferences, and, within the context of what they know, reach for any number of strategies that are internally consistent (even if others, similarly situated and motivated, might make other choices)—they are nevertheless rational muddlers, making guesses while invariably swimming in unfamiliar waters, not clean machines playing some version of computer chess. Thus the range of choices they might make can be plausibly anticipated, but, shaped as they are by varying, implicit theoretical models of how the world works and informed by distinct historical experiences, those choices are impossible to predict.

Classical Realism also holds to a reserved analytical modesty due to its dyed-in-the-wool sensitivity to the fundamental, unbridgeable distinction between the natural and social sciences. As a technical matter, because in the social world the choices made by the objects of analysis can shape outcomes, the behavioral relationships between variables are unstable: the speed of light is constant; but social relations are malleable and influenced by experience and ideas, even if human nature itself changes little over the centuries.[10] Because the choices made by states will be made in the context of their own historical experiences and because those choices will influence the environment in which other states make their choices, in world politics, the future is unwritten. Even as Classical Realism aspires to analytical rigor and searches for generalizable tendencies and productive anticipations, it does so chastised by the admonition of indeterminacy.

In short, Classical Realism is defined by its attentiveness to the inexorable dangers implied by anarchy (latent or present), a need to respect the realities of power (the capabilities of others, the inevitable limits of one's own), and an anticipation that world politics is characterized by conflicts of interest (with the resolution of one disputation soon followed by another), all in the context of irretrievable uncertainty.

It's (Almost) All in Thucydides

Much of the essence of classical realism was articulated by Thucydides, in his book, *The Peloponnesian War*—though certainly he did not use the word "realist" nor fancy himself a "theorist of international relations," concepts (and academic specializations policed by vigilant gatekeepers) that did not exist in his time. Yet his account of the epochal twenty-seven-year war (431–404 BCE) that took place between the Greek city-states of Athens and Sparta (actually two ten-year periods of active fighting interrupted by a simmering, unstable seven-year interregnum) was designed to explain and understand the origins, course, and context of the conflict, and as such is easily recognized speaking to questions of politics and international relations.

Why should contemporary scholars of international politics take Thucydides seriously? His *History* describes a war that took place millennia ago, an epic confrontation between two slaveholding city-states, filled with battles between spear-wielding hoplites and oar-driven triremes; it includes passages of contested provenance and ends abruptly in mid-sentence. Nevertheless, modern IR scholars (and students of politics more generally) are richly rewarded by studying with care *The Peloponnesian War*, which, to borrow a literary phrase, is a heartbreaking work of staggering genius.[11] The Athenian general, in exile for most of the war, had the time, resources, and, most important, the disposition to observe the war—and engage in a thorough inquest into its causes and course—so that future generations might profit from his exposition and insights. In these efforts he was astonishingly successful. And despite the fact that classicists report the prose is often very challenging, countless passages (in translation) are visionary, viewed in whole cloth the book is masterfully crafted, and Thucydides' commitment to accurately reporting the facts exemplary.

For the student of international politics, however—especially in the context of the purpose of this discussion—care must be taken not to be drawn into three Thucydidean controversies: did he get the facts right, did he get the war right, and did he have a distinct point of view? Regarding the facts, classicists and historians of ancient Greece have, understandably, devoted extensive attention to assessing, with laudable care and spirited contestation, the accuracy of some of Thucydides' claims. The allure of following the thread of these tantalizing debates is considerable, so much so that it becomes necessary to keep in mind what most matters for IR. In particular, for the game to be worth the candle—that is, if Thucydides is worth taking seriously—then two plausible assumptions must hold: that Thucydides was a prodigious thinker, and that he was committed to an honest exposition of the facts as he understood them. This means, for IR theory, it does not matter if he made some factual errors. What matters for IR is not the exact details of an ancient war but the wisdom to be found in what Thucydides had to say—though it is worth noting that Thucydides did go to heroic efforts to gather all the relevant material and to carefully adjudicate between competing accounts when they arose. Specialists tell us that what he reports is generally consistent with the fragmentary evidence (such as surviving inscriptions) that is available to contemporary scholars.[12]

As for the war itself, Thucydides offers, despite his "just the facts" presentation, an account that is inevitably interpretative. And that interpretation could easily have been wrong. Thucydides tends to blame neither side for the initial outbreak of the war, but rather stressed a systemic variable, the changing nature of the balance of power. (It should be emphasized that although Thucydides stresses this as the underlying cause of the initial war, his account of the conflict that followed—its contours, course, and, notably, its outcome—draws almost entirely on non-systemic factors, including leadership and domestic politics. And the central episode of the war for Thucydides, and the cause of Athens's ruin—the Sicilian adventure—was not a consequence of systemic pressures.)

But Thucydides need not have been correct about this. In *The Outbreak of the Peloponnesian War*, Donald Kagan—whose scholarship is often eager to contest Thucydides' accounts—contra Thucydides, blames Athens for the conflict.[13] And not so much as a result of its rising power, but due to its increasingly sharp elbows in a variety of international political disputes. For Kagan, Athens's serial troublemaking eventually "put the Spartan war party into power," and even then, a sluggish Sparta had to be roused into action by the Corinthians and other allies that had suffered at the hands of Athenian aggression.[14] In contrast, G. E. M. de Ste. Croix in *The Origins of the Peloponnesian War* reaches the opposite conclusion. Engaging Kagan explicitly as a foil, de Ste. Croix rejects the view "that Athens was the aggressive party in 433–1" and reports that he has "no doubt that the real aggressors were Sparta and her allies." Both scholars, if with somewhat different shadings, highlight the role of the Corinthians in considering the origins of the war.[15]

Thus Thucydides' conclusions are certainly contestable—as are the variables he chose to emphasize (or downplay). His account tends to place less emphasis on economic factors (among others) than others might. Some scholars of the war, for example, have placed great emphasis on the Megarian Decree—essentially economic sanctions imposed by Athens on Megara that Sparta clearly wanted lifted. It is widely understood that Thucydides downplayed the significance of the decree. As Robert Connor explains, Thucydides "never gives a full account of the matter; instead he introduces the decree obliquely"—an assessment universally shared by Thucydidean scholars.[16] Perhaps economic pressures and incentives were more significant to the causes and course of the war than Thucydides suggested. For classical realism, this matters not.

Consider the finest dozen of the flood of books that were published on the occasion of the one hundredth anniversary of the start of World War I. Most of these were written by accomplished historians marshalling facts and formulating arguments. Each of these accounts, written with scholarly integrity, is contested by others. Which is definitively correct? That remains an open debate, despite the fact that the documentary record is vast, commonly maintained with meticulous care, and widely accessible. In contrast, Thucydides' account of his ancient war remains the only substantive history that we have. Had ten other accounts been written at the time of the war, with each author making good-faith efforts to objectively present the evidence, Thucydides' arguments and interpretations would have no doubt been contested—he surely made errors, and certainly had a point of view. But we don't have access to that debate; moreover, tidying up various factual errors and omissions in *The Peloponnesian War* would not change what Thucydides has to offer IR theory: the lessons that he would have us draw from his account of the war. These remain whether or not his arguments regarding the causes of the war or his interpretations of events during its course are "correct"—something that, it should be noted, are likely unknowable, given the ancient nature of that conflict.[17]

Thucydides is distinguished by his admirable, even heroic efforts to learn the facts of the matter and look at them unflinchingly, but also by his point of view—and the latter remains of enduring practical relevance. No historical account can pretend to be simply a recitation of "just the facts." Indeed, this is where Thucydides' genius lies—and why his treatise remains so rewarding, even as the events he recounts recede ever further into ancient (and ultimately unknowable) history. As Jacqueline de Romilly observed, Thucydides "strives so impressively for perfect scholarly objectivity," but at the same time, "the author's intervention is profound. Everything in it is the product of his construction and his will. Every word and phrase, every silence and remark, serves to present a meaning made distinctive and imposed by him." Centuries earlier, Thomas Hobbes, one of the first to translate *The Peloponnesian War* into English, shared a similar revelation: although Thucydides never digresses "to read a lecture, moral or political, upon his own text," nevertheless, "the narration itself doth secretly instruct the reader and more effectually than can possibly be done by precept."[18]

Even assuming that every word reported by Thucydides was precisely accurate—an unrealistic standard for any work of history, and an impossible one for Thucydides, who often adjudicated between multiple oral accounts of events he did not witness, and by his own explicit acknowledgment at times recounted versions of speeches as he thought they would likely have been—there would still inevitably remain the weighty consequences of editorial choice. What to include, what to elide; what to dwell upon at length, what to summarize perfunctorily; what to juxtapose, what to hold apart—ultimately, implicit judgments about what events *mattered*, and which did not—none of these choices are a function of the facts. They are the essential craft of narrative nonfiction.[19] And in gleaning lessons from Thucydides, we need not shrink from this "narrative" element in play here. As one scholar observed, Thucydides most effectively uses a technique of "extreme narrative deceleration" to dwell on moments he wishes to invest with meaning.[20] Especially as the centuries pass, the space between Thucydides, the careful historian drawing on the craft of storytelling, and Tolstoy, the brilliant novelist drawing closely on historical events that he witnessed, is ever narrowing.[21] Which is not to suggest that Thucydides "just made stuff up"[22] but rather, like a documentary filmmaker, he had a point of view.[23]

Both explicit authorial judgment (relatively rare in *The Peloponnesian War*) and, more to the point, the power of narrative choices are apparent in Thucydides' treatment of Pericles. Thucydides' overt praise is clear: he considered Pericles among the Athenians the "ablest alike in counsel and action" (1.139.4) and offers a long, laudatory assessment of his life as "the best man for all the needs of the state" (2.65.4), one whose passing contributed directly to Athens's ultimate defeat (2.65.7). More subtle, and more rhetorically powerful, is the way Thucydides presents Pericles' three major speeches in the *History*—his advocacy for the war, the famous funeral oration, and a final, brilliant rallying of the citizenry during a difficult moment of public despair in the aftermath of the plague near the end of the second year of the war. Each time, Pericles speaks alone, as Thucydides withholds any other voices—what would often have been sharply dissenting voices. This is most obvious with Pericles' initial call for war. Thucydides tells us "there were many speakers who came forth to give support to one side or the other" (1.139.4), but he shares only the words of Pericles, who thus appears to stand alone and unchallenged on the stage. This inevitably privileges his perspective, in a speech that one prominent Thucydides scholar argues "could stand as a summary of Thucydides' thought in the whole first book."[24]

It is this, Thucydides' thought, his point of view, often only indicated by the ingenuous way he crafts his history, which is primordial of much of Classical Realism.

The Great Teacher

Thucydides, as noted, surely made his share of errors, and his accounts are necessarily filtered through the lens of his own distinct perspective. Nevertheless, *The Peloponnesian War* comes close to offering something of a Rosetta Stone for Classical Realism.[25] This section reviews ten foundational tenets of the paradigm expressed in those pages.

From start to finish, Thucydides reminds his readers of ***the stark consequences of anarchy***: behaviors may be restrained, norms may be respected, and actors might behave in a civilized fashion. But they might not—and nothing guarantees that the very worst will not come to pass. In one early episode, Thucydides pauses to make the observation that the Corinthians, after routing one adversary in battle, "butchered as they sailed through, not caring so much to take prisoners" (1.50.1). A military commander in the Athenian empire, Thucydides did not shrink from the prospect of war nor the bloodshed that combat would necessarily entail. But his revulsion at the wanton exercise of gratuitous violence is palpable—as is his awareness that such episodes are often the bitter harvest of anarchy. Thucydides also dwells at length on that moment when, "in the fury of the moment," the citizens of Athens voted to put to death "the whole adult male population of Mytilene, and to make slaves of the women and children" before having a change of heart after a second day of debate, in which the decision was narrowly overturned (3.36.2). But before the reader can exhale, the narrative shifts to Plataea, where the Spartans deliver the brutal fate that Mytilene avoided, for no other reason than Sparta's desire "to please the Thebans, who were thought to be useful in the war" (3.68.4). Other such episodes abound, such as the annihilation of Scione, as the Athenians "put the adult males to death . . . making slaves of the women and children" (5.32.1), and Sparta "killing all the freemen that fell into their hands" after capturing the Argive city Hysiac (5.83.2) before marching on to plunder Phlius.[26]

Thucydides also had much to teach about the imperatives of power and the exigencies of politics with passages that have not aged a day since he first articulated them. Everywhere, ***the balance of power profoundly shapes decisions***. Consider the peripheral conflict that emerges as the proximate cause of the war, the confrontation between Corinth and Corcyra. Should Athens allow itself to be drawn into the conflict, in defense of neutral Corcyra against Sparta's ally? Much talk ensues, but ultimately Thucydides, in the guise of reporting the events as they occurred, guides the reader toward the compelling logic: Athenian power rested on its naval dominance; Corcyra, the weaker power, possessed a formidable navy. And "no one was willing to see a naval power of such magnitude as Corcyra sacrificed to Corinth" (1.44.2). Similarly, Sparta's motivations in this confrontation were rooted in the importance of maintaining its relationship with Corinth, lest they, as threatened, be driven "in despair to some other alliance" (1.71.4), whereas, they assured, "if only you will act, we will stand by you" (1.71.6).[27] Once again, throughout the work, balance of power concerns routinely tip the decision-making scales: one reason Sparta agreed to the peace of Nicias was an awareness that its peace treaty with long-time Peloponnesian rival city Argos was about to expire. Such influences were common and widespread. Faced with a shared threat from Athens, the feuding cities of Sicily set aside their differences. Late in the war, Persia modulated its support for Sparta with an eye toward playing one rival against the other.

Attentiveness to power dynamics—that is, the notion that changes to the balance of power are much more consequential than its distribution at any moment in time—is Thucydides' most visible influence on contemporary IR theory.[28] "The growth of the power of Athens, and the alarm which this inspired in Sparta, made war inevitable" (1.23.6) is likely the most quoted sentence from his epic tome. It is eminently reasonable to quibble, as many specialists have, with the word "inevitable" (especially given Thucydides' general and steadfast rejection of determinism); moreover, as always, he could certainly have been wrong. And indeed that element of Thucydides has in fact been too influential, gestured at by scholars who would lazily reduce a nuanced and sophisticated thinker to a crude structural determinist, with ideas condensable to bumper-sticker friendly slogans.[29] But that Thucydides saw this as the true cause of the initial outbreak of the war is hard to dispute, and as if to make sure the point is clear he offers a reprise of the argument ("the Spartans out of fear of you want war," 1.33.3) and then doubles down explicitly on the claim (the Spartans chose war "because they feared the growth of the power of the Athenians," 1.88.1).[30]

In his exposition of seemingly endless political jockeying between rivals (and often erstwhile allies), Thucydides also illustrates the open-ended nature of international politics—described above as the realist tenet that ***there is no end zone*** in world politics, rather, the resolution of one conflict gives way to new clashes that had been lurking on the horizon, or just beyond. Disputes are not misunderstandings to be resolved but result from inevitable conflicts of interest—and the resolution of one contest simply reveals the next waiting in the wings. (Even Athens and Corinth, whose animosities were key triggers of the great Peloponnesian War, were close allies before 460, after which their relations soured over a number of issues.) That fluidity of contestations are the stuffing of international politics is most apparent in Books V and VIII of *The Peloponnesian War*, which are often criticized for their relative raggedness. But to some extent those parts of the book reflect periods where such political tumult was most salient: first after the peace of Nicias (which brought the first ten-year phase of the war to a close) and later in the turbulent aftermath of the Sicilian catastrophe. Regarding the former, many of Sparta's allies opposed the peace of Nicias, and the most intriguing development of an alliance between Corinth and Argos followed. Similar shifts fill the narrative of Book VIII, which anticipate Palmerston's nineteenth-century adage that Britain did not have permanent allies or enemies, only interests.[31]

Realists of all stripes embrace these first four Thucydidean tenets, but the balance of his grand lessons are associated distinctly and closely with Classical Realism. This is certainly true for Thucydides' ***emphasis on content and purpose***, and not simply power, in explaining the behavior of actors—which he famously roots to three principal motivations: fear, honor, and interest. In contemporary IR scholarship it is more common to limit the analysis to interest (and often the pursuit of individualist-egoistic, exclusively material interest). But Thucydides' anonymous Athenians speaking before a Spartan assembly (surely one of the passages he reconstructed, at best) attribute the factors that drive foreign policy: "fear being our principal motive, though honor and interest afterwards came in" (1.75.3). Interest certainly matters, but fear comes first, yet another reminder that all pursuits take place under the shadow of anarchy. And interest is formatively shaped by honor—what actors want, and how they pursue it, is influenced by a sense of what is honorable. This more than opens the door for—it demands attention to—the distinct social-cultural context of political action.

It ought not to be surprising, then, to learn that *The Peloponnesian War* lingers extensively on domestic-level variables, with Thucydides emphasizing ***the important role of regime type and*** (what would later be called) ***national character***. These arise on innumerable occasions, in matters large and small. Regime type is a crucial explanatory variable in *The Peloponnesian War*; one modest example among many is when two of Sparta's allies hedge their bets about joining an emerging coalition, "thinking Argive democracy would not agree so well with their aristocratic forms of government as the Spartan constitution" (5.31.5). Domestic politics are also at the root of Sparta's eventual disenchantment with the peace of Nicias, for "the ephors under whom the treaty had been made were no longer in office, and some of their successors were directly opposed to it" (5.36.1). And Thucydides also attributes the success of Syracuse—important in explaining the outcome of the war—to the fact that they "were most like the Athenians in character" (8.96.5).

This question of national character looms large. In the first great debate of *The Peloponnesian War*, featuring the foundational speeches of the Corinthians, the Athenians, and the Spartan leaders Archidamus and Stenelaidas, it is a central theme. The contrast of character of Sparta and Athens is stressed at length by the Corinthians (1.69–1.71)—in particular when expressing their frustrations with Athenian opportunism and Spartan passivity—and forcefully in Thucydides' own voice, appealing to "the wide difference between the two characters" in explaining how events unfolded. Scholars have argued persuasively that even Thucydides' account of the consequences of the changing balance of power can only be properly understood when filtered through his elaborate elucidations about the national characters of Athens and Sparta, the distinction between which is arguably the overarching theme of his entire *History*.[32]

Thucydides also expected democracies to behave differently than non-democracies, and not necessarily in a good way. Another common thread that winds its way through the narrative is his concern that democracies will be carried away by the malevolent schemes of charismatic demagogues. Such passages can be especially dispiriting to read today, but the point is more general, and again, at odds with other schools of realism and hyper-rationalist IR scholarship more generally—Thucydides clearly thinks that ***leadership and diplomacy matter***—not to fill in details but to explain outcomes (and once again, this a notable tenet of Classical Realism). The consequential role of leadership, good and bad, is never far from the narrative of *The Peloponnesian War*; savvy diplomatic maneuvers often bend the branch of history as well. In one passage Thucydides (2.65.11–13) underscores the crucial influence of both leadership and domestic politics, when, as Jeffrey Rusten argues, he "seems to trace Athenian defeat to a single cause, a lack of unity which began after Pericles's death."[33]

The Peloponnesian War also speaks to Classical Realism with its emphasis on the ***central role of uncertainty and contingency*** in explaining outcomes.[34] Thucydides goes to great lengths to show that things need not have occurred as they did. On numerous occasions votes on momentous issues are very close—and at times decisions reached are reversed (which certainly suggests that either result was plausible). Notably, even the initial decision that led to the war—the Athenian decision to come to the aid of Corcyra—was a close call, in which sentiments shifted over the course of two assemblies. "In the first there was a manifest disposition to listen to the representations of Corinth; in the second, public feeling had changed" (1.44.1). Similarly, the outcome of crucial battles is often determined not by the calculable correlation of forces but by the unforeseeable interventions chance and blind luck—an earthquake here, a storm there, an unplanned detour that proved decisive. Both of these elements were present in the Mytilene affair, which featured two close votes, the second of which overturned the brutal sentence of the first; Thucydides then provides a breathless account of how a second Athenian ship was "at once set off in haste" and overtook the first, tasked with "so horrid an errand" in the nick of time (3.48.2–4). Thucydides' emphasis on chance and radical contingency—that we don't know what's going to happen and things could have turned out very differently—even extends to his discussion of the Sicilian campaign. His suspenseful narrative, featuring dashing ships and races against time, suggests that, even there, things could have turned out differently—an acknowledgment that in no way undermines what is clearly understood and easily described as his position regarding Sicily: the way to avoid that "colossal disaster" was "not to invade in the first place."[35] Indeed and more generally, alertness to uncertainty also informs the realist instinct for prudence (about which more in chapter 4). The Spartan king Archidamus, whom Thucydides praises as "a wise and moderate man," advised against rushing into war with Athens, warning that "the course of war cannot be foreseen" (1.72.2, 2.11.4)—an adage illustrated by the narrative of *The Peloponnesian War* time and time again.

Finally, Thucydides offers two profound insights—really more warnings than lessons—about the ***fragility of civilization*** and the ***danger of hubris***. Of the many insights and admonitions to be found in *The Peloponnesian War* (and there are still more lessons than those ten highlighted for our purposes here), these most plainly fulfill Thucydides' ambition to offer, with his *History*, "a possession for all time" (1.22.4). Thucydides' concern for the fragility of civilized order is illustrated by the extent to which he lingers on the consequences of the plague that ravaged Athens in the second year of the war. With the tumult of the plague, "Men now did just what they pleased, coolly venturing on what they had formerly done only in a corner" (2.53.1). Similarly, during the Corcyrean revolution, men took to "butchering those of their fellow citizens whom they regarded as their enemies" and "death raged in every shape; and, as usually happens in such times, there was no length to which the violence did not go" (3.82.2). As Simon Hornblower argues persuasively, "the importance of this section for the student of [Thucydides'] own opinions cannot be exaggerated."[36] This concern helps explain why Thucydides so often dwells on peripheral events and atrocities, even those that take place in settings "of no strategic significance," such as the grisly, murderous rampage of the Thracians at Mycalessus.[37] Here and elsewhere Thucydides slows the narrative with passages that make clear how easily war can lead to the crumbling of that thin layer of civilization.

Thucydides was also deeply concerned about the consequences of years of war on the very character of Athens as he envisioned it. This explains one of his most dramatic "extreme narrative decelerations": the Melian dialogue. Obviously, Thucydides thought the encounter important—he stops the narrative of the war in its tracks for this digression. But any thoughtful reading of *The Peloponnesian War* must reckon with the question of why. Melos was a trivial backwater whose fate was of no military significance.[38] Nor was it necessary to dwell on the episode to illustrate the perils of anarchy—by this point in his *History*, Thucydides had provided numerous examples of polities that were similarly annihilated, too weak to resist their heartless, marauding conquerors; others would follow. Nor is the extensive Melian dialogue needed to teach about the stark implications of what centuries later would be called realpolitik. The Athenians lectured on this point in Book I, defending their behavior before the Spartan assembly: "it has always been the law that the weaker should be subject to the stronger" (1.76.2). As Mynott notes in his commentary, this would be "a recurring theme in the work."[39]

Melos stands out only for its narrative purpose. When contrasted with the debate over Mytilene in the fourth year of the conflict, the Melian dialogue, which takes place a dozen years later, illustrates how years of war have hardened and hollowed a once-admired Athenian society. Mytilene was a relatively well-privileged and capable ally; its rebellion was, from an Athenian perspective, treacherous, dangerous, and potentially precedent-setting. Melos, in contrast, was a small settlement on the periphery of the action, whose crime was simply that it sought to avoid subjugation. Yet over Mytilene the Athenians deliberated and then modulated their (still punitive) response; at Melos they were unreflectively barbaric.[40]

Politics in Athens would turn decisively ugly as the war reached its later stages. Not long after dispatching the Melians, Thucydides describes how "the Athenian people grew uneasy and suspicious" and became convinced that "oligarchic and monarchial conspiracy" was afoot (6.60.1). In the "state of agitation" that followed, mob rule prevailed and suspects were herded into prisons as "public feeling grew daily more savage." In a particularly chilling passage that echoes through the millennia to follow, one prisoner "was induced . . . to give information," but whether his coerced confession was "true or not," Thucydides reports, it is impossible "to say for certain" (6.60.2). Nevertheless, the Athenian people "at once let go of the informer and all the rest whom he had not denounced, and bringing the accused to trial, executed as many as were apprehended" (6.60.4). It is not so long a trip, it would seem, from civilization to barbarism.

And then there is the greatest lesson of them all: Thucydides' exposition of how, as Pericles had feared, it was not the power and designs of adversaries that led to Athenian defeat and ruin but rather hubris, in the form of reckless over-ambition. (Pericles, who died in the third year of the war, had assured the citizens of Athens's victory in the coming struggle with Sparta, "if you can consent not to combine schemes of fresh conquest with the conduct of the war," adding a phrase that would haunt innumerable military disasters over the following centuries: "indeed, I am more afraid of our own blunders than of the enemy's devices," 1.144.1). Thucydides clearly endorsed these sentiments.[41] And indeed Athens fell, not because it was overtaken by rivals (and not because it was overcome by systemic forces beyond its ability to influence) but because it became intoxicated with the idea of its own greatness, and could not recognize the limits of its own power.[42] There are two crucial moments in the text where Thucydides drives home this essential argument. First, in year seven of the war, Sparta suffers a disastrous setback at Pylos and offers terms to Athens, which they describe as "satisfactory to your interests, and as consistent with our dignity in our misfortune as circumstances permit" (4.17.1). The Spartans urge Athens to recognize that good fortune, not final victory, had contributed to their advantageous present circumstances—the underlying balance of power had not much changed, if, admittedly, Sparta had suffered a terrible setback. "Indeed, sensible men are prudent enough to treat their gains as precarious, just as they would keep a clear head in adversity" (4.18.3). Unfortunately, Thucydides reports, "the Athenians, however . . . grasped at something further" (4.21.2) and rejected the offer—though soon enough "they began to repent rejecting the treaty" (4.27.2).[43]

Grasping for more at Pylos is, of course, just a preview of the central episode of Thucydides' entire narrative—the disastrous decision to try to conquer Sicily. And here again, the Melian dialogue served a distinct and pointed narrative purpose, as with one final sentence Thucydides describes the annihilation of Melos; with the very next, he wrote, "The same winter the Athenians resolved to sail again to Sicily . . . if possible to conquer the island" (6.1.1). Melos captured Athens at the height of its arrogance; Sicily would be the site of its comeuppance.[44] This central episode is the topic of Books VI and VII of *The Peloponnesian War* (about a quarter of the work), as Thucydides, in the most closely argued passages of his opus, lavishes close and detailed attention on the campaign. The Athenians "were now bent upon invading; being ambitious in real truth of conquering the whole" (6.5.1).

This need not have been. Nicias—and it is very hard to argue that Thucydides does not fully endorse his perspective—urged against the enterprise in public debate, with compelling (and all too accurate) admonitions. "You leave many enemies behind you here to go there far away and bring back more with you," he warned. Athens "should not be grasping at another empire before we have secured the one we have already" (6.10.1–5). Although Nicias was (rightly) concerned that Sparta remained the principal danger to Athens, he also noted, wisely, that the Sicilians "even if conquered, are too far off and too numerous to be ruled without difficulty" (6.11.1), and urged the Athenians to reject this "mad dream of conquest" (6.13.1).[45] His advice, of course, was rejected. How did it go for the Athenians? In Thucydides' words: "They were beaten at all points and altogether; all that they suffered was great; they were destroyed, as the saying is, with a total destruction, their fleet, their army—everything was destroyed, and few of many returned home. Such were the events in Sicily" (7.87.6).

Hunter Rawlings argues persuasively that "Thucydides clearly regards the Athenian adventure in Sicily as the greatest event of his war, and its conclusion as the greatest event in Greek history."[46] Athenian arrogance and hubris turned one-time allies into unhappy, hostile vassals (just as the Melians predicted such behavior would); and at two critical junctures, from a position of relative strength and security, Athens foolishly and voluntarily embarked on adventures that led to its own destruction. It is Thucydides' most singular warning: the gravest threat to the security, integrity, and civilization of a great power lies not with the designs of its adversaries, nor the tragic implications of anarchy, but from the arrogance of power.

Forging Classical Realism: From Ancients to Moderns

Classical Realism as a school of thought of international relations theory was largely developed in the middle third of the twentieth century, timing that reflected the fact that IR theory in general, as a distinct scholarly discipline, itself only emerged in the twentieth century. The global horrors of modernity: the incomprehensible mass slaughter that was World War I, the immiserating catastrophe of the Great Depression (worsened considerably by the failure of international cooperation), the world-in-flames apocalyptic brutality of World War II, and, immediately following, fears regarding the all-too-real prospect of nuclear annihilation not surprisingly generated urgent imperatives for the systematic study of world politics.

Nevertheless, twentieth-century Realism was visibly influenced by the contributions of a number of primordial thinkers—philosophers and writers whose work transcended disciplinary boundaries (as such things did not yet exist) and are ill-suited to be described as "IR theorists" but whose influence on realism is unmistakable. It bears repeating that the purpose here and throughout, regarding the visitation of canonical figures, is not to be comprehensive or microanalytical, nor (most certainly not) to suggest the infallibility of or lockstep conformity across these thinkers. It is instead an attempt to distill some common themes and wisdom, especially as they pertain to the contemporary practice of Classical Realism.

Two thinkers who are commonly (and properly) associated with the disposition of realist international relations theory are Thomas Hobbes and Niccolò Machiavelli. Hobbes, who was enormously influenced by Thucydides (in explaining conflict, his emphasis on the motivations of "gain," "safety," and "reputation" clearly echoes Thucydides' triptych of interest, fear, and honor), articulated and explored the foundational notion of anarchy (the "state of nature") and its perilous consequences that characterize the setting of world politics.[47] (It should be noted that Hobbes largely focuses on anarchy between men, not states, and the leap from individuals to collectives profoundly complicates the implications of anarchy.) Machiavelli, a complex figure whose "true" positions remain actively contested (on many topics his two most enduring works gesture at opposing conclusions), is generally associated with the aphorism "the end justifies the means."[48] In an IR context, that ruthlessly chilling dictum reflects the position that given the ultimate implications of pitiless anarchy, any action taken to ensure the survival of the state is justifiable. This extreme conclusion is eminently contestable and, I would stress, plainly untenable; as noted this and other philosophical issues will be considered more closely in chapter 4. More comfortably and uncontroversially within the mainstream of realist thought is Machiavelli's urgent reminder that from anarchy, there is no escape, even if the barbarians are not yet visible at the gate. "A common defect of men," he warned, was their tendency "not to take account of the storm during the calm."[49]

Productive academic careers have been devoted to the close study of each of these two thinkers, but it is possible to briefly note some of the themes associated with their writings that look back toward Thucydides, and in turn inform the thinking of modern realism.[50] Both model individuals as more than just security seekers, but as harboring considerable ambition, and they stress the relative or positional grounding of those ambitions, and cravings defined not by endogenous needs but, both emphasize, by envy—people want what others have. Hobbes describes men "continually in competition for Honor and Dignity," with each invariably "comparing himself with other men"; Machiavelli stresses "the envious nature of men," observing that "men hate things either from fear or from envy." With characteristic pessimism, neither sees a possibility of ever satisfying such ambitions (Machiavelli declares "human appetites are insatiable"; Hobbes sees "a perpetual desire . . . of power after power").[51] This instinct, of course, has been the taproot of considerable misery throughout history, for if ambitious have no limit, the constant drive for "more" will surely invite overreach and finally prove self-defeating. Or as the notorious Alcibiades put it, advocating for the disastrous Sicilian campaign (deploying rhetoric the ultimate implications of which a more thoughtful person might have contemplated): "we cannot fix the exact point at which our empire shall stop; we have reached a position in which we must not be content with retaining what we have but must scheme to extend it for, if we cease to rule others, we shall be in danger of being ruled ourselves" (6.18.3).[52]

Two additional pre-twentieth-century figures have had a particularly salient influence on Classical Realism as it later emerged: Carl von Clausewitz and Edmund Burke. Again, neither of these thinkers are properly described as "IR theorists." Clausewitz was a military strategist; Burke was a politician, polemicist, and philosopher, whose legacy would have a formative influence on modern conservatism. More narrowly of interest here is Burke's emphasis on prudence, a concept of enormous significance for Classical Realism more closely considered in chapter 4, and which also importantly informed Keynes's approach to uncertainty, a condition essential to Classical Realist analysis and elaborated in chapter 2.[53]

Clausewitz bequeathed to Classical Realism two iron laws (these are not exclusive to Classical Realism, but they are central to its understandings). The first, once again plainly visible in Thucydides, is the crucial, inescapable role of uncertainty in both politics and war. The future is not only unknown, it is unknowable, even in a probabilistic sense. Regarding war, his area of practical expertise (a career military man, he was a prominent figure in many of the great battles of the Napoleonic wars), Clausewitz explained, "No other human activity is so continuously or universally bound up with chance." (Tolstoy, born three years before the Prussian general's death, obsessively researched those same battles for his magisterial *War and Peace* and reached a similar conclusion: "Every battle . . . fails to come off as those who planned it expected it to. That is inevitable.")[54]

A more distinctly Clausewitzian contribution was his understanding—which so many throughout history and to the present day have tragically failed to grasp—that the use of force only has meaning in its political context. The most famous quote from his magnum opus, *On War*, is "war is nothing but a continuation of policy with other means." But this particular homily does not most plainly capture his principal point. Better still is: "The political object—the original motive for the war—will thus determine both the military objective to be reached and the amount of effort it requires." That is, it's not whether you achieve military victories—or inflict severe damage on the enemy—rather, the metric of "success" with regard to the use of force is solely and simply the extent to which it achieves the political goals for which it was introduced. "The political objective is the goal, war is the means of reaching it, and means can never be considered in isolation of their purpose." And still one more, because the point is so foundational that it is hard to overemphasize: "No one starts a war—or rather, no one in his senses ought to do so—without first being clear in his mind what he intends to achieve by that war and how he intends to conduct it." In studying war, then (or for that matter, conflict more generally), it is necessary to understand the political purpose of its participants.[55]

Burke similarly informed Classical Realism (and again, one can imagine Thucydides nodding along) with his concerns regarding hubris and emphasis on uncertainty. It is perhaps counterintuitive to find the impressive might of one's own homeland to be a cause of concern, but it was indeed for Burke, because power is always dangerous, even in one's own hands: "Among precautions against ambition, it may not be amiss to take precaution against our *own*. I must fairly say, I dread our *own* power and our *own* ambition; I dread our being too much dreaded. It is ridiculous to say we are not men; and that, as men, we shall never wish to aggrandize ourselves in some way or another." As for uncertainty, Burke could not speak more clearly: "Circumstances are infinite, are infinitely combined, are variable and transient; he who does not take them into consideration is not erroneous, but mad."[56]

Defining Contemporary Classical Realism

Classical Realism emerged as a recognizable school of thought in the middle of the twentieth century, in response to international traumas of that time.[57] To establish the contours and core elements of the paradigm, I will draw principally on the contributions of five figures: E. H. Carr, George F. Kennan, Hans Morgenthau, Raymond Aron, and Robert Gilpin. In so doing, it remains necessary as always to take note of the usual truckload of qualifications, of which three in particular stand out. Certainly, many other scholars made important contributions to this tradition (and several of those will join the discussion that follows). Second, our interest remains in the themes, not the thinkers; so the engagements that follow are designed to sketch key arguments associated with each (which are commonly shared by all)—not to take deep dives into canonical oeuvres. Finally, and most important, this is not an exercise in hagiography—far from it. Realism envisions humans as not just fallible but routinely compromised and commonly flawed; realist thinkers enjoy no exemption from these qualities. Carr frequently disappoints, and it is an open question how someone who was so wrong about Hitler and so naive (at best) about Stalin might be permitted to be called a "realist"; a close read of Kennan reveals sentiments that cause the reader first to squirm and finally to recoil; as Stanley Hoffmann observed of his mentor Raymond Aron, "his tendency to see every side of every issue" at times muddied the analytical and moral clarity of his arguments. This list is easily extended.[58] Nevertheless, individually and collectively, these five thinkers set down the markers that well define classical realism.

The endless and inevitable conflict of interests. With his book *The Twenty Years' Crisis, 1919–1939* (first published in 1939), E. H. Carr can lay a claim to making the foundational statement of twentieth-century realism. Written, as most things were in the interwar years, under the imposing, pitch-black shadows of the Great War and the failed peace that followed, Carr's principal target was a version of liberalism, which he dismissed as utopianism. He rejected the hopeful aspiration that war could be replaced by international law, treaties, and well-intentioned international organizations. (The Kellogg-Briand Pact of 1928, for example, by which its signatories agreed to renounce the use of force to settle disputes, was an exemplar of the naive utopianism that *The Twenty Years' Crisis* sought to redress.) Carr's principal critique of a liberal/legalist approach to world politics was that, drawing from liberal economic theory that stressed the mutual gains from unfettered economic interaction, the utopians similarly imagined international politics as a venue where interests were again harmonious—and this was simply not so. Rather, he argued sharply, "the doctrine of the Harmony of Interest was tenable only if you left out of the account the interest of the weak who must be driven to the wall." And even more pointedly (since who would not see "peace" as a good and welcome thing), he rejected the assumption that "every nation has an identical interest in peace." In many instances, to insist on "peace" is simply to insist on privileging the status quo, and Carr (and Classical Realism more generally—Arnold Wolfers also articulated this point) is unwilling to assume that the status quo is any more legitimate than a given set of arrangements that might replace it. The assumption of the harmony of interests, Carr lectured, "evade[s] the unpalatable fact of a fundamental divergence of interest between nations desirous of maintaining the status quo and nations desirous of changing it." Rather, world politics boils down to this: "The clash of interests is real and inevitable; and the whole nature of the problem is distorted by an attempt to disguise it." (Reinhold Niebuhr, if more gently, also took as his point of departure the inevitability of divergent interests as the engine of political conflict between groups.)[59] Realism requires attentiveness to these inevitable clashes of interest, and, just as important, the discipline to not assume that one side or the other holds the higher moral ground. "A transaction, by becoming legal, does not become moral," Carr explained—more likely it reflects the balance of power between the participants at the time when the agreement was reached. And like Thucydides, he emphasized dynamics as a crucial cause of conflict. Carr's expectation was that as the balance of power shifted over time, disenchantments with ways of doing things based upon the old order would inevitably follow. Since war was normatively a bad thing—a waste of blood and treasure (here at least, Carr was willing to "pass judgment")—the fundamental challenge of world politics was to find a way to achieve "peaceful change" which, as a practical matter, was likely to require concessions from those who most benefited from the status quo.[60]

Seeing the world as it is. George F. Kennan, an influential American foreign service officer, Russia hand, and prolific, accomplished writer, is best known for his landmark essay "The Sources of Soviet Conduct," which had a formative influence on the emerging American policy of containment at the dawn of the Cold War. As an exercise in Classical Realism it is exemplary, combining structural variables (given the global distribution of power, the relationship between the United States and Russia would not much change even if communism vanished overnight) with particularistic factors (rooting the "sources" of that "conduct" to internal Russian politics, historical experience, the nature of the Russian character, and other particulars).[61] Kennan's principal contributions to Classical Realism, however, are found in two small, incisive books, *American Diplomacy, 1900–1950* and *Realities of American Foreign Policy*.[62] In these slim volumes, Kennan preaches the need to see the world as it is, not the world as one might wish it was. As he wrote in his memoirs, it was essential "not to recoil from the struggle for power as something shocking or abnormal." Very much with Carr, his tone is admonishing: "we will not improve our performance by failing to deal with its real nature or dress it up as something else." (Also similar to Carr, whose analytical if not political instincts he largely shared, Kennan was unwilling to genuflect before the status quo—rather, the opposite was required: "the task of international politics is not to inhibit change but to permit change to proceed without repeatedly shaking the peace of the world.")[63] The need for such a clear-eyed, unflinching understanding of the ways of the world was especially urgent because, with Morgenthau and Thucydides (who invariably cast rabble-rousing demagogues as the villains of various set pieces), Kennan was particularly wary of the ability of democracies to deftly navigate the dangerous currents of world politics.[64] Democracies (and especially American democracy) like to imagine their behavior as noble and their causes as just. This can make them clumsy, incapable of appreciating the ambiguities and nuances present in most international political challenges, and crusading, so that when roused, they tend to overreach. On both of these points Kennan's lectures are clear (and Classical): "Let us face it: in most international differences elements of right and wrong . . . are, if they exist at all, which is a question—simply not discernable to the outsider." And as for the "dangerous delusion" of "total victory" in international struggles, Kennan plainly channels Clausewitz: "Perhaps there can be such a thing as 'victory' in a battle, whereas in war there can only be the achievement or nonachievement of your objectives."[65] In all of these considerations, it should be noted, Kennan reaches for a medical analogy, stressing the need to have the disposition of a physician, with "an attitude of detachment and soberness and readiness to reserve judgment." This analogy (invoked by Machiavelli as well) has an important methodological as well as analytical implication. Understanding the vagaries of world politics requires judicious, context-specific wisdom. "We must be gardeners and not mechanics in our approach to world affairs," Kennan insisted.[66]

The primacy of politics and inescapable uncertainty. Hans Morgenthau was the most influential Realist scholar of the mid-twentieth century. His book *Politics among Nations* served as something of a textbook for two generations of students; but his greatest contributions are to be found in *Scientific Man vs. Power Politics* and *In Defense of the National Interest.* Morgenthau was a prolific writer over the course of a long career, but it is hard to overestimate the importance of *Scientific Man*, which, looking back over his estimable oeuvre thirty years after its publication, Morgenthau described as "the book I most favor."[67]

The title of *Scientific Man* efficiently captures two of the book's core arguments, which are foundational to Classical Realism. In the middle of the twentieth century, especially in the United States, especially after World War II, there was seemingly no problem that could not be solved by the can-do application of modern scientific analysis. Morgenthau saw this as folly—the social sciences in general, and international politics in particular, could not be properly understood following the methods and mindset of the natural sciences. He castigated "the illusion of a social science imitating a model of the natural sciences." The complexities and analytical interdependencies were much greater, behavioral relationships between variables were not constant, and the role of human agency, purpose, and desire, irrelevant to studying natural phenomenon, were essential for understanding the social world. As Reinhold Niebuhr argued similarly, "The radical freedom of the self and the consequent dramatic realities of history are naturally embarrassing to any scientific effort."[68] (Note, crucially, that Morgenthau does not reject the notion of social science—the search for tendencies, patterns, context-dependent generalities, and an understanding of the range of the likely, the plausible, and the possible—he simply renounces the notion, however aspirational, that the social sciences might be well served by converging toward a natural sciences style of analysis.)

The second half of the title, *Power Politics*, is similarly illuminating. Morgenthau defines his individual actors (and their aggregations) as motivated by *politics*. "Man is a political animal by nature," he argued, with a "longing for power" that is "a universal force inherent in human nature."[69] This rather dramatic assumption has led some to dismiss Morgenthau's perspective as "human nature realism," and as such of limited utility (since human nature is constant, but real-world outcomes and moments of war and peace vary dramatically). But to see actors as ambitious and motivated by political goals is not an explanation, it is an assumption that builds toward various efforts at explanation. (All approaches to social science have their abstract assumptions—structural realists tend to assume their actors are "security seekers"; economists model their agents as individual, egoistic, materialists.) This matters: all assumptions shape analytical expectations. Morgenthau (and classical realism more generally) does not envision actors as security seekers but rather as harboring political ambitions not easily satiated; instead, the limits of such ambitions are defined by the presence of countervailing power. "The selfishness of man has limits," Morgenthau observes; "his will to power has none." This again is in accord with the Classical disposition to see ambition rising with capabilities. Martin Wight held that it "is in the nature of powers to expand"; Nicholas Spykman similarly observed "the number of cases in which a strong dynamic state has stopped expanding or has set modest limits to its power aims has been very few indeed."[70]

Because Morgenthau sits at the epicenter of modern Classical Realism, it is not surprising that his work has enmeshed affinities with so many of the themes already enumerated. Similar to Carr, Morgenthau is wary of what international law can hope to achieve as an alternative to the resort to arms by the aggrieved, because conflicts between states will not commonly be amenable to resolution by legal rulings. More generally—if perhaps a caricature, but with the catastrophic failures of the League of Nations very much in mind—Morgenthau also echoes Carr with his critique of the perspective "that there is no international problem which cannot be solved by negotiations leading to compromise."[71] Instead, and again, world politics is characterized by basic clashes of interest, and when one conflict is resolved another will soon take its place. This is true both locally (regarding specific conflicts) and more generally: "That a new balance of power will rise out of the ruins of an old balance and that nations with political sense will avail themselves of the opportunity to improve their position within it, it is a law of politics for whose validity nobody is to blame."[72] And with Thucydides, Clausewitz, and others, and not surprisingly given his emphasis on uncertainty, Morgenthau also places great emphasis on the importance of chance in war; for these reasons, he echoes Kennan's ethos of "gardeners, not mechanics" with his own distinction between the statesman and the engineer.[73]

Defining the craft of Classical Realist analysis, Morgenthau observed (even in his most "scientifically" inflected text, *Politics among Nations*) that "knowledge of the forces that determine politics among nations, and of the ways by which their political relations unfold, reveals the ambiguity of the facts of international politics. In every political situation contradictory tendencies are at play." Once again the purpose of this statement is not to renounce methodical analysis but to distinguish between natural and the social scientific enterprises, and to be alert to the distinct challenges inherent to the latter. "The best the scholar can do, then, is to trace the different tendencies that, as potentials, are inherent in a certain international situation."[74]

The struggle for objectivity. The emphasis Classical Realism places on uncertainty and the unknowable also informs its approach to the study of world politics. A profound self-awareness about what can be known, and, in addition, the importance of understanding that events are interpreted differently when seen through distinct historical narratives and analytical perspectives, is common to the approach but has been most clearly articulated by Raymond Aron. Certainly Aron's work reliably checks the key boxes of the paradigm: the benchmarks touched on in his book *Peace and War* include admonitions about power and ambition ("History offers few examples of hegemonic states which do not abuse their force"); the National Interest ("not reducible to private interests or private collective interests"); skepticism that treaties do little more than "express the relation of forces"; the rejection of prediction ("The formal analysis we have just conducted does not afford us a means of forecasting but a kind of outline"); as well as appeals to Thucydides, the role of chance in war, and the distinction between military victory and the achievement of political objectives, before bringing the volume to a close with a hat tip to Kennan's "gardeners, not mechanics" ethos. And although most classical realists cite Clausewitz as an influence, Aron, no dilettante, wrote a celebrated book about him.[75] Nevertheless, Aron's most singular and enduring contribution to Classical Realism is dispositional—how the study of world politics ought to be conducted. In his memoirs, Aron writes of his aspiration "to understand my time as honestly as possible, without ever losing awareness of the limits of my knowledge." And looking back on his career, Aron affirms that key ideas in his first important book, *The Philosophy of History*, remain his guiding principles, including his steadfast opposition to determinism—which is more than "History is unpredictable, as is man himself," but also means that choices have consequences, and things could have turned out differently—and the need to acknowledge the "plurality of the possible interpretations." Classical Realism has a pessimistic streak, and Aron's work in particular can be described, in Tony Judt's phrase, as "a disenchanted realism," with a sensitivity to the fragility of civilization seen firsthand, as a witness (as was Morgenthau) to the collapse of the Weimar Republic and the harrowing radical polarization, political paralysis, and cultural decay that characterized France in the 1930s and contributed to its sudden, unexpected collapse when tested by Germany's invasion.[76] Crucially, however, Aron's particularly moody, everybody-has-their-reasons realism should not be misunderstood as morally vacant or postmodern nihilism. Rather, caution about moral judgments in the evaluation of International Relations stems from his brilliant observation that in politics "it is not every day that a Dreyfus Affair comes along justifying the invocation of truth against error."[77] And as for objectivity, it may well be unattainable. (That was Niebuhr's position: "complete rational objectivity in a social situation is impossible.") But that does not in any way preclude *striving* for objectivity—as Aron put it: "the more one wants to be objective, the more important it is to be aware of the viewpoint from which one expresses oneself and from which one regards the world." Such a disposition is essential for the productive study of world politics from any paradigmatic perspective (and exposes the folly of pretending that work is not rooted in some implicit or explicit paradigm).[78]

Dynamics over statics. Robert Gilpin was the last major Classical Realist scholar of the twentieth century. His seminal *War and Change in World Politics*, which focused on the rise and (relative) decline of hegemons and the international political contestations that follow, identified *changes to* the balance of power as the principal engine of conflict and war in world politics.[79] "The most important factor for the process of international political change is not the static distribution of power in the system (bipolar or multipolar) but the dynamics of power relations over time." In either setting, it is the "changes in relative power among the principal actors in the system" that are key. Kennan, who did not explore the argument systematically, held a similar position: "The unevenness of development is, in itself, a tremendous factor working for tension and conflict in international life." But Gilpin self-identifies his principal influences as Thucydides, who identified "the uneven growth of power among states [as] the driving force of international Relations," and E. H. Carr, whose work sought ways to resolve the resulting disequilibria through "peaceful change."[80]

Gilpin also articulates most plainly the realist emphasis on continuity over change in world politics. "The fundamental nature of international relations has not changed over the millennia," he insists. Innovations, ideologies, and interdependencies might shift cost-benefit analyses, but, then and now, autonomous states (or conflict groups) pursue their interests in the context of anarchy and are willing to fight over their differences. Gesturing at Thucydides' ambition to provide "a possession for all time," Gilpin imagines the Athenian general would have "little trouble in understanding the power struggle of our age." Implicit in this perspective is the assumption that people today are not better or smarter or wiser or more inherently civilized than in years past; nor does it harbor the expectation that history has an identifiable arc—it wobbles rather indifferently with regard to the fate of mankind.[81] Gilpin's work more generally is also robustly and recognizably classical. Regarding ambition, he holds as axiomatic "as the power of a state increases, it seeks to extend . . . its political influence." And his contributions are steeped in distinctly classical traditions, emphasizing the essential roles of both power and purpose in explaining behavior—with purpose only comprehensible through an understanding of domestic politics, sociological factors, ideology, and, always, history. The resilience of hegemons in decline, for example, is "limited by internal transformations in society," including "social conflict" and—a recurring Gilpinian theme—the "moral decay and the corruption of the original values that enabled the society to grow in the first place."[82] And although *War and Change* places great emphasis on states assessing the costs and benefits of various strategic decisions, Gilpin holds that these assessments are "highly subjective" and depend on "perceived interests." What shapes those perceptions? "Foremost," he states plainly, "is the historical experience of society . . . what lessons has the nation learned about war, aggression, appeasement, etc.?" Morgenthau similarly emphasized the importance of "political and cultural context" in explaining the choices states make. These factors are foundational, not marginal. Indeed, Gilpin distinguished realism from contrasting paradigms by noting its distinct emphasis on "national sentiment" and "political values" and stressed the role of ideology in shaping state choices. Similarly, as Martin Wight argued, "It is not possible to understand international politics simply in terms of mechanics." Because the character of choices made by states is informed not simply by "territories, raw materials and weapons, but also beliefs and opinions."[83]

Classical Realism in Theory and Practice

This chapter has introduced Classical Realism—an approach to understanding and explaining International Relations. Realism takes as its point of departure the implications and consequences of anarchy for world politics. Classical Realism, characterized by the analytical devices and assumptions described above, is ultimately distinguished within the realist school by three additional, foundational points of departure: the past is profoundly relevant, the future is largely unwritten, and, above all, politics matters. Politics are formative in that it is impossible to know how states will behave without understanding what they want—both power and purpose will shape the choices made by states. And as most states are not facing imminent threats to their survival most of the time, they enjoy considerable discretion with regard to how they will orient and conduct their foreign policies. Politics matters again in that those foreign policy choices will in turn influence the choices made by other states, by shaping their expectations and altering the calculus of the perceived costs and benefits of various courses of action. States, especially great powers, make basic international political choices, choices that are profoundly shaped by their historical experiences, ideational frameworks, and ideological dispositions.

Chapter 2 argues that the return to a revitalized Classical Realism is necessary due to the irretrievable shortcomings of two predominant paradigms: Structural Realism and the hyper-rationalist bargaining school. The failures of each are rooted in disfiguring assumptions at the core of their models: Structural Realism misapplies oligopoly theory, a proper understanding of which yields an indeterminism that can only be resolved by appeals to history, ideology, and purpose—variables that approach explicitly renounces. The Bargaining Model is little more than a misapplication of Rational Expectations Theory from macroeconomics, an approach which, even in economics, generates theories that produce results wildly inconsistent with real-world outcomes. And that deeply flawed theory, in any event, is singularly inappropriate to apply to questions of war and peace.[84] The following chapter then illustrates the utility of classical realism in practice, by looking at some great puzzles in modern international political history and demonstrating that these riddles are better understood from the perspective of classical realism. More generally, and throughout this book, we will see that the utilization of variables that classical realism emphasizes (and its principal intellectual adversaries forbid) and the embrace of classical realism's analytical disposition more generally are necessary and crucial to understand important events in world politics—always, but urgently now in the context of the uncertain and unfolding events of our time.

CHAPTER TWO

Reclaiming Realism

THIS CHAPTER CONTRASTS Classical Realism with two predominant approaches to contemporary International Relations theory.[1] The central argument here is that those approaches, Structural Realism and the bargaining model (which derives from the "Rationalist Explanations for War" framework), are characterized by foundational errors of analysis resulting from their fundamentally flawed embrace of different forms of economism.[2] Much of structural realism, for example, derives from the misguided adaptation of price theory (that is, microeconomic competition), with the scarcity constraints of markets seen as analogous to the disciplining constraints of anarchy. The minimalist assumptions of neorealism have also encouraged an all-too-easy reification of a style of analysis, now pervasive across many IR paradigms, that values prediction above explanation. (As this chapter will elaborate, it is not so much erroneous point predictions but an analytical disposition that values the aspiration of prediction, and one that imagines social science inquiry as akin to those undertaken in the natural sciences, that is at the root of the problem.) These same pathologies—flawed economism and aspirations to a natural science model—also characterize the second influential paradigm, derived from a purported claim to elucidate "rationalist explanations" for war, which reflects the hyper-rationalist turn in IR theory.[3] This approach reflects the uncritical adaptation of a certain type of macroeconomics: Rational Expectations Theory. But the limits to—one could go so far as to say the follies of—Rational Expectations Theory in economics (deductively elegant, empirically wrong) were revealed analytically for decades and ultimately exposed by the global financial crisis of 2007–8. Worse, even where the approach adds value to economic theory, it is particularly unsuited for adaptation to IR theory. Notably, the rise of structural realism and hyper-rationalism represented a rejection of the style of analysis associated with classical realism, with its emphasis on history, contingency, choice, ideology, uncertainty, and unpredictability, in favor of more purportedly scientific and, in particular, economistic approaches to IR theory. But these more modern paradigms are dubious in their logic and of limited utility when applied to real-world phenomena.

Exploring the flaws in Structural Realism and hyper-rationalism and articulating the contours of Classical Realism is essential because "isms" matter. They reflect underlying philosophical points of departure and are rooted in specific, explicit assumptions about how the world works. The very different expectations and conclusions of different theories often stem from the fact that those theories were derived from distinct, and contrasting, paradigmatic roots. To be self-conscious about those foundations is to understand the likely strengths, weaknesses, limitations, controversies, and specific attributes of various theories. In contemporary International Relations scholarship, there is a common claim that the discipline is "past paradigms"; many younger scholars are expected to recite this. But that is a political act, not an intellectual one. It reflects the influence and proselytizing of one particular paradigmatic perspective—one with specific analytical building blocks of individualism, materialism, and hyper-rationalism—which *is* a paradigm; and one that has been well described as an "intellectual monoculture."[4]

Classical Realism, as a point of departure for the study of world politics, is, not surprisingly, distinct from other schools of thought such as liberalism and Marxism, which are commonly understood to represent contrasting perspectives. In distinction to those paradigms, for example, Realism more generally places greater emphasis on political motivations rather than stressing predominantly materialist incentives.[5] (Thucydides reports that the Melians chose annihilation over subjugation—an extreme case to be sure, but one that is nevertheless representative of the realist expectation that actors in world politics have a strong and general preference not to be subject to political domination by outsiders, a value irreducible to material interests.) But in exploring the contours of Classical Realism the objective here is not to rehearse familiar differences between realism and liberalism (although the last section of this chapter will situate Classical Realism in relation to some other paradigms and approaches). Instead the emphasis is on the ways that Classical Realism is distinct from its realist cousins—that is, from the predominant practice of structural realism (also known as neo-realism) and its closely affiliated variants. All declensions of realism share common orienting principles regarding the significance of anarchy, attentiveness to the balance of power, an embrace of the notion of the national interest, and the central role of politics in explaining the behavior of actors in international relations. As seen in chapter 1, however, in contrast to its brethren, Classical Realism is markedly distinguished by a number of additional attributes, including, importantly: that structure matters, but it is irretrievably indeterminate; the central role of history in understanding world politics; and attentiveness to content (that is, to both power *and* purpose)—all of which imply that attention to aspects of domestic politics and ideational variables are necessary to understand state behavior. In addition, Classical Realism anticipates that great powers seek more than just security, and they are instinctively opportunistic; and that international politics—that is, the choices made by states—are uncertain, contingent, and consequential. Each of these attributes either violates core tenets of structural realism or attends to factors it deems superficial or ephemeral.

Classical Realism also contrasts sharply with another dominant approach in contemporary International Relations theory—the hyper-rationalist turn—which is characterized by an extremely strict (and misguided) definition of "rationality" that it imposes on the actors whose behavior it aims to model. In particular, classical realists hold radically different (and more empirically defensible) assumptions about rationality—and from there, about the predictive capabilities both of rational actors in world politics and of the scholars that hope to model them—than does the hyper-rationalist approach.

Each of these movements (the rise of structural realism and hyper-rationalism) reflected aspirations to grasp for more purportedly scientific and, in particular, economistic approaches to IR theory. The ironic if not surprising consequence of these changes was the devaluation, and in some cases abandonment, of political factors in explaining behavior in world politics. An unfortunate and less appreciated attribute of structuralism and hyper-rationalism is that they commonly feature the misapplication of economic theories and analogies to the study of IR. Understanding these errors both exposes the consequential flaws of these approaches and illustrates the important differences between these paradigms and Classical Realism.

The Inescapable Indeterminacy of Structural Realism

Classical realists have an acute sensitivity to the balance of power, which must be recognized and attended to, since it establishes the constellation of potential security threats. But unlike Waltzian neo-realism, which became the hegemonic voice of realism in the 1980s (to the extent that, even among specialists, structural realism is often conflated with realism), classical realism aims to "put structure in its place"—that is, to understand its strengths and (considerable) limitations as a tool for understanding world politics.[6] From a classical perspective, to insist that analysis be limited to the "systemic" level (a consideration of states as like units differentiated only by their relative capabilities) is to demand the sound of one hand clapping. Waltz, however, is dismissive of any appeal to variables at other levels of analysis—"it is not possible to understand world politics simply by looking inside of states," he insists. "The behavior of states and statesmen . . . is indeterminate."[7] This may be true. But, it need be emphasized, this is also true for the system.[8] Thus, as noted, Classical Realism is very alert to the structure of the system, because in the context of anarchy and the possibility of war the balance of power conditions states' fears and expectations and influences the pattern of interactions between them. Nevertheless, classical realism also holds that it is simply impossible to understand world politics simply by looking outside of states. The implications of systemic forces are inherently and irretrievably indeterminate.

This is the case for international relations—just as it is true for the microeconomic theory (as applied) that serves explicitly as the intellectual template for neo-realism. The international system does indeed impose constraints on states in a way analogous to how market forces limit the range of choices available to firms. And the market (like the international system) on the one hand derives from the collective behavior of its participants but on the other generates pressures that are beyond the control of any particular actor. But this analogy is imperfect, and upon reflection, self-negating as it applies to international relations. Even assuming an idealized abstract market, with similar firms seeking singular goals (maximizing profits or market share), the deterministic implications of systemic market pressure are dependent on very strict assumptions of "perfect competition"—which holds when there is a very large set of actors, each so small that they have no market power but instead are "price takers." But as the idealized assumption of perfect competition is relaxed, market forces remain vital but individual choices—idiosyncratic choices—become increasingly central to explaining behavior. In particular, large firms in oligopolistic settings, while certainly not unconstrained by market forces, nevertheless enjoy considerable discretion as to how they will pursue their goals.[9]

The problem for neo-realist IR theory is even more subversive than this. It is true, and problematic for neo-realism, that oligopolists are *not* price takers, and thus have discretion over what course of action they choose—or, put more plainly, they are not simply presented with market pressures; *their choices also contribute to the shape and definition of those pressures*. Even worse (for neo-realism) is the fact that, once oligopoly (or duopoly) enters the picture, we can't even make the most basic predictions, or even derive expectations about that most elemental aspect of neo-realism: balancing behavior. Great powers may tend to balance against each other (and classical realists would expect this, just as structuralists do), but this does *not* necessarily follow from the relevant economic theory that structural realism embraces. In fact, microeconomic theory is suggestive of the opposite: theories of imperfect competition tell us that oligopolists and duopolists have *more* to gain by colluding with each other than they do by competing with each other. (Thus rather than balancing against one another, great powers, especially in bipolarity, face great incentives to form a condominium and divide the spoils.) This danger is so great in the economic sphere that there are very commonly laws against such collusion within domestic societies. Economic theory can't tell us which will occur—collusion or competition—numerous, varied, specific, and contingent factors make one or the other more likely. This has been widely understood by economists, well before the emergence of structural realism: "it has long been recognized that oligopolists may achieve monopolistic results by means of an explicit agreement, and that they may well behave in an essentially monopolistic way even without any explicit collusion. It is also widely appreciated, however, that some form of economic warfare is an alternatively possible outcome." Even Nobel laureate George Stigler, the Chicago school economist who was tireless in his efforts to emphasize the efficiency of the unfettered market, began his classic paper on oligopoly by accepting "the hypothesis that oligopolists wish to collude to maximize joint profits," which is rooted in the fact that their "combined profits . . . are maximized when they act together." Stigler was motivated to probe the limitations of such collusion (thus reducing the need for government intervention) but readily acknowledged the fact that it commonly occurred, even when firms have to resort to complex and hazardous strategies designed to evade (that is, break) the law.[10]

Returning again to International Relations, that considerable discretion is especially true for great powers, which, it should be noted, attract the lion's share of analytical attention from realists of all stripes—and Waltz in particular, who holds that "a general theory of international politics is necessarily based on the great powers."[11] But most states generally, and great powers in particular, look *much* more like large oligopolists regarding the behavior of each other than tiny firms facing disembodied constraints under perfect competition. (There are of course basic differences in the nature of the competition between firms and states—but nevertheless it remains shattering that the central analytical analogy of *Theory of International Politics* is fundamentally misapplied, and as a practical matter, what remains pertinent tells us nothing new.)[12] And, again, oligopoly fundamentally changes the metaphor, and demands attention—requires attention—to more than structure. As Raymond Aron observed, "The structure of the international system is always *oligopolistic*. In each period the principal actors have determined the system more than they have been determined by it." Oligopolistic competition implies indeterminate outcomes, and also means that agents' choices shape the systemic environment. This is another crucial point, because it means that not only do states have choices, but those choices made by states *matter*—not simply for filling in colorful or minute details but in shaping the pressures that in turn affect other states.[13] In International Relations, that indeterminacy, and system-shaping behavior, is of even greater consequence than when dealing with firms and markets, because despite their common attributes, states in world politics are less similar to each other than are firms of the same industry, and despite a common desire for survival, as classical realists have observed in the past, states pursue a broad range of goals (certainly more diverse than the goals of firms), the content of which will vary from state to state.[14] And even in pursuit of that most narrow, common goal, survival, states are still less predictable than firms, because they typically have considerably more latitude—firms are selected out of the system with much greater frequency than are states. (When was the last time you traveled on Eastern Airlines, not all that long ago one of the largest and most profitable carriers in the world?)[15]

In sum, the balance of power (and changes to it) and the systemic pressures generated by an anarchic political order more generally inform importantly the environment in which all states act. But in that context, all states, and especially great powers, enjoy considerable discretion with regard to how they will pursue their goals and what sacrifices they will make in the face of constraints. It is thus impossible to understand and anticipate the behavior of states by looking solely at structural variables and constraints.

Frustrated by the stubborn truth that neo-realism had, like the Pied Piper, led its large following down a blind alley, a number of scholars have attempted to retrofit its core analytical machine, bolting a few ad hoc variables onto the engine of neo-realism in the hope of salvaging some practical application of the approach. Prominent among these efforts is "neo-classical realism," which takes as its point of departure the observation that "states occasionally respond inconsistently with systemic imperatives," and welcomes a handful of variables, such as misperception, some domestic political constraints on foreign policy practice, and other selected factors to help explain why states might at times respond suboptimally to the urgent obligations presented by systemic forces. But although neo-classical realism has produced some excellent scholarship, as a friendly and gently modified version of neo-realism it remains trapped in the same corner into which structural realism has painted itself. The ethos of neo-classical realism is found in its explicit embrace of "the positivistic scientific rigor that structural realism introduced to realism," and with its wholehearted endorsement of the "causal primacy of the international system."[16] Ultimately, then, neo-classical realism is modified neo-realism (neo-neo-realism?), and its analysis and apparatus do not reflect a deep engagement with the central elements and tenets of classical realism, including the essential roles of history, uncertainty and contingency, purpose, and of course the subversive fact that the systemic pressures presented by structural forces are not simply exogenous (as would be suggested by the inapplicable market analogy of perfect competition) but are also shaped by the endogenous choices made by states. Again, and with respect for the commendable scholarship undertaken in this tradition, as James Tobin said of a group of eminent scholars who self-described as New Keynesian, "If I had a copyright on who could use the term 'Keynesian' I wouldn't allow them to use it."[17]

To explain world politics, it is necessary to seriously engage a host of factors, including domestic politics, history, ideology, and perceptions of legitimacy. To many modern ears this sounds incongruous, because the dominance of structural realism has left the impression that "realists can't do that." But classical realists can—and do—take domestic politics seriously. And they also understand that state behavior is shaped by the lessons of history (right or wrong), ideas (accurate or not), and ideology (good or bad), and that (as discussed further below) states are not best understood as hyper-rationalist machines but make choices conditioned by those influences, and in the context of irretrievable uncertainty.

It is thus necessary to dig below the surface, and understand that state choices are informed, as Gilpin argued, by historical experience and filtered through ideological lenses. Different states, as political animals, see the world in different ways. Classical realists, then, place great emphasis on domestic politics, and take seriously the role of historical experience, and of ideas, norms, and legitimacy in explaining International Relations. Indeed, as a paradigm of IR theory, realism is distinguished from varieties of liberalism and Marxism by rejecting a reductionist emphasis on individualist materialism in favor of a foundational focus on political goals and collective ambitions.[18] As seen in chapter 1, Thucydides expected actors to behave differently based on their system of government, quality and composition of leadership, factional conflicts within societies, and distinct "national character." Carr took very seriously the role of public opinion ("power over opinion . . . is a necessary part of all power"); Morgenthau attributed many of the pathologies of U.S. foreign policy to ideology and domestic politics; similar laments were a ubiquitous theme in Kennan's writing.[19] Most important of all, Classical realism stresses the role of history in explaining behavior: "No significant conclusions are possible in the study of foreign affairs—the study of states acting as units—without an awareness of the historical context," Henry Kissinger argued in his first and finest book. A state "achieves identity only through the consciousness of common history. This is the only 'experience' nations have, their only possibility of learning from themselves. History is the memory of states."[20]

These variables are incompatible with *structuralism*, but they remain robustly realist. Classical Realists do not assume ideas are "good" or that lessons are learned accurately. (As Kissinger observes, history is essential, but it "is not often that nations learn from the past, even rarer do they draw the correct conclusions from it. For the lessons of historical experience, as of personal experience, are contingent.") Similarly, ideas will shape behavior, but the dispositional cynicism of the paradigm anticipates that very often ideas, instrumentally or even perhaps unwittingly, often serve interests (what Carr called "the relativity of thought to the interests and circumstances of the thinker"). Nor does Classical Realism expect norms to prevent states from pursuing radically treacherous foreign policies. But it does expect that all of these things nevertheless affect, significantly, politics and behavior. Realists may withhold moral judgment on the merits of competing ideologies, but states' choices will nonetheless be deeply affected by the influence of one or the other. Norms will not stop states from engaging in horrifying acts of barbaric aggression, but historical experience and perceptions of legitimacy nevertheless condition the way in which states interpret the meaning of each other's actions; certainly this view was central, for example, to Carr's thinking.[21]

IR Theory and the Predictive Fallacy

A second fallacy, again rooted in the siren call of (and injudicious aspiration to) apparent economistic rigor, is the embrace of a predictive model. Common to structural realist approaches but a general characteristic (and ambition) of much contemporary IR theory, this wrong turn is once again rooted in the misguided conflation of the social and natural sciences (in particular those implicitly modeled on Newtonian physics and theories of general equilibrium). Classical Realism takes as a point of departure a fundamental and unbridgeable gap between the social and the natural world, and this informs how to best understand the former. The problem is not simply, as Reinhold Niebuhr observed, one of "causal complexity" (not to be underestimated), but that "human agents intervene unpredictably in the course of events," and in the social world even after the facts of the matter are plain to see, nevertheless a number of "alternative conclusions can always be plausibly presented."[22]

Neo-realism assumes that states are motivated by a desire for "survival" and crave "security" in order to assure that survival. Other than survival, their desires are, in Waltz's words, "endlessly varied." This "survival plus agnosticism" is the way in which structural realists model states. Even John Mearsheimer, touting a brand of Structural Realism ominously branded "offensive realism" (considered closely in chapter 6), explicitly models states as seeking nothing more than to assure their own security and survival. The "Tragedy" of "Great Power Politics" derives from the (postulated) awful consequences of rational, dispassionate attempts to satisfy these understandable and fairly benign instincts.[23]

In contrast, Classical Realism is also distinguished by its assumptions about the motivations of states and the influence of statesmen. In particular, it assumes that states want more than survival. Indeed, Classical Realism anticipates that great powers seek status and deference, and have a desire to shape the international environment in accordance with their preferences. These are all positional goods—and, all dependent on distinct *content* of those preferences, as Wolfers emphasized.[24] It should be noted that this suggests a more dangerous world than is implied by neo-realism—or, at the very least, a world of active, varied political contestation—because, however challenging it may be, it is possible to imagine settings in which two or more great powers can plausibly feel secure. But secure actors can still clash over status, primacy, and the orientation of global affairs.[25] For classical realists, then, international politics is less of an active, present struggle for survival (most great powers, most of the time, are not faced with threats to their survival) and more about the clash of interests, with outcomes determined by power. And more than just security, this perspective emphasizes that, as instinctively political actors, they are motivated by more than simply the accumulation of material things—they have a desire for power as an end in itself. As emphasized in chapter 1, in this envisioning of politics, there is no end zone, no ultimate goal achievement.

This emphasis on politics—and from there, on contingency, choice, and, consequentially, diplomacy—distinguishes classical from structural realism. For Classical Realism, the trajectory of state choices—especially of great powers, which have the most room for maneuver—is uncertain, and influenced by historical legacies, conceptions of interest, domestic politics, and, importantly, the choices made by other great powers, whose behavior shapes the nature of the opportunities and constraints presented by the system. This also exposes the false promise of chasing prediction. Scholarship following a Structural Realist tradition has been susceptible to the predictive fallacy because the minimalist conception of state goals lends itself to a false confidence about uniformity of likely behavior. But the problem is endemic to IR theory more generally.

Classical Realism, in sum, does not share a conception of inquiry that imagines a sequence of the stepping-stones of "description, explanation, and prediction," with prediction as the end goal and crowning achievement. From this currently predominant perspective, prediction absent explanation is not problematic, as poor explanation is irrelevant. If that poverty of explanation (or the unrealistic nature of assumptions) was consequential, then a better theory with superior explanation or more realistic assumptions would do a better job of predicting.[26] But the classical realist, although committed to rationalism, causality, the search for generalizable claims, productive hypothesis testing, and establishing the criteria by which arguments can be evaluated, nevertheless views forecasting the international political future as *impossible*, and thus redirects effort away from prediction—and, just as if not more important, away from orienting scholarship toward the idealized goal of prediction.

Indeed, it is the orientation toward and the idealized goal of prediction that is more consequential than specific predictions themselves. As a matter of practice, although there are notable exceptions, most IR theorists in their scholarly work do not make point predictions about specific outcomes in world politics. (It should be noted, however, that the entire hyper-rationalist enterprise is predicated on the idea that the actors it models *can and do* make shared, savvy, accurate [if probabilistic] predictions about *very* specific events.) But to the protestation "we are not making point predictions" one could offer the rejoinder expressed by John Lewis Gaddis: "It will not do to claim that forecasting was never an objective of these theories in the first place, because the theorists repeatedly set that task for themselves." But the issue is a larger one, because the problem is not simply with the presence or absence of specific predictions, but with that more general aspiration. Even though it is the case that most IR scholars tend to (very wisely) shy away from specific point predictions about future events, pernicious consequences flow from the orientation of research around some imagined predictive ideal. And much of IR scholarship is largely in the business of building analytical machines designed to improve predictive acuity, and generates theories that are evaluated on their ability to do so. And that idealized vision, which aspires to prediction over explanation, even in a probabilistic sense, even as a hope recognized as unreachable, encourages the pursuit of one set of and one type of questions over others, and reinforces a narrow set of criteria for how to evaluate theory.[27]

Rather than describe, explain, and predict, the social science of Classical Realism is characterized by a different set of objectives: *describe, explain, understand, and anticipate*. It is crucial to emphasize that "anticipate" is not a euphemism for "soft" prediction, or "probabilistic prediction" (probabilistic prediction *is* prediction).[28] Rather, *anticipate* refers to an alertness to the range of plausible consequences of events. In contrast to predict ("there is a 70 percent chance you will win this war"), to anticipate is to be attentive to what might easily happen next ("here are the likely consequences of winning [or losing] the war"). Anticipation is not about, however loosely, attributing some probability to that outcome but to call attention to its plausibility and likely consequences, such as the prospect that a defeated country will descend into chaos, empower regional adversaries, and undermine the political goals that motivated the resort to arms in the first place. Similarly and more broadly, anticipation is not about guessing outcomes of political conflicts; it is about looking past the resolution of that conflict toward the plausible range of cascading political consequences that will follow. (Recall that it is central to Classical Realism that there is no end zone, and one political conflict will soon be followed by another conflict or constellation of conflicts.)

This shift from "describe, explain, predict" (with the implication that "predict" is the most important) to describe, explain, understand, anticipate (with explanation and understanding crucial in and of themselves as well as essential for anticipation) is a dramatic shift in analytical orientation. But it is not an inherently radical move, nor is it a rejection of the scientific method, properly understood. Rather, it derives from an awareness of the fundamental difference between the natural and the social sciences, and to the unbridgeable gap between them—and as such, the expectation that approaches to social science rooted in the transplantation of a natural science disposition will inevitably fail. The social science of Classical Realism is also rooted in analytical modesty and a respect for the limits of what International Relations theory can hope to achieve. If there is one characteristic that all Classical Realists share, it is to draw a sharp and basic distinction between what E. H. Carr described as "the political sciences, which are concerned with human behavior," and the "physical sciences."[29]

Classical realism, then, as founded and practiced, has been committed to the "scientific" study of world politics. (This also requires a vigilant discipline when assessing hypotheses. If you are rooting for a theory, good science rarely follows.)[30] But "science" need not suggest the resort to test tubes and Bunsen burners, or the general chase of whatever technique is perceived as "cutting edge." Rather, it reflects a commitment to the objective, dispassionate analysis of international political behavior. The fundamental realist emphasis on acknowledging the reality of power gives pride of place to seeing the world as it is, not as one might like it to be. (As Raymond Aron put it, "If one wishes to think . . . in the political sphere, one must above all take the world as it is.") It also requires, *from an analytical perspective*, a recusal from labeling actions "good and bad" or "right and wrong." Critical theorists are skeptical of whether analysts can really achieve such "objectivity"; ethicists might suggest implicit, inescapable moral choices (and culpability) attendant to the enterprise.[31] (These and other important challenges, which are suggestive of the limits of realist analysis, will be discussed in chapter 4.) Nevertheless, as Carr plainly describes (and endorses), "Consistent realism . . . involves acceptance of the whole historical process and precludes moral judgment on it."[32]

But beyond this dyed-in-the-wool commitment to the objectivity and dispassion of a scientist, and a commitment to studied reason with the hope of intellectual progress, classical realists recoil from the notion that the social sciences might aspire to converge, in their practices and disposition, toward the model of inquiry offered by the natural sciences. Central to this essential temperament is the issue of *unpredictability*, a key source of what Hans Morgenthau saw as "the practical weakness of a political science which aims at emulating the natural sciences."[33] Orientation around a predictive model is at the heart of much contemporary social science, but it is incompatible with Classical Realism. It also, it should be noted, is an approach rejected by many of the seminal figures of twentieth-century economics. Frank Knight saw a belief in prediction as the basic flaw in economic theory, stressing instead "the inherent, absolute unpredictability of things, out of the sheer brute fact that the results of human activity cannot be anticipated." One important source of this "is the variation in the power of reading human nature, of forecasting the conduct of other men, as contrasted with the scientific judgment in regard to natural phenomena." Friedrich von Hayek also emphasized the distinction between the natural and social sciences, which informed his insistence that "in the study of such complex phenomena as the market," economists could expect to offer no more than "only very general predictions about the *kind* of events which we must expect in a given situation."[34]

Classical Realists sing in harmony with this tune. For George F. Kennan, "the greatest law of human history is its unpredictability"; in Gilpin's assessment, like evolutionary biology, "ours is at best an explanatory and not a predictive science." Niebuhr spoke even more plainly. "No scientific investigations of past behavior can become the basis of predictions of future behavior," he declared; the causal chains are simply too complex, and one "can not predict which one of the many tendencies and forces which determine actions, may have a dominant place in the life of individuals and nations."[35] Once again Keynes, speaking of economics—and accentuating arguments that were at the heart of the Keynesian revolution—made these points incisively. Emphasizing the "sharp difference" between the natural and the social sciences, he warned that "the pseudo-analogy with the physical sciences leads directly counter to the habit of mind which is most important for an economist to acquire." Social science deals with "motives, expectations [and] psychological uncertainties." These do not exist in the natural sciences, requiring a fundamentally different approach to studying one as compared with the other. "One has to be constantly on guard against treating the material as constant and homogenous," he admonished. "It is as though the fall of the apple to the ground, depended on the apple's motives" as well as "on mistaken calculations on the part of the apple as to how far it was from the centre of the earth."[36]

Unfortunately, after misunderstanding oligopoly theory, chasing prediction is a second grand flaw of much contemporary IR theory. This is a problem that transcends intramural realist infighting. Prediction—for example, predicting war—with a greater or lesser emphasis on qualifying conditions is explicitly or implicitly the ambition of an enormous body of literature in International Relations, from a variety of theoretical orientations and methodological approaches.[37] It bears repeating that the larger problem is not that prediction in practice will slip beyond the grasp of the IR theorist—as it surely will—but that the chase of prediction, however rhetorically qualified, will send the analysis barking up the wrong tree. The predictive disposition is again microeconomic—it treats the behavior of states as if they were individual consumers, with tastes for war the same as tastes for ketchup, sensitive to shifts in supply and demand. And indeed in the study of consumer choice, causal factors can often be limited to a few, relatively pristine independent variables; there is commonly an enormous universe of nicely homogenous data available for analysis; additionally, in drawing confident conclusions about the implications of these variables, it can be comfortably assumed that behavioral relationships are stable.[38] Yet, once again, the transposition to IR falls flat, for even here, in this most favorable of analytical settings, "prediction" nevertheless refers to predicting the *average* behavioral response of a random actor drawn from large population making similar choices, and not to predictions about the behavior of any one specific individual, which can, and will, vary broadly. But in International Relations, the ultimate goal of the enterprise is capturing that elusive *individual* behavior (the behavior of a particular state at some significant moment in time) as opposed to the behavior of a hypothetical "average state." Moreover, it should be recalled, our imagined consumers in that microeconomic setting are drawn randomly from a vast sea of tiny actors operating under perfect competition—as opposed to the market-shaping oligopsonists that states in world politics are more properly modeled as.[39] This crucial distinction, between the individual and the average reaction, is largely inconsequential in the microeconomic realm of consumer choice theory, but is fundamental to IR in general and the study of great power politics in particular. It is also at the core of Classical Realist analysis, as will be discussed later in this chapter with its elaboration of the crucial "ketchup allegory."

Moreover, it should be recognized that even in economics—which arguably would at times offer settings much more analytically hospitable to forecasting future outcomes—there is good reason to be wary of prediction. Alfred Marshall, one of the founding fathers of the marginal revolution in economics, with all of the analytical precision that implied, was nevertheless profoundly skeptical of prediction, and this informed his approach to the discipline. Marshall explained how the problem of contingency—something even more prevalent in international politics than in economics (what Morgenthau called "the interminable chains of causes and effects")—severely circumscribes the prospects for all but the most limited efforts at prediction: "Prediction in economics must be hypothetical," Marshall insisted. "Show an uninterrupted game at chess to an expert and he will be bold indeed if he prophesies its future stages. If either side make one move ever so little different from what he expected, all the following moves will be altered; and after two or three moves more the whole face of the game will have become different."[40]

Once again, these types of obstacles are even more problematic (and intractable) in the vastly more complicated analytical setting of world politics. Consider, for example, theories designed to explain the "causes of war"—three additional challenges immediately emerge. First is the larger number of explanatory variables, some of which can be quite mercurial and idiosyncratic (such as the personal attributes of leaders—would there have been a Falklands War absent Margaret Thatcher? My answer is no),[41] and of which many are intricately interdependent rather than independent variables. Second is the lack of stability of these behavioral relationships over time, meaning that exactly the same set of circumstances that led to war in one period might not cause war in another, due to any number of factors. Third is the heterogeneity of the "dependent variable," that is, war. States choose to go to what we routinely (and accurately) call "war" for very different reasons.[42] The resort to war with different social meanings and purposes (compare, for example, the causes, motivations, and purposes associated with the first and second Gulf wars) is likely the result of distinct (and, again, contingent) causal logics.

Each one of these individual analytical challenges might, in theory, be addressed (with the likely exception of contingency, wedded as that is to uncertainty, as elaborated below). But can a "general equilibrium theory" of world politics be derived? For the classical realist the answer is an emphatic "No." As Aron concluded plainly, there can be "no general theory of International Relations." This absence of inviolable laws is ironically an iron law of classical realism: "The first lesson the student of international politics must learn and never forget," Morgenthau lectured, "is that the complexities of international affairs make simple solutions and trustworthy prophecies impossible."[43]

The trajectory of state choices—especially of great powers, which have room for maneuver—is uncertain, and contingent. Structural realists, however (not to mention, of course, hyper-rationalists), cannot distinguish between the Japan of the 1920s and the Japan of the 1930s; for them the former was necessarily pregnant with the latter (a basic error we will revisit in chapter 6). Nor can they distinguish between Weimar Germany and Nazi Germany; nor can they mourn the blunders of the Western powers in the 1920s, rooted in a tragically shortsighted and narrow (and unrealistic) conception of the National Interest. Classical realists, on the other hand, looking back tend to see the catastrophes of the 1930s not as the inevitable consequences of physical laws but rooted in the dismal political choices of the 1920s and shaped by the extreme economic upheavals that followed (crises that were made more likely by those poor political choices). A classical realist would have preferred measures designed to help facilitate an international environment where Weimar thrived and was reintegrated into the global economy, and, however a bitter pill this might be to swallow, to reemerge with some respect of its power and interests. In Kennan's view, "the great misfortune of the west . . . was not Hitler but the weakness of German society which made possible his triumph . . . which takes us back to the question of the attitude of the Western democracies toward the Weimar Republic" and the "lost opportunities" of the 1920s. For Morgenthau, "The German situation in 1932, for instance, contained essentially three such germinal developments: parliamentary democracy, military dictatorship, and Nazism," any one of which could have "finally materialize[d]."[44]

Which one? The classical realist can't be sure. It depended on "the contingent elements of the situation" and "could not be foreseen."[45] This remains true today. For classical realists, politics matters, and the future is largely unwritten. Ironically, the classical realist vision of an unwritten future, but a written (and consequential) past, is the opposite of the approach taken by neo-realism (and, indeed, much of contemporary IR theory, including, notably, the hyper-rationalist approach), which insists on the absence (or at least the irrelevance) of history and a more determined future. Structural realists model their states as amnesiacs, innocent of historical legacies; assume their policy choices are irrelevant in shaping incentives and influencing the choices of others; and model their statesmen as caretakers, arranging the deck chairs on ships guided by inexorable currents beyond their control.

An Irretrievable Error: Rational Expectations and the Hyper-rationalist Turn in IR Theory

The most consequential error in contemporary IR theory can be found at the heart of what is arguably the baseline, predominant, theoretical approach to the study of war: bargaining models rooted in the Rationalist Explanations for War (REW) perspective. The central premise of this approach is that "given identical information, truly rational agents should reason to the same conclusions about the probability of one uncertain outcome or another. Conflicting estimates should occur only if the agents have different (and so necessarily) private information."[46] Classical Realism rejects this proposition—and this is not simply a matter of intellectual disposition or analytical orientation or preference. Although the core REW proposition has a plausibly coherent internal logic, it crumbles under the weight of competing deductive claims and, not surprisingly, is easily and repeatedly falsified when put to an empirical test. Thoughtful, dispassionate experts looking at an identical, extremely rich information set *routinely* come to markedly different expectations about the probability of various possible outcomes.[47] This is a crucial engine of conflict in world politics, even as directed by actors considered rational by any reasonable definition of the term.

The fundamental flaw of the REW approach (and of the "hyper-rationalist" turn in International Relations theory more generally) can be found in its uncritical and intimate (if often implicit) embrace of the Rational Expectations revolution in macroeconomic theory. A central tenet of Rational Expectations Theory is that actors process information quickly, efficiently, and correctly—and, crucially, that they share knowledge of the (essentially) correct underlying model of the economy.[48] This approach took the economics profession by storm, and seemed to overthrow a preceding, Keynesian logic. It also presented a raft of empirically testable implications. But Rational Expectations did not test well; even leading anti-Keynesian economists concluded that "the strong rational expectations hypothesis cannot be accepted as a serious empirical hypothesis." Other mainstream economists concluded that "the weight of the empirical evidence is sufficiently strong to compel us to suspend belief in the hypothesis of rational expectations"; most attributed the empirical failure of rational expectations to the flawed underlying assumptions of the approach. These dissents have only increased as mistakes in the treatment of expectations and rationality came home to roost, as the limits to its deductive logic and empirical applications were most visibly exposed by the global financial crisis of 2007–8. Critics, armed with ever more evidence, have increasingly observed that Rational Expectations models have "turned out to be grossly inconsistent with actual behavior in real world markets."[49]

In contrast, a classical realist perspective typically models actors with what could be called "realistic expectations": it sees rational actors aiming to advance relatively stable, ordered preferences by drawing thoughtfully and logically on implicit models of how the world works. But, to repeat, REW's hyper-rationalist approach, grafted from Rational Expectations Theory, holds the view that rational actors must know and share the same (more or less) correct model of international politics (and so if they have the same information, they must reach the same conclusions).[50] In a world of Rational Expectations, in the words of founding father John Muth, "expectations, since they are informed predictions of future events, are essentially the same as the predictions of the relevant economic theory." Or as Thomas Sargent explains, "you simply cannot talk about" differences among people's models in the context of rational expectations. "All agents inside the model, the econometrician, and God share the same model."[51] This can't be emphasized enough. If there exist competing, enduring models, Rational Expectations Theory does not work, and REW does not work, full stop.

"Rational Expectations," by seizing the label "rationality" and defining it in a certain way, was remarkably successful—as a rhetorical device. After all, it implies that the alternative is to assume people somehow hold "irrational expectations." But Keynes (and others, and classical realists) did not argue that actors were irrational. Rather, he assumed agents were essentially rational, purposeful, and motivated—but not hyper-rationalist automatons who always have the right information, know the proper underlying model of how the economy will work, and as such can (probabilistically) predict future outcomes with canny precision, leaving space, of course, for randomly distributed errors that cancel each other out. (Rational Expectations Theory and thus REW envision a probabilistic world of known risk, and thus do not require actors to make exactly the same predictions, nor that those predictions turn out to be correct, but they require that actors anticipate exactly the same probability functions of those expected outcomes, which derive from that shared model.)[52] Actors as seen by Keynes will thoughtfully process information, but they will often guess, fall back on personal experiences, received "conventional wisdom," and various rules of thumb to help guide them through the cacophonous noise of economic activity and irreducible uncertainty.[53]

Much of the Rational Expectations revolution was caught up in active and politicized debates about Keynesian style policy management, especially in the context of the dismal economic performance of the 1970s. But it was a long trip from Keynes (who died in 1946) to Keynesianism, and more important, one need not embrace Keynes to reject Rational Expectations. Indeed, some of the greatest and most celebrated intellectual opponents of Keynes were economists who also explicitly rejected assuming such hyper-rationality and bird's-eye omniscience. As noted above, even with regard to economic phenomena, Hayek was profoundly skeptical of the prospects for prediction. And he was fine with that—in fact, he was rather insistent about it—his purpose to chastise the hubris of his fellow economists. "I confess that I prefer true but imperfect knowledge, even if it leaves much in-determined and unpredictable, to a pretence of exact knowledge that is likely to be false." Knight also stressed "true uncertainty," which is "unmeasurable" and which "must be taken in a sense radically different" from risk. He not only insisted on the fundamental distinction between risk and uncertainty (a distinction incompatible with Rational Expectations Theory, and the REW approach) but saw uncertainty as the very engine of capitalism, from which entrepreneurs find their opportunities for profit. Uncertainty brings about the "necessity of acting upon opinion rather than knowledge," and following one's own instincts, while trying to gauge the opinions of others for additional clues and insights.[54]

Thus REW and classical realism are rooted in two radically different conceptions of how to model the rational actor. Of these two competing perspectives, one thing we now know is that the foundation of the REW approach, Rational Expectations Theory, is wrong. That is, outcomes in the real world are inconsistent with *its* expectations (which should be of little surprise given the shaky deductive foundations of the approach). By 1999, even Sargent, one of the founding leaders of the movement, was forced to throw in the empirical towel. In *The Conquest of American Inflation*, he evaluated two competing macroeconomic models designed to explain the pattern of inflation in the United States, one a modified version of the old-fashioned adaptive-expectations model and the other based on the rational expectations challenge that discredited the former. It turns out, Sargent concluded, that the old-fashioned model, "which seems to defend discredited methods," is more successful than the rational expectations version of the natural rate model, which is "more popular among modern macroeconomists." Subsequent critics have spoken even more plainly, concluding that the grievous "empirical failures" of rational expectations models make clear that they are simply not in accord with real-world outcomes.[55]

The failure of Rational Expectations roots back to its extreme (and implausible) assumption about individual behavior and economic theory. In practice, rational individuals reach different conclusions when presented with the same facts. Knight, as quoted above, attributed this to the "inherent, absolute unpredictability of things" and expected that actors would display "diversity in conduct," rather than uniformity.[56] More dubious still is the assumption that all actors are aware of the "true" (and unchanging) underlying model of the macroeconomy.[57] But again, and this is a point worth belaboring, Rational Expectations Theory—and the REW approach—assumes that "the representative individual, hence everyone in the economy, behaves as if he had *a complete understanding of the economic mechanisms governing the world*." (For REW, crucially, substitute "political mechanisms.") But they don't. "No economist can point to a particular model, and honestly say 'this is how the world works,'" explains Mervyn King, former Governor of the Bank of England. "Our understanding of the economy is incomplete and constantly evolving."[58] And that's in economics, where many theoretical relationships, like that between the money supply and the inflation rate (which, actually, has its own problems in practice), are at least simple and solid enough to allow rational agents to make informed (if still varied and often misguided) predictions about future price levels.[59] In sum, the Rational Expectations approach, upon closer scrutiny (not to mention rather publicly slamming into a hard wall of reality in 2008),[60] revealed serious flaws and limitations as an approach in economics, which it had come to dominate. Worse, whatever its merits, it doesn't work at all as the foundation for IR theory.

Why is this approach wrong, and so particularly ill-suited for application to questions of war and peace? First and foremost, in the fantastically more complex setting of International Relations (compared to, say, macroeconomic forecasting), leaders, statesmen, and experts walk around with different, and competing (and typically implicit), theoretical models of world politics in their heads. And when confronted with the same information, even complete information—that is, all of the information that can be known at a given point in time—they will thus make different guesses, based on those disparate implicit models and theories. Actors will *not* have converged around the same, essentially correct models of war (what will cause them, how they will unfold). And "bad" or "inferior" theories will not be selected out, because of the enormous complexity of the assessments involved, the small number of cases to draw on, the heterogeneity of the relevant "sample" (and even possible disagreements about what is a relevant data point and what conclusions to draw about it)—and here even assuming behavioral stability among the variables over time (which is *extremely* unlikely).

Consider what the hyper-rationalist approach insists upon. Since its actors know, in advance (that is, share the same probabilistic expectations regarding), the costs of the not yet fought war, how those costs will be distributed, and what the outcome of the war will be, a rational actor would prefer to reach a deal to avoid the war, since there is money on the table and a mutually beneficial bargain can be reached. With no loss of blood and treasure involved, a bargained outcome must be Pareto superior to a war outcome. This purely materialist conception obviously strips the analysis of all politics—to take but one example, it is easy to imagine a rational leader even under these conditions who would find the political gains of fighting and losing to be larger than the gains associated with his portion of the bargained outcome. The shallow, indeed essentially vacant conception of politics of the hyper-rationalist approach more generally is of course deeply problematic, but the discussion here will stay focused on critiques that meet the approach solely on its own exceedingly circumscribed terms, because that is more than sufficient to reject the perspective.[61]

Think for a moment what the REW perspective requires. Recall again the core claim: "given identical information, truly rational agents should reason to the same conclusions about the probability" about all possible outcomes. Thus given identical information, all parties should agree (in a probabilistic sense) on the eventual outcome of the war, and the costs, to each side, of that outcome, *before a single shot is fired*. This claim simply disintegrates when confronted with its practical implications. Even a virtually omniscient vantage point fails to assure a convergence of expectations. Consider, for example, the fall of France in 1940. Expert historians, with unlimited access to not only reams of comprehensive evidence but the actual outcome of the battle itself, *still* disagree about whether Germany's victory was virtually inevitable or an unlikely stroke of luck.[62] These disagreements are not the result of private information, or the result of randomly distributed errors around the pretty much right, widely shared model, but are due to the multiplicity of causal models deployed by the experts, which are sustained by the absence, and practical impossibility, of a singular predictive model of war.[63] (And, it should go without saying, if actors disagree over questions as basic as who will win the war, the core of agreements that both sides will find satisfactory is likely to be a null set.)

Or consider what would have been necessary for France and Germany to reach an efficient bilateral agreement in order to avoid World War I. Given the astronomical costs of that war, not to mention the horrifying loss of life, surely there were antebellum agreements which each side would have found preferable to the actual outcome. But for the model to work, before the war started, French and German officials, assuming they were each given equal access to every bit of information available to either side at that time, would have had to come to exactly the same conclusions (that is, assigned the equivalent probabilities to)—the likelihood of the outcome (French victory and German defeat); the cost of that outcome, to each side, in blood and treasure—and, in addition, assign the same probabilities to events including but certainly not limited to (1) the failure of the Schlieffen Plan (and its consequences for the war); (2) the initiation and failure of the Gallipoli campaign (which A. J. P. Taylor called "an ingenious strategical idea carried through after inadequate preparation and with inadequate drive");[64] (3) Triple Alliance member Italy's entrance into the war on the side of the allies (and its consequences for the war); (4) the collapse of Russia into revolution and its withdrawal from the conflict, reaching a separate peace with Germany (and its consequences); (5) the American entry into the war (and its consequences); and (6) the failure of the German spring offensive of 1918 (which saw Germany's greatest territorial advance).

This sounds utterly implausible, because it is. War, in particular (as well as the steps taken toward its approach), is a plunge into radical uncertainty, and rational experts can and will disagree, profoundly, with regard to their expectations about its cost, course, and consequence, even in the most complete and symmetrical information environments conceivably imaginable.[65] Indeed, elite decision makers *within* states, sharing exactly the same information, disagree about the implications of war—how much it will cost, how it will unfold, how it might widen, what will be its ultimate outcome—as a perfunctory scanning of the minutes of cabinet meetings or military planning sessions on the eve of any conflict makes clear.[66]

If the first great lesson of Clausewitz is that the use of force can only be understood (and assessments of its utility only possible to evaluate) in its political context, his second great lesson is this: that war is a plunge into radical uncertainty. As noted in chapter 1, the Prussian general and military theorist saw war as the human activity most dramatically and distinctly influenced by unpredictability. "The element of chance, guesswork and luck come to play a great part in war," Clausewitz lectured. "The art of war deals with living and with moral forces" in a context of general uncertainty, with the result that (the italics are his) "*actual war is often far removed from the pure concept postulated by theory.*" His position could not be clearer: "In short, absolute, so-called mathematical, factors never find a firm basis in military calculations. From the very start there is an interplay of possibilities, probabilities, good luck and bad that weaves its way throughout the length and breadth of the tapestry." Expectations of how a prospective war might unfold is, if anything, an area where similarly informed experts are extremely likely to disagree. War unleashes the genie from the bottle, and what will happen next is, literally, anyone's guess. Otto von Bismarck—no shrinking violet on the use of force—nevertheless urged great caution in choosing war, even when the prospects for victory looked promising, because "one cannot see the cards of Providence far enough ahead to anticipate historical development according to one's own calculation." Or as Clausewitz put it plainly, "in war everything is uncertain." In such settings actors "can seldom predict the train of events they set in motion, and they frequently lose control over social and political forces," Gilpin observed. Note that Gilpin expressly models his decision makers as rational, who choose the resort to war as when it is perceived as the best way to advance their interests. Yet they rarely "determine or anticipate the consequences" of the conflict that is unleashed, and thus "they do not get the war they expect."[67]

A basic reason why the REW approach does not hold in practice is that there is simply too much space for different theories (that is, different implicit causal models) to exist, and to be sustained, and to be inadequately updated. From the hyper-rationalist perspective, through a process of learning (and/or perhaps a natural Darwinian elimination of those who hold the "wrong" models), there must be convergence toward the correct model. But in international relations, this will not be the case. If an expert is shown by experience that his prediction is wrong, given a probabilistic world (as REW assumes), the meaning of such an outcome can be contested. If a theory suggests that a certain outcome has a 70 percent chance of occurring, that means the theory holds that outcome won't happen 30 percent of the time. So when a "failure" is observed, was it the result of a flawed model or just a case of (slightly) bad luck? Either is possible, and it is very hard to tell with very small, heterogeneous "samples." As a result, competing theories are not easily selected out. Given that most experts have some level of confidence in their own expertise, they are in fact apt to be cautious about updating their models in the wake of just one such episode. More likely they will react as Tolstoy described: "in the failure of that war he did not see the slightest evidence of the weakness of his theory. On the contrary, the whole failure was to his thinking entirely due to the departures made from his theory."[68]

The implicit expectation of the REW approach with regard to updating provides still another example of the pitfalls of grafting an economic theory for use in International Relations, and is an illustration of the scientific overreach of the hyper-rationalists (in contrast to the conservative analytical modesty of classical realism). Theory updating requires a large set of similar trials. But the data set available to two sides approaching war: how large is the set of relevant trials, and how similar are they, given the passage of time, changes to force postures and new weapons (both untested in battle), different political elites, generals, and soldiers (also perhaps untested in battle)? Consider, for example, that the United States went to war in Korea in 1950, Vietnam in 1965, Iraq in 1990, and was fighting in Afghanistan in 2005—each setting, obviously, involving different troops, weapons, leaders, terrains, adversaries, and politics. Is this data adequate to produce a singularly accurate theory around which all experts would converge, designed to "predict" the capaciousness of U.S. troops or the choices made by U.S. leadership in wartime, say, in the pacific theater in Asia in 2025? Clausewitz would be deeply skeptical, to say the least, given his position that "every war is rich in unique episodes. Each is an uncharted sea, full of reefs." Nor would he anticipate the behavioral relationships between crucial explanatory variables to remain constant from one war to the next. Theories of war, to the extent that they can be valuable, apply only "in the light of the peculiarities" of a given historical moment, as "every age had its own kind of war."[69]

Compare this with the expectations for theory building and in turn shared (again, probabilistic) predictive capacity held by the very economists who champion Rational Expectations Theory. Eugene Fama, when asked if new financial instruments such as Collateralized Debt Obligations (CDOs) were increasing market risk, responded that there was simply not yet nearly enough good data "to come to any conclusions on these issues." Indeed, he explained, it might take as long as "another half century before we really know."[70] Fama, it bears repeating, is a hyper-rationalist—and he wanted fifty years of repeated trials of homogeneous episodes that would occur thousands of times on a daily basis before drawing any conclusions. Imagine if he'd been asked a question about the how the innovation of submarines, or aircraft, or tanks, or a volunteer army (to say nothing of a political upheaval) might influence the course of a future war. (Again, for REW to hold, experts must agree, completely and promptly, about the consequences of every innovation and transformation on the course and consequence of future wars. And without the luxury of access to decades of repeated trials of very similar events or the mountains of data provided by daily market trading.)

Finally, even those aspects of Rational Expectations Theory that "work" in economics are singularly unsuited for being grafted and applied to theories of war. This is because they are best suited for situations of *continuity*, when the coming future is most likely to look very much like the recent past. But to initiate a war is to dive headlong into the unknown or, at the very least, into the different. (Note how common it is to speak of "prewar" and "postwar" periods, because war represents the discontinuous juncture between the patterns of behavior to be found in one era as opposed to another.) It is the very moment when we would least expect a Rational Expectations–based theory to work well. This was certainly seen at the site of the global financial crisis. In the years before the crisis, macroeconomic theory had converged around an approach called Dynamic Stochastic General Equilibrium (DSGE), which was rooted in the microfoundations of individual actors with rational expectations. These models performed fairly well during normal times.[71]

But DSGE models did not anticipate the global financial crisis, and, more to the point, had no way to even account for the possibility of such a crisis. (Legend has it that one eminent financial historian had long been dismissive of the approach, because "it excludes everything I am interested in.") As the *Economist* explained, DSGE models "do badly in a crisis . . . because their 'dynamic stochastic' element only amounts to minor fluctuations around a state of equilibrium, and there is no equilibrium during crashes." Not surprisingly, after the financial crisis DSGE models came under considerable criticism.[72] But the relevant point here is that all Rational Expectations models work best in the context of continuity, not change. Such models require that the past is a reliable guide to the future and assume that things will generally and indefinitely continue to be as they were, that is, when things are "normal." However, and again drawing on a financial crisis analogy, in periods of innovation and change it is plausible, even likely, that behavioral relationships will change. At such moments, there is often very little past—as one observer asked, "How could the trajectory of a CDO squared be judged from past data when that 'past' was just two years old?" Similarly, financial models are at their best when the sailing is smooth, but are prone to "fail badly during times of panic, fear, and limited liquidity." This is why it became common for critics of financial models to ridicule their performance during crises—the 1987 stock market crash, for example, would have been predicted to occur once in a billion years—only to be added to a long list of other once-in-a-planetary lifetime disturbances in the decade that followed.[73]

But war is not tidy and certain, and is quite explicitly a departure from normal. It is the political equivalent to voluntarily initiating a moment of crisis, novelty, and discontinuity. And is thus exactly the moment when Rational Expectations–based models will have the least to say.

The Craft of Classical Realism

In sum, classical realists look at the microeconomic and macroeconomic stories told by contemporary IR theory and come to fundamentally different conclusions. From the perspective of Structural Realism and hyperrationalism, history, politics, content, ideology, and purpose can be dispensed with, because states are a homogeneous band of similarly striving materialists, who must respond to the uniform imperatives of anarchy (or be selected out of the system). Classical Realism reaches virtually the opposite conclusions, and from the same economic analogies, sees the central roles of fundamental uncertainty, consequential contingency, and inherent unpredictability. Thus while classical realist analysis remains alert to the consequences of anarchy and very sensitive to the basic role of power and wealth in conditioning state behavior, it nevertheless sees as essential those variables that competing (and predominant) approaches expressly forbid, if the choices made by actors are to have any chance of being understood.

As elaborated in this chapter, the distinct orientation of Classical Realism is rooted in fundamental departures from those more contemporary paradigms: the unbridgeable gap between the natural and the social sciences, the crucial distinction between irreducible uncertainty and actuarial risk, and, as a consequence of those two factors, an antipathy to prediction and to the conditioning analysis toward aspirations of prediction. Classical realism rejects chasing the false promise of prediction—both as the goal of the analytical enterprise (and the idea that better theories mean improved prediction) and with regard to the ability of actors in the moment (or even in retrospect) to agree on what *must* be the consequence of a given course of action.

None of these challenges will be ameliorated by "better" social science, because the problems inherent to those efforts do not reflect inadequate progress but are simply beyond the grasp of what social science can hope to achieve.[74] This, as noted above, is not a rejection of the scientific study of politics, properly understood, but reflects a judicious respect for the prospects and limits of social inquiry. Stanley Hoffmann (not coincidentally, a student of Raymond Aron) was another critic of the turn in International Relations Theory toward the "quest for certainty," and "the desire to calculate the incalculable," which in turn featured a "crusade to replace discussions of motives with such more objective data as word counts and vote counts." In his dissent, he clearly articulated the perspective embraced here: "International relations should be the science of uncertainty, of the limits of action, of the ways states try and manage but never quite succeed in eliminating their own insecurity. There has, instead, been . . . a quest for precision that turns out to be false or misleading."[75]

This, of course, echoes Morgenthau, with his emphasis—in both his groundbreaking, ambitious *Scientific Man vs. Power Politics* and his more conventionally social-science inflected textbook *Politics among Nations*—on "unique and unpredictable sets of developments" that drive politics, and the role of crucial events and episodes, factors that cannot "be foreseen with any degree of certainty." And again, this is especially the case with regard to choices made on the road to and in the midst of war. Thucydides quotes anonymous Athenians speaking before the Spartan assembly (surely one of the speeches he himself crafted) to underscore "the vast influence of accident in war," and that war, as it unfolds, "generally becomes an affair of chances, chances from which neither of us is exempt, and whose event we must risk in the dark."[76] Again, much of this roots to that unbridgeable gap between risk and uncertainty. "The orthodox theory assumes that we have a knowledge of the future of a kind quite different from that which we actually possess," Keynes explained. "This hypothesis of a calculable future leads to a wrong interpretation of the principles of behavior which the need for action compels us to adopt, and to an underestimation of the concealed factors of utter doubt, precariousness, hope and fear."[77]

The need to know the relevant history, attentiveness to context and content, the imperative of intellectual modesty given irreducible uncertainty—these notions cause would-be scientists of world affairs to squirm in their seats. What about parsimony—explaining the most with the least?—is a common rejoinder. If a simple analysis can explain 80 percent of the observed variation with a small handful of abstract variables, why back up a tractor-trailer of complexity to squeeze out a few more percentage points of explanation? To which the answer is: to the extent that more can be explained with less, parsimony is attractive. But that requires that more *is* being explained with less. In his landmark *Theory of International Politics*, Waltz insists on limiting the analysis to the systemic level—to modeling states as like units, dwelling in anarchy, distinguished only by their relative capabilities—no need to bother about history or content or purpose (beyond a desire to survive). But what does *Theory of International Politics* explain? Advocates of the approach invariably remind would-be critics that it has no "theory of foreign policy," and Waltz himself states plainly that systemic theory only tells us "a small number of big and important things." But it is hard to see what those big and important things are—that is, the "more" being explained by less.[78]

Put bluntly, it is incumbent on the defenders of *Theory of International Politics* to explain exactly what we understand after reading it that which we did not know before, and what can and cannot be achieved by a scholar armed with that knowledge.

Studying world politics is not easy, and, as a realist might say, wishing that something were so will not make it so. It is a complex, contingent, and often confusing enterprise. Instead of deploying an electron microscope, in the search for what Hoffmann described as false precision, Classical Realism reaches for a trusty tool kit—or, to return to the medical analogy, something like a doctor's bag, full of analytical devices capable of widespread application but deployed as tailored to the demands of each specific, idiosyncratic, and unique situation. Understanding those tools, and how best to deploy them, is the craft of Classical Realism.[79]

As Charles Kindleberger argued, in international politics, "it is futile to spend time at the over-all level," because "the total system is infinitely complex with everything interacting. One can discuss it intelligently, therefore, only bit by bit."[80] Kindleberger, an economist then writing about the discipline of International Relations, later in his career took this advice to heart, as his own interests migrated toward economic history—or what he preferred to call historical economics—and he articulated a methodology that is consistent with the approach of Classical Realism. Kindleberger argued that "there is not one all purpose economic theory or model that illuminates economic history," and emphasized instead economics as a "toolbox" in which the practical economist is armed with a large set of theories (such as the law of one price, or Gresham's law) that are applicable to and provide insights into a variety of settings. Historical economics is an exercise in developing and honing (and possibly circumscribing or discarding) those tools—in particular by considering "how general are economic theorems or laws, how well they fit case 2 if it is evident that they fit case 1 neatly." But despite the search for general tendencies, he nevertheless explicitly rejected prediction, and argued further that Historical Economics "looks for patterns of uniformity but is wary of insisting on identity."[81]

Situating Classical Realism

In considering Classical Realism, it will be helpful to distinguish distinct aspects of the paradigm, and to situate it within the framework of international relations theory more generally. Three succinct but crucial elaborations should be further clarifying: regarding the consequences of endogenous preferences, the role of content, and models of rationality.

Regarding preferences—this is a crucial consideration that returns to the core themes of the distinction between the natural and the social sciences, and how best to deploy analogies from economics to better understand international politics. Economic analogies, properly deployed, can offer insights into international politics; and an understanding of relevant economic theory is an important part of any Classical Realist's tool kit (aspects of this will be elaborated in chapter 5). But as Susan Strange urged in her (unheeded) Presidential Address to the International Studies Association, international relations scholars should learn more economic theory but should not "try to ape the methods of equilibrium economics."[82]

General equilibrium economics—which, as noted, draws its inspiration from Newtonian physics—is a singularly unhelpful approach to apply to world politics. Once again, a basic problem is that in the natural sciences it is very often sufficient to understand the average behavior of particles, whereas in International Relations, the "average" response to stimuli is almost always irrelevant—especially when trying to understand the likely reactions of large powers. Kindleberger, well ahead of the intellectual curve, saw this clearly: "in physics, for example, the behavior of the mass of molecules is several orders simpler as a problem than the prediction of the behavior of the separate molecule." International relations, he explains, is doubly challenged, because "one of the major handicaps of international politics is that it deals with a narrowly limited population." Thus, not only is it more difficult to establish with confidence the "average" reaction, but—and this is everything—in IR, it is understanding the elusive individual or particular reactions that is of paramount importance.[83]

As noted earlier in this chapter, consumer choice theory illustrates this clearly—and also shows how an economic theory that is quite successful when applied to important questions relevant to economics can be of almost no utility when applied to International Relations. To reprise this vital point: theories of consumer behavior can tell us much about the behavior of the "average" actor but practically nothing about a particular actor. And to put it plainly, *there are no average actors in world politics*—or, to phrase this key point in a more qualified way, perhaps in theory the average reaction to some stimuli is vaguely calculable, but knowing what the average reaction to a given political phenomenon will be in world politics is almost invariably of no practical value. (Raymond Aron, citing Clausewitz approvingly, notes that the purpose of the use of force is to get the adversary to submit to one's political will. But how much force will yield what degree of submission? That is only understandable on a

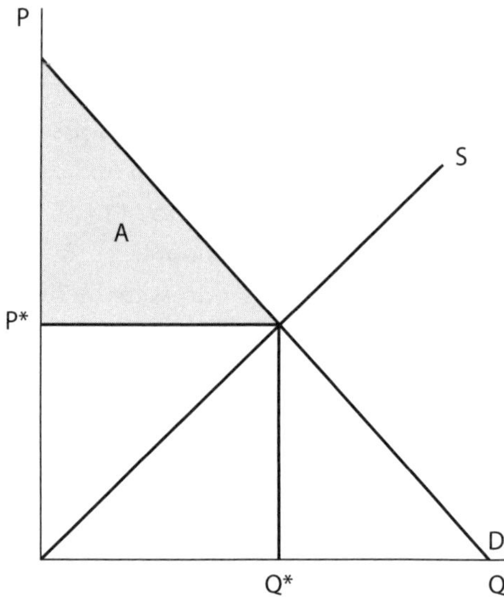

FIGURE 1. Supply and Demand for Ketchup.

case-by-case basis, because "the will to resist cannot be measured" and will surely be context dependent as well.)[84]

This can be illustrated by what I have dubbed "the ketchup allegory." Consider the market for ketchup, as illustrated by the standard supply and demand diagram in Figure 1. Note the familiar contours—the amount of ketchup provided by suppliers increases as the price increases; the amount demanded by consumers moves in the opposite direction. The standard "Marshallian Cross" shows the intersection that establishes the equilibrium level of quantity (q*) and price (p*), which are a function of the aggregate behaviors of all participants. Alfred Marshall labeled the shaded area "A" as "consumer surplus" because right up to the equilibrium point, each consumer is paying less for their ketchup than they would have been willing to. How much more would they have been willing to pay? That would depend on their individual preference for ketchup, which would situate them in their particular place along the demand curve. (Note of course there is an analogous "producer surplus" in the [unshaded] triangular region below the area of consumer surplus.)

Now consider a policy measure that raises the price of ketchup (say, for example, the imposition of a tariff). This, too, is a familiar story, which is illustrated in Figure 2. The consequences of this are also well established and need not be fully rehearsed here—the relevant point is that the effects on the equilibrium price and quantity are clear: price will go up, and the aggregate

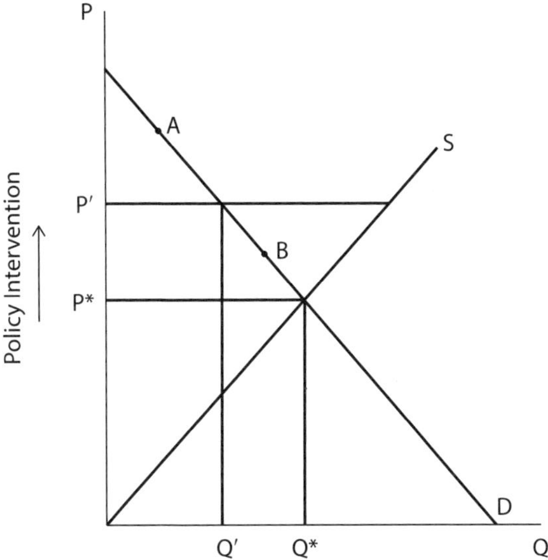

FIGURE 2. Supply and Demand for Ketchup with Policy Intervention.

quantity demanded will fall.[85] These forecasts are essentially airtight. But they are forecasts of *aggregate* demand. They do not tell us about the behavior of specific consumers. Aggregate demand falls because some will no longer buy ketchup (the price is above their willingness to pay), but others will continue to buy ketchup—indeed happily so, as they would have been willing to pay even more, and still enjoy Marshall's consumer surplus. But in IR, *the behavior of the specific actor is the crucial question.* If I introduce a given international policy measure, how will other states react? It depends entirely not on the exogenous shock of the measure but in each actor's individual endogenous preferences, that is, where they fall on our allegorical demand curve regarding their taste for the behavior they are pursuing. As seen in Figure 2, the behavior of actor A will not change; the behavior of actor B will. Only by understanding the endogenous preferences of the actor will we be able to understand their behavior.[86] Content and purpose matter.

Content Matters—Situating the Constructivist Contribution

The Classical Realist assumption that preferences matter and that a range of plausible policy choices are not just possible but consequential in shaping international relations means that understanding the behavior of powerful actors in world politics requires attention to both power and purpose. This can be a source of some confusion among contemporary students (and even many accomplished scholars) of IR theory, whose instinct is to respond, "Isn't that constructivism?"—a question that implies that realism and constructivism are competing paradigms. But this widely held view is misleading. Realism and Liberalism are opposing paradigms. As paradigms rather than theories, it is perhaps better to say they are "contrasting approaches whose distinct assumptions and points of departure often lead to very different expectations." Liberalism, like realism, represents a rich constellation of affiliated but distinct branches that generate varied theories and expectations that do not march lockstep with each other. Most generally, liberal approaches tend to place less emphasis on the consequences of anarchy, anticipate that barriers to cooperation are often surmountable (at times facilitated by international intuitions), and typically see collective interests as aggregations reducible to individual and commonly material preferences. A liberal perspective is also likely to stress the mutual benefits and in turn relatively pacifying effects of international economic enmeshments, which disincentivize conflict.[87] It should be noted, however, that most if not all theories and theorists of liberalism and realism are best seen as falling along a continuum from idealized types with imagined notions of "pure liberalism" to "pure realism" at the distant extremes. Regarding the consequences of anarchy, for example, one would be hard-pressed to imagine a liberal who sees the possibility of war as impossible or irrelevant to state behavior; similarly few realists envision the world as an unmitigated state of war and naked struggle for power.[88]

Constructivism, however, represents an orthogonal dimension. As Jeffrey Checkel well and succinctly describes, constructivism holds that the environment in which states act "is social as well as material" and that setting can provide states "with understandings of their interests."[89]

Neither realism nor liberalism is inherently "constructivist" or not, nor is either necessarily incompatible with constructivism—though some schools of thought within those paradigms certainly are. The liberal school of "open economy politics," for example, is plainly anti-constructivist. Open Economy Politics is narrowly materialist; it models its actors as selfish egoists who want more stuff. Similarly, the narrow and exclusive materialism of structural realism has little space for factors that might influence assessments of interest.

On the other hand, the liberal theory of a "democratic peace"—that liberal democracies, almost as a law-like statement, tend not to go to war with one another—is an argument that depends on recognizing consequential distinctions in the perceived political identities of other states (and in self-identity as well). Similarly, classical realism, which, although it presumes an important place for material goals and incentives, nevertheless sees political conflict taking place over much more than that. "I may do well to remind you," Keynes noted in 1926, "that the fiercest contests and the most deeply felt divisions of opinion are likely to be waged in the coming years" about questions that "may be called psychological or, perhaps, moral."[90] Constructivism is helpful for understanding such conflicts, by asking instead a different question than reductive materialists ask: "What kind of things do actors desire?" And from there it assumes that what actors (states, groups, and people) want is influenced by their environment (history, ideology, culture, social norms, notions of honor and prestige, etc.). Instead of taking preferences and goals as given, and limiting study to the singular pursuit of those presumed objectives, constructivist analysis, among other things, sees the more politically interesting and consequential question to be finding out what actors want. Narrowly materialist conceptions of politics, on the other hand, are more inclined to assume preferences, disregard social influences, and work out the math.

Debates about constructivism will not be settled in this brief commentary, nor will the many related contestations be presently rehearsed at length. Simplifying dramatically for the purpose of this schematic overview, the relationship between liberalism and realism with constructivism can be represented (as seen in Figure 3) by the notion of whether or not "content matters." For those branches of liberalism rooted in economics (such as open economy politics, institutionalism, and the commercial peace), content matters little; for branches of liberalism that emphasize the influence of shared political affinities, it is a fundamental driver of the analysis. Similarly, for Structural Realism content is irrelevant; for Classical Realism it is essential. That Structural Realism is content-free provides one of the two reasons for the common fallacy that realism and constructivism are somehow inherently at odds with one another. When constructivism emerged as an intellectual force in IR theory, Structural Realism was so predominant *as* realism that many (erroneously) conflated the two. And as content is irrelevant for Structural Realism (or for any form of systemic or "third-level" analysis), *structural* realism (including, notably, the approaches championed by Waltz in *Theory of International Politics* and Mearsheimer in *The Tragedy of Great Power Politics*) is indeed incompatible with constructivism. A second factor that reinforced and even

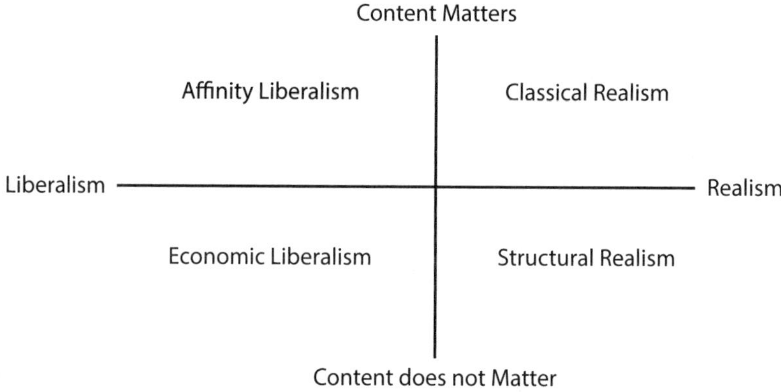

FIGURE 3. Liberalism, Realism, and Constructivism.

encouraged this false sense of rivalry between constructivism and realism was that constructivism arrived on the IR scene immediately following the end of the Cold War and the collapse of communism more generally. It was also initially presented as something of a dissent to mainstream approaches.[91] As such it was implicitly "slotted in" as a "replacement" for Marxism, a paradigm that was then rapidly fading from the scene (if perhaps primed for a comeback in the wake of twenty-first-century concerns about rapacious capitalism and attentiveness to profound inequalities of wealth). But it is more helpful, and especially clarifying for our purposes here, to highlight the ways in which the constructivist contribution sits not in opposition to realism (or liberalism) but rather how it illuminates differences between distinct branches of those paradigms.

Modeling Rationality

Finally, it is important to clarify and situate the way in which Classical Realism models the rationality of its actors. This chapter has already established the grounds for rejecting hyper-rationalism, that is, an envisioning of rationality rooted in Rational Expectations Theory (RET), that was then implicitly transplanted to the "Rationalist Theories of War" perspective and the bargaining model more generally. This approach, it should be recalled and underscored, is misguided. RET is deductively suspect in most settings (especially in macroeconomics, nominally its home field); routinely confronted with falsifying evidence when tested empirically; and singularly unsuited to be applied to questions on International Relations. Again, those additional, irretrievable problems with applying RET to questions of international politics are threefold. (1) The data is simply not—and will never be—adequate to provide the similar, repeated trials necessary to generate convergence around a shared model (a problem further complicated by the fact that in the social sciences, even an imagined, idealized model will be constantly in flux, as behavioral relationships can shift across time and context). (2) Hyper-rationalist approaches of all stripes require a world of risk, not uncertainty. But with Keynes, Hayek, and Knight—and consistent with the world we see around us—Classical Realism understands the analytical setting as one of uncertainty, in which RET-type models simply cannot apply. (3) Although we can recognize some areas of economics where RET might provide insights into the behavior of the average actor, for the most important questions in IR—political and (especially) military confrontations between states—are exactly the moments when hyper-rationalism is least likely to be able to provide such insights: war in particular is a plunge into radical uncertainty. We have no singularly shared theory of what will happen in the next war, and we never will.

Still, Classical Realism models its actors as rational. It simply articulates a more nuanced and sophisticated understanding as to what rationality is. In this conception, the rational actor (perhaps better described as the "reasonable actor" or the "rational muddler") can order its preferences and pursue its goals based on these preferences in a way that has an internal logical coherence in the context of the knowledge structure the actor is drawing upon—a logic structure that is observable to the outsider, who may not share those causal beliefs, and, of course, with agnosticism regarding the merits of the particular goals being pursued. A rational actor can also make mistakes. Uncertainty continues to play a central role in this conception: as Keynes argued, in the context of uncertainty, when pressed to select a course of action from a plausible menu of possibilities, actors are often left groping in the dark, doing the best they can to process often inherently ambiguous information by making guesses about the sentiment of the crowd, drawing on varied, implicit models, and falling back on rules of thumb and instincts derived from distinct and varied personal experiences.[92] Keynes was here thinking of investors, but Classical Realism applies these same notions to decision makers in states.

In considering participants in world politics, then, Realists of all stripes envision the actors as rational. Still, it should be noted, there are some qualifications to this. Ever alert to the perils of anarchy, Realists cannot rule out that dangerous actors might yet behave irrationally—for Raymond Aron, who saw firsthand the collapse of civilization in Weimar

Germany, "National socialism . . . taught me the power of irrational forces." In a different spirit, Waltz is careful to argue that his minimalist approach "requires no assumptions of rationality"; rather, those who fail to pursue their interests rationally will likely be selected out.[93] This is perhaps aesthetically pleasing in its analytical minimalism, but, as a practical matter, when explaining world politics, scholars working in a Structural Realist tradition more or less universally assume a baseline level of rationality among their actors, and in trying to have anything to say about international political behavior in the real world as a working assumption it is more or less essential—otherwise it would be impossible to anticipate any behavior of any actor. This holds true for Classical Realism as well. Without embracing the hyper-rationalism of Rational Expectations–derived theories, Classical Realists and Structural Realists are on the same page here, if with an acknowledgment that there may be exceptions to this general rule.

Where these contrasting approaches to realism part company, however, is on the separate dimension of the possibility for the role of what Albert Hirschman called the influence of "passions" in shaping behavior.[94] Variants of Structural Realism, here in accord with Bargaining Models, rule out this possibility. Classical Realism leaves open the door for such prospects, however. Again an appeal to Keynes is clarifying of these differences. One element of the Keynesian revolution was its embrace of the influence of emotional states—such as the role of "animal spirits" in influencing investment. This was not an isolated innovation. Looking back on his earlier assumptions of rationality, which he described as "our code"—an understanding of humanity shared with his peers—Keynes would later consider that it "was flimsily based, as I now think, on an a priori view of what human nature is like, both other people's and our own, which was disastrously mistaken." In particular, the error of "attributing an unreal rationality" to people's feelings and behavior "led to a thinness, a superficiality" of analysis and understanding that skewed and truncated their vision. Embracing a "pseudo-rational view of human nature" blinded them to "certain powerful and valuable springs of feeling."[95]

Similarly, certain "springs of feeling" can be relevant for Classical Realism. Thucydides, for example, describes an episode when Pericles, "seeing anger and poor judgement" among the Athenians, "and confident in his wisdom," avoided calling an assembly when one might have been expected, "fearing the fatal results of a debate inspired by passion and not by prudence" (2.22). More generally, Classical Realism anticipates that states will be motivated by fear, pride, and, as Thucydides emphasized in particular,

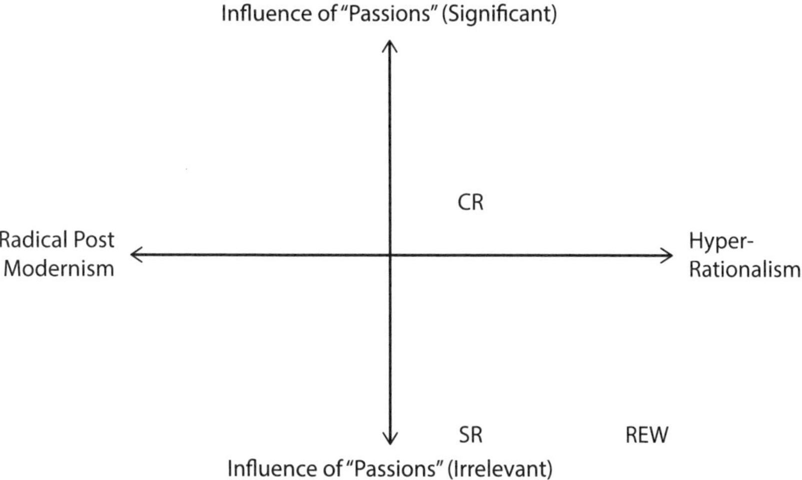

FIGURE 4. Envisioning the Rationality of the Actor.

hubris. "Fear" as used here refers to something different than alertness to the dangers inherent to anarchy, but an emotional state that a society can share and which can affect behavior. Pride suggests that actors will bear costs to avoid taking actions that, regardless of their material benefits, they would perceive as humiliating, and will take exception to others whom they perceive to be imposing humiliation upon them. Hubris, of course, is the passion of the arrogance of power, grasping for what cooler heads might see as beyond one's reach—and as will be illustrated further in chapter 3, is an important explanatory variable for classical realism.

Once again, a diagram can be used to situate Classical Realism in relation to other perspectives—here structural realist and hyper-rationalist approaches. In Figure 4, the horizontal axis represents notions of rationality, with radical postmodernism at one extreme and hyper-rationalism on the other. (Radical postmodernism, at its frontiers, suggests the impossibility of objectively assessing the "rationality" of specific actions.)[96] Figure 3 situated paradigms generally within assigned quadrants; here the positioning of the perspectives on the scatterplot is indicative. Regarding definitions of rationality, REW is to the extreme right, with Classical Realism and Structural Realism assuming the baseline reasonable actor/rational muddler described above. As for passions, some role is permitted for them by Classical Realism, but they are forbidden by the others. Admittedly they are difficult to measure, but there is no shame in including consequential factors simply because they are less tangible than others (though there should be in trying to pretend that such things don't matter simply on the grounds that they are hard to elegantly model). As Hirschman wrote, "After so many failed prophecies, is it not in the interest of social science to embrace complexity, be it at some sacrifice of its claim to predictive power?"[97]

Having demonstrated the distinct contours of (and urgent need for) Classical Realism in theory, chapter 3 turns similarly to applications of the perspective in practice.

CHAPTER THREE

Why We Need Classical Realism

ENDURING PUZZLES

CHAPTER 2 DEMONSTRATED THAT the principal approaches to the study of world politics that claim to have superseded classical realism—structural realism and hyper-rationalist bargaining models—are fundamentally and irretrievably flawed at the theoretical level. This chapter illustrates how classical realism is of practical value, by doing a better job at explaining important puzzles that have eluded other perspectives. It examines two catastrophic foreign policy blunders made by great powers—British appeasement of Nazi Germany and the American war in Vietnam—and shows that these events are beyond the grasp of the mainstream, predominant approaches but well understood by a classical realist perspective.

Why did Britain appease Nazi Germany? The two best structuralist explanations are that (1) given the multipolar order, coupled with the expectation that defensive strategies against invasion would be effective in any future war and thus such a war would be a long one, Britain (and France) engaged in "buck-passing"—trying to pass the political (and especially economic) burden of preparing for war with Germany onto others; (2) given the lack of preparation to face the German threat (which itself ought to be a puzzle for structuralism and hyper-rationalist theories—lack of preparation to defend the homeland against a major, proximate threat?), British appeasement was a strategy designed to "buy time" in anticipation of a future war, at a moment when the balance of power would be more favorable. But these explanations are wrong. Britain was not buck-passing—its motivations for restraining defense spending were rooted in a prioritization of financial rectitude, not hopes that France could be nudged into bearing a larger share of an implicitly joint concern. And British leadership—the Conservative party that dominated government through the appeasement era—was not trying to "buy time" (this was more of a post hoc rationalization than a strategy)—its goal was to avoid war at almost any conceivable cost (save the loss of the British Empire). Ultimately, British appeasement of Nazi Germany can only be explained by two variables that are expressly forbidden by structural realism but are embraced by Classical Realism: history and ideology. That is, it is not possible to explain British behavior without understanding the influence of World War I (not on power, but on preferences) and the vehement anti-communism of the British right (and its relative comfort with fascism).

Why did America fight in Vietnam? Here again this chapter looks closely at still another notable structural explanation, the leading exemplar of a cluster of contributions that fall under the rubric of "power cycle theory." Varieties of this influential approach tend to focus on the issue of "hegemonic decline," and elaborate how and why the changing costs and benefits of maintaining the status quo turn the tide against hegemons facing rising challengers. Power cycle theories have much to offer in illustrating the general realist expectation that underlying shifts in the balance of power are to be expected, and that such dynamics can be so destabilizing. But these often elegant, abstract analytical machines simply do not well explain the ruinous catastrophe of the Vietnam War—which, once again, is better understood from a classical perspective. The most grievous wounds suffered by the United States as a hegemonic power—as seen again in the disastrous decision to wage a preventive war against Iraq in 2003—were not the result of external checks on American power due to tectonic shifts in the underlying balance of power but from, if anything, exactly the opposite: a preponderance of power and the temptations such lack of constraints can invite. History, ideology, temptation, ambition, and hubris—these factors are central to explaining the great puzzles of world politics. They are forbidden by structural realism and hyper-rationalism; they are the stuffing of classical realism.

The Puzzle of British Appeasement of Nazi Germany

Great Britain came very close to losing World War II. There are few if any theories of International Relations that do not presume that the primary goal of the state is to ensure its own survival. Yet Britain, one of the world's mightiest powers, came within a hair's breadth of being subjugated by one of the most brutal and horrifying regimes in history. What to make of that prospect? Winston Churchill, as prime minister, told the cabinet on May 28, 1940, "If this long island story of ours is to end, let it end only when each of us lies choking in his own blood upon the ground."[1] How could Britain, one of the world's greatest powers, with its mighty navy, economic muscle, and vast overseas empire, have gotten it so wrong?[2] True, Britain had been dealt a difficult hand. Victorious in World War I, the Great War nevertheless left the country financially and physically exhausted, with more rather than fewer overseas commitments, and facing new challenges (in particular, erstwhile ally Japan was emerging as a significant geopolitical rival in Asia). Nevertheless, Britain emerged from the war as a great and secure power, and with its traditional adversaries weakened. Russia had turned inward toward the convulsions of its civil war and consolidation of Bolshevik authority; as for Germany, a country that suffered two million dead and five million wounded—its bitter serving for losing the war, imposed at the point of a gun and on the brink of starvation, left that country demilitarized, dismembered, and stripped of colonies and assets. Yet from those ruins the Nazi menace would emerge in 1933—abetted by the one-two punch of socially destabilizing hyperinflation in 1924 and descent into Great Depression in 1928 (in 1932, unemployment in Germany soared to 25 percent)—and for the next six years Britain dithered as that mortal threat grew.

A key claim of this book is that the future is unwritten. Thus it was impossible for British leaders to *know* that Hitler would embark on a militarized project to dominate Europe (the prevention of which was seen as the linchpin of British security for centuries) and quite possibly beyond. But it was also grossly irresponsible not to recognize the likelihood of such a prospect, and to act accordingly. Hitler was not a riddle. He was a messianic, militant, charismatic demagogue who spelled out his intentions explicitly in his prison memoir *Mein Kampf*, and from the very beginning his deeds matched his words—horrors plainly visible to see to anyone who could be roused to pay the slightest attention. Hitler was appointed chancellor on January 30, 1933, and on March 24, the Reichstag passed the enabling act, which essentially granted him dictatorial powers that he would consolidate over the following year. Violet Bonham Carter, daughter of former British prime minister H. H. Asquith, shared these thoughts at a conference of the Liberal party on May 18: "In Germany, freedom as we conceive it seems to have perished in the last few weeks, in the twinkling of an eye, almost without a struggle, and given place to a nightmare reign of force whose horror we can hardly conceive." Months later, she warned that the Nazi system threatened "not merely the soul of a people, but the peace of the world," and in December lamented that "we in this country have looked on with dazed astonishment."[3]

The implications of the Nazi regime were known at the highest levels of the British government—or at least they certainly should have been. Horace Rumbold, the British ambassador in Berlin, sent a lengthy and insightful dispatch to London on April 26, 1933, that offered an alarming report about the new regime. Prime Minister Ramsay MacDonald thought the missive was important enough to circulate to the cabinet, which then included Neville Chamberlain, who served Chancellor of the Exchequer from 1931 until 1937, when he became prime minister. In late June Rumbold cabled with an even more critical report. His successor in Berlin, Eric Phipps, who served from 1933 to 1937, witnessed the same brutality and sent home similar warnings, arguing that it would be foolish to make concessions to Hitler and urging British rearmament.[4]

In 1933 it was clear that Germany was violating the armaments limits set by the Versailles Treaty, but the provocation was overlooked (as was Germany's unilateral withdrawal from the League of Nations in October). By March 1934 Germany's continuing increases in defense spending leapt ahead so dramatically that France felt compelled to make the gesture of withdrawing from ongoing disarmament talks, but neither Britain nor France followed suit with renewed spending initiatives of their own.[5] And on March 16, 1935, Germany reintroduced compulsory military service, and announced that its army would expand to thirty-six divisions, more than five times the ceiling mandated by the Versailles Treaty. The meaning of all this, again, was not hard to decipher. As Ernest Hemingway wrote at the time, soon there will be war: "Not next August, nor next September; that is still too soon," he warned. "But the year after that or the year after that they fight." There will be war not because countries want war, he explained. But "Italy is a man, Mussolini, and Germany is a man, Hitler." And their ambitions will eventually and inevitably lead to war. It is important to note that although Hemingway would later emerge as a militant anti-fascist, actively supporting the loyalists in the Spanish Civil War and subsequently witnessing the Normandy landings, in 1935, with the pointless ruin of the Great War fresh in his mind, Hemingway was not itching for the fight—just the opposite, he was urging the United States to steer clear of the inevitable conflict.[6]

Hitler's next provocation, especially in retrospect, marked a crossing of the political Rubicon. The remilitarization of the Rhineland on March 7,

1936, was, among other things, a devastating and sobering blow to the notion that France would, in theory, press a military advantage against Germany in support of the defense of its eastern European allies. But the measure was also an alarming harbinger in that it was not simply a violation of the Treaty of Versailles, which Germany signed under duress, it was a violation of the 1925 Treaty of Locarno. The Locarno pact, which was designed to normalize and pacify European international politics after the tumultuous years that followed the Great War, was a sweeping, multilateral agreement that reflected a series of measures intended to provide reassurances and stability across the continent—and was negotiated with Germany as a peer, not a defeated adversary, and celebrated by Nobel peace prizes in both 1925 and 1926. Thus while it can be argued that some of Hitler's initial measures were overlooked by British elites because they had tacitly (or explicitly) embraced the view that the Versailles Treaty had been inappropriately severe in its treatment of Germany, this could not apply to naked violations of Locarno. This distinction is an important one, as the severity of the Versailles settlement is hotly contested in debate to this day, with some scholars blaming John Maynard Keynes's book *The Economic Consequences of the Peace* for overstating the case that the measures imposed on Germany were too harsh. Although Keynes did favor lower reparations payments, this critique misinterprets Keynes's key arguments and overstates the influence of a then-obscure Treasury official, one whose proposals that were articulated in his book, it should be added, were roundly ignored by all parties. Keynes's principal objective was to call attention to what the treaty failed to do—and on these points he was unquestionably correct. The treaty, he wrote, "includes no provisions for the economic rehabilitation of Europe—nothing to make the defeated Central empires into good neighbors, nothing to stabilize the new states of Europe," nothing to restore "the disordered finances of France and Italy." And even worse than the reparations were the debts between the allies themselves, which were "a menace to financial stability everywhere," imposed a "crushing burden," and would be "a constant source of international friction." An international financial order that was little more than a tangle of debts and reparations could hardly "last a day." Most prescient still, he argued, "It was not obvious that it would do anyone any good if the structure of the German State were to collapse and if disorder under the opposed banners of Communism and Reaction were to plunder the rest of Europe on the other side of the Rhine."[7]

In any event, the remilitarization of the Rhineland could not be attributed to Versailles revisionism; to the contrary, it was a rejection of the spirit (not to mention the letter) of the more celebrated Locarno pact. Yet again, neither Britain (nor France) lifted a finger in response, a decision that has been called "the first capitulation," and one that is all the more tragic in retrospect because Hitler was taking an enormous gamble—he did not then have the ability to resist any military countermeasures taken against the maneuver, and the humiliation of being forced to turn tail and run might easily have brought his end in a Germany not yet purged of all of his potential adversaries in the military and elsewhere. For Raymond Aron, this "crucial capitulation" was even more consequential than the Munich disaster. It was the best opportunity to stop Hitler, although, he recalled, "taking into account what France was like at the time, I was convinced that France and Great Britain would not do what was necessary to prevent a war."[8]

Fascism was not subtle, or shy, or ambiguous in its embrace of militarism, as seen in Italy's attack on League of Nations member Ethiopia, a brutal war of imperial conquest that featured the use of (banned by international treaty) mustard gas, which outraged public opinion in Britain and France. This forced Western diplomats to become secretive about their efforts to placate Mussolini, which became a source of some embarrassment when those machinations became public, ultimately forcing the resignation of British foreign secretary Samuel Hoare, who was replaced by Anthony Eden.[9] From 1936 Germany and Italy provided active military support to Francisco Franco in his effort to overthrow the Republican Spanish government. Legions of idealistic Westerners flocked to Spain to fight on behalf of the Loyalists, including George Orwell, who was grievously wounded. (Thousands of them, including Julian Bell, the nephew of Virginia Woolf, who served the cause as a volunteer ambulance driver, lost their lives.) The British government, however, at least as wary of communist elements among the Republicans (who received assistance from the Soviet Union), maintained a posture of strict neutrality as the Italian and German armed forces participated in the fighting.[10]

Neville Chamberlain, upon acceding to the position of prime minister in May 1937, did not invent the policy of appeasement, which had broad support across the Conservative party, but as a powerful Chancellor of the Exchequer he had embraced it fully, and as prime minister he came to personify it. In command of a large majority in Parliament, Chamberlain, whose most ardent defenders would not hesitate to describe him as confident and arrogant, single-handedly directed the course of British foreign policy until well into the first year of World War II. Chamberlain's dedicated application of appeasement reached its apogee in 1938. He watched calmly as Hitler seized Austria and added it to the Reich—German tanks rolled across the border on March 14. With Austria absorbed, Hitler immediately set his sights on Czechoslovakia, and crises on that front brewed for months, until the final fiasco of the Munich accords of September, which ceded the Sudetenland region of the country in exchange for the promise that the remnants of the republic would be left unmolested. Munich is a story so familiar it need not be rehearsed here, other than to note its fruits: within two weeks Germany announced still another major expansion of its rearmament program, and much of the world gasped in horror at the atrocities of Kristallnacht that soon followed. (Chamberlain was unmoved; in the words of one account, he "was not prepared to abandon his entire policy simply because of domestic German beastliness.")[11] In March 1939 Hitler seized the remnants of Czechoslovakia, breaking the consensus about appeasement in Britain and leading to its guarantee of Poland's territorial integrity, the German violation of which in September finally led Britain to declare war.

"The failure to perceive the true character of the Nazi regime and Adolf Hitler stands as the single greatest failure of British policymakers makers during this period," one recent account of appeasement concluded. "The real nature of the Nazi regime was . . . obvious."[12] Why did Britain get this so wrong—at the peril of its very existence? The predominant explanations are unsatisfactory.

Structuralist Explanations for British Appeasement

There are two major realist/rationalist explanations for Britain's catastrophic failure in the 1930s: buck-passing and buying time. The former derives from a sound deductive argument that can be plausibly applied to the 1930s, but does not in fact capture what was actually taking place. The latter is simply wrong. Both explanations are handicapped by their unwillingness to allow for history and ideology as explanatory variables.

The buck-passing argument is most closely associated with a seminal paper written by Thomas Christensen and Jack Snyder. An effort to explain alliance patterns under multiparty, the authors advance Waltz's analytically paralyzing minimalist structuralism by adding the variable of perceptions regarding whether offensive or defensive military doctrines are seen to have the advantage. The essence of this innovative argument can be quickly summarized. If the offense has the advantage, then aggressors might win wars that erupt quite quickly; the opposite is true when defense dominates. Thus in a world of perceived offensive advantages (like the "cult of the offensive" before World War I), one must promptly come to the defense of allies—as Robert Jervis argued, these are dangerous "shoot first and ask questions later" settings. With regard to alliances, this leads to the pathology of "chain-ganging" whereby the most militant and aggressive state can drag its allies into war, as well as the allies of its adversaries, and their allies, and so on. Alternatively, if everybody expects that defenses will be robust and conquest difficult, states can take a "wait and see" attitude when their allies get into trouble. But this can contribute to the pathology of "buck-passing"—engaging in suboptimal levels of military preparation in the hope that this will nudge allies to shoulder a larger share of the burden, confident that, if war does actually emerge, there will be time for a robust rearmament effort then, while well-defended allies hold the fort.[13]

This is a plausible argument; even in the late 1930s, Britain had incentives to buck-pass—surely it was very much hoped that France would bear the brunt of any land war on the European continent. Consider that in World War I, Britain committed sixty divisions to the western front. For the next war, should it come, it now pledged two, with the suggestion that perhaps as many as two or three more might be forthcoming if circumstances dictated. And of course France wanted desperately to ensure that Britain would participate in any future European war, and so any measures that incentivized British rearmament were in the French interest.

But neither the timid diplomacy nor, crucially, the sluggish pace of rearmament by Britain and France can be attributed to buck-passing ("let's spend less and thus force the other to spend more"). Buck-passing was simply not a plausible strategy for France. A front-line state, it did not have the luxuries that its ally (apparently) enjoyed: between Britain and Germany stood a very large European army (France's), and beyond that the protection afforded by the English Channel. Nor could France as easily entertain the notion (which Britain, plausibly if misguidedly, might) that if Nazi Germany were to consolidate its power in eastern and central Europe and come to dominate the continent more generally, well, that might be regrettable but something that with the right air defenses, naval supremacy, and vast overseas empire one could learn to live with.

In fact, for both powers, domestic economic priorities (and, importantly, economic ideology)—not calculations of the potential contributions of others—were the key motivations that restrained defense spending. In France, a widely held fetish for economic and monetary orthodoxy was the driving force behind all budgetary decisions, and for much of the 1930s this led to wave after wave of deflationary policies and budget cuts—misguided policies that inevitably and tragically starved defense spending.[14] As for Britain, it was an article of faith, especially in the Conservative party, that too much defense spending would imperil the stability of British finances, the soundness of which was seen as the vital "fourth arm of defense" and necessary to preserve should a war actually occur. (Such a posture also well served the perceived economic interests of the party's political base.)

The sensitivity of the government for the need to maintain confidence in the financial sector (with which the Conservative party was intimately associated) imposed restraints on government borrowing and spending and inhibited rearmament. As one study concluded, "the decision to limit defense expenditure . . . had its roots in economic assumptions shared by the Treasury and the financial community."[15]

These perceived constraints limited British rearmament and reinforced the policy of appeasement. Despite the breathtaking pace of German rearmament, obvious from 1933 and immense from 1935, Britain lagged dangerously behind, even as the Nazi war machine raced ahead. Military spending did pick up in 1936, but only reached 8 percent of gross domestic product in 1938 (the level Germany reached in 1935) and was not engaged with urgency until well into 1939.[16] And at all points, even at the very end, finance was pressing at the brakes. In 1935 Prime Minister Stanley Baldwin pledged that Britain would maintain parity with the German air force (this was an urgent matter, as the palpable fear of devastating air strikes against the homeland was widespread throughout the country—thus the "starvation of the British army" was one thing, but restraining the air force budget could not be attributed to buck-passing). But even this pledge was soon forgotten. In 1935 Germany produced over 5,000 aircraft, as Britain built fewer than 2,000; and when war was declared in 1939, the Luftwaffe had 3,000 combat-ready planes, as compared with 1,400 for Britain.[17]

As Chancellor of the Exchequer from 1931 to 1937, Neville Chamberlain was "preoccupied by the economic constraints on British rearmament," and as prime minister, he "played a major role in efforts to keep defense spending at the lowest possible level." He was even more stringent than his Treasury advisors, who managed to force a slowdown in military spending in the second half of 1937, citing fears of inflation. Moreover, although looking back, Chamberlain's defenders often emphasize his role in shoring up Britain's vital air defenses, upon assuming office he dismissed Baldwin's eighteen-month-old parity pledge as ancient history, and routinely clashed with his Secretary of State for Air, Philip Cunliffe-Lister (Lord Swinton), who was persistent in his efforts to increase the air force budget beyond the strict ceilings imposed by the prime minister. Swinton was marginally successful in squeezing a few pounds more for the air force from the Treasury, and an emergency cabinet meeting was held in March 1938 to evaluate his "scheme K," to expand the potential capacity for aircraft production. But Swinton's proposal was rejected, and Chamberlain dismissed him from office in May.[18] In sum, the relentless budgetary pressure on British defense spending in the years leading up to the war and the relatively sluggish pace of its rearmament were driven by an overzealous commitment to financial orthodoxy, not an attempt to elicit greater spending from France. (And had buck-passing been a motive, surely Britain would have long recognized the utter failure of such an effort. France, if anything, was even more lethargic in responding to the existential threat of Nazi Germany, a failure that must be attributed to a crisis within French society, a general theme that will be revisited in chapter 7.)[19]

Was Chamberlain buying time? Chamberlain's posthumous defenders and apologists have attempted to untie the puzzling knot of appeasement by rallying around the revisionist claim that the prime minister and his supporters were not naive; rather, they were clever, and playing a bad hand well. The Munich Agreement, especially, in this revisionist assessment is reinterpreted from the shortsighted, foolish humiliation that it was, and reimagined as a savvy far-sighted strategy: Chamberlain recognized that Britain was not well equipped to fight Hitler in 1938, and so he used the Munich accords instrumentally to buy time for rearmament, and thus confront the Nazis militarily at a time when the country would be better prepared and thus the odds would be more in its favor. In International Relations scholarship this position is best associated with Norrin Ripsman and Jack Levy, who argue that "British appeasement was not based on a naïve understanding of Hitler's intentions or on wishful thinking about the possibility of establishing a lasting peace with Germany." Rather, appeasement (here centrally over Munich) was "a means of buying time for rearmament, thus delaying the likely confrontation until Britain was adequately prepared for war."[20] Setting aside the obvious retort that it was the appeasers' reluctance either to check Hitler's ambitions or to rearm from the mid-1930s as Germany galloped ahead with its massive military expansion that left Britain unprepared in the first place, this argument simply does not stand up to scrutiny, undermined by two essential flaws. First, the breathing space between September 1938 and September 1939 did not shift the balance of power in the allies' favor. If war it was going to be, better to have fought in 1938. Second, and fundamentally, the policy of appeasement was not designed to buy time for a future war. It was designed to make sure that war would never occur.

This is plainly illustrated by the actions and words of Chamberlain and his affiliates—over Munich, after Hitler's shredding of the accord with Germany's absorption and dismemberment of the rest of Czechoslovakia in March 1939, in the final buildup to war that summer, and in the immediate aftermath of Germany's invasion of Poland. A careful look at the evidence makes clear that appeasement indeed was based on a fundamental misreading of Hitler, and the desire to come to understanding with the Nazi regime and forge a lasting peace between Britain and Germany.

"Buying time" at Munich did not tilt the balance of power in Britain's favor. Indeed, Ripsman and Levy readily admit that "Germany made better use of the delay in war than did Britain." This is no small concession, and merits a modest review of the changing military situation. Britain did increase its arms spending after the Munich accords, and still more after Germany's subsequent invasion of Prague. But at all points both Chamberlain and the Treasury pushed to moderate the rate of increase—an odd strategy for a nation imagining itself ramping up for war. And always, finance came first. Days after Munich Chamberlain reminded the cabinet of his long-standing and continuing concern that "the burden of armaments might break our back." (Thus even wise decisions, such as the production of fighter planes, were based on the desire to avoid investing in what would have been a much more expensive heavy bomber program.) Even more damning, the buying time for rearmament argument must reckon not simply with British preparation but with devastating counterarguments, in particular, the relative weakness of Germany in 1938, and the consequences of the neutering of Czechoslovakia. Hitler was in no position to win a general European war in 1938—he would have had his hands full with a fight over Czechoslovakia, with its large, well-equipped army stationed behind mountainous fortifications, not to mention the prospect that France and Russia might fulfill their treaty obligations and come to Czechoslovakia's defense. The ceding of the Sudetenland abandoned those fortifications and the country's industrial centers. The balance of the republic was left defenseless after Munich, and, with the subsequent occupation of Prague, not only was the formidable Czech military subtracted from the ledger of the allied forces, but the Nazi war machine added its industrial capacity, raw materials, arms production complexes (Czechoslovakia was a major arms exporter), and large cache of weapons. In sum, with regard to buying time, "there is no basis for such an argument."[21]

But even more important, the simple fact of the matter is, Chamberlain was not buying time. He was, quite sincerely (if misguidedly), trying to avoid war altogether—when he proclaimed that his diplomacy had achieved "peace in our time," he meant it. As Chamberlain's devoted parliamentary private secretary (and future prime minister) Alec Douglas-Home put it, Chamberlain and his confidant and influential advisor Horace Wilson "believed that by the sacrifice of Czechoslovakia they could achieve permanent peace and that Hitler would be satisfied." Looking back, Wilson could not have stated it more plainly: "the aim of appeasement was to avoid war altogether, for all time.[22]

Chamberlain blundered appallingly at Munich, done in by his robust ego and obtuse inability to see Hitler for what he was. In the words of Robert Self, editor of *The Neville Chamberlain Diary Letters*, whose disposition is generally very sympathetic to his protagonist, "It is unquestionably true that Chamberlain profoundly misjudged Hitler and fell easy victim to his calculated flattery." After his first encounter with the Fuhrer, the prime minister boasted to his sister that, according to Wilson, by all accounts Hitler was "very favorably impressed" with him. This was not true, but, conspicuously, the converse was—in Hitler, Chamberlain saw "a man who could be relied upon when he had given his word."[23]

In Hitler, Chamberlain confidently assessed that he had found a partner with whom he could achieve his heartfelt goal, peace in his time. Certainly, he would concede, the Fuhrer was a bit of an ill-tempered rogue, with perhaps a spot of blood on his hands, but he was a reasonable fellow, and a deftly handled combination of generous concessions, combined with just enough rearmament to persuade Hitler that attacking Britain would be more trouble than it was worth (and provide some insurance should the nightmare of war actually come to pass), would carry the day. Hitler walked away from the bargaining table with the Sudetenland; Chamberlain, in turn, took home Hitler's promise that he would seek no more than that and, most important to him, with the Fuhrer's hurried scrawl on a document that avowed of "the desire of our two peoples never to go to war with one another again." Chamberlain was not buying time, he was buying peace. Days after Munich, he approached Lord Swinton, his dismissed Air Minister, seeking his support. "I will support you," Swinton responded, "provided that you are clear that you have been buying time for rearmament." Chamberlain was puzzled by the notion, responding, "But don't you see, I have brought back peace." On October 31, the prime minister articulated his vision plainly: "Our Foreign Policy is one of appeasement. We must aim at establishing relations with the Dictator Powers which will lead to settlements in Europe and a sense of stability." In the press and around the country, he admonished, a considerable amount of "false emphasis" had been placed on rearmament. But although increased defense expenditures were necessary, the next objective would be arms control, not an arms race. The following day, Wilson explained that "putting the aircraft industry on a war footing would be contrary to the Munich declaration that Anglo-German disagreements would be settled peacefully."[24]

This disposition was plain to see. Ivan Maisky, the Soviet ambassador in London and an often insightful observer of British politics and foreign policy, met with Chamberlain on March 2, 1939. In his diary, Maisky wrote that the prime minister shared that "he remained an 'optimist' despite everything," and "the general situation is improving." Both Hitler and Mussolini, Chamberlain explained, had given him "their personal assurance" of their peaceful intentions, and the prime minister was confident that "Hitler and Mussolini are afraid of war."[25] Thirteen days later German troops marched into Czechoslovakia. This was a turning point in Britain—whatever Hitler may or may not have promised at Munich, the accords had been shredded and few could continue to deny the true nature of Germany's aggressive behavior and intentions. Even Chamberlain's ever faithful partner in the implementation of appeasement, Foreign Minister Edward Wood (Lord Halifax), wavered in his confidence about the direction of British foreign policy. After the absorption of Czechoslovakia, British rearmament finally picked up in earnest and public opinion began to shift in favor of a more assertive foreign policy.[26] Britain soon guaranteed the territorial integrity of Poland—finally, it would seem, drawing a clear line in the sand. Remarkably, however, there was more continuity than change in British foreign policy. Halifax was perhaps newly wary of Hitler, but his political instincts endured. He was still the man who found himself charmed by Hitler's right-hand man, the murderous sociopath Hermann Göring, in November 1937. Halifax was "immensely entertained" by Göring, whose personality he described in his dairy as "frankly attractive." And the Treasury still sought to press the brakes on rearmament at every opportunity. And Neville Chamberlain would not be dissuaded from his strategy of appeasement. "I bitterly regret what has now occurred, but do not let us on that account be deflected from our course," he told the House of Commons after the occupation of Prague. Acknowledging that British policies needed to be reassessed, his fundamental disposition was unchanged. "I am no more a man of war today than I was in September," he declared. "I trust that our actions . . . will prove a turning-point not towards war . . . but towards a more wholesome era when reason will take the place of force."[27]

Chamberlain continued to misread Hitler, and his remarkably enduring if hopelessly misguided goal was to find a way to accommodate the Fuhrer's demands and somehow satiate his appetite for expansion, in order to avoid war at almost any cost. His letters to his sisters illustrate this plainly. On May 28, 1939, he wrote, "I myself still believe that Hitler missed the bus last September and that his Generals won't let him risk a major war now." On July 15, he expressed "little doubt that Hitler knows quite well we mean business." One week later he was characteristically confident: "One thing I think is clear, namely that Hitler has concluded that we mean business and that the time is not ripe for major war. Therein he is fulfilling my expectations." By staying this course, Germany will "come to realize that [war] never will be worth while." That same month, Britain turned down a request from the Polish government for export credits and a cash loan.[28]

Astonishingly, Chamberlain's attempts to reach a settlement with Hitler and find a way to avoid war endured after the Nazi invasion of Poland, and even into the early months of the war. The day after Germany's invasion of Poland on September 1, Chamberlain gave a tepid and uninspiring speech before an uproarious session of the House of Commons, in which he referred to the prospect of a diplomatic solution brokered by Italy. The performance so disturbed some cabinet members that a dozen of them, as if in a movie, descended on 10 Downing Street in the pouring rain as midnight approached, demanding an audience with the prime minister. The following morning at 11:30 on September 3, Chamberlain finally announced that Britain was at war.[29] Even technically at war, however, the prime minister still searched for a way out—and continued, remarkably, to misread Hitler. As the Nazi war machine stormed across Poland, Chamberlain wrote his sister that "communications with Hitler and Goring looked rather promising at one time but came to nothing." The man who took the Fuhrer at his word was at a loss to explain why. "Was Hitler merely talking through his hat and deliberately deceiving us while he matured his schemes? I don't think so." Chamberlain anticipated that peace talks would not be far off, and a general European war could still be avoided. This was reflected in his passive "phony war" strategy, with Halifax fully on board—by avoiding military measures that might only provoke Germany and dash the hope that the Nazis might come to their senses. Well into 1940, Chamberlain "continued to delude himself the conflict would remain limited," one critic summarized. "His abhorrence of war has not grown any weaker."[30]

In sum, the puzzle of appeasement eludes explanation by structuralist theories. Britain was not buck-passing, and it was certainly not buying time. Ripsman and Levy assert that "Chamberlain and Halifax would have been pleased by German reciprocity and a durable peace, but they viewed that outcome as highly unlikely." As briefly reviewed here, this is simply inconsistent with the evidence, and forcefully contradicted by Chamberlain himself, in the remarkable public confession he offered in his address to the House of Commons at the outbreak of the war: "Everything I have worked for, everything that I have hoped for, everything that I have believed in during my public life, has crashed into ruins."[31]

Explaining Appeasement with Classical Realism: History and Ideology

The poor leadership of Neville Chamberlain, however, cannot account for years of foreign policy blunders that risked Britain's very survival. Rather, history and ideology are the factors that explain the puzzle. The relevant history was World War I. It is not possible to understand British (or French) foreign policy in the 1930s without taking this into account. The Great War was a traumatic experience for the nation, even in victory. And although with the passage of time scholars and historians can point to underlying economic and social factors, and destabilizing changes to the balance of power, that can dispassionately account for the intensity of that conflagration, for those swept up in the moment it was an unfathomable horror caused by an obscure and unlikely chain of events (an assassination, a crisis in the Balkans, a regional war that quickly spread across the continent as commitments and alliances drew states onto the conflict). Perhaps worse, the war seemed to settle nothing, with even the winners bled white, the vanquished embittered, and economic and political disarray across the continent.

The scale of the war, and the waste of young lives—and the appalling brutality with which the bodies of a generation of men were torn to shreds, for uncertain purpose and pyrrhic victory—was unprecedented and unimaginable. In 1915, at the battle of Loos, thousands upon thousands of British soldiers lost their lives in what were essentially human wave assaults against fortified, well-entrenched machine gun nests—at one point in that engagement Britain suffered 8,000 causalities out of 10,000 men in a four-hour period. On July 1, 1916, the first day of the Battle of the Somme, over 20,000 British soldiers would perish in a similar fashion, sprinting into machine gun fire; allied forces would suffer over 600,000 casualties during that campaign, which pushed the front forward seven miles. Among those wounded was future prime minister

Harold Macmillan, a member of a battalion tasked with attacking a German machine gun stronghold. Felled by multiple wounds, he tumbled into a muddy shell hole which provided cover from the projectiles flying above. As a distraction from his suffering, Macmillan pulled out a book from his pocket (Aeschylus's *Prometheus*) and passed the time reading, playing dead whenever enemy troops approached. For years after the war he avoided returning to Oxford, because it was "a city of the dead. Almost everybody I knew there seemed to have been killed." These were common experiences. In 1917, over 370,000 British soldiers died in the Third Battle of Ypres, a campaign that netted forty-five square miles of blood-soaked muddy fields. Over the course of the war the country of forty-five million suffered nearly a million dead and 1.6 million wounded—most of those, of course, men between the ages of twenty and thirty-five. French losses were considerably worse, with 1.7 million dead and 4.26 million wounded from a population of forty million, in battles fought largely on its home soil. In 1918 there were 630,000 war widows in France.[32]

It is not surprising that few in Britain wanted to repeat the experience of the Great War. "Never again" was the mindset (especially regarding European entanglements), and pacifism the order of the times. Notoriously, at an Oxford Union debate in February 1933, the motion "This House will under no circumstances fight for its King and country" passed by a vote of 275–153. Perhaps that could be dismissed as a fluke, or a joke, but a subsequent motion to expunge that resolution was defeated 750–138. If the Western powers were slow to meet the Nazi threat, it was in part because they simply could not bear the thought of another war. During the Munich Crisis, Virginia Woolf fretted, "one shot at a policeman and the Germans, Czechs, French will begin the old horror." Unlike Chamberlain and his men, Woolf was under no illusions about the brutality of the Nazis—nevertheless, she was terrified at the prospect of another great European war. As Raymond Aron reflected, it would certainly have been wise to try to nip Hitler in the bud, "but the consequences of the previous war were enough" to effectively rule out that prospect. Even as late as 1938 and 1939, "the French and British alike were still haunted by the horrors of war."[33]

This explains the general public reaction to Chamberlain's triumphant return from Munich and his promise of "peace in our time": adulation, and enormous relief—followed increasingly by a sense of shame. ("Shame and relief" was how Isaiah Berlin recalled his father's reaction to the news.)[34] Consider an instinctive pacifist like Keynes, who, with his cohort, was traumatized by the Great War and more than keen to avoid another. Keynes had little stomach for war and feared its civilizational consequences, and he would not have favored fighting to protect Czechoslovakia from Germany in September 1938. Nevertheless, unlike the appeasers in the Conservative party, he was under no illusions about the malevolence of what he called the "brigand powers," and he favored ambitious rearmament and a more assertive foreign policy.[35] The international situation is "critical and dangerous," he wrote to a friend in 1937; "our sole and overriding purpose should be made quite sure of countering the fascist powers at long last." Castigating the prime minister in the *New Statesman and Nation* in March 1938, Keynes explained, "We have assumed that a negative pacifism . . . would prevail against a positive militarism," adding, presciently, that Chamberlain "is not escaping the risks of war. He is only making sure that, when it comes, we shall have no friends and no common cause."[36]

Thus although, as noted, Keynes would not have used force to stop Germany from seizing the Sudetenland six months later, he thought that British policy should be to "bluff to the hilt; and if the bluff is called, back out," noting, accurately, that even on their own, the Czechs would be able to put up a good fight. Of the subsequent Munich accords, he did not see "peace in our time"; his private correspondence expressed the tumult of mixed emotions increasingly shared by many: "intense relief and satisfied cowardice joined with rage and indignation." In the pages of the *New Statesman* he was more blunt: "we and France have . . . sacrificed our honor and our engagements to a civilized and faithful nation, and fraternized with what is vile."[37] But for memories of the Great War, appeasement could not likely have been sustained as long as it was.

The Weakness of Structuralism Illustrated: Content and Purpose Matter

The attempt to appease Nazi Germany also exposes the poverty of structuralist attempts to understand international relations. Because the practice of "appeasement" as a strategy is in the abstract not inherently problematic, nor inconsistent with realism—to the contrary, there are times when it will prove to be the wise policy choice.[38] In other settings, as in the 1930s, it can be disastrous. It depends largely on *whom* one is trying to appease. But since the essence of structuralism is to model states as "like units, differentiated only by their relative capabilities," such analyses are incapable of making this crucial distinction. This is why E. H. Carr blundered so miserably on this question in the 1930s, and why Aron and Hans Morgenthau got it right. Carr considered only the structural variable (recognizing changes to the balance of power, and the prospect of making peaceful adjustments to restore equilibrium); Aron and Morgenthau understood there was something distinctly dangerous about the Nazis and the insatiability of Hitler's ambitions.

Carr's *The Twenty Years' Crisis, 1919–1939* was not only, as discussed in chapter 1, an early and major statement of modern realism—it was also, published in 1939 before war broke out, a full-throated defense of the Munich accords (the references to which were altered or deleted in the second and standard edition of the book, published in 1946). The 1939 edition, replete with a laudatory introduction by Halifax, also reflected the awful shadow of the Great War. As Realism was about seeing the world as it was, not as one wished it to be, in a world where states harbored ambitions and the underlying balance of power shifted over time, a mechanism of change was required. If differences were not to be settled by war (readers at the time would have had little difficulty finding an alternative to that appealing), then there must be a mechanism for "peaceful change." Thus, Carr lectured, "If the power relations of Europe in 1938 made it inevitable that Czecho-Slovakia should lose part of her territory, and eventually her independence, it was preferable (quite apart from any question of justice or injustice) that this should come about as the result of discussions around a table in Munich rather than as the result either of a war between the Great Powers or of a local war between Germany and Czechoslovakia." (Note here that Carr is pushing the appeasement envelope, defending Munich *after* Prague, when most finally understood that appeasement was not going to work, as well as rejecting not only a general European war but the Czech right to self-defense—the capacity for which, as noted, was formidable.) Carr's realism is wise and robust in his unwillingness to sanctify the status quo with moral legitimacy (as opposed to simply a reflection of the preferences of the established and the powerful), and the need to shed the idealism of trying to impose one's hopes into the unyielding winds of power realities, and further with his aspiration to avoid unnecessary, ruinous wars. Thus at the purely abstract level, the deductive logic of his defense of "the negotiations which led up to the Munich Agreement of September 29, 1938" as "the nearest approach in recent years to the settlement of a major international issue by a procedure of peaceful change" is plausible in theory. But it was also, in its specific application, ruinously, catastrophically wrong—and it was so because Carr limited himself to structural variables, essentially assuming that all states were "like units," which more or less behaved the same way and wanted the same things. He could not see that the Nazis were different.

Rather, he naively (idealistically?)[39] wrote, "Since the Munich Agreement, a significant change has occurred in the attitude of the German and Italian dictators." They now favor peace, and "it would be a mistake to dismiss such utterances as hypocritical." This is the willful blindness of looking solely at power and not also at purpose.[40]

But fascism was different, as was plainly visible to those unwilling to avert their eyes. As Hans Kohn wrote at the time, "Fascism is not only the glorification of power without moral restraint, but also of the insatiable will without rational limitations." These characteristics were not lost on Hans Morgenthau or Raymond Aron, who were able to see Hitler plainly. The German-born Morgenthau emigrated to the United States in 1937; his opposition to Munich was rooted in this understanding. Aron, who as a young academic spent several years in Germany (and who heard live speeches by Hitler and Goebbels on the radio), noted the difference in that country with the Nazi rise to power. After 1933, he recalled, "the problem no longer was the madness of the earlier war; my problem—my obsession—became: How to avoid the coming war?" It remained Aron's credo—and good realism—that "to reflect upon politics, one must be as rational as possible." Nevertheless, the rise of Hitler forced him to understand "the fundamental irrationality of mass movements, the irrationality of politics." Part of seeing the world as it is, and not as one wishes it would be, is to be disciplined by both of these admonitions.[41]

The Ideological Foundations of British Appeasement

British appeasement of Nazi Germany, however, is still not explicable without the appeal to another variable forbidden to structural realism: ideology. British conservatives were able to sell appeasement to a mass public determined to avoid another war. But they pursued that strategy well past the point when its failures were obvious due to a more shameful attribute. The British Right may have been appalled by the worst excesses of fascist brutality—but actually, they were very comfortable with most of it. Stated plainly, Chamberlain and his cohort fundamentally misread Hitler, but part of the reason for that was that they were quite unperturbed by the notion (and contrary to the touchstone of British grand strategy for centuries) that a fascist German state would dominate the continent of Europe. Thus the strategy of appeasement was not designed to pass the buck or buy time, it was an effort to accommodate Germany—a strategy rooted in an affinity with fascism abroad, a skepticism of France, ambivalence about America, and an implacable abhorrence for the Soviet Union.

The personification of these traits could be seen in Chamberlain's man in Berlin, Ambassador Neville Henderson. After five years of receiving accurate and alarming missives about Germany's intentions from Horace Rumbold and Eric Phipps, in May 1937 the prime minister, in one of the most common blunders in diplomatic history, decided he would prefer to hear the voice of someone who shared and would reflect his preexisting views. If Chamberlain was duped by Hitler, and Halifax charmed by Göring, Henderson was not fooled by the Nazis at all—he was a fan, a disposition not uncommon on the British Right. (In March 1938, the *Manchester Guardian* warned of "the dangerous reactionary temper of large sections of the Conservative party, to whom a virtual alliance with the dictators would not be altogether distasteful.") Shortly after his arrival in Berlin, Henderson actually raised a toast to "the great social experiment" underway in Nazi Germany. In contrast to his predecessors, he wrote to Halifax, "We must drop all fears and suspicions. . . . The main point is that we are an island people and Germany a continental one. On that basis we can be friends and both can go along the road to its own destiny without the clash of vital interests." When illness forced Henderson to return to Britain in October 1938, chargé d'affaires George Ogilvie-Forbes, acting in his place, send back a series of more alarming dispatches; one in January referred to Goebbels as "that vile and dissolute demagogue." But upon Henderson's return to Berlin in February 1939 he rebuked Ogilvie-Forbes, sent reports back "correcting" his deputy's dispatches, and resumed sending a steady stream of more optimistic assessments of Nazi intentions. Over time many in the Foreign Office grew weary of Henderson's cheerleading, joking in private that he was more the Nazi ambassador to Britain rather than the British ambassador to Germany. But he was Chamberlain's faithful servant, carrying out his wishes and reflecting the prime minister's vision. There was little intellectual space between the two men, and there was a much darker side to all of this, as suggested by Chamberlain's go-to response whenever he was asked by a reporter about Nazi atrocities or Hitler's untrustworthiness—which was to chastise "such an experienced journalist" for being so "susceptible to Jewish-Communist propaganda."[42]

The comfort level that British elites had with Nazi Germany was notable in the business community as well. Raymond Aron recalled that despite his expectation from 1936 that war was very likely, "After 1938 . . . the most intelligent man I ever knew, Alexandre Kojeve, did not believe there would be a war. He felt that Great Britain, that British capitalism, had already put Europe in Hitler's hands." And notably, although appeasement was a political strategy, it had an economic element, orchestrated by

British finance. The aversion to war of the City of London, as the financial community was known, long predated the 1930s. The City did not need the experience of the Great War to recoil in horror from the thought of a new war with Germany—before the first war, "perhaps the most persistent economic lobby for good Anglo-German relations were the financial circles in the City." And when that war materialized, "the City was a very sick man, dazed and feverish," in Keynes's estimation, "too much overwhelmed by the dangers, to which they saw their own fortunes and good names exposed, to have much wits left for the public interest and public safety."[43]

The City was perhaps wise in its judgments in 1914—but it was shameful in its behavior leading up to World War II, not only rallying behind appeasement but practicing what would become known as "economic appeasement," an effort by the City, the Treasury, and the Bank of England to keep Nazi Germany integrated with the international financial system by granting it one-sided economic concessions. One notorious episode (which caused a dustup in Parliament) that was the source of some embarrassment when it became public months after the fact occurred immediately after the shock of the occupation of Prague. Having absorbed and dismembered the balance of Czechoslovakia, the Nazis now demanded that the six million pounds' worth of Czech gold reserves held at the Bank of England be transferred to the German Reichsbank—a demand to which the Bank of England promptly acceded, despite the nominal order to freeze all Czech assets held in the United Kingdom in the wake of the German invasion on March 15, 1939. But more consistently throughout was the maintenance of the "standstill agreements," the provision by British banks of short-term credits to Germany in order to finance trade that would otherwise have been frozen in the wake of the global financial crisis of 1931. Economic appeasement was also aimed at empowering the German "moderates" such as the enigmatic president of the Reichsbank Hjalmar Schacht. But the resolute commitment of the City to avoid war with Germany outlived any reasonable hope that the strategy was working. Despite coming under increased criticism from members of Parliament, the standstill agreements were renewed every year through 1938—and negotiations for their extension took place in May 1939—by which point Schacht had been removed. (In January he was replaced by longtime Nazi and future war criminal Walther Funk.) As one study noted, "In 1939 the Treasury recognized that there were grounds for renouncing this agreement: it was contrary to Britain's interests to allow Germany to collect the considerable proceeds of her export surplus in free sterling which enabled her to buy potential war materials." But the influence of the City kept the agreements alive, and the "Bank of England itself was prepared to go to extraordinary and clandestine lengths to ensure the success of the payments agreement." In fact, the arrangements were not officially terminated until the British declaration of war on September 3.[44]

The British upper class and the City of London were also motivated by a shared, visceral hostility toward the Soviet Union. Indeed, fear of communism (and, well short of that, fear of the power and potential influence of the British labor movement) informed the policy of appeasement. Large-scale rearmament, for example, would require coordinating with and empowering trade unions, possibly unleashing broader social changes. "The real opposition to rearming comes from the rich classes in the [Conservative] party who fear taxation," Halifax's private secretary wrote in his diary in November 1938. Finding the Nazis more palatable than communists or socialists, they realize that "any war, whether we win or not, would destroy the rich idle classes and so they are for peace at any price." Again the poverty of structuralism is exposed. It is not possible to understand the British behavior in general and its disposition toward both Germany and Russia in this period without accounting for this fact.[45] Consider the following counterfactual: holding all other factors constant (like capabilities and foreign policy behavior), if after World War I Germany had gone communist and Russia fascist, would basic British foreign policy choices have been different? A structural realist account requires that the answer would be no. But in fact it is very hard to argue against the expectation that under such circumstances Britain would have rather swiftly aligned with Russia against the German threat.

But of course the communists were in Russia and the Nazis ruled Germany, and Chamberlain, and much of his party, and British elites more generally (as well as their respective counterparts in France) feared the distant, disheveled Bolsheviks more than the proximate, militant fascists. (In fact many saw fascism as a crucial bulwark against the global spread of communism.) These roots ran deep, and it is hard to explain the pattern of appeasement without them. "Our capitalists," France's ambassador to Russia told his hosts plainly in 1934, "are afraid of you." When Hitler remilitarized the Rhineland, "France might succeed in crushing Germany with the aid of Russia," Prime Minister Baldwin informed his cabinet, "but it would probably only result in Germany going Bolshevik." At the time of the Munich crisis, France and Russia—not surprisingly given their overlapping interests—each had a defense alliance with Czechoslovakia. Such a triumvirate would have been more than the Germans could then have handled, but France, following Britain's lead, ruled out coordinating with the Soviet Union at that time. (Within a year an increasingly desperate France would reverse its position, but the British remained adamant in their opposition to such measures.)[46]

Chamberlain in particular had a profound suspicion of Russia, as his letters to his sisters reflect. In late April 1939, he would write, astonishingly, "Our chief trouble is with Russia. I confess to being deeply suspicious of her." Curiously, among his doubts were that the two countries had any common interests; more curiously still, he counted among the reasons for his suspicions the Soviet "lack of any sympathy with Democracy as such." Throughout May his letters returned to his "suspicions" and "deep suspicions" about Russia. Of course, it was more than eminently reasonable to be suspicious of Stalin's Soviet Union. But consider who Chamberlain was not suspicious of—Hitler and Mussolini—and it becomes clear that ideology is driving British behavior—at the clear expense of British security. Hitler was, famously, in Chamberlain's eyes "a man who could be relied upon," and his endless attempts to woo Mussolini—even after the latter's invasion, conquest, and absorption of Albania in the weeks before Chamberlain wrote those letters—was foolish, and little short of humiliating. But by the prime minister's assessment the Italian fascist was worth eagerly courting, and ideally counting on to check German power, with little concern for Il Duce's lack of "sympathy with democracy."[47]

This would become enormously consequential as war approached. Through the spring and toward the summer of 1939 the prospect of an alliance between France, Britain, and Russia became increasingly plausible (and logical). Such an alliance could not be presumed, but pursuing the possibility made enormous sense, and, not surprisingly, France in particular was eager to explore the prospect—and the British public overwhelmingly supported the notion. France and Russia each made serious overtures toward a possible pact, but Chamberlain dragged his feet. Indeed in July he approved secret back-channel negotiations with Germany. During that same month—within six weeks of the Nazi invasion of Poland and the British declaration of war—in private correspondence he expressed that he remained "suspicious" not of Germany but "of [Russia's] good faith" and that he was "so skeptical of the value of Russian help." It bears remembering that without Russia's ultimate participation, the European war would surely have been lost. But on July 15, Chamberlain was reluctant "even to talk to them." France, unwilling to act alone, was reduced, like a desperate lover, to checking in now and then, asking whether Britain had found the opportunity to review their modest proposal for a tripartite alliance. Sensing British wariness, Soviet foreign minister Molotov suggested a watered-down arrangement, a strictly defensive agreement of mutual assistance should one of the three parties come under attack, which, again, gained no traction in London. Russian ambassador Maisky concluded in his diary that Chamberlain would oppose any such alliance because "it would once and for all throw him in the anti-German camp and would put an end to any projects to resurrect 'appeasement.'" Ultimately the bitter adversaries of Hitler's Germany and Stalin's Russia would stun the world with the announcement of the Nazi-Soviet non-aggression pact on August 23, leaving the Western powers painted still further into a geopolitical corner.[48]

In sum, it is not possible to explain one of the great puzzles of modern International Relations—why did Britain, one of the world's most powerful states, pursue policies that threatened its very survival and led it to approach the very precipice of invasion, exposure to pitiless barbarism, and utter ruin—without appealing to the variables of ideology and historical legacies. The trauma of the Great War, and the hostility of the British ruling class to the notion of associating in any way with communists (as opposed to consorting with fascists), meant that British conservatives decided, until it was very nearly too late, that the best course of action available to them was to accede to the Nazi domination of Europe.

Misunderstanding the Limits of American Hegemony

Among the great puzzles in modern international political history is why did the United States, the world's greatest power, engage into two acts of foolish geopolitical self-mutilation: its war in Vietnam from 1965 to 1973, and its preventive war against Iraq that began in 2003. In each case the wars were viewed as illegitimate abroad, tarnishing America's international reputation (this mattered especially during the Vietnam War, because winning "hearts and minds" globally was taken seriously during that Cold War—indeed, the Vietnam War would not have been fought but for its Cold War context). More important, each of these wars of choice was ruinous, and hollowed out the American military physically and U.S. foreign policy psychologically (with the scarring and exhaustion of its soldiers and the public more generally). These distant wars of dubious-at-best urgency left the United States weaker and less politically influential. The leading theories of International Relations do not explain well U.S. behavior in either case. Vietnam was both remote and strategically insignificant—yet the United States poured the bulk of its military (not to mention its reputation) into fighting and losing that war. Iraq was a preventive war—it was explicitly fought in the absence of a pressing imperative. America actually had to invent a new and radical doctrine—the Bush doctrine of preventive war, which announced that the United States would fight wars against threats "before they were fully formed." Read dispassionately, this is easily seen as an invitation to strategic error, overreach, and disaster.[49]

Hyper-rationalist theories of International Relations are, not surprisingly, unhelpful in explaining massive, sustained blunders. Actors can make errors from such a perspective, but those errors should be randomly distributed around good decisions, not result in collective, wild lurches into obvious folly. Structural approaches do somewhat better, but even the best of these stumble—which is the focus of the discussion here. In the 1970s and the 1980s, as U.S power seemed to be relatively eroding, a large body of scholarship emerged that focused on the question of "hegemonic decline." Packaged theoretically, these studies were nevertheless motivated to understand what was then perceived to be the American experience, and how the United States seemed to be on a trajectory to follow a cycle of the rise and decline of empires and great powers recognizable throughout history. (Actually, this widely shared perception turned out to be wrong, as the unexpected collapse of the Soviet Union and the stalling of Japan's economy led to the resurgence of American hegemony in the 1990s.)[50]

In general, in International Relations theory, explanations of such power cycles, at the systemic level, are fellow travelers of structural realism, which explains world politics by looking at the distribution of power between states. That approach tends to be a snapshot, a focus on the static distribution of power at any moment in time (most commonly, "is the system bipolar or multipolar?"). A different type of systemic theory is *dynamic*, in which the driving explanatory variable is *changes to* the balance of power. (Recall E. H. Carr's emphasis on how changes to the balance of power undermine the sustainability of the status quo, generating political pressures that would find expression in war if a mechanism for peaceful change was not found.) Classical realism in general tends to place greater emphasis on dynamics rather than statics. And dynamic systemic theories of the relative decline of great powers tend to focus on the increasing costs of maintaining a formal or informal empire at its frontiers, which leads to strategic overextension. This spawned a vast literature, but the seminal articulation of the theory of hegemonic decline is found in Robert Gilpin's *War and Change in World Politics*.[51]

Developed in the 1970s and published in 1981, the book was written directly into the experiences of the Vietnam War (and the economic distresses of the 1970s and the increasing geopolitical assertiveness of the Soviet Union). *War and Change* remains one of the great realist statements of the last half century, though it is flawed in part. Intellectually, it is something of a hybrid, combining a then period-fashionable structural framework with Gilpin's own classical instincts. Not surprisingly, the structural machine turned out to be wrong. It also poorly explained America's strategic blunders. Hubris, not the deterministic mechanics of relative decline, best explains the grievous wounds suffered by the United States during the seventy-five years of its hegemony (approximately 1945–2020), injuries that were entirely self-inflicted. The United States was not an overextended Britain, exhausted by wars rooted in challenges to the status quo by emerging rivals—it was an arrogant Athens, embarking on not one but two misguided Sicilian adventures.

Why did the United States make such colossal blunders, and not once but twice? A closer look at *War and Change* shows how its mechanistic structural dressing gets the story wrong, and should be discarded, but the real stuffing of the book, its classical elements, provides enduring insights into this puzzle and remains an essential contribution to the study of world politics.

The Limits of Structuralism Redux: Gilpin's War and Change in World Politics

War and Change is a shotgun marriage of two books. One reflects the careful articulation of a structural machine, a model that is clean, pristine, and logically coherent—and wrong in its principal prediction. But the other is a brilliant, modern expression of classical realism. The former anticipated a "hegemonic war" between the declining United States and a rising Soviet Union; the latter illustrates why, more generally, the assumptions of structural realism and hyper-rationalism—even in Gilpin's hands—will invariably get the big questions wrong.[52] A consideration of *War and Change*, featuring a comparison of Gilpin the classical realist with Gilpin the structural realist, offers an ideal opportunity to explore the basic differences between the two approaches—and once again illustrates the flaws of the latter disposition and need for scholars to return to the wisdoms of the former.

In the preface to *War and Change* Gilpin explicitly reflects on this basic tension in his book, describing the strengths and weaknesses of contending "economic" and "sociological" conceptions of the study of international politics, and expressing his intention to "draw on both the sociological approach and the economic approach."[53] It is an uneasy mix, with classical exposition often at odds with an austere, structural framework. Despite articulating a minimalist and strictly rationalist structural model, Gilpin's elaborations check every box that distinguishes classical from structural realism. (Recall from chapter 2 the ways that classical realism parts company with structural realism, with its understanding that structure matters but on its own it is irretrievably indeterminate; that history and purpose, and thus domestic politics and ideational variables, must be included in efforts to explain behavior; that great powers are assumed to be ambitious and opportunistic; and that politics matters, and shape the contingent and consequential choices made by states.)

Gilpin wears his classical realism on his sleeve, stating plainly that "both the structure of the international system and domestic conditions of societies are primary determinants" of state behavior. And in *War and Change* (and in Gilpin's writings more generally), domestic politics, social forces, ideology, and the perceived lessons of history are all crucial to understanding world politics. Choices in the international arena "depend ultimately on the nature of the state and the society it represents," and are profoundly shaped by varieties of "domestic social arrangements." Even the appeal to cool calculations of cost-benefit analysis, which is at the heart of the book's deductive model, requires an understanding of domestic politics in order to answer what Gilpin poses as the crucial question, "profitable (or costly) for whom?" Gilpin takes another giant step away from a narrow conception of rationalism by arguing further that the assessment of costs and benefits is also "highly subjective" and depends on "perceived interests"—perceptions that are determined "foremost . . . [by] the historical experience of society" and the lessons learned from those particular experiences. And large swaths of the book are devoted to domestic factors that include "moral decay" and "the corruption of . . . values," variables that would surely elude any analysis restricted to assessing the balance of material power between states.[54]

War and Change also presumes that great powers are ambitious and will eagerly seize opportunities to expand their influence when presented with them—as elaborated presently, that is a principal instinct that drives his model. And their choices will be informed by ideology—which will influence how states will define their interests, shape the character of a given hegemonic order, and affect the prospects for war and peace. In Gilpin's assessment, for example, the ideological character of the superpowers was "a greatly underappreciated factor in the preservation of world peace" during the Cold War. *War and Change* is also unmistakably and fundamentally classical in its modeling of rationality (actors are assumed to be imperfect, rational muddlers, not hyper-rationalist automatons), its skepticism of prediction, and, most important, with its embrace (à la Thucydides, Gilpin's "favorite realist") of the central role of irreducible uncertainty in shaping outcomes. At the very start of the book, Gilpin stresses how "unique and unpredictable sets of developments" render prediction beyond the means of the student of world politics; toward the end he reminds the reader that "in truth it must be said that uncertainty rules the world." Along the way he emphasizes how "decisions are made under conditions of uncertainty," and the "rush of events" are shaped by "gnawing fear" and "anxiety" and further buffeted by "unintended consequences." Rather than seeing through the veil of uncertainty, statesmen quickly lose control of the forces they unleash when they choose to embark on war, and are routinely surprised (and often dismayed) by the trajectory and outcomes of those conflicts. Nor can these events be explained by systemic forces alone: "Ultimately, international politics still can be characterized as it was by Thucydides: the interplay of impersonal forces and great leaders," Gilpin concludes. "Though always constrained, choices always exist."[55] This is classical realism.

Revisiting the Assumptions of War and Change—*Too Clean a Machine*

Yet *War and Change*, of enduring value as a classic text, failed with regard to its specific application and expectations. But these failures are illuminating. A review of the book's five core assumptions reveals how the paradoxes and contradictions generated by its lean framework are rooted in those moments when its informal model veers most closely toward structural realism and hyper-rationalism—and are resolved when they are revisited through classical lenses. Gilpin's abstract argument is built around five core assumptions. Three of these are consistent with classical realism (and a number of other perspectives as well). Two others, however—the suspect assumption 3 and the enigmatic assumption 4—are problematic, and are the source of unresolved puzzles in the book. Together they account for the ghost that has always haunted the machine of *War and Change*: how, in the blink of an eye, the hegemonic power transforms from an actor that orchestrated the flawless expansion of its international political power and influence to one that finds itself dangerously overextended, rattled, and unable to bring its commitments back into line with its capabilities. Similarly, only an appeal to classical variables, as opposed to hyper-rationalist calculation, can account for the historical regularities that Gilpin is most concerned with: the tendency for hegemonic powers to overexpand (that is, for their political reach to exceed even their impressive material grasp), why relative decline and the emergence of rising challengers present such enormous and commonly intractable political challenges, threatening the stability of the international system, and why the coveted achievement of "peaceful change" often proves so elusive.

Consider the five core assumptions of *War and Change*. As noted, assumptions 1, 2, and 5 are neither controversial nor problematic:[56]

> (1) A system is stable . . . if no state believes it is profitable to attempt to change [it].
> (2) A state will attempt to change the international system if the expected benefits exceed the expected net costs . . .
> (5) If the disequilibrium in the international system is not resolved, then the system will be changed . . .

These assumptions are rooted in expectations that states are ambitious, essentially rational, and uninhibited in the pursuit of their goals. If states perceive opportunities in the international system (which typically arise from underlying economic changes that alter the balance of power and capabilities) they will pursue them with all of the means at their disposal, including the resort to force. Most International Relations theorists, and almost all realists, would find these reasonable building blocks (although structural realists reach for the assumption of "security seeking" and are agnostic as to whether states actually crave "more").

Assumptions 3 and 4, however, although not obviously unreasonable, on closer consideration, and especially from the perspective of classical realism, invite contestation.

> (3) A state will seek to change the international system through territorial, political, and economic expansion until the marginal costs of further change are equal to or greater than the marginal benefits.
> (4) Once an equilibrium between the costs and benefits of further change and expansion is reached, the tendency is for the economic costs of maintaining the status quo to rise faster than the economic capacity to support the status quo.

Specifically, assumption 3 is inconsistent with the expectations of classical realism; assumption 4 (and the dangerous disequilibria it generates in world politics) can only be understood by the resort to explanations inconsistent with structuralism and hyper-rationality.

A classical recasting of assumption 3 would be that states tend to systematically overreach. That is, they don't stop expanding until they are *clearly beyond* the point where costs equal benefits, because it is only when they are well past the point that they belatedly realize that costs have considerably exceeded benefits. Why? Because in the real world (to say nothing of the messy practice of foreign policy even directed by the most capable hands), the data and evidence used to assess costs and benefits will be noisy and lagged (and, as a technical point, foreign policy "stopping points" will almost invariably be discontinuous).[57] These observations are not at all controversial—the question is whether, given these limitations, there will be a tendency to err on the side of "too cautious" or "too assertive." The classical departure is to expect that in this context states, and especially great powers, will typically overreach. Because all that data will not simply be noisy but contested in its interpretation, and a rising power, especially one near the height of its power (and thus well accustomed to winning, and having things go its way, and likely optimistic about its future prospects), will be primed to interpret setbacks as temporary, and aberrant.[58] Stated plainly, great, rising powers near their apogee are almost certain to suffer from a hubris cultivated by a long string of successes.[59] They will be naturally overconfident, and slow to process experiences that suggest anything to the contrary. Or as Boss Jim Gettys said to a similarly disposed Charles Foster Kane, who simply did not understand that he had been beaten: "If it was anybody else, I'd say what's going to happen to you would be a lesson to you. Only you're going to need more than one lesson. And you're going to get more than one lesson."[60] So it is true for hegemons at the apogee of their power, overconfident and utterly unprepared to process the fact that they stand at the precipice of overreaching. Again, crucially, this adjustment is inconsistent with security seeking, affectless structuralism, which would assume dispassion and expect much more prudence from a great power; it is also fundamentally at odds with a hyper-rationalist approach which simply cannot abide the possibility of systematic biases. At the heart of rational expectations theory, it should be recalled, is the idea that any errors made are unbiased, that is, randomly distributed around the correct (or at least best) model. Thus hegemons should be just as likely to stop too short as expand too far, and certainly sentiments like hubris are expressly presumed *not* to influence decision making.

Assumption 4 is, if anything, more problematic—indeed it presents the paradox that has always gnawed at the psyche of *War and Change*: if at equilibrium costs will begin, cumulatively, to outweigh benefits, why does the hegemon—modeled up to this point as a savvy, efficient, rational calculator—fail to anticipate this or, at least, aptly adjust to it?[61] Gilpin is aware of this puzzle and, leaning heavily on his classical side (in addition to reviewing a number of external factors that work to the hegemon's disadvantage), introduces a host of debilitating domestic political and social changes that he argues are common to mature hegemons.[62] But this does not unpack two lingering puzzles, even if Gilpin is correct about the emergence of the external and internal problems he elucidates: the failure of a hegemon, in ascendance (when it is rationally and efficiently calculating costs and benefits), to anticipate problems on the horizon; and the failure of the hegemon in relative decline to properly adjust.

Far-sightedness presents a paradox that Gilpin wrestles with on several occasions. He argues that (liberal, capitalist) hegemons will bear the costs of establishing and maintaining an open international order, for the good realist reason that, given their economic advantages and position, they expect "to benefit *relatively* more than other states." This is the basic motivation of the hegemon, as Gilpin and others have emphasized. Yet he also notes that "trade and investment between advanced economies and less developed economies tend to favor and develop the latter." Subsequently Gilpin acknowledges this apparent contradiction, noting although he had argued that "a world market economy tends to favor and to concentrate wealth in the more advanced and more efficient economy," this is only the case for the "short run." In the long run, "a world market economy fosters the spread of economic growth," and "new centers of economic growth . . . frequently overtake and surpass the original center."[63] This may be true, and Gilpin gives good reasons why. But it leaves open the question of why the hegemon did not act more forcefully to preserve its advantages, or perhaps behave in a more predatory fashion during that period when it was reaping most of the advantages. More generally, structural and hyper-rationalist approaches might appeal to "time inconsistency" or a "discounting of the future." But this is unsatisfying; it is plausible that such pathologies may arise, but the analytical problem remains that they result in a systematic error (an error biased in one direction, repeatedly); moreover they are errors that contrast with the hegemon's previous skillful, unbiased forecasting of costs and benefits (forecast by assumption 3). Additionally, from a realist perspective, the state is supposed to have a long time horizon—that is one of the public goods it provides to society. For classical realism the paradox is less vexing, as it anticipates systematic errors based on overconfidence. Even more important, a classical realist approach is untroubled by the apparent puzzle of why an equilibrium point suddenly becomes a disequilibrium point. As discussed, it offers a different engine for the hegemon's troubles at this stage: having expected the hegemon to overextend, by the time it stops expanding, it has already fomented the disequilibrium. Costs have already run far ahead of benefits, presenting formidable burdens for the hegemon and opportunities for potential challengers.

A second lingering puzzle that flows from assumption 4 is why hegemons faced with relative decline typically fail to restore equilibrium through retrenchment—bringing costs and benefits back into alignment by reducing their commitments. Gilpin argues that disequilibrium is most commonly resolved by hegemonic war—which is puzzling from a hyper-rationalist perspective, since such wars are obviously horrifying and (more to the theoretical point) enormously costly, and therefore all sides should be able to agree to a mutually beneficial settlement that is better for all parties than the resort to arms.[64] Moreover, Gilpin does not see hegemonic war as a rational war but rather, as noted, influenced by "gnawing fear" and "anxiety"—as well as "passions" that "can easily escape from human control." As a normative matter, Gilpin expresses the notion—citing Carr approvingly on the general theoretical point—that a mechanism for bringing about peaceful change would be preferable to war. Recall that Carr, however misguided in his specific application, cogently articulated the realist position that "defense of the status quo is not a policy which can be lastingly successful"; moreover, as Gilpin summarizes Carr's argument approvingly, the dominant state, not the challenger, has "a moral obligation to make the greater concessions."[65] But despite this, and despite Gilpin's praise for British retrenchment before World War I, he argues that retrenchment is "a course seldom pursued by a declining power." Why? Setting aside structuralism and affectless rationalism, Gilpin finds the answer in politics, hubris, and fear. Retrenchment is "*politically* difficult," even if it is the wisest course of action. One source of the political difficulties derives from the classical assumption that declining powers and their challengers—as well as various political actors *within* those states—will look at exactly the same information and reach different conclusions about its implications. There will thus be basic disagreements, both within and between states, about whether, and how much, retrenchment and adjustment is needed. And beyond that there is what can be called the hubris/fear paradox: "Until a state is pressed by others, it has little incentive to make concessions for the sake of peace." But once faced with a real challenge, it fears that such concessions "will only whet the appetite for still greater concessions."[66] (This dilemma will be revisited in chapter 6.) In sum, hegemons are too arrogant to make concessions when they should and too frightened to make them when they must. Thus despite its structural machine, *War and Change* thus roots its central problem—the difficulty of adjustment—in a classical grounding.

Armed with this reassessment of *War and Change in World Politics*, it is now possible to explain America's disastrous wars attendant to its hegemonic experience—its wars of choice in Vietnam and Iraq. They were not the tragic consequences of hegemonic overextension as costs came to exceed benefits, due to technology diffusing abroad and the logic of uneven economic development relatively empowering others. Rather, they are better explained by Gilpin's favorite realist Thucydides, who, as emphasized in chapter 1, singled out hubris as the basic, mortal threat to great powers, whose "general extraordinary success" makes them "confuse their strength with their hopes." Reckless foreign adventures are the true graveyard of empires. However powerful a country might be, fighting on the road, especially with aspirations for conquest, is more difficult than a reading of the raw balance of power would suggest. "Not that confidence is out of place in an army of invasion," Thucydides warned, "but in an enemy's country it should also be accompanied by the precautions of apprehension."[67] As with Athens in Sicily, in Vietnam and Iraq, the United States failed to heed that admonition.

Vietnam: The Paradox of Having Too Much Power

Into the 1960s, the United States was still near the height of its post–World War II hegemony (the economic recovery of its allies in Western Europe and Japan reduced U.S. share of world GDP, but that was surely not a blow to its relative power in the context of the Cold War). What occurred in that decade was not an example of the United States increasingly struggling with the rising costs of defending the status quo—but the tragic, foolhardy blunder of a hegemon unwilling to recognize the limits of its own capabilities. Only an abundantly secure state with a vast surplus of power would even be in a position to throw so much bad money after good long past the point that a country with real security concerns possibly could. Too much power and too much arrogance explain the American war in Vietnam.[68]

Moreover, Vietnam mattered to the United States solely due to its Cold War context—the front lines of which were in Europe. Viewed in isolation, Indochina was an obscure, geopolitical backwater. But even as the United States poured unimaginable amounts of blood and treasure into that war—23,000 U.S ground troops introduced in January 1965 became 180,000 by December, and then 380,000 one year later, and finally over 500,000 troops at the end of 1967—America was no closer to winning the war or, more important, to achieving its political goals. But over the course of the effort it hollowed out its military, damaged its economy, weakened its defenses in Western Europe, and undermined its political standing around the world. Ultimately, a war fought to advance U.S. interests in the Cold War undermined those interests considerably and across the board. Thus even if the Vietnam War had somehow, against all odds, been "won" (though it remains difficult to imagine how), it still would have nevertheless been an unmitigated failure by the only metric that matters—the weighing of the costs of the effort against the political goals that would have been achieved. American hegemony was not undone by reaching an equilibrium point at the frontiers of its geopolitical influence, and then having costs rising faster than benefits; it was undone by the United States obtusely grasping for too much, and trying to exercise its power long past the point that the costs of doing so exceeded the benefits.

Warning signs against intervention in Vietnam were clear from the beginning. In 1947 the State Department understood "the unpleasant fact that communist Ho Chi Minh is the strongest and perhaps ablest figure in Indochina." Four years later Congressman John F. Kennedy reached a similar conclusion. After visiting Vietnam in October 1951, he reported that "we have allied ourselves to the desperate effort of the French regime to hang on to the remnants of an empire." Were a free election to be held, he noted, all experts agreed it "would go in favor of Ho and his communists."[69] But despite U.S. misgivings, especially as the early Cold War increased in intensity, America was invested in bolstering its political and military affiliations in Western Europe, which in turn meant supporting the French effort in Vietnam. That effort, however, was doomed to fail, and after losing a decisive battle at Dien Bien Phu in May 1954, France was forced to abandon its effort to reconquer Vietnam. The terms of the French withdrawal were established by the Geneva Accords of 1954, which stipulated that the country would be temporarily divided at the seventeenth parallel. After a brief period, free elections would be held; in the interim, strict limits would be placed on the presence of foreign troops.

From this point on the Vietnam War fell under the American purview, although President Eisenhower was under no illusions as to Ho's widespread popularity (especially compared to the U.S.-backed Ngo Dinh Diem), and the former General of the Army, fearful that the jungles of Indochina "would absorb our troops by divisions," was unwilling to commit U.S. forces to a ground war in Asia. Nevertheless, he saw the conflict as an important frontier in the ongoing Cold War. A new strategy would be required. In 1955 Diem repudiated the Geneva Accords, and the goal of U.S. policy was now to create a new country—South Vietnam—a self-sustaining entity that would stem the tide of communism in South East Asia.[70] But the goal of establishing a politically viable South Vietnam would elude four presidents, and the challenges would only mount over time. Eisenhower had kept the number of U.S. advisors in Vietnam to a Geneva-limited 685; at the time of Kennedy's assassination, there were over 16,000 U.S. military "advisors" in the South. Still, the war was being lost.[71] President Johnson gambled on the notion that "bombing the North would save the South" (despite the widespread international condemnation that such a measure would engender), and when that failed, he made the fateful decision to introduce U.S. ground troops as well. By the end of 1967 not only were there 500,000 American troops in the country—a staggering figure—but the United States had dropped nearly half a million tons of bombs on North Vietnam and over a million tons on South Vietnam itself.[72]

It was a disaster that any good realist could have seen coming—and all good realists did. Raymond Aron was an early critic of France's war: "we have brought into being . . . the very thing we should have feared above all else: an endless war against an Indo-Chinese resistance which, though led by communists, is supported by a majority of nationalists," he wrote in 1951. France "is squandering its resources in an adventure" to an extent that was not justifiable "in terms of the self-interest of the country." Of the American war, Hans Morgenthau was a visionary critic, expressing deep reservations as early as 1956, and he would emerge as a vociferous opponent of the U.S. effort well ahead of most others—and for reasons instantly recognizable as rooted in the tenets of classical realism. In 1962, he explained "the only viable alternative" to our current "primarily military approach" is "the subordination of our military commitments to, and thus their limitation by, our political objectives in South Vietnam." In March 1964 he articulated "The Case against Further Involvement," and three months later he warned, "It is tiresome but necessary to say again what has been said so many times before: The problem is political and not military." Without solving the political problem, it will be "impossible to win the war in Vietnam." The implications were not hard to see: "Only humiliation or catastrophe awaits us" if the United States continued down this path. (He also bemoaned that savvy diplomats of the past, such as Bismarck, "would not have allowed themselves to get committed in a civil war which cannot be won short of a political miracle.") Morgenthau's consistent, published opposition was voluminous enough to be collected in a small book in 1965—criticisms that were taken seriously enough for National Security Advisor McGeorge Bundy to debate him on national television in June of that year.[73]

George F. Kennan also expressed public doubts about the war in 1965, and in February 1966 (at a time when the war still enjoyed broad public support), he testified forcefully before the U.S. Senate. Kennan urged the United States to "liquidate" its involvement in the war, which was damaging American foreign relations, and described himself "bewildered" by the U.S. commitment to South Vietnam, as well as "what that commitment really consists of, and how and when it was incurred." Reinhold Niebuhr also spoke out publicly against the war weeks ahead of Kennan's testimony; he would lament a year later that the United States had allowed itself to get "drawn into a civil war in an obscure nation of Southeast Asia," observing that "only our plutocratic wealth allows us to commit these stupidities in International Relations."[74]

With the Tet Offensive in 1968, it was finally and indisputably clear that the United States was not going to achieve its objectives in the war. The massive wave of attacks across South Vietnam failed to achieve their military objective—but they exposed the limits of American power.[75] Eager to seize the initiative, American commander William Westmorland put in an urgent request for an additional 200,000 troops. Hoping to press what he claimed to be an advantage and an opportunity, at the same time he nevertheless reported, ominously, that "a setback is fully possible if I am not reinforced and it is likely we will lose ground in other areas." Johnson was at a crossroads. The shocking request for a 40 percent increase in troop strength would require the mobilization of the reserves, threaten economic stability (the dollar was already under serious pressure), and contribute further to the atrophy of U.S. forces worldwide. He asked Defense Secretary Clark Clifford, a long-time supporter of the war, to study the entire situation with fresh eyes. On March 4, Clifford reported to the president that neither more troops nor more bombing could assure victory, that the end was not in sight, and that he was now "convinced that the military course we were pursuing was not only endless, but hopeless." At the end of the month Johnson shocked the nation by announcing that he would no longer seek another term as president.[76]

Even American power had its limits. By 1968, Richard Nixon, running for president, reached a similar conclusion. Nixon had been a consistent hawk on Vietnam throughout the war, but the savvy politician knew a loser when he saw one, and even before the Tet Offensive, he was repositioning. In a prominent essay, "Asia after Vietnam," Nixon deemphasized the war, focusing instead on his vision of a broader (and more modest) "American policy toward Asia." And after Tet, he abandoned talk of victory in Vietnam; instead, starting with a speech on March 5, he pledged to "end the war and win the peace in the Pacific."[77] Henry Kissinger, who would become Nixon's National Security Advisor and his intimate collaborator on questions of foreign policy, had known for years the Vietnam War was a lost cause. In October 1965 he wrote in his diary, "No one could really explain to me how even on the most favorable assumptions about the war in Vietnam the war was going to end." Quietly, he told some of Johnson's advisors "we couldn't win." Shamefully, however, Kissinger actively supported the war in public, calculating that such professional malpractice was the best way to secure the plum political appointment he so craved in the next administration, Democratic or Republican. But by 1969 he got with the new program as well. Writing in *Foreign Affairs*, Kissinger laid out clearly what had gone wrong with American policy, and what a future settlement would look like. "Our military operations . . . [had] little relationship to our declared political objectives," he explained, returning to the safe intellectual harbors of Realism 101. "We have been unable so far to create a political structure that could survive military opposition from Hanoi after we withdraw." An American "commitment to a political solution . . . and a negotiated settlement" was now "inevitable." Fortunately, the parties in the conflict "have a fairly wide area of agreement on some basic principles." In particular, Kissinger emphasized a return to the basic understandings of the Geneva Accords, the "ultimate" withdrawal of American forces, and the reunification of Vietnam as a result of negotiations between the local parties themselves. The main disagreement at present had to do with "the status of Hanoi's forces" (in the South).[78]

Unfortunately, superpowers are unaccustomed to losing wars, and so in an effort to achieve the "negotiated" settlement that would provide a fig leaf for the inevitable American withdrawal, Nixon sought to cover his steady draw-down of U.S. troops with various measures that actually widened the war: secret, massive bombing campaigns against Cambodia and then Laos (and a trebling of bombing within South Vietnam); an enormously controversial incursion into Cambodia in 1970; and, in February 1971, participation in a South Vietnamese invasion of Laos. After some initial gains that offensive stalled into a costly draw, followed by an embarrassing, hectic retreat during which the United States lost 168 helicopters and saw more than 600 others damaged.[79] At some point in this bloody mix the administration set its sights still lower, now seeking something that could be called "peace with honor," which would provide a "decent interval" between the final U.S. withdrawal and the inevitable conquest of the South. But an agreement negotiated in Paris by Kissinger proved to be a hard sell to the South Vietnamese, who saw the settlement as "tantamount to surrender"—and their public opposition to the emerging deal would undermine claims to "peace with honor." So to placate the reluctant South and perhaps provide them with some breathing space by wounding the North, in 1972 the Americans engaged in two massive bombing campaigns (in the spring and then later with the widely condemned "Christmas Bombings"), fulfilling Nixon's promises that he "would not go out whimpering" and to bomb "those bastards . . . like they've never been bombed before."[80]

Ultimately, in January 1973 Nixon and Kissinger signed a peace treaty that essentially ratified America's defeat and sealed the fate of South Vietnam: cease-fire, the withdrawal of U.S. forces, the release of American POWs—and no clause requiring the withdrawal of North Vietnamese forces from the South. (After the American withdrawal, violence in the South continued, until a final offensive by the North in early 1975 reunified the country.) It was a deal that could have been reached in 1969. Only a preternaturally secure state with a massive, surplus military capacity could even imagine continuing a foreign military campaign against a tiny, impoverished nation 8,000 miles from its shores, for four years after it understood it had lost, for no other reason than it didn't yet want to admit defeat. Consider the twelve days of the Christmas bombing, initiated to force cosmetic changes to a final settlement that had been agreed to by both sides months previously: 739 B-52 sorties dropped 15,237 tons of bombs, at a cost of fifteen B-52s lost along with eleven other aircraft—not to mention the death and destruction rained down on the North.[81] Obviously these war materials were not urgently needed elsewhere.

What can explain such behavior? Certainly not hyper-rationalist theories, or structural realism, nor can the ruinous American adventure in Vietnam be attributed to hegemonic decline (the war undermined U.S. power and influence but was not caused by its relative decline). How "can one conceive the inconceivable and render the disaster intelligible—the Sicilian-like expedition on the twentieth century scale?" Raymond Aron asked rhetorically. "First, by invoking hubris." The American effort in Vietnam arose "from an illusion of omnipotence."[82]

Echoes in Iraq

A quarter century after the last U.S. troops left Vietnam in defeat, another cycle of American hegemony met with a similar fate. With the unanticipated collapse of the Soviet Union, the unexpected eclipse of the Japanese miracle (the juggernaut of the Japanese economy had been an obsession for those focused on notions of hegemonic power cycles in the 1980s), and the renaissance of the U.S. economy in 1990s, the American decline widely forecast since the late 1970s did not come to pass. Instead, the United States entered the twenty-first century more powerful than ever before—not simply a hegemon but routinely described as a hyper-power, the colossus of a unipolar world.[83] Yet within a decade after emerging as perhaps the greatest power the world had ever seen, America was bloodied, overextended, debt-ridden, exhausted, and in the process of losing two wars against distant, weak adversaries. And once again, this stunning reversal of fortune did not come about because the United States expanded its reach until the benefits of doing so finally touched up against the equilibrium costs of maintaining its position, after which those costs increased. Rather, disaster occurred, as it did before, largely due to hubris—again rooted not in the constraints on its power but in the lack of them. In particular, by embarking on an imprudent and catastrophic war of choice against Iraq (while its war in Afghanistan was still ongoing and unresolved), the United States radically overestimated its ability to use force to remake the world as it would have liked it to be.

International Relations theory does not have a good off-the-shelf explanation for why the United States chose to embark on what amounted to a second Sicily in 2003. The enduring puzzle of the Iraq war is reflected in the considerable confusion of competing efforts to explain it, none of which are satisfactory and many of which are bizarre.[84] Moreover, it is hard to craft an explanation for the war that does not rely on the exogenous shock of the September 11, 2011, terrorist attacks on the United States to serve, at a minimum, as a crucially permissive factor (which, understandably, is not ideal for theories that aspire to generalizability).[85] But short of providing a definitive explanation for the war, it is informative here to note the essential role of the familiar variables of unrestrained power and unchecked hubris. In this instance, almost certainly, the pathologies associated with the arrogance of power were exacerbated by passions, including, in this instance, not just hubris but fear (and not the measured, prudent sensitivity to an inherently dangerous world but the anxiety of a great power, attacked on its homeland for the first time in sixty years, and uncertain of what shoes might fall next, which likely exacerbated a collective sense of existential insecurity).[86] It is not surprising that frightened great powers suddenly feeling a general sense of vulnerability might wildly lash out.

Of course, lashing out is only possible if a state has the power to do so. And the United States was the only country in the world that *could* have launched an Iraq war in 2003—sending a large army halfway around the world to mount an ambitious military invasion. Even if others might have wanted, for some imagined purpose, to do such a thing, anywhere, no other actor had such capabilities; in addition, and crucially, the Americans also enjoyed an uncommonly massive surplus of security, lacking peer military rivals for which its own military resources would need to stay on guard against, or at least remain alert to. As with Vietnam—indeed perhaps to an even greater extent—the war against Iraq is not well explained by structural constraints or rationalistic calculations, but the tendency, which has often preoccupied classical realists, of great powers to overreach.

The foolhardiness of the Iraq war was illustrated by the need to invent a new doctrine to justify it: the Bush doctrine of preventive war.[87] Unlike preemptive war—striking at an adversary just as they are poised to attack you—preventive war is waged against those it is imagined might be the source of a potential security threat at some point in the future. These are of course by definition wars of choice, not urgency—preventive wars in particular are leaps into the unknown. Rarely prudent (to invoke a term closely associated with classical realism), preventive war was famously described by Bismarck as "like committing suicide out of fear of death." Another warning sign that went unheeded was the potential implications of the fact that the confrontation between the United States and Iraq also reflected a radical asymmetry of power. But asymmetric wars are also commonly traps that great powers stumble into.[88]

It is much easier for a great power to start an asymmetric war than to finish it—the early fighting typically favors the powerful, and this bright prospect looms larger for decision makers facing tough choices than do distant clouds on the horizon. But wars are fought for a reason, and after the first battles are won the question remains open as to whether the victors will have the skill and wherewithal to impose their political vision. Moreover, short of imperial absorption (and often even then), the attention span, interest, and motivation of occupying powers from distant lands to stick with the effort indefinitely correctly have their limits—whereas local actors are . . . local actors, who are unlikely to simply leave, and will be fighting on their home turf, navigating intricate political contexts with which they are familiar. These challenges are even more likely to emerge in a preventive war, which amounts to a policy of "shooting first and asking questions later," a line that might sound good in a movie but an attitude in geopolitical life that is an invitation to political disaster. Once again, with Clausewitz, winning military battles does not guarantee achieving political success (and might generate shock waves that reveal new and daunting political challenges). Recall the realist admonitions regarding both inescapable uncertainty and the absence of political end zones. It is impossible to anticipate the range of consequences brought about by war, but one thing is certain: politics never ends, and one conflict is likely to be followed by a new set of contestations. Thus it is always essential to have a clear vision regarding the political objectives for which the use of force is to be introduced. But when the case for war is less clear-cut—as it necessarily will be in a preventive war—the likelihood is even greater that there will be an enormous chasm between military victory and political success. Regarding Iraq in particular, there was little doubt that the United States could steamroll over that country's modest, rusty, and decrepit military. But there were scandalously few careful considerations of the politics that would follow in the days after—despite the fact that there were good reasons to be alarmed, and to recognize that in the longer run, such a war and the ensuing chaos that would follow from there would more likely undermine than advance U.S. political objectives. This is not twenty-first-century 20/20 hindsight but was a common understanding of international relations scholars at the time. In April 2003, after the swift fall of Baghdad and just weeks before the United States announced its "Mission Accomplished"—and when support for the war in America touched its all-time high of 80 percent—I wrote the following: The war "was very unlikely to achieve, and in fact would probably undermine, the broader political objectives for which it was fought," and that eventually "a fatigued and impatient America" would finally distance itself from "the chaos that ensues."[89]

In one sense, the United States made exactly the same mistake it did in Vietnam—perhaps to an even greater extent. In Vietnam the political goal America aspired to (but never came remotely close to achieving) was to leave behind a stand-alone, self-sustaining, legitimate local government that would have a disposition amenable to the preferences of the United States. In Iraq, the political "strategy" was to decapitate the regime, assume that a friendly government would take its place, and reap the benefits generated by the performance of American military supremacy—in particular, expecting that local adversaries would be swiftly intimidated into acceding to broader U.S. policy preferences in the region.[90] (Technically, this was a belief that local powers would "bandwagon" with American power, as opposed to balance against it.)

Not surprisingly, as with Vietnam, American realists of all stripes were uniform in their opposition to such a patently transparent blunder. As the Bush administration was laying the groundwork for war, Kennan, then ninety-eight, spoke out forcefully against the prospect. He failed to see a plausible case for war and found the Bush doctrine of preventive war "a great mistake in principle." He also observed that "war has a momentum of its own," and although the United States might know how to start a war in Iraq, "you never know where [it is] going to end." Robert Gilpin, whose shy, scholarly disposition usually rendered him cautious about wading into debates about public policy, did not mince words. The "costly and reckless war" represented a grave threat "to the security and wellbeing of the United States." The war "has not only undermined the social and political stability of the Middle East," he also noted, presciently (and with the eagle eyes of a classical realist), that it "significantly exacerbated dangerous social, cultural, and regional fissures in US society." He attributed the catastrophe to the "hubris, ambitions, and incompetence of the ideological amateurs" then managing U.S. foreign policy.[91]

Although all card-carrying realists opposed the Iraq war—as well they would—distinct styles of realist analysis do not speak with one voice, or with equal insight, in their ability to grasp the events as they unfolded. Only classical realism comes close to having the capacity to comprehend such a catastrophe—structural realist and hyper-rationalist perspectives are simply incapable of accounting for or explaining such a patently foolish and monumentally costly act of geopolitical self-mutilation. Structural realism models its actors as security seekers; hyper-rationalist approaches anticipate that all hands will pursue their goals with cool heads and sharp eyes, armed with a well-informed understanding of the likely probabilities of all possible outcomes. These approaches offer little if any insight into the most wrenching and consequential choices about war and peace made by the United States as the world's leading power. In contrast, classical realism anticipates that states, especially ones that are potent and secure, will harbor ambitions, and seek much more than simply an assurance of their basic security—and that the greatest powers, driven by hubris, will commonly overreach, and blunder into misguided adventures.

History and hubris, intentions and ideology—as this chapter has shown more generally, it is not possible to explain and understand events in world politics, past and present, or to anticipate the range of prospects likely to emerge in the future with two analytical hands tied behind the back. Narrow structuralism may be aesthetically appealing; assuming a forced and implausible interpretation of rationality might facilitate the construction of elegant and sophisticated models. But neither approach will give much purchase into actually understanding and explaining the great puzzles of the past, or those events in the real world that are of the greatest and most pressing interest to students of International Relations.

CHAPTER FOUR

The Limits of Classical Realism

CHAPTER 2, BY REVEALING the irretrievable theoretical shortcomings of its would-be successors, demonstrated why a return to classical realism is urgently warranted. Chapter 3, which revisited stubborn puzzles associated with some of the great events in international political history, illustrated how a classical realist approach could provide insights into these upheavals that had eluded those other perspectives. And as we shall see, the advantages of embracing a classical realist perspective are also noteworthy for understanding and explaining pressing issues of contemporary international politics, such as the consequences of the rise of China.

Nevertheless, classical realism as well can and should be interrogated with dedicated attentiveness and a sober self-awareness of its own limitations and shortcomings. Some of these challenges, not easily resolved, are common to all flavors of realist analysis. But they can appear to be especially relevant for classical realism compared to more abstract realist approaches (and thinkers), which imagine they can safely set such questions aside, or bracket them off with simplifying assumptions. This chapter, then, engages some of the basic challenges, dilemmas, and paradoxes that have often vexed realism in general and classical realism in particular both in theory and in (would-be) practice. Principal among these are wrestling with the issue of morality (a significant quandary for any approach that imagines itself "realist"); the potentially paradigm-subversive malleability of the core concept of the "National Interest"; the crucial imperative of disentangling descriptive and prescriptive aspects of analysis (never easy in the social sciences, this challenge is virtually inbred in studies of international relations, as they almost invariably have implications for foreign policy); and, following that, the stubborn limitations of realism as a guide to purposeful action (as opposed to providing a valuable guide regarding what *not* to do).[1]

Lies That Life Is Black and White

Questions of morality (and charges of immorality) have perennially haunted realist analysis—and for good reason. Because realists tend to stress the possibility that actors in world politics will at times behave utterly without moral restraint, and anticipate that the bottomless dangers of anarchy will require even the best-intentioned states to resort to regrettable measures to protect themselves and ensure their survival, some self-professed "realists" see foreign policy behavior as distinctly unbound by concerns for ethics and morality. But that conclusion does not necessarily follow, even if we permit that there is a significant moral difference between the behavior of an individual person within a society and that of a state dwelling in anarchy.

Nevertheless, there are good reasons why realists are profoundly reluctant, from an analytical perspective, to call balls and strikes regarding which behaviors by states in world politics are "good" or "bad." Certainly there are some easy exceptions—genocide would be an obvious example—but as a rule of thumb, like Bill Murray in *Ghostbusters*, realists are invariably "a little fuzzy on the whole good/bad thing." Realists tend to see conflict as rooted in the clash of interests between two parties, as opposed to the distinctly nefarious attributes of one of the participants in a dispute. Moreover, it is likely that each side will have a competing narrative of history and events, and although such positions can be introduced cynically and instrumentally, getting at "the truth" can actually be harder than one might think. Most contestations—although, again, obvious exceptions easily leap to mind—are not reducible to pristine distinctions between black and white but feature muddied, shadowy shades of gray. Recall Raymond Aron's enduring, admonishing observation from chapter 1: "it is not every day that a Dreyfus Affair comes along justifying the invocation of truth against error." (But note that this also implies that on some days, it does.) And recall as well Aron's sensitivity to the need for any analyst of social relations to be attentive to the limits of their own objectivity.[2]

As a practical matter, "the whole good/bad thing" is indeed often much murkier than imagined. For example, it is not even possible to confidently label the aggressor in a war as being in the wrong. If the status quo is unjust, and the contented guardians of the way things happen to be are unwilling to yield, the resort to force might be understandable, and even morally justifiable. (This does not preclude, of course, the possibility that a war was initiated to advance the aggressive designs of wicked men—a prospect no realist would disregard.) Thus rather than fight their way through a thicket of competing claims in a jungle of hypocritical posturing, realists prefer to sidestep these questions and, following Morgenthau, refuse "to identify moral aspirations of a particular nation with the moral laws that govern the universe" and reject "the sentimental notion that foreign policy is a struggle between virtue and vice."[3]

Much of the complications attendant to assessing morality in international affairs derives from two interrelated concepts—one regarding the differences between people and states, the other recognizing the distinct challenges faced by the latter in the self-help conditions of anarchy. The first is most closely associated with Reinhold Niebuhr, who as a theologian and an ethicist took questions of right and wrong very seriously. He endeavored to reconcile what could be understood as appropriate behavior in the perilous, rough-and-tumble arena of world politics with the tenets of his deeply held faith—exploring and articulating the perspective that would become known as "Christian Realism." Niebuhr, without renouncing moral concerns, nevertheless emphasized the "sharp distinction" between the morality of individuals and groups, one that was informed by a sensitivity to "the brutal character of the behavior of all human collectives."[4]

The second complication realists face in engaging questions of morality, which in its most naked form is best attributed to Machiavelli, circumscribes the imperatives of moral restraint on state behavior with a competing moral concern: the responsibility of the state to protect its citizens. From this perspective, given the present or latent dangers of subjugation and annihilation, acts necessary to preserve the integrity of the state take on their own moral purpose. As the lives of the citizens of the state are valued more highly than the lives of others (and the presumption that this value system is common to most if not all other political entities), actions taken in the name of security must be evaluated in this context. As Machiavelli warned in *The Prince*, "A prince who wants to maintain his state is often forced not to be good." He speaks even more plainly in *Discourses of Livy*, which carries even greater weight, as *Discourses* is generally seen as the more nuanced, reasonable, and even Republican of his major writings. Nevertheless, even here the notion is virtually sacrosanct: "for where one deliberates entirely on the safety of his fatherland, there ought not to enter any consideration of either just or unjust, merciful or cruel, praiseworthy or ignominious; *indeed every other concern put aside*, one ought to follow entirely the policy that saves its life and maintains its liberty."[5]

Few perhaps would press this point as far as Machiavelli; indeed most people of character can imagine measures they would *not* be willing to take, even if the survival of the state was on the line. But the broader point, that state survival presents a competing moral imperative, is not vacuous and the theme is a consistent one in realist thought. For states (as opposed to, say, firms), self-preservation is not simply a preference, or an instinct, or an objective, but indeed is a moral responsibility—human lives, not marginal profits, are at stake in many basic foreign policy choices. This responsibility for self-protection must be weighed against other values, and, at times, all states will, inevitably, have to engage in disreputable or at the very least deeply regrettable behavior in the name of security. As Machiavelli lamented, here more deftly, "For a man who wants to make a profession of good in all regards must come to ruin among so many who are not good"—a sentiment shared by the young Bruce Springsteen, in reference to anarchy of a different type: "it's hard to be a saint in the city."[6]

Nor does this exhaust the reasons for realist wariness of placing moral concerns at the forefront of international political practice. Even the best-intentioned actors will find themselves, in the real world, with choices such that either one of which will leave them with dirty hands. This is because politics in general, and, as noted, foreign policy in particular, is almost never, as Aron lectured, a conflict between "good and evil, but always a choice between the preferable and the detestable." (Realists often rhetorically label their intellectual opponents as "utopians"—for Aron it was indeed utopianism to compare "present realities with theoretical ideas rather than with other realities.") Thus even when guided by normative concerns, the objective often reduces to choosing the least evil action—with inaction no escape from the dilemma, as that choice will also often cost innocent lives as well.[7] And there is also the realist sensitivity to the realities of power—not simply the respect for the power of others, though this is of course essential, but the limits of one's own.[8] In particular, "doing good" might be harder than it looks. Consider the following thought experiment: you are walking along a dock and hear a drowning man calling for help. A life preserver is visible nearby. Surely there is a moral obligation to toss the life preserver into the water. All too often in international relations, however, the would-be Good Samaritan gets his feet tangled in the rope and is sent plunging into the water as well. Or, perhaps worse, and even more commonly, what looked like a life preserver was actually a concrete ring, which struck the poor fellow in the head, killing him. This happens more often than we would like to admit. Certainly it is the story of America's disastrous intervention in Libya in 2011—which looked like an ideal candidate for the judicious application of well-intentioned force: an unambiguously bad guy posing a severe threat to innocents (and to potentially promising endogenous regional political developments), plausibly remediable via a low-cost, low-risk, clearly contained, logistically feasible military operation executed in a broadly permissive international political environment, and unmuddied by attendant ambitious geopolitical designs. Yet the result was disastrous.[9]

For all these reasons, then, on questions of right and wrong, realists tend to follow the admonition of Hans Morgenthau and reject the naive "illusion that a nation can escape, if it only wants to, from power politics into a realm where action is guided by moral principles rather than by considerations of power." Instead, with George F. Kennan, they are inclined to "refrain from constant attempts at the moral appraisal" of the behavior of others and, in weighing foreign policy decisions, follow instead the lodestar of "the gentle civilizer of national self-interest."[10]

That sounds good. And surely it is often right. But it is also much too easy, and it is a non-trivial problem that too many realists think they can superciliously hand out such "get-out-of-jail-free" cards to each other and call it a day. Classical realist Arnold Wolfers—who could paint a rather dark picture both of human nature and of the perils of anarchy—nevertheless offered a withering critique of the notion that morals can be set aside in the practice of international politics. States may have a moral obligation to ensure their survival, but "nations engaged in international politics are faced with the problem of survival only on rare occasions." Most of the time, most foreign policy practices—especially those of great powers—are directed at the pursuit of a much broader range of national interests. (Wolfers can be credited with introducing the important notion of "milieu goals": foreign policy measures that are taken to influence world politics in ways that make the international environment conducive to the thriving of national values and one in which political allies feel secure and content in their shared affinities.) Thus even if states can be forgiven (or at least held to a less stringent account) for a certain ruthlessness regarding measures taken in the name of national survival (though even here, Wolfers's absolution is qualified by the observation "Even national survival itself . . . is a morally compelling necessity only as long as people attach supreme value to it"), this waiver does not naturally extend to the pursuit of other objectives, which, again, is the stuffing of most foreign policy in practice. If anything, the danger runs in the opposite direction, as "attempts to evade, silence or ignore moral judgment merely play into the hands of those who relish the uncriticized use or abuse of their power." Wolfers was writing in 1949, but this moral abyss is clearly evident, for example, in the bloodstained hands of Nixon and Kissinger, as seen in the bombing of Cambodia, complicity in the atrocities in Bangladesh, and cozy relationship with the brutal Chilean dictator Augusto Pinochet.[11]

There is a real danger here for realism as a vocation, akin to one observable in economics. Students in introductory microeconomics classes generally learn that the discipline models agents as selfish egoists: that they care only for themselves and not for others. A (presumably unintended) consequence of this abstract modeling device is that undergraduates who take such courses actually "learn" to be more selfish in their own behavior.[12] Similarly, lectures on realism that model state behavior as amoral can inadvertently teach students—and those who would proffer foreign policy advice derived from realist principles—that foreign policy *should* be conducted without concerns for its moral implications. Again, these are two very different things.

Finally, realists also need to be wary of conflating the assumption that actors in world politics might act without regard for moral concerns with the distinct notion that morality is irrelevant for understanding the behavior of states. It is an almost universal characteristic that leaders across time and place have felt the need before domestic (and international) audiences to couch their foreign policy choices as conforming with virtuous social norms—rarely do they say, out loud, "this is evil, but to our advantage." It must be that such efforts to legitimize foreign policy choices are seen as necessary, and thus consequential.[13] Nor can a student of world politics, however wary of the enterprise, utterly renounce moral judgments about the nature of states in assessing their intentions. As discussed in chapter 3, E. H. Carr proffered a sophisticated realist approach to peaceful change, and one with considerable and enduring value. Nevertheless in application he stumbled badly, fatally misjudging Hitler (and subsequently Stalin—no small errors these). Morgenthau, clearly not one to be easily distracted by normative appeals, nevertheless was not dismissive of them—not at all. Indeed, he attributed Carr's "monumental failure" to the fact that his mechanistic approach offered a "relativistic, instrumentalist conception of morality," which blinded Carr's ability to see things as they were. "It is a dangerous thing to be a Machiavelli," Morgenthau lectured. "It is a disastrous thing to be a Machiavelli without *virtù*."[14]

That cutting observation, of course, does not settle the matter. Which is exactly the point. For all the reasons discussed here, realists are indeed quite properly and understandably fuzzy about the whole good/bad thing. But it is another thing entirely to think that such questions can easily be set aside—and that practice must be acknowledged as a common realist vice.

Depending (on) the National Interest

Another concept central to realist thought is the National Interest (a notion so important it gets its own capitalization). And like moral diffidence, it is another flag prominently planted which upon closer inspection is frayed with loose ends that, when tugged, threaten to unravel an entire tapestry. Yet it remains essential. Thus this is another dilemma for realism not easily resolved but one which again must be acknowledged, and navigated in practice with attentiveness and sensitivity. Realist analysis depends on the perils of anarchy—without the danger of war, however latent, realism has not much to offer. Beyond that, it also depends on the notion that groups, not individuals (or aggregations analytically reducible to individuals), are the unit of analysis.[15] Most commonly, in the modern era, those groups are states, although as Robert Gilpin emphasizes, they need not necessarily be. All realism requires is organized political units (which make distinctions between who is and who is not a member of the group), with capacities for violence, dwelling in anarchy.[16]

But by whatever name and institutional structure, realism requires that the unit of analysis is the group. As Aron states plainly, "The national interest is not reducible to private interests or private collective interests." The national interest is also not reducible to economic interests. Although individuals, subgroups, and coalitions within states inevitably have economic interests and are often highly motivated to pursue those goals, "Politics is never reducible to economics even through the struggle for the possession of sovereign power may in many ways be linked to the mode of production and the distribution of wealth."[17] Realism requires politics. The basic preference for sovereign units in world politics to avoid subjugation by others must derive from a desire for independence and autonomy that is not reducible to material goals. These attributes (irreducibility and politics) yield the central realist notion of a "national interest."

The distinct nature of the National Interest can be clarified with an analogy from economic theory: it can be conceptualized as a "public good." Public goods are things whose consumption or enjoyment is non-rivalrous and non-exclusionary. That is, the utilization of or pleasure derived from the good (or service) by one person does not impinge on the availability of that product to others; and once provided, there is no way to stop people from benefiting from it. (A pristine example of this is traffic lights; once put in place, not only is their utilization non-rivalrous and non-exclusionary, as a practical matter they are only effective if everyone has unlimited access to them.)[18] But because of these two qualities, the free market, left to its own devices, will underprovide public goods—because voluntary contributions to pay for them will tend to fall short due to the free rider problem, and entrepreneurs will not invest in enterprises that can't turn a profit. Thus even the most orthodox, libertarian-leaning economists hold that it falls to the state to provide public goods—and national defense is often held out as a classic illustration of such a necessity. (If a state's borders are protected from foreign invasion, all citizens enjoy that benefit, and each individual's enjoyment of that "security" does not impinge on the amount of security enjoyed by others.)

The National Interest, then, which certainly includes the territorial integrity of the state—that is, assurances of protection from invasion by outsiders—clearly has this public quality and thus gives basic credence to the notion that a distinct and irreducible "national interest" exists. Territorial integrity, in turn, is only truly meaningful if it implies some level of domestic policy autonomy, so measures taken to protect that surely fall under the broad umbrella of the National Interest as well. And not far beyond that lie Wolfers's milieu goals—as noted, aspirations to shape the international political environment so that national interests and national values might thrive; measures taken to advance these ends implicitly if indirectly enhance physical security and policy autonomy. Although the pursuit of milieu goals is ultimately a less pressing imperative than ensuring territorial integrity and domestic policy autonomy, such actions are nevertheless derivative of the National Interest (advancing broad, long-term goals) and, as noted, and especially for great powers, are what most foreign policy is about in practice. This is all also suggestive of another "public good" attribute of the National Interest: longer time horizons. Since states live much longer than people, concerns about "the long run" will tend to be underprovided if left entirely in the hands of self-interested individuals. Thus states are charged with keeping an eye on assessing (and implementing) measures that might be necessary to sustain collective interests over time, another component of the National Interest.

In defense of (the concept of) the National Interest, it is not hard to point to practical illustrations of the phenomenon. For centuries, it was in the British National Interest that no single power achieve political hegemony on the European continent, as such an entity could pose a real threat to the home islands. From this naturally yielded the tendency for Britain to provide political and military support for the weaker coalition in continental confrontations. In a similar spirit, it was surely in the U.S. interest that no single power come to dominate the Eurasian landmass, which informed its foreign policy choices during World War II and the

Cold War.[19] In the nineteenth century, the United States might not have had the capacity to enforce the Monroe Doctrine, but the notion that the European powers ought to steer clear of the Western Hemisphere made good sense from a general national security perspective. For one hundred and fifty years it has been in the interest of France that German power be either checked or tamed. It is in the interest of almost all states that non-state actors do not come into possession of nuclear weapons.

Many other examples could be easily added to this list. Nevertheless, it is also possible to look at articulations of the National Interest the way Marlene Dietrich looked Orson Welles up and down in *Touch of Evil* and reach a similar conclusion: "You're a mess, honey." To begin with, once again we have the classical realist admonition that the imperatives of anarchy, which must inform the National Interest, are rarely sufficient to explain how states will define it. As prominent late twentieth-century realist Samuel Huntington observed, looking at the balance of power is certainly a reasonable point of departure, but it has "severe limits" and "does not get one very far" because states do not "perceive their interests in the same way or act in the same way."[20] Even granting this qualification (that the National Interest is not exogenously and uniquely determined), problems with the notion endure. All too often, as a practical matter the concept as appealed to is intolerably vague. Despite the examples offered above, a cursory review of the relevant history will reveal the National Interest to be commonly malleable over time, variable in trajectory, and contestable in articulation—and even when agreed upon, still subject to robust debate as to which policy measures will best serve it. In addition, even as we hold to the notion that the National Interest is not reducible to either economic concerns or the disproportional influence of subnationally motivated domestic political coalitions, as seen in the discussion of "Hirschman effects" in chapter 5, economic interests—especially broadly based economic interests—cannot be dismissed as irrelevant in shaping the National Interest.

Gilpin and Wolfers—neither of whom, it should be stressed, is prepared to dispense with the concept—nevertheless offer trenchant critiques of its casual invocation. Gilpin calls attention to the extent to which such interests can be defined in a number of possible ways. In *War and Change in World Politics*, unsurprisingly he invokes the national interest, and the notion that the pressures of anarchy limit the definition of that interest within some plausible, circumscribed range—but nevertheless holds that its content, directionality, and tactical pursuit can take a number of distinct forms. Indeed, Gilpin goes so far as to say that "shifts in domestic coalitions may necessitate redefinition of the 'national interest.'" Especially in countries where political lines of contestation are often divided along regional lines, such as the United States for much of its history, it is possible to imagine competing visions of what the National Interest might be.[21]

Gilpin, then, embraces the National Interest but insists that, in the absence of unambiguous, pressing, existential threats to security (that is, for most great powers most of the time), it can be interpreted and pursued in a number of ways. For Wolfers, and this anticipates a challenge for both descriptive (how states will behave) and prescriptive (how states should behave) realist analyses, the problem is one of underdefinition. "In a very vague and general way 'national interest' does suggest a direction of policy," he notes, appropriately invoking those measures which prioritize the imperatives of a country as a whole rather than the particular interests of "subnational groups." But without the articulation of specific goals and attentiveness to their political context, he argues, "normative admonitions to conduct a foreign policy guided by the national security interest are . . . ambiguous and misleading."[22]

Disentangling Is and Ought

A problem for all scholarship in International Relations (and an issue for the social sciences more generally) is dealing with the distinction between descriptive and prescriptive analysis. This is, at the broad philosophical level, a large and enduing conundrum that has been engaged by prominent thinkers throughout history, notably David Hume and Max Weber.[23] Such grand and timeless questions will not be settled here. But they must be raised and reckoned with, as those engaged in international political analysis almost invariably have a hand in each. This is understandable—it is exceedingly rare for a scholar drawn to theoretical problems pertaining to world politics to be innocent of or indifferent to their practical implications. Indeed the formal discipline of International Relations was forged by normative concerns, in particular a desire not to repeat the ghastly, senseless bloodletting of World War I, and later given urgency by the specter of nuclear annihilation. In pursuing theoretical puzzles, then, lives are at stake—potentially millions of lives—in getting the answers right, as implications for policy will necessarily flow from the most dispassionate, aspirationally value-neutral theoretical analysis.

The primary calling of scholarship must be analytical: efforts to describe, explain, and understand world politics, and to be alert to causal patterns that make it possible to anticipate the range of likely and plausible consequences of different events. That is certainly the ambition of this book. And always, following Aron, it remains essential to be disciplined and attentive to the stubborn limits of objectivity—even the choice of the units of analysis, to take one example among many, carries inescapably normative implications. (This is true in economics as well, scholarship which often, naively and self-soothingly, likes to imagine itself above such untidy and "unscientific" moral dilemmas.)[24] Nevertheless, if muddied at the margins, description is a different enterprise than prescription, which is the advocacy of measures that states *should* pursue (which presumably flow from the logic of the descriptive analysis).

But the pitfalls here are enormous—and students of world politics commonly tumble into them, often willingly. Given the challenges of uncertainty and contingency (in addition to the essential "ketchup problem" emphasized in chapter 2—the fundamental difference between understanding average as opposed to individual behavioral responses), the prescriptive implications of a pristine descriptive analysis in a particular situation, even in the case of a theory widely shared (relatively rare in international relations theory), are open to considerable debate. And positions in that debate will be informed by normative dispositions.

Description and prescription are thus distinct, but oddly enmeshed. Consider the expectations of classical realism that great powers will harbor ambitions that will grow with their capabilities, and that they are prone to act rashly and be driven by hubris. Yet if there is a broadly shared classical realist policy disposition (about which more below), it is the call for caution and prudence. This makes sense—if the world is a dangerous place characterized by ongoing political contestation, best to keep one's power dry and marshal resources for the most pressing threats (and the ones that will loom beyond that). And if the hubris of great powers has historically been an important source of their undoing, then guarding against ebullient, wild-eyed foreign adventures is wise. But note the disjuncture between the expectation of the way states will behave (recklessly and ambitiously) and the policy advice of how they should behave (with measured caution and level heads).[25]

Efforts to grapple with the philosophical enigmas and pragmatic challenges of disentangling prescription and description can quickly take on a Talmudic quality, and are unlikely to ever be fully resolved. As a practical matter then, the imperative for scholars of international relations boils down to the need to be very cautious when flirting with policy advocacy, to make every effort to distinguish between the positive and (very often implicit) normative aspects of their analysis, and, above all and at all costs, to avoid the all-too-common danger of confusing and conflating positive with normative analysis. Especially for realism, which, as noted, often fancies that its theoretical apparatus flirts with an amorality that exempts it from normative questions, this is an analytical danger that must be taken very seriously.

Consider one prominent and influential self-professed realist, John Mearsheimer, who describes his theory this way: "offensive realism is mainly a descriptive theory . . . but it is also a prescriptive theory. States should behave according to the dictates of offensive realism, because it outlines the best way to survive in a dangerous world."[26] At one level this is simply somewhat puzzling, to say the least, because the "descriptive theory" on offer explicitly claims to be a deterministic one—and so policy advice should be irrelevant if the theory is correct, as states will inevitably behave in the way that they are predicted with certainty by the model to behave. (Newton did not say, "The apple will fall from the tree, and I urge it to pursue this course." Nor would he have chastised apples for failing to follow his advice, or attribute their foolish behavior to the disclaimer that some varieties of the fruit are squeamish about the implications of gravity.) But more important, combining description and prescription in this way is a basic subversion of good social science. If advocacy can change outcomes (and if it can't, why advocate?), then urging actors to behave as one's theory predicts is putting a finger on the analytical scale—like predicting a barroom brawl and then provoking one. As will be elaborated in chapter 6, there are fundamental flaws in the underlying logic of Mearsheimer's theory of offensive realism, and the approach should be set aside. But even if the theory had merit, Mearsheimer's conflation of is and ought gestures at still another all too common, and potentially disqualifying problem: once we start rooting for our theories, it is all over. To mobilize scholarly inquiry for the express purpose of supporting policy advocacy invites skepticism of the integrity of the enterprise. This is a complex and nuanced issue, and one that is not effortlessly resolved, since scholars cannot fully escape their own implicit value systems. Nevertheless, in the social sciences in particular, vigilance against a self-confirming bias is essential.[27] Because once scholars are rooting for their theories, or are deploying their theories instrumentally in support of a favored policy, the floodgates are opened for personal preferences and inclinations to implicitly motivate nominally theoretical claims and conclusions—especially because in studies of world politics, available evidence will often lend itself to multiple interpretations.[28]

Another pitfall of prescriptive realist analysis—suggestions regarding how foreign policy ought to be conducted—is that, ironically, it is vulnerable to its own form of utopianism. In particular, classical realists have often favored foreign policy dispositions and measures that are simply not politically feasible. Such a conceit stems from an imagined foreign policy that somehow stands apart from politics and process. But of course there is no such thing, and if foreign policy prescriptions are incompatible with the possibilities of real-world practice, then they are of little practical value.

Relatedly, any assessment of the limitations of classical realism must reflect upon the undercurrent of elitism that is shared by many if not most of its greatest thinkers. In particular, classical realists are terrified by the ease with which masses can be moved by unscrupulous demagogues, and, it must be acknowledged, their writings often suggest a wariness of democracy itself—or at the very least the notion that foreign policy should be left to the untidy, mercurial whims of the democratic process.

Anxiety about demagogues, especially in democracies, is a leitmotif as old as realism itself. It was a principal theme of Thucydides' *The Peloponnesian War*, as illustrated in his emphasis on the disastrous influence of numerous such figures, including his bête noir Cleon—prominent among those who were invariably "grasping for more." Thucydides saw great danger in the ways in which individuals could be radicalized, especially in times of distress, such as during the revolution in Corcyra. "Reckless audacity came to be understood as the courage of a loyal supporter; prudent hesitation, specious cowardice; moderation was held to be a cloak for unmanliness; ability to see all sides of a question incapacity to act on any," he described. In such settings, Thucydides added archly, "the blunter wits were most successful."[29] These concerns informed the wariness of America's founding fathers of what they saw as the fine line between direct democracy and mob rule. As Alexander Hamilton wrote in *The Federalist*, "History will teach us that . . . of those men who have overturned the liberties of republics, the greatest number have begun their career by paying an obsequious court to the people; commencing demagogues, and ending tyrants." James Madison shared similar apprehensions. "In all very numerous assemblies, of whatever characters composed, passion never fails to wrest the scepter from reason," he argued. "Had every Athenian citizen been a Socrates, every Athenian assembly would still have been a mob." Such alarms are routinely echoed in twentieth-century classical realism. "Our foreign policy is . . . threatened with a kind of apoplectic rigidity and inflexibility," Niebuhr lamented, which requires "the disavowal of precisely those discriminate judgements which are so necessary." These instincts are likely why classical realists at the time (even, bravely and prominently, Kennan, whose political instincts were very conservative and even authoritarian) were early and outspoken opponents of McCarthyism.[30]

Calling out demagogues, however, is one thing. Wariness about democracy is another. This matters, not simply as a normative observation that cannot be dismissed but, again, as a guard against utopianism. If one is going to proffer foreign policy advice to a democratic country, it would behoove the analyst to make those recommendations with an eye toward the possible, as opposed to the Platonic. (And if the suggestion is that non-democracies have "better" foreign policies than democracies, it would be requisite to show any research to back up that claim.) Thucydides had a reverence for Athens and its (bounded) democratic practices. But he had an even greater admiration for Pericles—or more generally, for the type of visionary leader who could tame democratic excesses. Early in the conflict, when Pericles was faced with mounting dissent and indignation against his cautious strategy, Thucydides lauds him for resisting the will of an increasingly hot-headed majority, which had "lost all patience" with his wise and prudent conduct of the war: "the whole city was in a most excited state; Pericles was the object of general indignation; his previous counsels were totally forgotten." Rather than, as would be expected, calling an assembly to discuss and debate the matter—the outcome of which would surely have been a vote that would have gone against him ("the determination was universal, especially among the young men")—Pericles managed to sidestep normal Athenian democratic procedures, and instead "he attended to the defense of the city, and kept it as quiet as possible." But leaders like Pericles don't grow on trees ("by his rank, his ability, and known integrity, [he] was enabled to exercise an independent control over the multitude . . . what was nominally a democracy was becoming in his hands government by the first citizen"), as Thucydides acknowledges: "With his successors it was much different . . . each grasping at supremacy, they ended by committing even the conduct of state affairs to the whims of the multitude."[31]

And frustration with the clumsy foreign policy practices of democracy is a common realist disquiet. Kennan leads the way ("public opinion, or what passes for public opinion, is not invariably a moderating force in the jungle of politics," he grumbles; rather it causes foreign policy to be "led astray into areas of emotionalism and subjectivity"). Kennan's distaste for liberal democracy leaves him as an outlier among his firmly anti-authoritarian peers, but he was not alone in bemoaning the incompatibility of realism with democracy. Morgenthau repeatedly expressed frustration with the inability of American foreign policy "to follow consistently certain standards of action and judgement in its conduct of foreign affairs," which he attributed, representing a broad chorus of classical realists, to the fact that the human mind "cannot bear to look the truth of politics straight in the face."[32]

Few classical realists would not share Kennan's longing for a world in which foreign policy was steered by professionals afforded the amenities of "privacy, deliberateness," and the luxury of taking the "long term approach." Surely that would have avoided the overreach of the Truman Doctrine, the dramatic articulation of an epochal, global struggle between freedom and communism that was deemed rhetorically necessary to secure the domestic political support for what was originally intended as a narrowly focused provision of assistance to Greece and Turkey. But to get that measured bill through Congress, Senator Arthur Vandenberg advised President Truman it would be necessary to "scare the hell out of the American people" and invoke rhetoric that was, in Secretary of State Dean Acheson's famous phrase, "clearer than the truth." The need to oversimplify and oversell foreign policy measures leads to lurching overreactions and suboptimal choices, what Niebuhr described as "fanatic distinctions between good and evil" that obscure "nuances of strategy."[33]

But it is not enough to point out the miscues of democratic foreign policies; following Aron, it is necessary to compare foreign policy practice not against an idealized vision of its imagined optimal execution but with the possibilities and outcomes that could be plausibly achieved with real-world alternatives.[34] And with regard to the imagined practice of foreign policy directed by a "star chamber" of wise men insulated from the vagaries of domestic politics, two problems loom very large. First, such Wise Men have been very wrong in the past, for example, in the bipartisan elite consensus regarding the Vietnam War, which was exactly and disastrously wrong.[35] Second, speaking specifically of classical realism, the flip side to the danger of democratic crusading—setting aside whether any society could sustain a grand strategy devoid of ideological content, purpose, and meaning—is the possibility that a "realist foreign policy" steeped in caution and prudence would be suboptimally *underresponsive*. That is, assuming there can be such a thing as a "Realist Foreign Policy."

Who Cheers for Prudence?

A final difficulty for realism is that it appears to have very little to offer by way of practical advice for purposeful action—at least, from a general paradigmatic perspective. Possibly, indeed probably as a function of the fact that it is so well attuned to avoiding foreign policy blunders (a talent not to be taken lightly), realism has much less to say about the wisdom of positive steps a country might productively take. All of that dispassion, deliberativeness, caution, and wariness of imbuing foreign policies with national values or moral purpose leaves little on the table to suggest what actually might be done with state power. But there is more to international politics than vigilance against potential threats, the moral equivalent of installing surveillance cameras, triple-locking the door, and never venturing outside. E. H. Carr, in his own critique of realism from within, noted that it lacked a number of "essential ingredients" for effective political practice, including, notably, its lack of content and purpose, and the absence of "an emotional appeal." Similarly, Martin Wight, while emphasizing the centrality of power as the final arbiter of international disputes, nevertheless argued that it was "equally true that power varies very much in effectiveness according to the strength of the beliefs that inspire its use." By the same token Niebuhr chastised fellow realists for failing to have a "proper regard for moral aspirations" in world politics, noting that "political power is a compound of which physical force, whether economic or military, is only one ingredient."[36]

But "most of all," as Carr noted, "consistent realism breaks down because it fails to provide any ground for purposive or meaningful action." On this point Morgenthau, in his otherwise devastatingly critical review of *The Twenty Years' Crisis*, was in full agreement. Morgenthau struck a similar chord in his more generous review of Aron's *A Century of Total War*, and the frustration is palpable. "An intellectual par excellence" (a phrase between academics that is akin to the sound of a sharpening knife), Aron's "purpose is not to prove a thesis, to develop a system, or to tell a coherent story. Thus he presents no program for action, no political philosophy, no history, but rather elements of one or another as the occasion arises."[37]

There are three distinct challenges for realism here, the latter two of which elude easy resolution. First, it is important to recognize that there is no such thing as a (singular) "realist foreign policy"—realists will disagree on much. Second, the one disposition that is shared almost universally by realist thinkers—a veneration of prudence—is quite helpful at steering policy clear of blunders, but inherently ill-suited as a guide for action.

Finally, that much-admired quality of prudence, which, if heeded, will commonly serve states well, nevertheless can and often will be a source of policy paralysis. It is possible to be too cautious, and in world politics, leaving the initiative and opportunities to others will at times make a state less rather than more secure. It is too easy to conflate prudence with passivity, which are two different things.

No realist foreign policy. Realists, historically, have not been shy about offering foreign policy advice. But they have disagreed and will disagree on basic aspects of that advice—not that there's anything wrong with that. As classical realism urgently reminds us, irretrievable limits to knowledge will always prevent convergence around a single, shared model of understanding of how the world works; and even were such a singular model possible, that would not settle the question of to what ends foreign policy should be applied.[38] These are not small hurdles. Consider that neoclassical economists—an intellectually homogeneous cohort with aspirations to analytical precision—do not share the same theories of exchange rate determination (a much tidier topic than grand strategy) and even if they ever did, the policy advice that followed from such a common model would still depend on which, from a variety of objectives, different analysts privileged. Once again, purpose inevitably and forcefully matters.[39]

Even if realists were somehow able to avoid the treacherous analytical landmines just described, the prospects for a singular, distinct realist foreign policy would still remain remote. To offer specific policy advice, it is necessary to have theories that make generalizations about how other actors will behave in world politics, and, relatedly, theories about how other states will respond to the recommended foreign policy measures that are introduced. About such matters there will never be universal laws, given variation in historical and social political context, and because, it should be repeated, the foreign policies of states are functions of both power and purpose (the capabilities of states, and what they want)—this, again, something to which classical realism is especially alert and attentive. Political developments at the end of the second decade of the twenty-first century in the United States vividly illustrate this point. American power did not change all that much (and assessments of that power vary widely)[40] but its purpose—whom it chooses to call friend and foe, what commitments it is likely to fulfill, the ends for which it will use military force, which institutions it will support—changed radically. This is problematic because, as a general measure, it is much easier (if still difficult in practice) to assess power, and it is also reasonable to anticipate that it will change relatively slowly, than it is to measure to purpose, which can also shift more rapidly. And regarding purpose, beyond the fundamental imperative of survival, realism is largely agnostic. Indeed structural realism renounces the concept of purpose, modeling states as like units, differentiated only by their relative capabilities; classical realism embraces purpose—but assumes that such purpose is informed by varied and contingent historical contexts.

Thus although the desire to survive is Realism 101, that does not get us very far in explaining the foreign policy choices of states (or, more to the point here, as a foreign policy guide), especially when attempting to explain the behavior of great powers. The survival of great powers is very rarely at risk, and thus it is not typically the imperative that informs most of their foreign policy choices. The stuffing of great power foreign policy is almost invariably about much more than self-defense. As Morgenthau observed, "the goals that might be pursued by nations in their foreign policies can run the whole gamut of objectives any nation has ever pursued or might possibly pursue." And great powers enjoy the broadest discretion in this regard and have the greatest capacity (and luxury) to pursue Wolfers's milieu goals—again, the pursuit of which in most circumstances will account for the lion's share of foreign policy practice.[41] Consider the contemporary United States. With its gargantuan military, enormous economy, enviable geography, and robust nuclear deterrent, if all the United States cared about was physical security and domestic autonomy, it would not even need a foreign policy. To design an American foreign policy that ventures beyond those first two items on the checklist (or, alternatively, for others to anticipate the foreign policy of the United States), it would be necessary to know what it wants—or have a theory of what else it should want. Similarly, China in 2020 was literally orders of magnitude more powerful and secure than it was two generations before that. If defending the homeland was its only national security imperative, China would need less foreign policy—and less foreign policy analysis—once it emerged as a great power. But of course the opposite is true.

In sum, articulating a singular, distinct "realist foreign policy" is inhibited by the fact that the behavior of states—their responses to the opportunities and constraints presented by the international system—is shaped by the way that the foreign policy choices of great powers inform those opportunities and constraints, and filtered through historical experience and ideological lenses. Uncertainty, the broad range of plausible and sustainable behaviors and responses, and distinct contingent circumstances leave room for contestation regarding both foreign policy advice and expectations about behavior. This rules out the possibility of a consensus about iron laws regarding foreign policy, even within the realist community. President Truman was reputed to have longed for a one-armed economist who would be incapable of saying "on the other hand"; but it remains inescapable that the realist response to even the most primal foreign policy choices must be "it depends." Consider the basic and perennial IR question: should an apparent provocation be met with firmness or conciliation?[42] It depends. Morgenthau was an opponent of the Munich accords, because he saw clearly the consequences of trying to accommodate Nazi Germany in the 1930s. But the problem was not with the policy of making concessions more generally—as Morgenthau made clear, and quite provocatively so, at the height of the Cold War. "Future historians will have to decide whether the Western world has suffered more from the surrender at Munich," he admonished, "or from the intellectual confusion that equates a negotiated settlement with appeasement and thus discredits the sole rational alternative to war."[43] Realist foreign policy advice will necessarily be contingent and qualified, and require well-informed, contextually grounded, situationally specific discretion, rather than urging general adherence to some imagined universally applicable rules. Recall Kennan's notion that we are gardeners, not mechanics.[44] As well it should be—this is not a problem to be solved but a quality that must be acknowledged and embraced.

A realist foreign policy disposition. Although there is no such thing as a singular "realist foreign policy," the analytical building blocks of realism are strongly suggestive of a particular foreign policy disposition. Attentiveness to the inexorable dangers implied by anarchy (latent or present), a need to respect the realities of power (the capabilities of others, the inevitable limits of one's own), and an anticipation that world politics is characterized by conflicts of interest (with the resolution of one dispute soon followed by the emergence of another), all in the context of irreducible uncertainty, lead, logically, to an imperative of prudence. Machiavelli is a potential outlier in this regard—although as always he can be hard to pin down. In *The Prince* he encourages embracing fortune ("it is better to be impetuous than cautious" in seizing opportunities when they suddenly arise, he counsels). This advice can perhaps be domesticated and shoehorned into accord with classical realism more generally by noting the important role in this analysis of the unpredictable, as well as a reflection of expectation that states are ambitious and will take advantage of opportunities when they arise—but in general passages in *The Prince* suggest a more impulsive temperament, and one that is uncommon among realists more generally. (And as always, it is better to acknowledge the outlier rather than offer post hoc rationalizations for it in the hope of imposing a uniformity and tidiness that does not exist.) But the Machiavelli of *Discourses*, which is invariably his more insightful and reflective contribution, returns to the traditional realist fold, holding that Republics are "more prudent, more stable, and of better judgment than a prince," and because they move more slowly and deliberately, they make "lesser errors than the prince, and because of this can be trusted more."[45] And the admonition to proceed with caution, weigh alternatives, identify and prioritize interests, and anticipate, as best as possible, the plausible range of the tumbling consequences of proposed foreign policy measures is the calling card of classical realism. As Morgenthau puts it, "Realism, then, considers prudence—the weighing of the consequences of alternative political actions—to be the supreme virtue in politics," sentiments echoed by Hobbes, Niebuhr, and of course Kennan, among others.[46]

This dyed-in-the-wool instinct for prudence is grounded further in two additional tenets that are closely associated with (but not distinct to) realism: great attentiveness to the essential relationship between force and politics, and a profound wariness of hubris and the arrogance of power. The former is most closely associated with Clausewitz, and his sagacious observation that the assessment of the merits of the use of force cannot be judged by the achievement of apparent military victories but the extent to which those achievements on the battlefield advanced the political goals for which they were introduced. This requires an almost myopic, forward-looking consideration of what the likely political situation will look like after the war is over and a sensitivity to the fact that political contestations—old and new—will continue long after the guns have been silenced.[47] More colloquially, this can be described as the "day after tomorrow question." Meaning, a state has used force, and perhaps even achieved its military objectives, but what happens next? The use of force will not only result in (unpredictable) countermeasures but also unleash a cascade of political consequences. Some of these may be good and even welcome—but in a world where politics and political conflict never end, the range of these consequences must be thoughtfully anticipated in advance. As for hubris, anxiety about the arrogance of power is perhaps the singular strand that weaves its way through realist thought throughout history.

Along these lines there is of course the Rosetta Stone of realist prudence, Thucydides' *The Peloponnesian War*. For all the casual (and cavalier) invocations of the notion of a "Thucydides Trap," as we have discussed, the greatest lesson that Thucydides wished to impart with his magnum opus was the mortal danger of hubris. Recall from chapter 1 that Thucydides makes abundantly clear that it was indeed hubris, not a mechanistic trap generated by power dynamics, which brought Athens to ruin. To Thucydides' palpable lament, the ambitious city-state repeatedly and tragically "grasped at something further," blunders that anticipated what would be the most grievous mistake of the war, the Athenians' wildly ambitious and ultimately disastrous scheme to conquer Sicily.[48]

For foreign policy, however, prudence, the national interest, and the primacy of politics yield less by way of practical advice than might appear at first glance. As seen in chapter 3, realists opposed the Vietnam War on all of these grounds, questioning the interests at stake, and the wisdom and prospects of trying to impose a military solution on an intractable political problem.[49] Similarly, an uncommonly overwhelming consensus among realists was reflected in their early, emphatic opposition to the 2003 Iraq war, as it was obvious that a relatively easy military victory would not translate into the achievement of broader objectives—in fact, quite the opposite.[50] And correspondingly, it is hard to imagine realists signing up for a U.S. military strike against Iran's nuclear program, for example, following familiar, Clausewitzian "the day after tomorrow" reasoning.[51] Nevertheless, and notwithstanding the considerable merits of being right about those disasters, Vietnam, Iraq, and Iran (and Sicily) are pretty low-hanging fruit—the sage advice of "avoid obviously foolish military adventurers" only gets you so far. Once again, realism is much better at suggesting what not to do than when and how to take positive action.

Moreover, gesturing at the wisdom of Thucydides in general, and invoking Sicily in particular, can with regard to some more general issues of foreign policy practice raise as many questions for realism as it answers. Consider Sicily. Many realists in American foreign policy debates who favor a posture of "restraint" invoke that catastrophe in defense of the proposition that there is an affinity between realism, one that can be traced all the way back to Thucydides, and their advocacy for a more restrained U.S. grand strategy. And it is quite correct to observe that Pericles, as described by Thucydides, would have never embarked on the Sicilian adventure had he lived to speak out against it. But Pericles (and implicitly, Thucydides) was a strong proponent of the initial war with Sparta—a war that Athens arguably provoked, and which was sparked by crises that Athens could have easily taken measures to mollify but chose not to. The debate for war in Athens was a close call, and Thucydides reports that Pericles' arguments (which his narrative privileges) were decisive in carrying the day. In the public debate before the war, Pericles spoke out forcefully against the notion of compromise or negotiation, and argued instead, "It must be thoroughly understood that war is a necessity"; according to Thucydides, Pericles' passionate advocacy for this war of choice was crucial in securing the majority vote necessary for Athens to take up arms.[52] Pericles' cautious, patient, warfighting strategy was surely prudent, but his enthusiasm for the war is not well characterized by that notion. Certainly all good realists would have opposed the Sicilian expedition—but it is more likely that they would have been divided over the very distinct debate over whether go to war with Sparta seventeen years earlier.

From prudence to paralysis? Recognizing the virtue of prudence as an abstract concept is different from the practice of a foreign policy, nor does it necessarily or invariably imply passivity or timidity. Just as monetary policy can be described as irresponsibly (or imprudently) "too loose," resulting in excessive inflation, it can also be (and has often been) "too tight"—and as a result impose an unnecessary and painful contraction of economic activity. Similarly, although many foreign policy blunders are the result of imprudence, foreign policy can also be too cautious, and such mistakes can place the state in danger as well. As seen in chapter 3, Western underresponsiveness to the German threat in the 1930s was a millennial catastrophe. Machiavelli, as noted, had a higher tolerance for risk taking than is typical for classical realists, but nevertheless it is hard to reject his contention that no state should "ever believe that it can always adopt safe courses." And in lauding the realist instinct for prudence, it needs to be recognized that one danger implicit in that realist predisposition is the prospect of important opportunities lost to an overabundance of caution.[53] The American forging of the international order after World War II was an active, ambitious, unprecedented, and even audacious undertaking. And in weighing its costs and benefits in retrospect, it was arguably also the most successful grand strategy in the history of grand strategy. But it was also opposed, on good realist grounds, by George F. Kennan at almost every turn. Kennan opposed the formation of NATO, favored a neutralized, demilitarized Japan, and (with the important exception of the first phases of the Korean War) was invariably eager to bring U.S. troops hope and reluctant to assert American political power abroad.[54]

It does not take a Machiavelli to suggest that Kennan took his prudence too far. Niebuhr, while rejecting a foreign policy of "adventurism" that failed to acknowledge the limits to power, nevertheless criticized fellow realists who "are so impressed by the force of the perennial problems of politics . . . that they are inclined to discount both the necessity and the possibility of new political achievements." And gesturing at milieu goals (and explicitly criticizing Kennan), Niebuhr argued that "the national interest when conceived only from the standpoint of the self-interest of the nation is bound to be defined too narrowly and therefore to be self-defeating."[55]

In sum, realists, ever alert to reconciling ends with means, will surely routinely err on the side of avoiding overextension—but "underextension," and too much caution, risks inviting dangerous foes to fill power vacuums left behind (a concept that will be explored more fully in chapter 7). As always, the wisest and most prudent course of action is dependent on context and contingent factors, and the national interest will not invariably be best served by caution. Stubbornly, the point remains that the common lineage that realists share does not translate into a clear foreign policy road map. In particular, "prudence" does not necessarily translate into "restraint" (though at times it may). In fact restraint, when it involves the scaling back of existing commitments—often wise, sometimes necessary—is not always the prudent thing to do.[56] Retrenchment is a shaking up of the box, an invitation to others to assert power and gain influence, and comes with it the elimination of any political benefits and regionally stabilizing effects that were attendant with the presence, participation, and commitments being withdrawn. That does not make it unwise.[57] But it is a leap into uncertainty, from the familiar to the unknown.

It is a limitation of classical realism that in a world of uncertainty and contingency, and properly humbled by analytical modesty, beyond proffering valuable (and all too often disregarded) counsel against folly and hubristic adventures, a realist disposition will very rarely translate into hard and fast policy advice. Once again, this is a problem more to be expressly acknowledged than easily resolved. "A statesman differs from a professor in a university," Edmund Burke once explained. "The latter has only the general view of society; the former, the statesman, has a number of circumstances to combine with those general ideas."[58]

CHAPTER FIVE

Realism, Economics, and Politics

FOR MOST OF modern history, and certainly in the twenty-first century, it is simply not possible to understand world politics without close attentiveness to economic issues. At the most basic level, the end of the Cold War is incomprehensible without recognizing the crucial role of the stagnation of the Soviet economic system; similarly, the only reason why there has been an explosion of interest in the implications of China's emergence as a great power is because of its three decades of spectacular economic growth. Had during those decades the Russian economy thrived while China's stagnated, the geopolitical world today would be fundamentally different. To note some additional, obvious examples: the oil shocks of the 1970s had observable and profound geopolitical implications and contributed to the causes of several large regional wars; efforts to understand the emergence of militaristic fascism and the origins of World War II must include a consideration of the consequences of the Great Depression and the global financial crisis of 1931; and scholars of world politics would be remiss if they failed to process and account for the international political implications of the global financial crisis of 2007–8 and its aftermath.[1]

Economic issues thus influence, routinely and at the most basic level, aspects of world politics, and thus cannot be safely set aside or bracketed off by students of international relations. Perhaps this was plausible, or at least arguable, in a bygone era when the economies of the two superpowers were practically sealed off from one other. But even then, and always, consider that analysts and practitioners of "grand strategy" are engaging in an explicitly microeconomic exercise—how to apportion finite resources most efficiently to achieve desired goals.

Additionally, and too often underappreciated, the relationship between economics and politics runs both ways. An attentiveness to the inescapable politics inherent to economic affairs is among E. H. Carr's foundational contributions to modern realism. Two of Carr's claims in particular provide the underpinnings of "realist political economy." First is his observation that "the science of economics presupposes a given political order, and cannot be profitably studied in isolation from politics." This derives from his dissent, which came naturally to Carr (whose economic instincts grew increasingly heterodox), against the presumptions of classical and neoclassical economics, which implicitly or explicitly assumed that market economies emerged spontaneously and operated apolitically. As Jonathan Haslam observes, "*The Twenty Years' Crisis* was the product of bitter disillusion with the liberal world order and all that went with it, including classical economics," and the easy, comforting assumptions that accompanied it.[2] Second, and related, pertains to Carr's development of realism as a critique of liberalism. At times his approach could be heavy-handed and slip into a caricature of liberal "utopianism"—but his dissent from liberal economics, which did celebrate a "harmony of interests" (that all benefit from unfettered economic exchange), especially as applied to international relations, was on the mark. It is not necessary to share Carr's view that "Laissez-Faire in international relations as in those between capital and labor, is the paradise of the economically strong" to recognize the important role of power in shaping economic relations.[3] Bringing politics to economics is the basis of realist political economy.

Having said that, however, it must be acknowledged that realism in general has tended to stumble on questions of political economy—while there have been notable exceptions, economics has been something of a blind spot for both ancient and modern thinkers. Once again, this pedigree—here something less to boast about—can be traced all the way back to Thucydides, who tended to downplay and even ignore economic factors that contributed to the causes and course of the Peloponnesian War. Most notoriously, as noted in chapter 1, Thucydides elided the significance of the Megarian Decree, economic sanctions that Athens imposed on an ally of Sparta. Some prominent specialists view the Athenian measure to have been a significant provocation, and one that contributed importantly to the likelihood of the war. Scholars of Thucydides tend to disagree on many things, but on this broad omission they speak with one voice—Thucydides did not seriously engage economic issues here or elsewhere in *The Peloponnesian War* more generally. Regarding Megara in particular, some have speculated that Thucydides was reluctant to call attention to Pericles' obstinacy on the issue, which would shift still more of the responsibility for the war on his shoulders, but this would not account for Thucydides' general tendency to downplay or ignore economic factors.[4]

Other eminences of the realist pantheon followed Thucydides' lead; figures like Hobbes, Machiavelli, and Clausewitz, for example, were largely silent regarding economic matters. And although there were some notable contributions pertaining to questions of economics and national security among more modern thinkers, for the most part even leading mid-twentieth-century realists, such as Kennan and Morgenthau, shied away from seriously engaging economic aspects of international politics.[5] Even Raymond Aron, who was much savvier on such matters and had a sophisticated command of the Keynesian revolution and its implications—and was capable of smartly unpacking and assessing the economic crises of the 1970s—nevertheless did not often draw this arrow from his quiver. It is possible that some of this reticence, especially in the case of Morgenthau and Aron, derived from their investment in emphasizing the distinct political roots of and motivations for behavior.[6]

International Relations would emerge as a distinct academic discipline after World War II, but the subfield of international political economy would not take shape until the late 1960s and early 1970s. There were both material and ideational reasons for this. With the golden age of capitalism in the quarter century that followed the war, and the relatively modest influence of the international economy (and potentially politically charged trade pressures) on the hegemonic U.S. in that same era, economic challenges (other than the drive to compete with the Soviet Union as a model for others) did not seem to impose on politics. Also not to be underestimated was anti-communism and McCarthyism, which had a chilling effect on the American academy through the 1950s at least—even in the 1960s, scholarship that explored the intersection of economics and politics was presumed to have a Marxist inflection.

By the turn of the 1970s, however, economics was encroaching on politics in ways that could not be denied, with the slowdown in global economic growth, concerns in the United States about pressures on the dollar and the economic consequences of the Vietnam War, increasing inflation, and, finally, the oil crisis that emerged in the wake of the 1973 Arab-Israeli War. Not surprisingly, the subfield of international political economy (IPE) was developed conterminously with these events. At the moment of its creation, IPE was not necessarily or even primarily realist, but as it did essentially involve, initially (things would change), the bringing of politics to economics, many of the seminal contributions of the enterprise, by scholars such as Robert Gilpin, Klaus Knorr, Susan Strange, and Charles Kindleberger, are well described as realist.[7]

Robert Gilpin in particular can be seen as the founding father of contemporary realist political economy. Influenced enormously by Carr, his "second favorite realist" (after Thucydides), Gilpin's scholarship, as noted previously, emphasized dynamics over statics (in particular how changes to the balance of power, brought about by underlying economic shifts, were the principal engine of great power conflict) and stressed the role of political factors in shaping the pattern of economic activity. In one of the founding statements of the subfield, Gilpin distinguished realist political economy from liberalism and Marxism by noting that in contrast to those other, more economistic perspectives, realism took politics as formative, and the point of departure for analysis. (And as a classical realist he placed great emphasis on "national sentiment," "political values," and an array of sociological and domestic political factors in explaining the patterns and prospects of political economy.) Echoing Carr, with a particular observation that could be applied to his analysis more generally, Gilpin explained that "every international monetary regime rests on a particular political order."[8]

It bears repeating that in explicating the political economy of realism, the purpose here, as always, is to define a classical realist perspective, not to insist that "realism" is superior to "liberalism" or other paradigms—which is not a productive enterprise. Recall from chapter 2 that realist and liberal dispositions are best envisioned as falling along a continuum, as opposed to representing hermetically sealed categories. Few liberals would hold the view that power politics are irrelevant; no good realist would fail to respect the enormous weight and influence of market forces. Recall as well that the principal intellectual opponents of classical realism are structural realism and hyper-rationalism. This latter point is especially relevant here because the hyper-rationalists (once again integrating misguided, obsolescent assumptions of rational expectations, embracing risk instead of uncertainty, and narrow, egoistic materialism over any ideological content) have come to dominate scholarship in international political economy in general and its liberal cohort in particular—but for classical realists, at bottom the irresolvable intellectual conflict is with the hyper-rationalists, not the liberal perspective per se. (Though of course the two grand paradigms clearly have basic dispositional differences.) More generally, of course, realist political economy remains a minority position—paradigmatically distinct from liberalism and incompatible with hyper-rationalism. Gilpin, if more successful in inspiring similarly minded scholarship in this vein than was Carr, nevertheless saw realists largely fail to embrace political economy, and the academic mainstream of the IPE subfield, ironically, given the impetus of its founding, became increasingly apolitical, save for the most narrow conceptions of distributional conflict, and increasingly focused on explaining politics via economics.[9]

Once again, as seen with the shadow of McCarthyism, the peculiar attributes of the Cold War are responsible for the disfiguring of the study of international political economy. Even as the subfield flourished in the 1970s, the distinct aspects of the confrontation between the United States and the Soviet Union nudged the scholars of world politics to retreat to separate corners. For security studies, the bipolar struggle dominated the agenda. But that confrontation was between two states with very little economic interaction—indeed the USSR did not even have a market economy. Most Cold War specialists could therefore comfortably marginalize, or at least bracket off, economic issues, and realists, not surprisingly, tended to gravitate intellectually toward that defining great power conflict. As Kenneth Waltz wrote, "Never in modern history have great powers been so sharply set off from lesser states and so little involved in each other's economic and social affairs." Similarly, liberal approaches tended to be overrepresented in political economy—and the action there was mostly among the very large economies (and political and military allies) found in Japan, North America, and Western Europe. Following Robert Keohane, such scholars were likely to share the view that "it is justifiable to focus principally on the political economy of the advanced industrialized countries without continually taking into account the politics of international security." In addition, a thriving sub-specialization of international political economy focused on "North-South" issues, where the principal motivating axis was rooted in the politics of economic development.[10]

It is remarkable that three decades after the end of the Cold War, the separation of international political economy and security studies largely endures. Liberal approaches can certainly do better—there is no reason why theories derived from a liberal tradition need be hyper-rationalist and narrowly materialist (especially as evidence mounts against the utility of that perspective).[11] But the concern here, of course, is with realism, and the balance of this chapter will focus on establishing what distinguishes realist political economy, and from there, on why, within the paradigm, approaches rooted in classical realism will avoid many of the blind spots and analytical cul-de-sacs that have characterized the limited engagements with political economy associated with structural realism.

Morgenthau, as noted, did not focus much on economic matters. Partially that was because in his postwar articulation of realism, like Aron he was eager to distinguish it from schools of thought that emphasized economics, or, more to the point, an economistic mindset. He distinguished realism from other approaches by the way that it saw the "landscape of international politics" as "interest in terms of power." Just as the economist was concerned with wealth, lawyers, law, and moralists, morals, he explained, "the political realist asks: How does this policy affect the power of the nation"—and subordinates other concerns to this question. (Morgenthau makes explicitly clear that these are all dramatic oversimplifications, but drawing these distinctions sharply is helpful for calling attention to the differences between these mindsets.) Gilpin, later articulating the foundations of realist political economy, would share this emphasis on the realist rejection of economism. The other primary approaches to questions of international political economy, liberalism and Marxism, he argued, certainly have their differences but share an inherently *economistic* perspective: individuals are motivated by desire to maximize their personal wealth—they want more stuff—and individual behavior is best described, explained, and predicted by the rational pursuit of more stuff. Gilpin was not alone in noting this basic affinity between liberalism and Marxism. Marx, after all, right down to his labor theory of value, was essentially a classical economist, which is why Paul Samuelson could summarily dismiss him "from the viewpoint of economic theory . . . as a minor post-Ricardian." Keynes's break with economic orthodoxy offered a similar but much more pointed critique, rejecting the classical liberal "Benthamite calculus, based on an over-valuation of the economic criterion," and "the final *reductio ad absurdum* of Benthamism known as Marxism." Realist expectations of human behavior, in contrast, are first informed by politics and also by anthropology, sociology, and cultural context.[12]

Once again, this perspective does not dismiss the considerable significance of material incentives and ambitions. As Gilpin readily notes, "the struggle for power and the desire for economic gain are ultimately and inextricably joined," yet another reminder of the practical impossibility of falsifying paradigms, which are philosophies and dispositions that can generate theories but are not theories themselves. In that spirit, what distinguishes realist political economy is its emphasis on three familiar foundations: the state, pursuing the national interest, in an environment defined by anarchy. As will be elaborated in this chapter, these attributes are interrelated. Realists see an autonomous state—that is, a state that is neither the sum of individual interests a la liberalism nor the implicit or explicit representative of certain privileged interests within society anticipated by Marxism. And that state pursues the *national interest* (a concept that was interrogated in chapter 4 and revisited here)—which is distinct from a pluralist vision that derives the national interest from the aggregation of individual interests, or from the more critical charge that the national interest is a cloak for the advancement of particular interests.[13]

Continuity in the Realist Perspective over Time

Realist political economy can trace its intellectual lineage back hundreds of years, to the writings of the mercantilists. Realism, it must be stressed, is not the same thing as mercantilism, or even the more sophisticated neomercantilism (the reformation of mercantilist analytical instincts after some key propositions of mercantilism were utterly shattered and rendered unsustainable by Adam Smith's devastating critique of that perspective in *The Wealth of Nations*). But the affinities of realism with its parallel dissents from the application of liberal economic theories are informative and worthy of some consideration.

Mercantilism is too easily oversimplified.[14] But as a theory of international trade, it blundered on two points in particular: first with the belief that trade was a zero-sum affair ("foreign trade, well conducted, has the necessary effect of drawing wealth from all other nations"); and second with its focus on the balance of trade as the key indicator of successful trade policy, rooted in the misguided notion that precious metals (the accumulation of which would be the result of a trade surplus) were the source of a nation's wealth. These were neatly summarized in the subtitle of one of the most influential seventeenth-century mercantilist tracts, "The Balance of Our Foreign Trade is the Rule of our Treasure." There was an international political component to this as well, which reflected notions that align with realism, in particular the importance of the relative standing between states—epitomized by a quote from another prominent mercantilist of that era: "if our treasure were more than our neighboring nations, I did not care whether we had one-fifth part of the treasure we now have."[15]

In 1776 Adam Smith eviscerated much of this thinking. In a foundational statement of liberal economic thought, he established that wealth derived from productive capacity, not precious metals; that the economic effects of trade were positive sum, not zero sum; and that, consequentially, the balance of trade was not usually a crucial determinant of economic well-being.[16] Any invocation of Smith's magisterial contribution must recognize that it is also much misunderstood, and often intellectually abused.

As Jacob Viner cautioned and many are content to forget, "Adam Smith was not a doctrinaire advocate of laissez faire. He saw a wide and elastic range of activity for government." And more to the point here, there were significant continuities between the classical mercantilists and their liberal challengers. In particular, each school of thought sought to maximize both power and plenty (prominent among Smith's list of government interventions in the economy were the protectionist navigation acts and subsidies for defense-related industries), and each saw a long-run harmony between those goals.[17]

Nevertheless, Smith's contributions were revolutionary and, with regard to the importance of productive capacity and the positive-sum economic benefits of trade, irrefutable. Leading nineteenth-century neomercantilists, then—such as Alexander Hamilton, Friedrich List, and Gustav Schmoller—would not refute Smith's economics but instead integrate his contributions into reconfigured and politically inflected perspectives on trade and exchange.[18] Indeed Hamilton virtually absorbed Smith; his influential "Report on Manufactures"—a call for protectionist measures to support American industrialization—was profoundly influenced by *The Wealth of Nations*, and he explicitly couched his argument as identifying "exceptions" to the received liberal doctrine.[19] List, a German nationalist, followed in Hamilton's footsteps, both with regard to policy and with his integration, rather than rejection, of Smith. List explicitly embraced the core liberal tenet that "*the power of producing wealth* is . . . infinitely more important than *wealth itself*." And in advocating protectionist measures, List similarly couched his arguments as reflecting special cases that did not reject the underlying logic articulated in *The Wealth of Nations*. List specified clear limits with regard to the size, duration, and targeted nature of his proposed trade policies, saw the goal as eventually phasing out those measures (industries that could not ultimately survive without protection were not worth the cost of supporting), and, despite often sharply disagreeing with Smith, still stated plainly that "*we should by no means deny the great merits of Adam Smith*."[20]

In sum, neomercantilists and classical economists (as well as, it should be noted, both liberal and realist scholars of international politics) share the view that power and plenty are crucial, complementary, and ultimately inseparable aims of state action; that that power flows from productive capability and productive capability from economic growth; and that there are clearly identifiable mutual gains to be realized through international trade. The realist dissent is with liberal politics, not liberal economics.[21] "Adam Smith's Doctrine," List argued, "presupposes the existence of a state of perpetual peace and of universal union." But of course, as he emphasized, this is not the case. Thus while List recognized the benefits of free trade, he argued that the "influence of war" required states to deviate from some of the policy prescriptions of liberalism.[22] This is easily recognized as directly informing the concerns that characterize a realist mindset. It is not enough to understand that trade would be mutually beneficial from an economic standpoint—states also have to be concerned about the consequences of their engagement with the international economy for their national security. Free trade implied specializing in areas where a country has an absolute or, following Ricardo, a comparative advantage. But would such specialization create security vulnerabilities (perhaps by reducing defense autonomy or, more likely, by shifting production away from vital sectors and capabilities)? And although the static case for comparative advantage was airtight, what about dynamic comparative advantage (shifts in the prospects for comparative advantage over time)? This was at the core of both Hamilton's and List's concerns—and it is no coincidence that thinkers from Britain, the world's most advanced economy, espoused the benefits of free trade, whereas the most well-articulated dissents came from those quarters with the greatest potential prospects for emerging as peer economic competitors.

This pattern of policy preferences reflects a phenomenon that Carr (who took ideology seriously, it should be recalled) thought all too common and often underappreciated: the tendency for ideology to fall quietly and gently into alignment with interest. And with regard to economic ideology, it is no surprise to learn that he criticized "the natural assumption" of the "prosperous and privileged" to imagine that laissez-faire was not just sacrosanct but universal in its appeal. In this spirit, Schmoller, following Hamilton and List, offered the rather cutting observation: "Does it not sound to us today like the irony of fate, that the same England, which in 1750–1800 reached the summit of its commercial supremacy by means of tariffs and naval wars, frequently with extraordinary violence, and always with the most tenacious selfishness, that that England at the very same time announced to the world the doctrine that only the egoism of the individual is justified, and never that of states and nations; the doctrine which dreamt of a stateless competition of all the individuals of every land, and of the harmony of the economic interests of all nations?" Indeed as the tides of economic competition began to encroach on British shores early in the twentieth century, newly emerging critics of its liberal trade policy would offer similar arguments, arguing that mercantilist strategies had actually helped forge Britain's industrial dominance, after which the embrace and promotion of free trade allowed a relatively advanced England to "crush rival industries in every part of the world, by supplying the markets with goods produced on the better and cheaper methods which were only practiced in England."[23]

In their advocacy for protectionist measures, Hamilton and List emphasized what would become known as "infant industry" arguments. Hamilton warned that "the United States cannot exchange with Europe on equal terms." Contra Smith, he held that industry, left to itself, will not "naturally find its way to the most useful and profitable employment" because of the "difficulties incident" in initiating enterprise in the context of "superiority antecedently enjoyed by nations." Echoing Hamilton, List argued that "under a system of perfectly free competition with more advanced manufacturing nations, a nation which is less advanced than those, although well suited for manufacturing, can never attain to a perfectly developed manufacturing power of its own."[24] This perspective was in fact rather widely held, especially among those looking to "catch up" with those perceived to have had an economic head start. Sun Yat-Sen, the Chinese economic nationalist and first provisional president of the Chinese republic, held that "just as forts are built at the entrances of harbors for protection against foreign military invasion, so a tariff against foreign goods protects a nation's revenue and gives native industries time to develop"—a comment that also serves as a reminder that the geographic breadth of neomercantilist thought was, historically, considerably greater than is commonly presumed.[25]

But it should be emphasized that realist wariness of free trade is considerably broader than that (infant industry concerns, in practice, only offer a narrow and specific set of exceptions). In taking a somewhat more cautious look at uninhibited free trade, realists, here reflecting the difference between mercantilism and neomercantilism, although they do not much focus on the *balance* of trade, are nevertheless attentive to the *composition* of trade and the *distribution* of the mutual gains that it generates. Mutual gains from trade in an anarchic world are insufficient to grasp for them, from this perspective. If trade will relatively empower potentially dangerous adversaries (or as noted, hollow out sectors vital for national security), those economic gains might not be worth pursuing. Despite this realist instinct, it should be noted that although emerging great powers have indeed commonly pursued neomercantilist economic strategies, empirical support for the distinct and more general notion that states routinely and carefully mediate their international economic engagements with an attentive eye toward the distribution of the mutual gains generated is quite thin.[26] Nevertheless, if empirically suspect, it is a realist inclination/anticipation that should be acknowledged.

Another element of mercantilism that has affinities with realism—and here there is more continuity than change when mercantilism reemerged as neomercantilism after the liberal revolution—is the centrality of the state. This has been a less appreciated aspect of mercantilism in contemporary invocations of the concept, but it was foundational to the movement, and reflects a political vision of the state that has been embraced by realism but is inimical to the liberal archetype of a minimalist, reactive, and pluralist authority. Clarifying this distinction, one scholar observed that List sees "the state as an end in itself and the major end of policy, rather than as an instrument for the promotion of individual welfare."[27] Similarly, according to Heckscher, "The state stood at the centre of mercantilist endeavours developed historically: the state was both the subject and the object of mercantilist economic policy." In fact, more than half of Heckscher's elaborate and comprehensive study is devoted to the explication of mercantilism as a state-building enterprise and the emergence of the state as a powerful actor with interests distinct from other groups within society.[28] This remained a central theme for the neomercantilists, most visibly Schmoller, for whom "mercantilism in its innermost kernel is nothing but state making" and who argued "what was at stake was the creation of real *political* economies as unified organisms."[29]

States, as autonomous actors with their own interests, will often find those interests in conflict with the interests and preferences of other groups in society. Classical mercantilists routinely called attention to the potential incompatibility of public and private interests; List put great emphasis on this theme, repeatedly insisting that "the interest of individuals and the interest of the commerce of a whole nation are widely different things."[30] With regard to international politics, this is of particular relevance at moments when the state, due to its greater sensitivity to security concerns or its tendency to have a longer time horizon than individuals, is more willing to accept short-term economic sacrifices in order to reap greater long-run rewards. "The nation," List insisted, "must renounce present advantages with a view to securing future ones."[31]

Realist Political Economy: Dispositions, Assumptions, and Expectations

Realist political economy is characterized by two points of departure and three basic assumptions, which in turn yield a set of general expectations that distinguish realism from other perspectives.[32] At the risk of repetition, it cannot be stressed enough that although it is clarifying to contrast "realism" with "liberalism" in such intellectual exercises, these schools of thought remain idealized types which in practice reflect a continuum of temperaments. Neither realist nor liberal political economy is plainly "right" or "wrong," and an effort to adjudicate between them is not the purpose here—nor is any such effort likely to meet with much success. To underscore this point, consider for example the "theory of hegemonic stability," which holds that economic cooperation is more likely to occur when there is a dominant power in the international system. There are both liberal and realist (and even neo-Marxist) versions of this theory. Evidence for or against hegemonic stability would influence assessments of the utility of the theory, but not of either paradigm.[33]

As to be expected, regarding questions of international political economy realism takes as its point of departure a sensitivity to the consequences of anarchy—that although war might not be imminent or even likely, in a self-help system with survival ultimately at stake, the possibility that war could occur will importantly inform economic policy choices. The state will thus cast a jaundiced eye on international economic relations. Some mutually beneficial transactions might nevertheless leave the country less secure, and so realist perspectives are likely to anticipate that states will make a larger set of departures from those policies that maximize wealth and short-run economic growth in the name of national security. Of course this can be vexingly circular and non-falsifiable, as national security would also be imperiled if a country renounced beneficial economic engagements to the extent that it significantly impinged on economic growth.[34]

Such interventions in economic affairs are the purview of the state, and, as discussed above, a second point of departure for realist political economy (here aligned with much of mercantilist thought) is an emphasis on a crucial role for the state. It is not necessary to embrace the mercantilist ambition that imagines "the superiority of the state over all other forces within a country" to nevertheless envision and emphasize the state as a distinct entity, irreducible to the sum of pluralist interests (as it is in the idealized liberal model), with its own interests, capabilities, and inclination to pursue its own agenda.[35] In contrast, and with important exceptions where "market failures" occur (such as the underprovision of public goods or the overproduction of negative externalities), the idealized liberal vision anticipates that individual actors pursuing their narrow self-interests will yield, without purpose, plan, or direction, something close to socially optimal outcomes. Government is mostly there to provide the underlying structures and adjudicating mechanisms which in that context facilitate those outcomes. The divergence between realist and liberal imaginations of the state is illustrated by Stephen Krasner's conclusion to his major articulation of modern realist political economy: "This investigation has shown that the state has purposes of its own."[36]

Realist political economy starts off with these two dispositions (an emphasis on the consequences of anarchy and the influence of an independently purposeful state), and to them adds three basic assumptions. The first is not special to realism; it is in fact the post-Smithian "liberal-realist synthesis"—that power ultimately derives from an economic base. As one analyst put it, "National power depends in large measure upon economic productivity" and "military power depends upon economic strength." This opens up quite a Pandora's box of complexities, as the range of economic factors that can plausibly be argued essential to national security quickly proliferate. In addition to the trajectory of economic growth, scholars have attributed the outcome of major wars to industrial capacity, command over adequate energy resources and crucial raw materials, mastery of cutting-edge technology, and access to plentiful finance.[37] For national security, however narrowly defined, economics matters, and crucially so. Especially in the long run, then, the pursuit of political and economic objectives by states in world politics will be almost impossible to analytically disentangle.

Realism is more distinct from other perspectives with its two additional assumptions. The first of these (basic assumption number two), which has already been stressed in chapters 1 and 3, is the expectation that economic change (rooted in differential rates of growth across countries) is virtually inevitable and invariably destabilizing. The reasons for the latter effect are now familiar but become even more salient in the context of the discussion here: economics underpins power, economic change will thus alter the underlying balance of power, and because great powers are generally ambitious (their desires will tend to increase with their capabilities), changes to the balance of power are engines of international conflict. The final core assumption is that states prefer to retain as much economic autonomy as is feasible. Realist political economy can again get a little slippery here, which is a problem not easily resolved but needs, as always, to be acknowledged. To aver that states seek as much autonomy as feasible, while recognizing that economic growth is essential for the sustainability of security, is an open invitation for the post hoc rationalization of behavior that might appear inconsistent with a presumed motivation for an autonomy imperative. In fact, it is fair to assess that in the modern era states have relinquished more control over their economies than a typical realist analysis would have anticipated. In response to this plain observation, it is possible to argue, as many have, that the two great episodes of global economic liberalization that followed the end of World War II and the Cold War were orchestrated by the United States, which was so predominant in those moments that it was able to set aside concerns for autonomy and be driven instead by the expectation that its national security interests would thrive in an environment of openness. That claim can be deductively sustained, but questions linger, such as why others so willingly followed and, more pointedly, with the observation that the American drive for financial globalization would ultimately prove disastrous, and could not be attributed to underlying economic wisdom or a U.S. *national* interest, as opposed to the particular interest of certain sectors of the economy.[38] It is better to simply acknowledge the assumptions of realism and see where they lead; as noted in chapter 4, there are few greater or more subversive scholarly sins than putting a finger on the scale for one's theories.

The points of departure and core assumptions of realist political economy lead to a number of general expectations, of which three are particularly notable. First, as argued by Carr and Gilpin, international politics will formatively shape the nature of international economic relations. The functioning and patterns of the global economy, as well as its institutional structures, will reflect international politics. Water may seek its own level (a powerful force not to be underestimated), but man-made dams, levees, reservoirs, canals, and aqueducts will determine where (and to whom) it flows. Similarly, to understand the currents and flows of the global economy, it is necessary to look to its political underpinnings. To take two formative illustrative examples, even in countries with very modest trade barriers between them, to understand the pattern of economic activity between otherwise equidistant cities, it is necessary to look at national borders; despite economic theories of "optimal currency areas," authority, not efficiency, overwhelmingly determines which currencies are used where.[39]

A second expectation is that the interests of the state and the interest of private actors will commonly diverge, and in such circumstances the state will often intervene to defend its perceived interests. Again at a foundational level, as national defense is a public good, states will be more attentive to providing and securing it than individuals collectively would be, but these disputes can be considerably broader than simply the underwriting and maintenance of a military establishment and government attentiveness to trade in militarily sensitive sectors. Here the intellectual pedigree can be traced to concepts central to both mercantilism and neomercantilism: Thomas Mun warned of economic activities that might enrich individual merchants, "when nevertheless the commonwealth shall decline and grow poor"; List made the general point more bluntly: "the interest of individuals and the interest of the commerce of a whole nation are widely different things."[40]

Finally, realist political economy anticipates that international economic cooperation will be difficult to establish and maintain. Again two now standard qualifiers loom large. First, although there has been plenty of discord—some profoundly consequential, such as during the catastrophic interwar years—nevertheless a considerable amount of international economic cooperation is plainly visible over the past two centuries of world politics, almost certainly more than would have been anticipated by some imagined, default, realist expectation. Second, in practice, the differences between liberal and realist perspectives on this issue are actually narrower than casually imagined. Liberal perspectives also anticipate barriers to international economic cooperation and expect many mutually beneficial opportunities to remain unrequited. Liberal theorists tend to see these barriers as rooted in various forms of market failures exacerbated by the presence of anarchy (that is, by the absence of a world government to help resolve such problems), such as asymmetries of information, underspecified property rights, or the underremediated generation of negative economic externalities produced by inward-looking economic policies that inadvertently harm others.[41] Moreover, realists can also see distinct factors that can help overcome barriers to cooperation. In comparing the utter failure of the London Economic Conference of 1933 with the successful Tripartite Monetary Agreement of 1936, a realist perspective, for example, would emphasize the difference in the international security environment—here crucial in permitting cooperation. In 1936, the Roosevelt administration, widely blamed for the failure of the 1933 conference, saw the increasing assertiveness of the fascist powers in Europe as a new and key motivating factor for reaching an economic accord with Britain and France. Similarly, security concerns (that is, the emerging Cold War) were if anything even more essential in influencing the willingness of the United States to orchestrate the postwar international economic system.[42]

Structural Realism Stumbles over Political Economy

Structural realism, which was developed during the Cold War, was particularly tone-deaf to questions of political economy, both for the peculiar attributes of that dominant conflict already noted but also because the discipline of International Relations theory, bifurcated into political economy and security studies, also subsequently got bogged down in "paradigm wars." With the former sub-specialization dominated by liberal theorists and the latter by structural realists, each side sought to discredit the other in often bitter and barbed confrontations, a dispute at times so rancorous that it brings to mind Woody Allen's crack about intellectuals, "They're like the mafia. They only kill their own." But the dysfunctional result of this was that structural realists were too often invested in the business of "debunking" liberal claims, and thus marginalizing political economy as largely irrelevant for the "high politics" of international security. (Liberal scholars could be equally condescending and contemptuous, especially in the post–Cold War 1990s, when the very notion of consequential military confrontations between great powers seemed anachronistic.)

A particularly unproductive turn in this clash, which crowded out what might have been other promising avenues for research, was the ubiquitous debate over the question of "relative gains." This dispute found its modern point of origin with the publication of Robert Keohane's influential book, *After Hegemony*, in which he argued that, building from realist assumptions (an anarchic environment populated by rational, self-interested egoists), mutually beneficial cooperation could still thrive. Realists quickly retorted that Keohane's case rested on the notion that both sides would gain, disregarding the problem that, as noted above, was central from a realist perspective: the existence of mutual gains is not enough to promote cooperation—states must be alert to the distribution of those gains. As a principal critic of Keohane put it, "states in anarchy must fear that others may seek to destroy or enslave them."[43]

But rather than producing a "smoking gun" for championing the cause of either liberal political economy or structural realism, the issue of absolute versus relative gains was in fact an intellectual red herring. Showing that actors routinely pursued relative rather than absolute gains would not make the realist case—because that pursuit routinely takes place in the absence of anarchy, and is commonly observable in many if not most transactions between parties within societies negotiating without concern for the terrifying consequences of anarchy. Collective bargaining negotiations within peaceful societies are invariably informed by expectations of who else is getting what (what another union was able to extract from the same employer, for example) and about how the overall pie will be divided.[44] The labor agreement between the players and the owners of the National Basketball Association, for example, sets the "salary cap" for each team's payroll as a negotiated percentage of all "basketball-related income." The players do not insist on a relative share of the proceeds because they fear if the owners get wealthier than them at a faster rate they will invade and conquer them. Rather, the overall income generated by the enterprise provides a focal point for negotiations by making clear what's on the table, and fighting over the division of those spoils (and sometimes going on strike over the matter) is how each side assesses their own expectations of what they can and should receive.[45] And as a practical matter, in international politics, where anarchy is indeed a factor in shaping state behavior, disentangling the enmeshed motives at the root of bargaining behavior will generally prove impossible.[46]

Structural realists have also been distracted by efforts to reject "interdependence" theory, and in particular the notion that intimate economic interactions between states would make war between them less likely. This argument has its roots in the classical economists of the nineteenth-century Manchester School. The free trader and Parliamentarian Richard Cobden (of the Cobden-Chevalier Treaty that liberalized trade between Britain and France) articulated this perspective publicly in Manchester in 1848, and argued that free trade between nations would go hand in hand with peaceful relations between them.[47] (The Manchester brand would endure—it was at the Manchester Free Trade Hall that an angry fan would shout "Judas" at Bob Dylan during his legendary 1966 tour of Britain.)

Interdependence theory was revived in the 1970s as an important element of the liberal branch of the emerging subfield of international political economy. With hard U.S. military power humbled by the Vietnam experience, the increasing salience of apparently footloose, border-hopping multinational corporations, and pressures on the dollar leading to the collapse of the Bretton Woods international monetary system (which ushered in an era of powerful global capital markets that eroded the policy autonomy of states), such scholars imagined a world where state sovereignty was "at bay" and where many outcomes were increasingly determined not by ratios of hard power but by the vagaries of "complex interdependence."[48]

Structural realists rejected these ideas. They noted, almost gleefully, that the catastrophic, ruinous Great War had taken place between states that were highly interdependent. But the realists tended to overplay their hand. It is one thing to note that any theory which holds that interdependence prevents war has been clearly falsified—it is quite another to, from there, extrapolate that interdependence is irrelevant when it comes to questions of war and peace. Committed to showing the liberals were wrong, such scholars tended to focus on rejecting the strongest forms of interdependence theory, often at the expense of recognizing the eminently sensible partial equilibrium hypothesis, that all other things held constant, high levels of interdependence will raise the costs and opportunity costs of war, and thus represents one disincentivizing factor among the vast many that influence decisions about war and peace.[49]

A similar overreach is visible in the structural realist critiques of prominent pre–World War I pacifists, such as Norman Angell and Ivan Bloch. Waltz argues that Angell's famous book, *The Great Illusion*, published just three years before the Great War, insisted that war between the great powers was simply impossible.[50] But this is not what Angell or Bloch was arguing. If anything, they were arguing the opposite: that the countries of Europe were about to stumble into a ruinous war, and the "great illusion" was that war could achieve their political goals—which, they insisted, it would not. And indeed, in 1916 the *New York Times* would run a feature about Bloch under the banner "Prophet of Trench Deadlock Vindicated." Angell, similarly, was advocating for, not predicting, peace, on the grounds that modern war was no longer a rational method by which states could hope to gain in an economic sense. Included in those arguments were accurate assessments regarding the enormous economic disruptions that would (and did) accompany any such conflict. Had Angell actually thought war impossible, he would not have been motivated to put pen to paper in the first place.[51]

Skepticism of the political consequences of economic interdependence, which approached something of a litmus test for membership among structural realists during the Cold War, served realists poorly when they were confronted with the phenomenon of globalization that emerged in the 1990s and shaped the global political economy in the decades that followed. Primed to dismiss globalization as a rebooted notion of interdependence, most realists reached for hand-waving dismissals of the phenomenon, rather than invest in any sophisticated and sustained engagement with globalization and its potential for influencing world politics.[52] In addition to the visceral rejection of interdependence theory, realists tended to be skeptical of globalization, which manifested in ways that seemed at odds with its assumptions and expectations. Globalization, most obviously but by no means exclusively in the financial realm, represented an encroachment on state autonomy; and for decades, the United States and China, each eyeing the other as a potential and perhaps even likely and ultimately principal geopolitical rival, nevertheless permitted their economies to become intimately enmeshed with each other, with few apparent prohibitions rooted in their security consequences.[53]

Instead, realist scholars tended to reach for ad hoc qualifications and explanations—which were not without merit, but again were informed by an instinct to be protective of the paradigm, not a disinterested assessment of the facts. It was certainly arguable that globalization was a political project pushed by a powerful state which thought that it would relatively thrive in that environment—as noted, this was clearly the case with regard to the aggressive U.S. push for financial globalization in the 1990s and beyond.[54] It is also the case that as globalization advanced, the opportunity costs of closure increased, and since states must be concerned with their economic well-being, it can be argued, from a realist perspective, that states needed to reevaluate the trade-offs between autonomy and growth. But again, these protestations have the flavor of motivated, post hoc rationalizations of events inconsistent with baseline expectations. Similarly, globalization "skeptics" have also routinely pointed out that the phenomenon is neither novel (often gesturing to some parallels with 1870–1910) nor irreversible. But although both of these qualifications are eminently reasonable (especially the latter), it does not follow that students of international relations can or should safely disregard the political consequences of globalization, as this chapter will revisit and elaborate below. No claim of novelty or irreversibility is necessary to hold the conclusion that globalization significantly affects national security. Similarly, while many of the pressures brought about by globalization are quite powerful, globalization is not an irresistible force, nor an arbiter of unbending laws. To claim that it is snowing heavily, and that the snow will significantly influence travel, is not to insist that it has never snowed before, or that it will continue to snow forever. It is simply to observe that it is snowing now, and it will not be possible to understand travel patterns without acknowledging that plain fact.

It is also important to recognize that globalization is *not* interdependence 2.0. The two concepts should not be conflated—they are markedly distinct, and are suggestive of very different causal mechanisms and consequences for world politics. Interdependence refers to economic relations between two states (and theories of interdependence and war consider how these relations affect the prospects for conflict between them). Globalization, in contrast, is an external environment, or a condition. It reflects an array of phenomena that derive from unorganized and stateless forces which nevertheless produce general, system-wide pressures, constraints, opportunities, and incentives that are felt by states.[55] These pressures emanate from a bundle of mutually reinforcing processes: through the intensification of economic exchange (including the fragmentation of production and the astonishing rise of international financial markets); dramatic changes in the nature of information flows resulting from a confluence of innovations including satellites, smartphones, and the internet; and "marketization"—an implicit (and often conflict-generating) expansion of the set of social relations that are governed by market forces. And it is worth remembering, always, that from the perspective of classical realism, there is no expectation that states will respond uniformly or in a deterministic way to such influences; we are back again to the central "ketchup allegory"—the pressure, like a price increase, is uniform, but individual responses and reactions to those common pressures, however, will be idiosyncratic and contingent.

Crucially, the processes of globalization are distinct—and they are not "interdependence." Intense economic interdependence between states can take place in the absence of globalization; and relations between two states with extremely circumscribed bilateral economic interactions can nevertheless be significantly affected by the general condition of globalization. The processes of globalization reshape the costs, benefits, and consequences of pursuing different policy choices. Choices made by self-interested states pursuing national goals will be influenced by those changing incentives. Realist political economy can, and should, and while retaining fidelity to its first principles, seriously engage and understand the consequences of globalization for world politics, as this chapter will elaborate in its concluding section.

Classical Realist Political Economy—Shaping the National Interest

A notable element of realist political economy is its attentiveness to the ways in which economic relationships have political consequences.[56] Note the absence of a qualifier. It is not that economic relations *can* influence international politics—it is that they invariably will. (Once again, this does not mean that economic factors will be decisive, or in many cases, even significant factors in shaping outcomes. It simply means that in relations between states, economic flows have political implications.) The most dramatic illustration of this phenomenon was provided by Albert Hirschman, in *National Power and the Structure of Foreign Trade*—and is yet another essential aspect of world politics that a classical approach grasps but which eludes structural realism entirely, because of the former's more nuanced appreciation of the National Interest. Focusing on Germany's interwar trading relations, Hirschman described how that country cultivated a series of asymmetric economic relationships with its smaller neighbors in eastern and southern Europe. Germany's goals were to secure the raw materials necessary for war, enhance its economic autonomy in order to reduce its vulnerabilities to embargoes and blockades (which it experienced in bitter portions during World War I), and, crucially, ensure the political obsequiousness of those neighbors. Hirschman observed that, for example, because of their disparate economic size, trade between Germany and a country like Bulgaria could account for most of the latter's exports, while barely registering on the former's international accounts. This, Hirschman recognized, yielded a type of power, one that was observable in any asymmetric economic relationship: power that derived from (the largely implicit) threat by the larger state to terminate the relationship—the consequences of which would be disproportionately felt by the smaller. Germany did purposefully pursue such asymmetric, bilateral relationships, cultivating what Hirschman called dependence.[57] This term invites confusion, because it sounds like a concept associated with the neo-Marxist branch of the first wave of scholarship in international political economy, "dependency theory."[58] In fact, Hirschman's dependence is the converse of dependency. In the latter, dominant states use their power to impose and enforce a system of economic exploitation—power is the instrument, wealth is the objective. But, to coin a phrase, "realists aren't in it for the money." The cultivation of Hirschmanesque dependence, in contrast, is about the use of economic leverage to achieve political goals—and despite the long-run harmony between economic and political goals, realist analysis anticipates that great powers will routinely make economic sacrifices in an effort to enhance their political influence in this fashion. And Germany's economic strategy was indeed a money loser—economically inefficient, Germany also offered sweetheart deals to its trading partners, in order to entice them into channeling their economic relations even more disproportionately toward Germany, making them still more conditioned and dependent on its economy and especially vulnerable to the threat of any disruption in those exchanges.

Hirschman emphasized the cultivation of this leverage, that is, of the accumulation of coercive power by Germany. But—and here again is where classical realism offers insights derived from crucial analytical tools that structural realism abdicated—*National Power* also demonstrates how these relations can have profound consequences for political *influence*, which is unrelated to coercion. As noted above, the National Interest, one that is distinct from the sum of individual interests, is central to all realist analysis. But as discussed in chapter 4, the concept can be slippery. The National Interest is not unique, sacrosanct, or exogenously imposed by the imperatives of anarchy; for any society there are a number of plausibly imagined visions of the national interest—and the trajectory of the definition of the national interest can bend in different possible directions. From a classical realist perspective, in addition to an assessment of the international distribution of material capabilities, other factors—ideology, the implications of and opportunities presented by the behavior of other states, and domestic politics (which includes competing economic interests)—shape perceptions of the national interest.

And it is at the level of domestic economic interests where Hirschman's analysis gets especially interesting for understanding world politics. Because *National Power*, which emphasized the vulnerability of small states to coercion, also illustrated how the economies of those countries can become *conditioned* upon the economies of their larger partners, and how this conditioning can lead to a change in those states' definitions of their own interests. And as a phenomenon in world politics more generally (and as a close reading of Hirschman reveals), this is both the more cultivated prize and more consequential outcome. The logic is as follows: If the flow of economic relations is channeled in a particular direction, then inevitably those domestic actors who are particularly engaged in those relations will thrive, and other actors will also respond to the incentives produced by that expanding activity. This will enhance the domestic political influence of those actors and shape the political coalitions that invariably form within societies. More actors will become stakeholders in a pattern of economic relations defined by the increasing importance of its dominant partner. In Hirschman's words, such "regions or industries will exert a powerful influence in favor of a 'friendly' attitude towards the state to the imports of which they owe their interests." This phenomenon was visible to observers at the time not simply in Germany's satellite states in Europe but among its trading partners in Latin America, where similar tactics were deployed.[59]

"Hirschman effects" in world politics are distinct from, but can be understood analytically as loosely akin to, what Joseph Nye has labeled "soft power"—instead of forcing others to do what you want them to do, soft power (and Hirschmanesque influence) is about "getting others to want what you want." Nye's conception of these concerns was broad, and included various aspects of attraction including cultural appeals (such as the mythical America represented in Hollywood films and varieties of its popular music).[60] But as a key concept for realist political economy, this type of power (the cultivation of influence) is more narrowly focused on the calibration and contestation of interest.[61]

There are several notable objections to emphasizing Hirschman effects in world politics. First is the admonition that one should be wary of building a general theory based on Nazis—as discussed in chapter 3, one of the things that distinguishes classical from structural realism is that the former can see plainly that Nazi Germany was a different and distinct actor in world politics. (Attempts to draw general conclusions from the distinctly distressed and circumscribed economic environment of the Great Depression should also give pause.) Second, some realists insist that for it to be of real consequence, any enhanced political influence that might follow from economic enmeshments must derive from, and take place in the shadow of, underlying, implicitly militarized coercive power (as it did in interwar Europe). Finally, assessing the significance of Hirschman effects is very difficult to illustrate in practice. The whole point of political influence is that if it works, you don't really see it happening. (And great powers will be reluctant to exercise overt coercion by cutting off dependent states, because that would mean the end of efforts to cultivate political influence.)[62]

But these reservations, appropriately suggestive of analytical caution, do not undermine the case for the significance of Hirschman effects and their cultivation. Implicit or explicit military power may be central elements of attempts at coercion (though this need not always be the case—consider the possibilities of economic sanctions, for example). But, again, influence and coercion are two very different things—the former is not about twisting arms, it is about changing perceptions of self-interest. Even Nazi Germany—which was, to put it mildly, not shy about engaging in acts of overt coercion—was shopping for politics, not simply power, in these relations. The goal of its foreign economic policies was to nest its dependent neighbors in a political-economic sphere of influence as an essential component of its strategy for an anticipated war with others, not to press its boot to their throats (thus the sweetheart deals). Moreover, as noted above, German economic diplomacy extended to Latin America, where the implicit threat of military force could not be a factor in shaping the interests (or achieving the submission) of its partners. And the extension of Nazi economic machinations to South America left some states there behaving as if their economies were enmeshed with Germany's (this was especially visible in their interventions in international currency markers). Nor was it hard to see the primacy of politics at work; Germany commonly "lost money" on many of these transactions, but as the *Economist* observed at the time, each of its business partners in Latin America became "a spokesman of German interests with his own government—an aspect not overlooked by Germany."[63] Additionally, although the cultivation of Hirschmanesque influence may have been a signature policy of Nazi Germany, hard to quantify in effect, and easier to practice in hard times, history provides innumerous examples of its general practice.

An illustration of the deployment of economic levers to enhance political influence can be seen in the U.S. Marshall Plan—an effort that cost the Americans no small fortune (well over $150 billion in 2020 dollars), the magnitude of which was well understood at the time.[64] The bold and generous initiative can be seen (beyond the short-run humanitarian aspect) as an exemplar of the pursuit of far-sighted, enlightened self-interest—in this instance designed not only to prevent an economic catastrophe but also to influence the precarious balance of domestic political power within postwar European societies—a very Hirschmanesque endeavor. Many of the countries of western Europe at that time had robust, competitive communist political parties, and Marshall Aid was designed, most narrowly, to stave off the economic problems in which they might thrive politically. More subtly but not inconsequentially, it was also intended to enmesh the economies of Western European states with the U.S. economy, and within those states to empower actors who favored internationalism over more inward-looking styles of national capitalism. George F. Kennan, then at the State Department and a principal architect of the plan, understood and embraced these objectives.[65]

More generally, international monetary relations have routinely been shaped by efforts by states (often at considerable cost) to place themselves at the center of arrangements in which their currencies would be relied upon by others—again with more than one eye on the anticipated political benefits of such arrangements. There was an important monetary element to Germany's interwar geopolitical economic vision, which went hand in hand with its trade strategy—but once again, the cultivation of "monetary dependence" requires neither Nazis nor economic closure.[66] From the 1860s, efforts by France to establish the Latin Monetary Union were rooted in an "express desire to see all continental Europe united in a franc area which would exclude and isolate Germany." This motivated efforts to manage and sustain the Union; the more modest (and economically misguided) interwar championing of a "gold bloc" was a reprise of those ambitions. France also cultivated the use of the franc or franc-based currencies first in its colonies and later, at considerable expense, in a "franc zone" of its former colonies. In the interwar years not just Germany but also Imperial Japan extended their monetary influence in support of a larger grand strategy. The British pound functioned as the world's money for over a century—that this was valued by British elites is suggested by the retreat to the sterling area and then the sterling zone (which provided a vital mechanism that helped finance World War II). The United States, long before it developed a fully mature financial system of its own, was nevertheless not averse to throwing its macroeconomic weight around early in the twentieth century, extending its monetary reach in the Caribbean, promoting New York City as a financial center, and more than nipping at the heels of rival sterling as an international currency. And of course the United States would go on to orchestrate, at some cost and effort, the Bretton Woods international monetary system. And even after immolating those arrangements by its own hand (President Nixon would renounce the commitment of the United States to the system in 1971), it would still jealously guard the primacy of the dollar as the world's currency. It would not go to the lengths suggested by internet conspiracy theories, but note the swiftness with which the United States crushed the efforts of its political and military ally, Japan, to create an "Asian Monetary Fund" in the wake of the Asian financial crisis of 1997–98.[67]

What was the United States seeking to protect? In a phrase, the Hirschman effects that derived from the dollar's dominance. Susan Strange, taking on this phenomenon from a slightly different angle, refers to the benefits of "structural power" which she describes as "the power to decide how things shall be done, the power to shape frameworks within which states relate to each other." And again, such power is in no way dependent on draconian financial regulations, economic closure, military threats, or dramatically asymmetrical relationships. Indeed, while the collapse of the Bretton Woods monetary system was at the time the occasion of much hang-wringing about the erosion of American power and the end of the American order, Strange saw it differently (and, in retrospect, correctly), observing "to decide one August morning that dollars can no longer be converted into gold was a progression from exorbitant privilege to super-exorbitant privilege." By renouncing the constraints of its own system with the wave of a hand, "the U.S. government was exercising the unconstrained right to print money that others could not (save at unacceptable cost) refuse to accept in payment."[68]

What remained in place was the fact that, Bretton Woods or not, states and other actors that use the dollar, hold dollars, and rely on a dollar-centric international monetary order develop vested interests in the endurance of and stability in the greenback. This followed the Hirschmanesque logic cheerfully articulated by Nixon's Treasury Secretary John Connolly to less than cheerful American allies, "the dollar may be our currency, but it's your problem." A world of dollar hegemony is a world in which many participants in the global economy are likely to become stakeholders in the future of the dollar—and will thus often act in ways that account for American interests, whether they like it or not. Thus although measuring Hirschman effects is no easy task, that the United States reaped such rewards was plainly illustrated at crucial junctures, such as during the global financial crisis of 2007–8. At a moment when the global financial system teetered on the abyss, Russia approached China with the idea of dumping American securities, exacerbating the crisis for the purpose of undermining U.S. power. But China was more than just a geopolitical rival of the United States—it was also a stakeholder in the dollar and the American system more generally, and did not see how its own interests would be advanced by such a measure.[69]

The political consequences of economic relations will remain an essential part of world politics regardless of how the global economy evolves. These effects will be ubiquitous. But in the 2020s, the most significant of them will involve China. In the span of just a few decades, the People's Republic has gone from being a modest player in the world economy to an economic powerhouse; by 2020 it was the world's second largest economy—and, more to the point here, the world's second largest importer. China emerged as the largest export market for numerous nations, including Australia, Brazil, Burma, Chile, Indonesia, Iran, Saudi Arabia, and Taiwan, and the second largest market for Japan and a host of other countries.[70] These realities politically complicate the strategy proposed by John Mearsheimer (discussed in chapter 6) that the United States should make every effort to damage China's economy—because even if such a strategy was somehow successful, by taking the wind from the sails of China's demand for imports it would leave in its wake an angry mob of exporting countries in distress, who would (correctly) blame the United States for their distress.

China's economic relations are transforming the patterns of world economic activity—and the country also seems interested in using its economic power to enhance its political influence, through measures large and small. The Asian Infrastructure Investment Bank is a modest effort at institution building—notable mostly for the fact that a stampede of nations rushed to join it, despite active U.S. efforts to dissuade them (tidily illustrating how the world had changed since the days of Japan's would-be Asian Monetary Fund). China's potentially more far-reaching Belt and Road Initiative, the details of which are murky and in considerable flux, is in its most ambitious articulations suggestive of a more orchestrated and purposeful effort to draw nations into the country's economic and thus ultimately political embrace.[71]

From the perspective of classical realism, as a practical matter these factors will arguably rival if not eclipse the role of militarized economic conflict in shaping the trajectory of regional political affairs in East Asia and beyond. Especially interesting in this regard is South Korea, which is a virtual laboratory for Hirschman effects. On the one hand, South Korea is an intimate, long-standing military ally of the United States; on the other, the gravitational pull of its increasing enmeshment with China's economy might prove an irresistible force. China is eager to bend the arc of South Korea's political loyalties—at a minimum away from the United States and toward a more neutral position. That would be an enormous geopolitical prize. And by the 2010s, trade with China was a predominant influence on the South Korean economy. In 2014 China's imports from that country ran to an astonishing $145 billion, accounting for 25 percent of all of South Korea's exports, and also representing its largest trade surplus (and was more than double the level of U.S. imports from Korea)—figures that were essentially unchanged over the balance of the decade that followed. And just as Hirschman would have expected, as one study concluded, "A 'China lobby' within South Korean business circles emerged that sought to protect South Korea's relations with China." Other scholars report that "South Koreans understand that their economic future is tied to China." At the same time, the emergence of a less predictable United States and the visible resurgence of its long-dormant neo-isolationist instincts cannot help but force an "active debate" in Seoul over fundamental aspects of its grand strategy, including whether it "will have to pursue alternative strategic pathways," if American commitments lose credibility.[72]

Classical Realist Political Economy—Globalization and the Social Economy

Even while retaining realist foundations—a state-centric perspective, continuity regarding expectations of states' motivations and (lack of) inhibitions, the pursuit of the National Interest in a dangerous anarchic world—and a focus on national security traditionally (even narrowly) defined, globalization matters for world politics, and classical realism is analytically well equipped to understand how and why. When the condition well characterizes world politics, a failure to account for the influence of globalization will make it difficult to understand changes in the balance of power, the prospects for war, and the strategic choices embraced by states. Shifting the setting doesn't eliminate intense and potentially dangerous interstate competition, but contexts are not neutral. Baseball and basketball are both zero-sum games with clear winners and losers. But one of the greatest basketball players in history was a mediocre minor-league baseball player.

Nor is there anything inherently reassuring about the political implications of globalization (the characteristic that made many structural realists respond so viscerally to claims about the international political consequences of interstate interdependence). As Stanley Hoffmann observed, "Globalization, far from spreading peace . . . seems to foster conflicts and resentments." Similarly, a wave of research on "weaponized interdependence" emphasizes the new and distinct conduits of interstate conflict facilitated by a highly enmeshed world economy.[73] More generally, reflecting an array of pressures that derive from unorganized and stateless forces, globalization affects traditional national security issues in three principal ways: by reshaping *state capacity*, recasting *relative power*, and revising calculations about the *costs and benefits of the use of force* in different settings. Globalization affects state capacity (in many ways increasing their capabilities, especially with regard to the domestic surveillance of political adversaries) and state autonomy (often reducing it, commonly seen with regard to macroeconomic policy). Because it does so unevenly, globalization thus alters the balance of power between states, reshuffling relative capabilities and vulnerabilities. It also generates new incentives and disincentives for war and political violence more generally, privileging some expressions of violence over others, and creates distinct axes of conflict.

Globalization—the increasing size and reach of the international economy, the growing pressure of market forces, and the tidal wave of border-indifferent information flows—is inherently disruptive, in the value-neutral sense of the term. Such forces more generally tend to disorder traditional patterns of activity, and widen or alter disparities between groups within societies. And times of rapid change—even change for the better—are often associated with political instability for this reason. As some thrive and others do not, the dissatisfied and vulnerable will demand redress and call for resistance—especially when unwelcome changes can be attributed to demonized "outsiders" both within and beyond a country's borders.[74]

The principal conduits of globalization are flows of information and commerce. As noted, with regard to the former, they can be empowering of states (and also weaponized); the latter are neither irreversible nor irresistible, but do raise the opportunity costs of closure. Nor should they be understood as in any way apolitical in origin or implication. State choices, especially those of the preponderant United States in the 1990s (but, with regard to finance, stretching back to the 1970s), were crucial in unleashing these forces—as one journalist pointedly observed at the time, "Globalization is the narcissism of a superpower in a one superpower world."[75]

But the unleashed forces of globalization, abetted by technological advances that cannot be un-invented, are quite formidable and, since the end of the Cold War, remarkable, as witnessed by the growth in (and fragmentation of) production and trade, and the soaring size and power of global financial markets.[76] Trade has consistently outpaced growth in global economic output, with the result that merchandise trade, which accounted for 32.4 percent of world GDP in 1990, rose to 44.9 percent in 2004 and then 60 percent in 2019—with trade in services growing even faster. And the level of global economic integration did not simply rise, it also changed qualitatively as dramatically increased intrafirm international trade, joint ventures and alliances, blurred, melded, and fragmented much of the world's business enterprises. The global stock of Foreign Direct Investment, valued at 6 percent of world GDP in 1980 (and 9 percent in 1995), grew to 22 percent by 2003 and 38 percent in 2019.[77] As for the rise of global financial markets, although integrated world capital markets and financial globalization are not novel and have arguably existed previously in history, developments since the 1980s are little short of breathtaking. In 1979, for example, the daily turnover in world currency markets reached an unprecedented $100 billion; in 1989 that figure had quadrupled to $400 billion. Around 1994 daily turnover exceeded $1 trillion, approached $2 trillion in 2004, and reached $6.6 trillion in 2019. Other changes in international finance, regarding the size of gross private capital flows and the magnitude of overseas investment finds, tell similar if less eye-catchingly spectacular stories.[78]

Innovations in information flows are perhaps even more transformative, and less likely to be reversed (though certainly they may be harnessed by powerful authorities). Once again, information revolutions are nothing new (consider the consequences of the invention of movable type, the telegraph, the telephone, mass circulation newspapers, radio, and television)—and in the present, as in the past, such transformations have profound consequences for both national security and, especially, for the autonomy and power of the state with regard to actors within society. As with baseball and basketball, different media environments relatively empower or disfavor distinct players and tactics. (A concentrated media environment with high cost of entry and operation will yield a very different information culture than one which is fragmented, inexpensive, and of uncertain origin.) The current "hypermedia" environment, characterized by a dizzying array of innovations, but seen most plainly in the proliferation of smartphones and the ubiquity of the internet, inevitably affects the relative balance of power of social forces within states, as well as the balance of power between them, sometimes in unexpected ways. (At the dawn of the hypermedia age, some thought that closed, repressive regimes, which almost fetishized the control of information, would be relative losers—but the rise of the surveillance state has if anything enhanced the chilling powers found in the authoritarian's toolbox.)[79]

It is possible to deduce a number of observations about the national security consequences of twenty-first-century globalization, which would elude analytical approaches that only consider states as like units distinguished only by differences in their raw material capabilities. Five in particular stand out. First, the international environment is characterized by considerable disincentives to old-fashioned great power war (that is, for large-scale militarized engagements designed to conquer adversaries). The fragmentation of production and the increased importance of knowledge-based economies suggest that the gains of conquest are less than they were when economies were dominated by their agricultural or (more narrowly national) industrial sectors. The disruptive effects of great power war also suggest that its opportunity costs are particularly high, as is the likelihood that financial markets will recoil from states embarking on such adventures.[80]

At the same time, a case can be made that the weak are getting dangerously weaker—that the processes of globalization have created an environment that will undermine the governance of states with already weak capabilities relative to other actors within their societies. Such settings are conducive to insurgency and civil war, empower transnational criminal networks and irregular armed forces operating within, across, and independent of titular state authorities, and create distinct opportunities and incentives for political violence. Understanding the political behavior of such states may need to attend to the greater salience of internal threats for such regimes, rather than simply traditional balance-of-power behavior concerns.[81]

These first two observations are suggestive of a third—that realists may need to revisit our traditional conceptions of geopolitics, which, historically (and wisely) distinguished between the core and the periphery. Traditionally, the central focus and objective of grand strategy (as articulated by Kennan during the Cold War, for example) was to ensure (ideally through political measures) that no single hostile power would come to dominate the world's key centers of industrial activity. Without setting aside this enduring wisdom, it may be (especially in a nuclear age, where the vulnerability of great powers to peer invasion is reduced but the proliferation of such weapons to the periphery is alarming) that militarized threats to great power security are more likely to emerge from the periphery.[82]

Despite a number of observable factors that create disincentives for great power war, classical realism nevertheless anticipates no recession in the ambition of states, their conflicts of interest, or pitiless implications of anarchy. Thus although the economic strands of globalization raise the costs and reduce the benefits of a traditional tanks-and-troops war between great powers (especially those with complex, highly modernized economies), the information revolution yields no such respite. Indeed, given the new vulnerabilities presented by reliance on computer networks (and perhaps even encouraged by the search for an outlet for hostilities given the relatively reduced appeal of territorial war), cyberwarfare might easily become a more common and consequential arena for bitter and costly great power conflict.[83] Finally, and distinctly, globalization will leave societies—some more than others—vulnerable to information warfare that undermines social cohesion, an important element of state strength. And it may be that democracies are more vulnerable than autocracies to such measures.[84]

This last issue raises a distinct question of realist political economy (unrelated to globalization, though clearly affected by it) that, again, is visible to classical realism but eludes entirely a structural perspective: the role of social cohesion as an important factor in any assessment of a nation's power. These are questions, for lack of a better term, of the social economy—and they can be important, and in some cases decisive, in explaining the outcome of confrontations between states. There will often be a crucial disjuncture between the raw material capabilities of a given state, and the ability of that state to "actualize" that power—that is, to effectively mobilize its resources to advance foreign policy objectives (and to fight wars). Additionally, the outcome of military struggles can often be greatly influenced by the relative capacity for endurance—not simply by how much distress one side can inflict on the other but by how much either side is willing (or able) to endure in order to achieve their objectives. (It is difficult to explain the French and American wars in Indochina without reflecting on this variable.)[85]

These factors are not easy to measure—but that is an inadequate excuse for not taking them seriously if they are important in explaining the outcomes of wars and the prospects for pursuing far-sighted grand strategies; the former is self-evidently essential for students of world politics, the latter is at the very heart of the conception of an analytically meaningful National Interest. Consider two cases that will be revisited in chapter 7: interwar France and the United States in the twenty-first century. In the former setting, there is the puzzle of the collapse of French power—a formidable military machine that quickly gave way to defeat, surrender, humiliation, and relatively docile occupation. A narrowly materialist conception must attribute the entire catastrophe to a highly contestable argument about innovative German military tactics.[86] (And even that would not account for the nature of the surrender and the collaboration that followed.) But, in addition to the vital role of history (the trauma of the Great War), France in the 1930s must be understood as a deeply damaged, traumatized, and divided society—a period well described as "hollow years" characterized by an "embrace of unreason." To understand the behavior of France as a power in world politics, as Raymond Aron observed (see chapter 3), it is necessary to understand "what France was like at the time."[87]

Similarly, by the second decade of the twenty-first century, the difference between (colossal) American power and its ability to harness and channel that power in the service of foreign policy goals was considerable. As always, history matters—it would be impossible to anticipate and understand U.S. choices about the prospective exercise of military power without reference to the weight of the prosecution of its two long, unsuccessful wars. But equally important is its (unraveling) social cohesion. In 1998, I argued that "the single greatest security threat" to the United States was "the internal atrophy of its national vitality," and that its growing inequality "would intensify distributional conflicts and make it more difficult to pursue far sighted national goals."[88]

Increasing inequality, sustained and cumulating over the course of more than four decades, is a defining characteristic of the American economy. It is not possible to draw straight lines from income inequality to foreign policy, or draw easily generalizable conclusions—as perceptions of inequality, cultural norms about fairness, and assessments of opportunities, absolute well-bring, and life prospects surely matter. But the long-term secular stagnation of median household incomes, combined with a dramatic increase in the wealth of those at the very top, will have social consequences and will inform debates over interpretations of the national interest and which foreign policy postures are best suited to pursue those interests.[89] Especially since globalization and its embrace are not unrelated to these phenomena—as with all economic processes, it generates winners and losers, in ways that have exacerbated these outcomes.[90] And once again history matters, as resentments about the global financial crisis of 2007–8—especially the (divergent) experiences that followed in its wake (the rich did just fine, the rest got the great recession)—further fueled the reemergence of America's isolationist instincts and contributed more generally to dysfunctions in its domestic politics.[91] In sum, it will simply not be possible to understand the foreign policy behavior and disposition of the United States without taking into account its domestic political economy (and, as noted above, the distinct vulnerabilities of its polity to the consequences of the hypermedia environment).

It remains a central tenet of classical realism, and one that distinguishes it from structural realism, that purpose matters—and as discussed here and revisited in chapter 7, social and economic factors will shape the nature of that purpose, and prospect.

CHAPTER SIX

Classical Realism and the Rise of China

THERE ARE FEW challenges more unsettling in world politics than the emergence of a new great power in the international system. In particular, realists of all stripes view this phenomenon as distinctly dangerous and destabilizing. Classical realism observes the emergence of new great powers in the system with enormous apprehension, because it expects the ambition of rising states to expand along with their capabilities, and also because of the anxiety that this expectation will provoke in their neighbors and potential adversaries. As emphasized throughout this book, from this perspective, changes in relative power, which ultimately derive from long-run variations in economic growth, are a mainspring of international political conflict. Economic change redistributes relative power over time, creating a natural tendency for divergences to emerge between power and privilege in world politics, which encourages rising states to challenge the status quo. A central problem in International Relations is addressing these changes to the balance of power, which historically has commonly been resolved by war.[1]

Classical realism is particularly alert to this concern because it tends to emphasize changes to the balance of power as the principal engine of political conflict, rather than focusing on the consequences of its static distribution. It is more common for structural realists, following Kenneth Waltz, to put greater explanatory emphasis on statics, and in particular, to share his assertion that bipolarity is more stable than multipolarity. Waltz argued that bipolarity was more stable (less prone to great power war) than multipolarity because the self-reliance of two great powers on their own balancing efforts avoided pathologies generated by the need for alliances, and that a bipolar system was, appealingly, more durable because of the vast gap in capabilities between the two dominant actors and the rest. But once again, as seen in chapter 5 regarding his treatment of interdependence, Waltz, proffering an abstract general theory, was extrapolating from the Cold War experience, and he was wrong. Anticipating, as was the broad presumption at the time, that the smaller Soviet Union would grow faster than the United States, he projected that the bipolar order would thus endure indefinitely. But in fact it was the Russian economy that soon grew more slowly, and the Soviet Union, and with it bipolarity, vanished within ten years of his assured prediction. Moreover, drawing on the Cold War setting to infer the appeal of bipolar orders more generally was always fraught with analytical peril—a large number of factors (including but not limited to stable nuclear deterrence) contributed to the relative stability of relations between the United States and the Soviet Union. Similarly, looking beyond the first half of the twentieth century, it is clear that other multipolar orders have been associated with long periods of peace. Ultimately, it is hard to draw generalizable conclusions about the relative stability of bipolarity or multipolarity. Thus as emphasized, classical realists, following Robert Gilpin, hold that the "most important factor" for understanding world politics is not the static distribution of power but the "dynamics of power relations over time."[2]

Without doubt then, understanding and anticipating the consequences of the emergence of China as a great power is one of the great challenges for observers of contemporary international politics.[3] And once again, a closer look illustrates the appeal of and insights offered by a classical realist perceptive. This chapter follows a similar pattern to chapter 3, which contrasted the explanations offered by structural and classical realism as applied to vexing puzzles of twentieth-century international politics. Here I consider closely two prominent and influential structural realist perspectives, in this instance John Mearsheimer's *The Tragedy of Great Power Politics*, which derives and articulates a variant of structural realism known as "offensive realism," and Graham Allison's *Destined for War: Can America and China Escape Thucydides's Trap?*, a structural approach that purports to apply the analysis of *The Peloponnesian War* to contemporary U.S.-China relations.[4] *Tragedy* argues that China will inevitably make a militarized bid for regional hegemony and that the United States, for the sake of its own security, must take dramatic measures to resist and to slow the rise of its emerging rival; *Destined for War* sounds an alarm that the two powers might stumble blindly into a destructive war, just like the great powers of Europe did before World War I.[5]

Both perspectives, however, are fundamentally flawed, with errors of analysis that can be traced to their dedicated structuralism, which blinds their analyses to the crucial role of history in informing assessments of interest, and eliminates the significance of the role of choices made by states—and of any influence of domestic and international politics—in shaping outcomes. As this chapter will illustrate, the theory of offensive realism is deductively unsound, misguided in its mechanistic determinism, and plainly and exactly wrong in its appeal to E. H. Carr in support of its analysis. As for *Destined for War*, it misreads *The Peloponnesian War*, is incorrect with regard to the key "sleepwalker" analogy it seeks to establish, and is inattentive to the real "Thucydides Trap" that might lead to a tragic war—that of great power hubris.

A classical realist analysis, in contrast to these approaches, emphasizes the crucial roles of politics, contingency, and choice. These factors will shape the trajectory of states' basic foreign policy dispositions and orientation, especially those of great powers. The experience of interwar Japan (considered below) vividly illustrates once again the poverty of narrowly structuralist approaches, both in general and as would be applied to understand the implications of the rise of China. The disastrous path pursued by Japan in the 1930s was not inevitable (nor explicable solely by looking at the distribution of power or changes to it). Rather, it was fundamentally shaped, and arguably disfigured, by major exogenous shocks—the Great Depression and the global financial crisis of 1931—upheavals that were filtered through Japan's fraught domestic political contestations at that time, in particular its polarized and stressed social economy. In the 1920s, Japan's future was unwritten, as is the destiny of China's foreign policy a century later.

Nevertheless, although classical realism offers more insight into the delicate and often tense twenty-first-century Sino-American relationship, it does not necessarily tell a happier tale. Recall that unlike structural realism, which assumes that states are security seekers, classical realism assumes that as states grow more powerful, they will typically tend to want, in a word, more—more authority in settling the outcomes of disputes, greater influence in shaping the international political environment, increased status, and implicit deference. Rising powers will also commonly seek positional goods, over which it is harder to compromise and split the difference. Moreover, although classical realism assumes a baseline of working rationality in the pursuit of a chosen course of action, recall that it also includes some role for what can be called "passions." Thus classical realism also anticipates that rising powers will be arrogant and difficult, and that great powers in relative decline will be temperamentally ill-equipped to appreciate the limits of their own power.

As a more practical matter, classical realism—with its emphasis on uncertainty, contingency, and politics, focuses not on the inevitability of outcomes but on how domestic politics and foreign policy choices will shape the trajectory of international relations—is suggestive of foreign policy dispositions that are the opposite of the recommendations associated with offensive realism. With regard to rising powers, even the most casual reading of history (forbidden by structural realism) vehemently admonishes against a militarized bid for hegemony. As for established states faced with an emerging great power, again, contra offensive realism, as a general rule (from which there will necessarily be occasional exceptions), classical realism, however inherently wary, pessimistic, and skeptical (very, always), seeks to accommodate rising power. This accommodation is rooted in three familiar core tenets of classical realism: first, and always, the acknowledgment of the reality of power, which is part of seeing the world as it is, not as we would like it to be; second, an unwillingness to automatically privilege the perspective of those that would defend the status quo; third, the belief that *politics matters*, and that therefore the future is largely unwritten. Unlike structural realists, classical realists are alert to the consequences of domestic politics (and here developments in both the United States and China are disquieting) and the ways in which foreign policy choices of great powers shape and inform the choices made by others.

The Fundamentally Flawed "Theory of Offensive Realism"

Realists in general must be pessimistic about the implications of an emerging great power in the international system, anticipating that newcomers will be arrogant troublemakers (it is hard if not impossible to find a rising power in history that wasn't, and that certainly includes the United States). But as always, realists can and will part company with regard to aspects of their analyses and, almost invariably, with regard to any policy prescriptions that they might derive from their models.[6] One prominent realist, for example, offers admirably unambiguous and irresponsibly overconfident answers to these questions. John Mearsheimer, drawing conclusions from a structural realist theory he derives and labels "offensive realism," states plainly that "China cannot rise peacefully." Instead, as its capabilities increase, China will become "an aggressive state determined to achieve regional hegemony." The inevitability of this—and "inevitability" is a key word here; this is a theory so deterministic it would make a physicist blush[7]—is such that policy measures designed to shape international incentives that China might face, or influence the contours of its domestic political deliberations, are "misguided" and "doomed to failure." Given this, the United States should direct its foreign policy to make its emerging, implacable adversary as miserable as possible, and "do what it can to slow the rise of China."[8]

As noted in chapter 4, Mearsheimer builds his theoretical framework on some very shaky analytical ground, conflating positive and normative analysis (a huge no-no), and immediately reaching for ad hoc variables explicitly ruled out by his model to try to account for plainly obvious empirical inconsistencies. Thus *The Tragedy of Great Power Politics* offers an explanation of how states *will inevitably behave*—in particular, the model concludes that the United States will be irresistibly drawn to confront China and take measures to prevent its rise—but then immediately notes that, actually, the United States might not. (This ought to introduce the possibility that China might not behave as expected as well, but Mearsheimer seems to be making an "American Exceptionalism" argument—something that is expressly forbidden by a structural realist analysis such as offensive realism, which models states as "like units.") The United States might depart from its predetermined path because, despite the core assumption of offensive realism that states are rational, in reality, sometimes they "do foolish things." Similarly, although it is assumed that great powers invariably "act as realists," and as such variations in domestic politics or ideologies are irrelevant, Americans are ideologically predisposed to "dislike realism," a disposition than can lead to foreign policy aberrations. Thus the need for the subversive analytical sleight of hand—the theory is presented as deterministic (states *will inevitably* behave this way), but when in doubt, it falls back to policy advocacy (states *should* behave this way). Of course, if the future is determined, policy advocacy is irrelevant. But if the future is unwritten, then policy choices can shape outcomes, sometimes disastrously. This issue has been raised earlier but bears repeating—it is one thing to predict that the apple will fall from the tree; it is very much another to yell at the apple for failing to do so. And with *Tragedy* Mearsheimer is out in the orchard giving a rousing pep talk: "States *should* behave according to the dictates of offensive realism, because it outlines the best way to survive in a dangerous world."[9]

But Mearsheimer is wrong. Working with assumptions that are individually reasonable, he draws conclusions from them collectively that are logically incoherent, and in turn offers policy prescriptions that are dangerously misguided. Many of the errors of offensive realism are rooted in its structuralism, and as such, it productively illustrates the pathologies that can result from an overreliance on structural variables.

The theory of offensive realism is built from five "bedrock assumptions." Each of these are, indeed, fine realist assumptions, although a classical realist analysis would find two of them overly restrictive. Nevertheless, they are all well and good as reasonable points of departure for realists of any stripe—the first three are bedrock assumptions of any realist analysis: the existence of anarchy (and thus, ultimately, of a self-help system, in which there is no guarantee that the behavior of others will be restrained); that other states, regardless of their apparent present intentions, have the potential to be dangerous; that the intentions of other states are uncertain, and you can never know for sure what other states are going to do, especially in the future. The fourth and fifth assumptions are eminently reasonable (even if classical realists might differ)[10]—and it is crucial to attend to them carefully, because it is the proper respect for Mearsheimer's own assumptions that ultimately undermines the conclusions that he would draw from his model. Assumption four is the goal of survival: "*survival is the primary goal of great powers*. Specifically, states seek to maintain their territorial integrity and the autonomy of their domestic political order." Assumption five is rationality: "great powers are rational actors."[11]

From these assumptions, Mearsheimer concludes that states, motivated to ensure their own security, will recognize that the safest position in the system is one of regional hegemony. (Global hegemony would be even safer but as a practical matter is simply not attainable. Here again a classical realist perspective agrees—as George F. Kennan argued, "No people is great enough to establish world hegemony.")[12] Only a regional hegemon is secure in the knowledge that it will not be conquered by others. Thus, given the anarchic nature of the international system, states that can plausibly make bids for regional hegemony will do so, as a matter of their own assessment of their best chances for survival. "States quickly understand that the best way to ensure their survival is to be the most powerful state in the system," Mearsheimer argues. "Only a misguided state would pass up an opportunity to be the hegemon in the system."[13]

But in the space between those two assertions Mearsheimer makes a giant and illogical leap, one that drives his entire argument—and is an irretrievable and fatal flaw. What Mearsheimer elides is that there is a fundamental distinction between *being* a hegemon and *bidding* for hegemony. It may indeed be that "the ideal situation is to be the hegemon in the system." But according to his theory, "survival is the number one goal of great powers."[14] Thus the crucial, essential, behaviorally determining question for a great power mulling a bid for hegemony is not "if I was the hegemon, will I be more likely to survive?" Rather, it must be, following the logic of the model, "if I make an aggressive bid for regional hegemony, will I be more likely to survive than if I do not embark on such an adventure?" And here the answer should be obvious, to any rational great power (and, again, assumption five assumes great power rationality)—bidding for hegemony is one of the few and rare paths *to* destruction for a great power. Most great powers are extremely likely to survive; most great powers that bid for hegemony do not.

In contemporary practice, the facts on the ground expose this basic contradiction of Mearsheimer's argument, rooted in assumptions about the primacy of the survival goal and of rationality. Is China's "survival" really in jeopardy if it does not aggressively bid to dominate all of Asia? Will the United States not "survive" if it fails to reach across the Pacific Ocean in an effort to crush a rising China before it is too late? (Puzzlingly, the United States, as a regional hegemon should have already have achieved Mearsheimer's big brass ring of preternatural security.) What exactly threatens the survival of these great powers? Given their military establishments, their nuclear deterrents, their economic might, their continental size, and their vast populations, is their survival really imperiled if they do not act as offensive realists? Or is it *only* imperiled if they irrationally act as offensive realists, pushing everything, including the few precious chips that hold the prospects for their destruction, across the poker table in a reckless bet to win it all?

But the problem is more general than that. Only a power with a complete ignorance of history would be eager to embark upon a bid for hegemony, if survival was its main goal. After all, most states in modern history that have bid for hegemony—with one exceptional exception—have antagonized their neighbors and eventually elicited an encircling coalition that, indeed, utterly destroyed them, leading to the loss of their territorial integrity and the autonomy of their domestic political order, the two things Mearsheimer says states hold most dear. The inability of states over centuries of modern history to attain regional hegemony ought to suggest that it is exceedingly hard to achieve. And for reasons that do not surprise realists, who assume that states have a primal preference not to be pushed around, and thus when they are able, will resist efforts by would-be hegemons to dominate them. The one "success" story, the United States, achieved its regional hegemony because it was distinctly lucky to be surrounded by weak neighbors and even weaker adversaries, and separated by vast oceans from other powerful states. No other geopolitical neighborhood, past or present, looks anything like that setting.

As Mearsheimer observes, five modern states sought regional hegemony. The United States succeeded; all of the others—Imperial Japan, Napoleonic France, Wilhelmine Germany, and Nazi Germany—failed and were utterly destroyed. It is hard to imagine that a rational great power with the primary goal of survival would fail to draw the conclusion that bidding for hegemony is perhaps the only thing that can possibly threaten its survival—its territorial integrity and domestic autonomy—and thus that such follies should be avoided. Yet Mearsheimer assumes as a law of nature (and failing that, advocates) that powerful states will behave in such reckless and likely catastrophic ways, which would appear to violate assumption five of offensive realism, that of rationality.

One source of this paradox is again rooted in the weakness of structural realism, which cannot allow for history, or learning. Classical realists would expect states to understand that throwing their weight around—not to mention a bid for hegemony—might be self-defeating; whereas states acting as structural realists expect them to make the same foolish choices over and over again, because the past is irrelevant and all that matters is the distribution of power. But classical realists place great weight to historical referents. Referring to European history, Raymond Aron observed the self-defeating nature of this sort of excess ambition, which invariably excites "the fear and jealousy of other states, and thereby provoking the formation of a hostile coalition. In any given system there exists an *optimum of forces*; to exceed it will produce a dialectal reversal. Additional force involves a relative weakening by a shift of allies to neutrality or of neutrals to the enemy camp." Thucydides observed a similar phenomenon in reporting the widespread "indignation felt against Athens," rooted in apprehension about its imperial aims, "which left men's feelings inclined much more to the Spartans."[15]

Mearsheimer tries to circumnavigate the stubborn truths that achieving regional hegemony is extremely rare and that aggressive attempts to attain it are exceedingly, mortally, and uniquely dangerous by misleadingly conflating the prospects for success in a given military confrontation between two states with the prospects for success in a bid for hegemony. In particular, Mearsheimer reports statistics that show the initiator of military conflicts in modern history won about 60 percent of the time, and from that observation he concludes that history does not support the contention that resorting to the offensive is unwise. These figures actually could be read as suggesting a much more cautionary tale (and suggest a good bit of folly on the part of those 40 percent who started a war and lost).[16] But framing the analyses in this way distracts from and obscures a larger and more basic point: to start a war is not the same thing as to bid for regional hegemony—the overwhelming number of initiations of militarized conflicts were and are indeed *not* bids for hegemony. With regard to the latter, the scorecard remains unchanged: one success and four (catastrophic) failures, which clocks in at a more discouraging 20 percent.[17] And even within these episodes, Mearsheimer cherry-picks the wrong metric. He observes that the Nazis won their wars against France and Poland, but lost against the Soviet Union. Are we to count this as a 66 percent "success" rate for the offensive?[18] No. These three wars were part of *one* bid for hegemony, which failed. Moreover, at times Mearsheimer suggests that it was a mistake for Germany to take on Russia (though at other times he suggests the opposite), but this simply fails to recognize, somewhat surprisingly given that offensive realism would predict it, that the whole point of all those wars was to bid for hegemony, which required confronting Russia. A similar sleight of hand is found in the remarkable, even breathtaking claim that "a careful analysis of the Japan and German cases reveals that, in each instance the decision for war was a reasonable response."[19] This is contestable, to say the least—within one six-month period, Germany declared war on the Soviet Union and the United States; Japan, in the midst of a wildly ambitious effort to conquer all of China, simultaneously declared war on the United States and the British Empire. Neither of these choices is easily characterized as "reasonable" (or likely to take home ribbons for "wise grand strategy choices")—but they were part and parcel of those states' bids for hegemony, which failed miserably.

Mearsheimer concludes that while the success rate of one out of five is "not impressive" (to say the least), he nevertheless insists the take-home point is that "the American case demonstrates that it is possible to achieve regional hegemony," thus proving the naysayers wrong. Instead, "the pursuit of regional hegemony is not a quixotic ambition, although there is no denying it is difficult to achieve. Since the security benefits of hegemony are enormous, powerful states will invariably be tempted to emulate the United States and try to dominate their region of the world."[20]

Offensive Realism—Suicide Solutions

Or not. Given the enormous security risks entailed in a bid for hegemony, rational states would not blithely assume they could simply re-create the U.S. historical experience at will. Rather, a rational power would carefully assess the particulars of the American experience, and weigh the extent to which those features applied to their own situation. Crucially, given all five cases available for comparison, a rational state would consider whether its geopolitical setting looks more like one in which the United States was able to achieve regional hegemony (weak neighbors, weaker adversaries, secure insulation from other strong states) or more like the environments in which the other four would-be regional hegemons—all of whom were ruined and utterly destroyed by the effort—rolled their dice. Given the exceptional attributes of the American case and the commonalities clearly visible among the failures, it strains credulity to think that a great power, motivated principally by a primordial desire to survive, would be "invariably be tempted to emulate the United States" and disregard the sobering experiences of all the others.

Even without focusing on the exceptional attributes of the American case (the only example of a successful bid) and limiting the analysis to a consideration of the abstract, deductive argument, the entire "inevitable aggressive drive for regional hegemony" theory still collapses under the weight of its own illogic. Once again assuming, as the theory of offensive realism does, that states are rational actors whose primary motive is survival, the bet is a foolish one. The key calculation is not "will I be more secure if I successfully achieve regional hegemony?" It is, what maximizes the probability of my survival, a militarized bid for regional hegemony or a more cautious approach? (Such as, for example, a measured marshaling of military capabilities and political influence to shape the regional political environment in desired ways.) Consider that any state in a position to even plausibly consider a bid for regional hegemony must be a very secure state, in historical perspective. For the effort not to be utterly foolhardy, it must be the strongest state in the region—probably by a considerable margin, because bids for hegemony commonly elicit countervailing coalitions if such possibilities exist—and our regional titan must also be confident that more distant adversaries pose no mortal threat even if it throws the weight of its military power around in a local adventure that might expose its flanks to peer competitors abroad. A state in that position is a very secure state, one that is extremely likely to survive. Were regional hegemony to be achieved, it is reasonable to concede, with Mearsheimer, that such states will be even more secure still. But the crucial questions remain: How much more secure (given that the state was already exceedingly secure) would they be? And what are the risks of making a militarized bid for hegemony? Most states that have tried it have failed, and indeed were conquered and ruined. For a rational power that prioritizes its survival and autonomy, a militarized bid for hegemony thus seems much less like an "inevitability" and more something to be avoided at all costs: a fantastically risky life-or-death gamble taken in the pursuit of a very marginal increase in state security—a prize won only by the long-shot chance that they are able to pull it off.

And that is just the abstract theory. Consider now the poor application of the model for the case which it was designed to explain (and serve as a vehicle for policy advocacy regarding). China is a nuclear power. As Mearsheimer observes, "states with survivable nuclear weapons are likely to fear each other less"; he also notes that "there is no question that MAD makes war among the great powers less likely."[21] Scholars can debate the meaning of, and the limits to, the nuclear revolution in world politics—but the implications for offensive realism, especially in this instance, are compelling.[22] China, with its potent nuclear capability, has one less reason to think that its security depends on achieving regional hegemony—and it also must reckon with the fact that the actual or latent nuclear capabilities of other regional powers might make such a bid still more difficult, dangerous, and counterproductive. (This also raises the question of why the United States, with its own massive, robust, and secure nuclear arsenal, must, to ensure its own survival, act swiftly, immediately, and forcefully to stop China's potential bid for regional hegemony before it occurs.)

Mearsheimer thus offers illogical predictions about, and, worse, dangerous and self-defeating policy prescriptions for, both China and the United States. Consider China. Recall again that following the theory of offensive realism, the inevitable militarized drive for hegemony derives not from grand ambitions, "wicked motives," or inherently aggressive designs but rather and nothing more than as the best way to maximize the prospects for the country's survival (thus the "Tragedy" of great power politics). Following the discussion above, however, the first question to ask of this claim is, what are the baseline expectations for China's survival against foreign threats in the foreseeable future? They would already seem extremely high. The issue, then, is to calculate the benefits of the added security from achieving hegemony, weighed against the risks of pursuing the bid. And again, a crucial question here is, does China's neighborhood look more like the one that characterized American experience or that of those who tried and failed?

The answer is obvious. China lives in a very crowded neighborhood. It shares a very long border with Russia, with whom, as Mearsheimer notes, it has fought in the past and which he codes as a "great power" (although this is arguable), and which has a very large and potent nuclear force.[23] Japan is also very close by. Mearsheimer also codes Japan as a great power, and he properly notes the mutual suspicion between the two states. If frightened or provoked, Japan has the capability to swiftly develop an independent nuclear force, and it is difficult to imagine a realist account that would not expect them to do so in such circumstances.[24] China also borders India, a very large, also rising, and nuclear armed state, and again one with whom China has fought in the past and eyes warily, and which has a latent economic potential similar even to that of China's own. China also shares a frontier with Vietnam—not a great power, but no pushover, and yet another state with whom China has fought in living memory. And even without unification, a nuclear-capable South Korea is another regional player in the neighborhood. Regarding Korea, in making calculations about the costs and benefits of foreign policy choices, again and always, *politics matters*. In chapter 5 we observed the increasingly important economic relationship between China and South Korea, and how, following "Hirschman effects," the latter's international political preferences might increasingly bend toward those of China, absent any coercion. On the other hand, the presence of overt or veiled coercion might undermine rather than enhance the prospects for achieving that political prize.

In sum, for China, the imperatives of offensive realism—rationality and the primacy of the survival objective—not to mention a host of other political factors, imply the opposite of what Mearsheimer postulates. Given its military prowess, economic capacity, continental size, and vast population, it is hard to imagine the foreign power that threatens its very survival. Indeed, the only thing that might bring it to ruin—as Thucydides would surely warn—is if it embarked upon reckless and unnecessary military adventures. And even if somehow, against all odds, China managed to pull off such a dangerous and unlikely feat, how much "more" secure would it be after all was said and done? The difference would be marginal at best, and certainly not worth the high-stakes gamble. China's survival would not be threatened, as Mearsheimer suggests, if it failed to act according to the tenets of offensive realism; to the contrary, acting like an offensive realist would be one of the very few paths that might threaten its survival.

As for contemporary American policy, Mearsheimer's logic is on even shakier ground. Again, it is the assumption that "survival is the number one goal of great powers" that takes much of the wind from the sails of his advice to the United States. Mearsheimer wants the United States to do everything it can to slow China's growth, but why? Aside from the fact that China is unlikely to achieve militarized regional hegemony in Asia, even if it somehow did, Mearsheimer makes a convincing case that, while the

United States might find this at times irritating, this would not threaten the survival of America. And since survival is its primary motive, from that position of security it should enjoy the luxury of choosing its China policy from a broad range of possible options.

After all, the reason why states want to be regional hegemons in the first place is because that position provides them with incredible security, even from other similarly situated powers. As Mearsheimer notes, "regional hegemons certainly pack a powerful military punch, but launching amphibious assaults across oceans against territory controlled and defended by another power would be a suicidal undertaking." Yes, indeed. Mearsheimer elaborates, repeatedly, the secure status of the regional hegemon, and in particular the distinct and enviable security of the United States as an "insular state," protected by the impressive "stopping power of water," which he appeals to numerous times as a law-like statement. Indeed and in sum, "the best outcome a great power can hope for is to be a regional hegemon."[25] Thus, even before we even put the U.S. nuclear deterrent on the table, its survival is simply not threatened by China, even one that somehow, against the odds, achieves regional hegemony.

Mearsheimer raises the notion that if China did achieve regional hegemony, it would find it in its interest to distract the United States by trying to foment trouble in America's backyard, and this might jeopardize U.S. regional hegemony. But this is a very problematic fallback position, for two reasons. First, there is nothing to stop China from doing that even without being a regional hegemon, as the behavior of Russia (with a GDP smaller than Italy and military spending about one-tenth that of the United States) in parts of South America illustrates (to say nothing of its active and consequential information warfare efforts to undermine the United States from within). Second, and more to Mearsheimer's point, such meddling is extremely unlikely to undermine America's position as a regional hegemon, not only because of the realities on the ground in North America but also because the durability of regional hegemony, once achieved, is extremely robust—after all, that's the engine that motivates the entire theory of offensive realism.

Even by Mearsheimer's own logic, then, it is simply hard to fathom why the United States, to ensure its own survival, would be compelled to reach halfway around the globe and try to make life as miserable for China as possible. As a great power the United States enjoys the luxury of choosing from a broad menu of policy postures and positions. And so we are back to the basic question, not of what it must necessarily do, but what choices are most likely to advance its interests. Setting aside (false) concerns for survival, would an overt attempt to disfigure China's economy advance the national interest of the United States? The answer is not obvious. As seen in chapter 5, China's economy is an important engine of growth for many countries, including many that have good relations with the United States. Hurting China's economy will harm those states as well. As one hard-nosed China expert observed, even if U.S.-China relations could be described as a zero-sum competition, such a strategy would be "counter-productive," because its political ramifications would leave the United States "much weaker in the region in relation to China."[26]

In sum, as this chapter emphasizes throughout, a classical realist perspective looks at China's rise with considerable alarm. But the deductively unsound theory of offensive realism urgently offers policy prescriptions to both China and the United States that are misguided, dangerous, and undermining of their basic national interests.

Getting Thucydides Wrong

In considering the implications of changes to the balance of power (in addition to a host of other questions regarding international politics), scholars have long drawn on Thucydides—and for good reason.[27] As quoted in chapter 1, the Athenian general states plainly in his *The Peloponnesian War* that "the growth of the power of Athens, and the alarm which this inspired in Sparta, made war inevitable" (1.23.6). A closer reading of Thucydides, of course, backs up a truckload of qualifications to this simple declaration—Thucydides was generally hostile to deterministic arguments, and his analysis of the causes of the war features a bevy of explanatory variables operating across all levels of analysis, including, especially, the distinct and contrasting attributes of the antagonists. Nevertheless, Thucydides makes very clear that he saw this shift in the balance of power as a basic cause of the initial conflict (recall that the war lasted twenty-seven years, in three distinct phases). Thucydides, who chose his words with care, repeats the argument twice in Book I, which is concerned with the origin of the first phase of the war.[28]

In is not surprising, then, that Graham Allison's *Destined for War* is an attempt to apply the lessons of *The Peloponnesian War* (and other historical episodes of "power transitions") to current tensions between China and the United States. Unfortunately, it fails in its efforts to do so. *Destined for War* is a poorly executed book, riddled with basic errors.[29] More important—and largely as a function of its embrace of minimalist structuralism, which reduces the wisdom of a subtle, sophisticated magnum opus to a simplistic slogan—Allison gets Thucydides wrong—fundamentally and consequentially wrong. *Destined for War* attempts to shoehorn selected fragments drawn from *The Peloponnesian War* into an ill-fitting argument that is at odds with the content and lessons of the original text.[30] The war itself, motivated in part by Sparta's fears of a rising Athens, is an awkward analogy for contemporary U.S.-China relations, as the United States more resembles Athens and China Sparta. And this is no small thing, given the enormous emphasis that Thucydides places on "national character" in explaining the contrasting behavior of the two antagonists he considers—a theme, central to *The Peloponnesian War*, that is of course invisible to structural analysis.[31]

A larger issue is the problematic effort of *Destined for War* to establish an erroneous "sleepwalker" analogy to the Peloponnesian War, which can then in turn be applied to contemporary international politics. Sleepwalking is the notion, often associated with (if actively debated as a cause of) World War I, that great powers can in some instances stumble into a conflagration they all wished to avoid; the concept is also relevant for how, during the Cuban Missile Crisis, the superpowers almost fell purposelessly into a cataclysmically ruinous conflict—the two episodes are repeatedly invoked in the pages of *Destined for War*.[32] In a similar spirit (war as an unintended, avoidable tragedy), Allison also suggests that a failure to grasp the security dilemma (that actions taken without malign intent might be unwittingly threatening to others) contributed to the outbreak of the Peloponnesian War, when he claims that "like so many others, Athens believed its advance to be benign." But although it is almost certainly the case that if the United States and China ever went to war, it would be an outcome of a crisis, perhaps exacerbated by the dynamics of the security dilemma, that spiraled out of control and which neither side hoped to fight, this does not describe what happened between Athens and Sparta. Allison reimagines the Peloponnesian War as a tragedy that both sides wished to avoid. He asserts that Athens and Sparta each made "repeated attempts to avoid it," and made "their best efforts" in the pursuit of a peaceful solution. Allison even goes so far as to claim that Athens's leading citizen Pericles opposed the war, but his hand was forced, as he finally "bent to popular pressure and reluctantly drew up plans for war."[33]

This is all simply and exactly wrong. Neither side made their best effort for peace. As noted in chapter 4, Pericles was in fact a leading advocate for the war. Nor did he come to this position reluctantly, goaded on by an aggressive public. And he was under no illusions about how Athenian power was perceived by others, stating plainly to his fellow citizens, "For what you hold is, to speak plainly, a tyranny; to take it perhaps was wrong, but to let go is unsafe." Explicitly rejecting compromise and proposals for a negotiated solution, Pericles rallied the more cautiously inclined public with a rousing speech, urging them to share his view that the choice for war was an absolute necessity. Furthermore, and again contra Allison, the people did not sway Pericles—rather, in open debate, with both sides represented and the final decision uncertain, Thucydides reports the opposite: that the public voted for war because they were "persuaded of the wisdom of his advice."[34] Nor did the Spartans search eagerly for a peaceful solution. In contrast, they refused the offer of arbitration (a measure that would have been in accord with the terms of the existing Thirty Years' Peace). And they came to regret doing so, acknowledging explicitly that they were in the wrong. According to Thucydides, years later, on the precipice of the war's resumption after the Peace of Nicias, the Spartans were keen not to make the same mistake twice: "In the former war, they considered that the offense had been more on their own side" for several reasons, including "their own refusal to listen to the Athenian offer of arbitration, in spite of the clause in the former treaty that where arbitration should be offered there should be no appeal to arms." In sum, Athens and Sparta did not sleepwalk into an unwanted war. Indeed, the Spartans, as was their wont, moved with caution and deliberation, to the consternation of many of their more hotheaded allies that harbored grievances against Athens. The road to the Peloponnesian War was paved by Athenian arrogance and Spartan intransigence.[35]

Once source of the sleepwalker analogy blunder derives from *Destined for War*'s shallow attention to context and history. No realist analysis would rule out the prospect that war might occur, at any time, or anticipate that normative understandings will prevent states from engaging in acts of aggression and barbarism. Nevertheless, in ancient Greece, war was a common, normal, and legitimate course of action. In contrast, between advanced societies today, while the resort to arms remains a possibility, and facilitating diplomatic and political blunders are all too common, war between great powers is nevertheless approached with greater caution now than it was in the distant past, due to a clear sensitivity to the enormous costs (and opportunity costs) that such a conflict would entail, and a sensitivity to the notion that naked aggression is less generally recognized to be a legitimate method of advancing interests.[36]

In reaching for lessons about contemporary international politics, the problems with *Destined for War* go far beyond its unsatisfactory treatment of the origins of the Peloponnesian War. They run deep, and they are dangerous. In seeking insights into power transitions more generally, the ambition of the book is to provide a comprehensive historical analysis of all cases where the "Thucydides Trap" might apply—that is, episodes where a predominant power was confronted with the prospect of a rising challenger. *Destined for War*, as its subtitle relates, wants to apply the lessons of the Peloponnesian War and these other occurrences to the twenty-first-century case of rising China and superpower America. The news is grim. Allison and his team of research assistants identify sixteen cases in which an "ascending power challenged an established power," twelve of which resulted in war. Moreover, he warns, "we can be certain . . . that the dynamic Thucydides identified will intensify in the years ahead."[37]

But these claims are undermined by Allison's tissue-thin reading of history, an inherent vice of structural analysis. *Destined for War* is an exemplar of exactly the kind of work that Paul Schroeder so keenly warned of. The book illustrates "an attitude toward history not uncommon among scholars of many kinds: an unconscious disdain for it, a disregard of its complexity and subtleties and the problems of doing it well or using it wisely; an unexamined assumption that its lessons and insights lie on the surface for anyone to pick up, so that one can go at history like a looter at an archeological site, indifferent to context and deeper meaning, concerned only with taking what can be immediately used or sold."[38] Indeed, Allison's manifestly unsatisfactory treatment of key cases, such as the confrontation between the United States and Japan before the Pacific war, raises serious doubts about the utility of conclusions he might reach on the basis of these episodes.[39] And the more distant historical sections of the book inevitably raise the question of the extent to which general conclusions for contemporary application can be confidently drawn from those experiences. The aspiration to make generalizable claims is certainly the appropriate ambition of much IR theory; nevertheless, caution is always in order. Are the factors that caused war between the kingdoms of Europe in the fifteenth through eighteenth centuries (roughly half of the cases in the "Thucydides Trap Case File") the same that would cause war between the United States and China today? Even Allison seems skeptical, noting, with Mearsheimer, that nuclear weapons are game changers, and "*have no precedent*."[40] They don't make armed conflict impossible, but the causal pathways that might lead to war between two great powers with robust nuclear deterrents are likely different than they were between conventionally armed rivals in the distant past.

Even if we were to set aside all of these concerns for the sake of argument, ultimately *Destined for War* is undermined by its misguided notion that there is an off-the-shelf, easily portable "Thucydides Trap," derived from its structuralism. But as elaborated in chapter 1, although Thucydides placed clear emphasis on the importance of changes to the distribution of power in explaining events in world politics, he was not, by any stretch of the imagination, the crude structuralist he is often caricatured as by careless or superficial readers of his work. In explaining the origins, course, and consequences of the Peloponnesian War, Thucydides placed enormous emphasis on numerous other factors, including the decisive influence of national character, domestic politics, and the role of leaders in formatively shaping states' choices. His *History* clearly reflects the classical conception that theories which operate solely at the systemic level are "theoretically useful but incomplete." This criticism, of course, does not apply to Thucydides, whose analysis is steeped in those first- and second-level variables noted above.[41]

In addition, and also as emphasized throughout this book, if there is a Thucydides Trap, it derives from a concept that is central to classical realism but incompatible with structural realism (and hyper-rationalist approaches to international politics)—that of great power hubris. A reader of *Destined for War* would be forgiven in concluding that Thucydides was warning his readers about a "trap" that Athens and Sparta fell into when war first broke out between them in 431 BC. But Thucydides, a great admirer of war-advocate Pericles, did not situate the Athenian tragedy in the initial decision for war—but rather in subsequent Athenian follies rooted in its gluttonous over-ambition. For Thucydides, the tragedy was not that the war took place but rather that Pericles' wise (and prudent) war-fighting strategy was abandoned after he left the stage in the third year of the conflict. The Athenians did in fact fall victim to a terrible trap, and one that has undiminished contemporary relevance and application: over the long course of the war, Athens repeatedly and catastrophically "grasped for more," and ultimately caused its own undoing, initially on the heels of its great victory at Pylos in the seventh year of the war and then, definitively, sixteen years after the initial outbreak of the war, over Sicily—which was for Thucydides the singular and defining episode of the entire conflagration.[42] This denouement, with Athens destroyed not because of the merciless logic of power politics or the schemes of its enemies abroad but by blunders of its own doing, fueled by unchecked, intoxicating hubris, passes unnoticed in *Destined for War*. This is indeed a trap that great powers are ensnared by over and over again. And if the United States and China come to blows, it is likely that they will have failed to learn Thucydides' timeless teachings about the arrogance of power. This is why we need to appeal to classical realism to better understand events in world politics throughout history, as well as the pressing issues of the present day.

The Rise of China through Classical Realist Lenses

Once again the errors and limitations of structural realism demonstrate the need to appeal to a classical perspective. What stands out from such a comparison is something of a paradox: classical realism is, on the one hand, even more pessimistic about the implications of the rise of China for international stability, but on the other, is strongly suggestive of the need to find ways to *accommodate* that rise. This is not because a classical realist analysis is naive or optimistic about the prospects of success for such a strategy (it is hard to overstate the wariness of classical realism on this issue). Rather, an approach that tries to carefully manage and deal with, rather aggressively confront and crush, China's growing capabilities is the wisest strategy in the only context that ever matters to realist analysis—that approach compared to the likely consequences of other options. (As often, realism reduces to trying to find the least bad option.)

The emphasis on accommodation, with eyes as much on political variables and measures as they are on the raw correlates of military capabilities, derives from two foundational classical realist tenets, and two consequences of those beliefs. First is the need to always acknowledge power: both the reality of the power of others and the necessary limitations of one's own. Related to this is the central importance of accommodation in classical realist thought (and it is on this basis that realists chastise the utopians and idealists). Second is that politics matters: both domestic and international. That is, choices made by states are affected by what goes on inside of them, and choices made by states are also affected by choices made by other states. Related to this, as illustrated in chapter 2, is the fundamental indeterminacy of structural analysis: in systems with small numbers (duopolies or oligopolies in economics, bipolarity or multipolarity in international politics), it is simply impossible to predict basic behavioral choices on the abstract—tastes, preferences, and designs will vary from state to state, just as they will across individual consumers or competing firms. Those choices will be shaped by the incentives presented by the decisions made by others. Since politics matters, and policies can be chosen, despite the fact that anarchy and the balance of power must powerfully inform state behavior, there are a number of very distinct trajectories along which the foreign policy of a great power can develop. For classical realism, the future is unwritten, and so wise policy matters.

Nevertheless, classical realism expects nothing but trouble from a rising China (and anticipates clumsiness from the United States in responding to that challenge). For even though states behaving as Mearsheimer expects them to act look like they are hopped up on a cocktail of steroids and amphetamines, their aggressive behavior is not some unhinged expression of belligerent rage but rather, according to his theory of offensive realism, is simply the outcome of rational, dispassionate calculation, motivated by nothing more than a desire to assure their own security.[43] Classical realists, on the other hand, see politics as the clash of interests, with states harboring competing ambitions and driven by political motivations and an appetite for power and primacy as ends in themselves, not simply reflecting instincts for self-protection. States are certainly well aware that they must provide for their own security in an anarchic, self-help world, but the ambitions of great powers are stirred by more than that—they have a mindset well summarized by the title of Stanley Kubrick's first film, *Fear and Desire*. Great powers have the luxury of indulging their desires.[44]

Thus we are back to Gilpin, and his axiom that "as the power of a state increases, it seeks to extend . . . its political influence." Rising powers in particular are potential sources of instability because the self-definition of their interests will expand along with their increasing capabilities (and expectations of still greater power to come); classical realism also expects them to seek not just security but status, prestige, and even deference from others—ongoing disputations over competing interests, not because great powers feel vulnerable due to anarchy (no tragedies of circumstance here) but because great powers are ambitious, and there is typically no obvious point at which they might not want still more. Aron warned that world politics was a "game for gangsters"—and the desires of such outlaws are rarely satiated.[45]

And the ambition and the extending stride of emerging powers must inevitably encroach on someone else's toes. Worse still, of course, is the fact that those others, unfortunately, may see things differently; in addition, from a realist perspective, even if those toes remain unmolested, other states can't help but be wary of a rising power, simply because it represents, at the very least, the latent potential for such a threat. Thrown into this mix (and recall that here, crucially, classical realism parts company with hyper-rationalism and its misguided insistence that all actors read all shared information in exactly the same way) is the fact that states will routinely disagree—and not just about interests but also about narratives, history, legitimacy, and justice, as well as assessments of relative power, especially in the context of the great uncertainties associated with economic change.

States will have—and often be motivated by, and disagree about—contrasting historical narratives and their implications, which can make disputes more difficult to resolve. This can be reflected even in the subtleties of language. To speak of China's "rise" is suggestive of a threat to the status quo, whereas embracing, as many carefully do, the term "reemergence" of China as a great power implies more of a return to the normal order of things; after all, for hundreds of years, until the nineteenth century, east Asia was largely a Sino-centric system. More pointedly, few professors of Chinese foreign policy fail to vividly lecture their students on the role of the national narrative of "the century of humiliation" (China's degradation at the hands of Western and other outside powers such as Japan from the start of the opium wars in 1839 until the victory in 1949 of the communists in the Chinese civil war) in informing that country's foreign policy choices and its perception of the legitimacy of the international order.[46]

Thus as a general phenomenon and in particular circumstance, a classical realist perspective must be viscerally alarmed by the consequences of the rise of China, and it will anticipate increased and dangerous international political friction and contestation as a result. But such a perspective does not view war as inevitable, nor does it lead to the prescription of superficially obvious policy recommendations.

What's a Classical Realist to Do?
(I) The Instinct for Accommodation

Classical realists speak clearly and with one voice on the need to acknowledge the realities of power. Morgenthau, who considered the Soviet Union to be a present military threat (more present, more clearly defined, and more dangerous than anything China currently approaches), nevertheless wrote at the height of the Cold War—and the height of McCarthyism—that "military preparations must join hands with an accommodating diplomacy." Morgenthau's Cold War policy was rooted in general lessons: "We must be strong enough to resist aggression and wise enough to accommodate foreign interests which do not impinge upon our own," he explained, and urged policymakers to remember, above all, that "no nation's power is without limits, and hence that its policies must respect the power and interests of others." Kennan's perspective was similar. At the height of the same hysteria, he favored the (then scandalous) position of seating the Chinese communists at the UN but was "shouted down." For Kennan, what mattered was not what the United States might have wished for but what was, and the "significant reality was created when the Chinese communists overran the mainland of China." The realities of power had to be acknowledged, they could not be wished away; moreover, states with the capacity to do so will generally seek authority over local affairs. Thus Kennan, like Morgenthau, was also quick to support, recognize, and respect the spheres of influence of other great powers, even (especially) those of potential adversaries.[47]

E. H. Carr was, if anything, the realist champion not simply of the need to acknowledge power but of the wisdom—indeed the imperative—of accommodating rising power. Recall in particular his admonition that the maintenance of international order as the underlying balance of power shifted requires that those at the top make "sufficient concessions."[48] Carr's advice—the central theme of his foundational book—is illustrative of the incoherence of offensive realism. Mearsheimer considers *The Twenty Years' Crisis* to be "a seminal realist work," and he defines Carr "as a realist on the basis of his arguments" in that book, which is also why, he explains, Carr "is widely—and correctly—seen as a realist." Mearsheimer, an often condescending critic of liberalism, enthusiastically celebrates Carr for exposing "the utopian," who "believes in the possibility of more or less radically rejecting reality, and substituting his utopia for it by an act of will," thus committing the cardinal sin "of ignoring power almost completely."[49]

But just who is the utopian here? Who is ignoring power, and hoping to reject reality—those who would seek to stop the rise China, or those who would acknowledge reality and seek to find a way to best accommodate it? In cheerleading for confrontation with China, Mearsheimer turns Carr's advice on its head. In its policy prescriptions offensive realism is in fact a form of utopianism, ignoring the realities of power—and as such it is as reckless and irresponsible as those who would unilaterally disarm when confronted with a mortal threat and simply hope for the best. China's power has increased; realism demands that stubborn fact be acknowledged and reckoned with. Carr's perspective on such issues is worth plainly repeating, as it is unambiguous—and the opposite of Mearsheimer's: "defense of the status quo is not a policy which can be lastingly successful. It will end in war as surely as rigid conservatism will end in revolution." Thus wisdom requires "adjustment to the changes of the balance of power"—which, again, must come from the top: "Those who profit most by that order can in the long run only hope to maintain it by making sufficient concessions" if there is to be any hope that inevitable adjustments will take place "as far as possible in an orderly way."[50]

As discussed in chapter 3, classical realists such as Carr and Kennan were so committed to the notion of acknowledging the realities of power that they foolishly supported the disastrous Munich accords. Carr saw the agreement as an exemplar of the mechanism for peaceful change that he was advocating. For Kennan, applying an icy logic, Czechoslovakia was "a central European state. Its fortunes must in the long run lie with—and not against—the dominant forces in this area." Adjusting to this "painful" reality was a better solution than "the romantic one of hopeless resistance."[51] But this massive blunder is instructive in three ways. First, as illustrated previously, Munich reveals the follies of structuralism: it was only possible to support the accords if one embraced the willful blindness of that approach and looked exclusively at the distribution of power. Structuralism, necessarily and by design, failed to understand the nature and intentions of the Nazi regime—whereas classical realism insists that content and purpose matter, factors which will vary from case to case.[52] Second, Munich illustrates the classical rejection of the notion that there are off-the-shelf rules that are applicable in every situation. There is no "one-size-fits-all" foreign policy—the particular context always matters. Third, and relatedly, the central role of context underscores the witlessness of invoking Munich as proving the "failure" of the strategy of accommodation more generally. Morgenthau, in contrast to Carr and Kennan, was exactly right about Munich—but the catastrophe of that blunder did not change his perspective on the importance, more generally, for the need to respect and accommodate power whenever circumstances would safely permit it. He was a consistent and vehement critic of "the crusader," for whom "compromise is a synonym for appeasement," and thus foolishly abandons the "middle ground of compromise and peaceful settlement." Never wavering in his harsh critique of the Munich accords, Morgenthau was nevertheless tellingly dismissive of those who would subsequently trot out the Munich trope to discredit all attempts at accommodation. He quoted Winston Churchill's 1950 speech before the House of Commons approvingly: "Appeasement in itself may be good or bad according to the circumstances. Appeasement from weakness and fear is alike futile and fatal. Appeasement from strength is magnanimous and noble and might be the surest and perhaps the only path to world peace." Morgenthau, of course, could not possibly have had offensive realism in mind when he argued, repeatedly, in favor of the need to recognize the power and interests of others, but as a withering indictment of Mearsheimer's general argument he could not have been more on target. In 2010, Mearsheimer pointedly borrowed the title of the first volume of Winston Churchill's history of World War II, *The Gathering Storm* (which reviewed the inexorable rise of the Nazi threat and the appalling failure of the British policy of appeasement to meet that mortal challenge), to insist, yet again, on the inevitability that "China cannot rise peacefully."[53]

In sum, naive idealists come in many stripes: not all of them are doe-eyed well-wishers; some are dangerous crusaders who have a cavalier attitude regarding the inherent limits of power and a lack of appreciation for the ubiquity of politics (and in particular, that actions will have consequences). Offensive realism is more reckless than realist, but rejecting a strategy of obstinate confrontation does not assure a smooth path forward. As noted in chapter 3, Gilpin, anticipating a clash between obstreperous newcomers and stubborn, satisfied guardians of the status quo, summarizes (and endorses) Carr's position as holding that the leading state, not the challenger, has "a moral obligation to make the greater concessions." Yet he is pessimistic about the willingness of established great powers to choose this path, which can be "politically difficult" for a great power long accustomed to getting its way. As always, hubris is a perennial problem for great powers. Moreover, in such settings there is often plenty of hubris to go around, as rising powers, often enjoying a string of successes and sensing that the tide of history is on their side, can also be quite arrogant as well. (A reminder that if there is a "Thucydides Trap," it does not derive from the risk of sleepwalking into unwanted war but from the boisterous overconfidence of great powers too eager to sow their wild oats.) And in addition to hubris, there is fear—what I earlier dubbed the "hubris/fear paradox": great powers are reluctant to make concessions when flush with confidence, dismissing emerging rivals as transient whippersnappers; but then, and not without reason, once it becomes indisputable that the balance of power has shifted to their disfavor, they come to fear that offering concessions and compromise will only signal weakness and encourage the rising power to demand even more.[54]

What's a Classical Realist to Do? *(II) The Primacy of Politics*

Ultimately, offensive realism and classical realism are fundamentally incompatible due to the specious determinism of the former. As emphasized in chapter 2, classical realists emphasize uncertainty—the essentially unknowability of what is coming next, even in a probabilistic sense (though Mearsheimer dispenses even with probabilistic outcomes, insisting that his projected outcomes will necessarily happen). The gap between risk and uncertainty—as emphasized in economics by Keynes, Knight, and Hayek and in IR theory central to the writings of Morgenthau and Aron among others—is unbridgeable, and uncertainty in particular and essentially leaves space for a wide variety of plausible choices and outcomes.[55] Classical realism also parts company with offensive realism with its view that, in a world of multiple possible futures, politics matters in shaping those potential trajectories. Domestic politics matters (recall the malleability of the national interest from chapter 4), and, in turn, international politics, including the consequences of wise or clumsy diplomacy, can create (or foreclose) opportunities, and at times incentivize the belligerent foreign policy choices of others by reducing the opportunity costs of pursuing them. Ultimately the theory of offensive realism offers dangerous and self-defeating policy advice to both China and the United States; in a world where politics matters and state choices shape systemic pressures, offensive realism is less a predictive theory revealing deterministic factors tragically beyond the influence of any state than it is an impetuous prescription that promises a dystopic, self-fulfilling prophecy. History is littered with horrors that need not have been, and which were made more likely by poor policies, not irresistible forces.

The foreign policy horrors of the interwar years need not have been. Classical realism can distinguish between Weimar Germany and Nazi Germany, and the Japan of the 1920s from the Japan of the 1930s—structural realism cannot. But the fragilities of the 1920s, followed by the Great Depression and the collapse of the global economy in the 1930s, shifted the domestic balance of power within societies away from moderate forces and contributed to (which is not to say it caused) the rise of fascism. The failure to reintegrate Germany into and actively repair the shattered European economy after World War I exacerbated and accelerated the economic stresses of the 1920s (first hyperinflation, then depression) that made a radicalization of German politics highly likely. The experience of interwar Japan is especially illustrative of the need to understand politics and history, in particular with regard to how economic and political changes polarized its domestic society, conflicts that were exacerbated by economic policy choices and then magnified by the global financial crisis of 1931. Any attempt to explain Japanese foreign policy choices in the late 1930s, and especially the early 1940s, that does not attend to these crucial factors will be woefully incomplete. Yet it is all too common for structuralist accounts (such as Allison's, in *Destined for War*) to center the narrative much too late, and focus on the proximate rather than the essential underlying causes of this cataclysmic, calamitous upheaval in world politics.

A closer look at this important episode underscores the need to carefully attend to the relevant history, with a sensitivity to the role that domestic conflict, contestation of strategic vision, and contingency play in shaping the trajectory of foreign policy. Japan in the 1920s was an emerging great power and, as realists would anticipate, one that had not been shy about using force to advance its interests, as witnessed by the Sino-Japanese War in 1895, the Russo-Japanese War in 1905, and its measured, productive association with the allied powers during World War I. Nevertheless, there was a fundamental difference between Japanese foreign policy and purpose in the 1920s and the 1930s.[56] In the 1920s, with the blessing of influential affiliates in the West, Japan aspired to emerge as a responsible great power in the international system, not without notable ambitions, but which were in accordance with and in the context of the norms and conceptions of legitimacy of the era. Outward-oriented economic interests in Japan were able to access international financial markets and, importantly, international allies in the United States and Britain, and this helped them achieve considerable influence in shaping Japanese foreign policy. American international bankers, eager to support their Japanese counterparts and encourage liberalism and openness in Japan, not only extended credit to the Japanese government but used their influence at home to help ensure that Japan's political concerns would be represented in international negotiations, such as those that led to the Washington Naval Treaty of 1922.[57] The radical, aggressive turn in Japanese foreign policy a decade later was not preordained, nor was it a function of the country's growing power—it was the result of bitterly contested domestic political conflicts. The outcome of these conflicts, and with it the trajectory of Japanese foreign policy, could have broken in either direction, but for the consequences of the Great Depression and the global financial crisis of 1931, which decisively tipped the domestic balance of political power and formatively contributed to the radicalization of the country.[58] In addition, each of the two moments in the 1930s when Japan's imperial ambitions leapt disastrously forward, in 1931 and 1937, were associated with violent domestic political crises that were resolved in ways that enhanced the power and authority of militarists within the country.

In both decades, economic and foreign policies were intimately intertwined, and economic conflicts within the country (and the erosion of its social economy) mirrored differences of opinion over foreign policy. Japan emerged from the Great War as a nascent, partial democracy, and in the 1920s parliamentary power passed back and forth between two dominant political parties; during those years the preferences of the modernizing, internationally oriented urban centers shaped the overall direction of public policy.[59] As with most European societies, a lodestar of economic policy was the desire to restore the gold standard, which had been suspended during World War I. Thus during the 1920s, usually directed by the influential Ministry of Finance and its allies in the Bank of Japan, government spending was kept in check—in particular, military spending was scaled back from its wartime highs and then held steady at a moderate level. A grand strategy that avoided unnecessary arms races with the Western powers went hand in hand with this broader economic vision.[60] Under the guidance of influential figures such as Bank of Japan governor Inoue Junnosuke, working with like-minded international bankers such as J. P. Morgan chief executive Thomas Lamont and Benjamin Strong (the powerful governor of the Federal Reserve Bank of New York), many Japanese elites saw in naval arms reduction talks a broader "Washington System" that would integrate Japan as a prominent hub in a larger, harmonious international financial order. This vision reached its apogee in 1929 as (then finance minister) Inoue announced his plans to finally restore the gold standard on January 1, 1930. His party returned to power having campaigned on an enmeshed policy cocktail of economic austerity, arms control, conciliation (and caution regarding China policy)—and the promise to return to gold.[61]

That restoration, however, would come at price—it would require austerity and costly deflation, in the form of further cuts to government spending and additional interest rate increases, which amounted to nothing less than an engineered recession. Inoue understood this, as did his allies; as one prominent banker explained at the time, "adjustment could not be achieved without great hardships; good medicine is bitter to the taste." But the return to the gold standard was an economic disaster and a political catastrophe. It was, to say the least, very poorly timed, coinciding with the advent of the worldwide Great Depression (not an ideal time for austerity), and it unleashed a fundamental domestic political crisis in Japan because those who were expected to bear the costs of austerity had already suffered a decade of economic distress.[62]

In aggregate, Japan's economy performed well over the course of the 1920s. But as is often the case, the overall growth of national income is a misleading statistic, and almost invariably, it masks politically consequential distinctions. (And as discussed in chapter 5, it would be a mistake to disregard domestic social-economic issues in explaining a state's behavior in the international arena, in the 1930s—or the 2020s.) Thus although many in the country, especially in the urban industrial sectors, did extremely well in the 1920s, at the same time, the agricultural sector suffered enormously. In the second half of the decade, the real income of the average farmer fell by over 30 percent, a staggering decline. Since in 1930 agriculture still accounted for half of Japan's employment, for a very large segment of Japanese society life was, as one study described, "hard and miserable." Rural depression, combined with industrial consolidation, contributed to the emergence of a "dual structure" to the Japanese economy, characterized by increased disparities in the distribution of wealth and well-being.[63]

The crisis in agriculture served to promote the radicalization of the armed forces, especially among younger officers who had only recently left their homes in the farming villages. Not surprisingly, economic policies that purposefully orchestrated an economic slowdown into the teeth of the deepening international depression at the dawn of the 1930s only served to heighten these tensions even further.[64] With the great slump agricultural prices fell still further, as they did throughout the world. Broad sectors of the Japanese economy were negatively affected—with agriculture leading the way. Average household income fell from an already low ¥1,326 in 1929 to an impossibly threadbare ¥650 in 1931.[65]

And things would only get worse. In 1931, a financial crisis triggered by the failure of the leading bank in Austria spread across the European continent, as the financial panic quickly moved on to Germany—what Keynes would describe as "the shattering German crisis," a banking crisis that was "precipitated, no doubt, by political events and political fears." Upending German finance, the panic continued apace, and dramatically, in September, Britain was forced off the gold standard in the absence of a temporary wartime suspension for the first time in two centuries. It is hard to overstate the domestic and international political consequences of the 1931 global financial crisis. During the initial Austrian turmoil, which would implicate affiliated German banks, financial journalist Paul Einzig presciently warned that a "collapse of the Reichsmark is certain to bring about a complete political upheaval in Germany. It is highly probable that the extreme nationalists or the communists will then acquire power." The crisis, the collapse of the international financial system, and the fall into the abyss of the Great Depression could not but upend already fragile domestic political orders. In the words of Zara Steiner, "The annus terribilis, 1931, was the watershed year that unleashed a systemic crisis of unexpected depth and severity." Thus although much emphasis has been placed, and not unreasonably, on the trauma of the Great War, the embittering peace, and then the hyperinflation of 1923 in utterly dislocating Germany's political stability, nevertheless, as is widely understood, it took the Great Depression and the global financial crisis to bring the Nazis to power.[66]

A similar tragedy was brewing in Japan. The government, having longed for so many years to restore the gold standard, would not soon abandon it without a fight. Even after Britain's unprecedented suspension of convertibility Inoue would not follow suit, pursuing instead still more austerity, cutting spending further, and raising interest rates in October and again in November, triggering a major political crisis.[67] As the Finance Ministry planned to cut defense spending, in September the military initiated the "Mukden Incident," sabotaging the South Manchurian Railway and blaming Chinese forces for the alleged provocation, which it used as a pretext to unleash a full-scale Japanese invasion of Manchuria. No longer willing to have issues of national security beholden to concerns for financial authority, the military raced ahead with an imperial project designed to change the facts on the ground. Meanwhile, on the home front, in October, a plot by mid-level officers to overthrow the government was exposed, and in November Prime Minister Hamaguchi was shot by a militarist dissident. The grave wounds Hamaguchi suffered removed him from the political scene and sent the government into disarray—it would collapse in the following month, setting the stage for new elections which took place in an increasingly dangerous and chaotic environment. Campaigning in February, Inoue was murdered by a radicalized urban refugee from the rural depression; weeks later the director of the Mitsui Bank was gunned down outside of its Tokyo headquarters. Finally, on May 15, 1932, Prime Minister Inukai himself was assassinated by a group of young military officers, precipitating the resignation of his entire cabinet and bringing an end to the era of party government in Japan—although civilian officials serving in military-led cabinets retained considerable influence over the next five years.[68]

Of those civilians, the most important was the venerable Korekiyo Takahashi, who in the tumult of 1932 assumed the still powerful and independent office of finance minister. It can be argued that Takahashi single-handedly pulled the Japanese economy out of the depression with a package of policies that would have been endorsed by Keynes: immediately breaking with the gold standard, slashing interest rates, and rapidly increasing government borrowing and spending. The economy quickly powered forward, growing at over 4 percent annually from 1932 through 1936, with improvements in the (still lagging) agricultural sector buttressed by special expenditures earmarked for emergency relief. Military spending also increased, more than doubling within five years, from ¥462 million in 1931 to ¥1,089 million in 1936.[69]

Unfortunately, Takahashi's economic successes did not resolve the deep, underlying social-political tensions seething in Japan, and once again a domestic political crisis and confrontation—the outcome of which was not inevitable—was resolved in favor of the most radical elements in Japanese society and associated with another giant step forward in its aggressive imperial ambitions. Under the finance minister's guidance, increases in military spending slowed and then finally leveled off by the middle of the decade. Takahashi, who had faithfully served his country for decades (he traveled to London to successfully raise funds for Japan's war against Russia in 1905), was no wide-eyed militarist—he was a pragmatist, and a thoughtful proto-Keynesian. Increasing military spending initially helped stimulate the economy, but within a few years he assessed that the economy was approaching capacity and risked overheating, and so following the same logic he cooled the jets of his economic stimulus. Takahashi now only grudgingly—and with accompanying public lectures about the need for financial prudence—doled out modest increases to the defense budget. The armed forces were not pleased with this turn of events, nor were the still struggling agricultural communities. In an increasingly tense and heated political environment, elections were called for February 1936—and to the surprise of many, the results delivered a major endorsement of the course that Takahashi was steering. But just four days after the votes were counted, on February 26, over one thousand troops, led by junior officers who hailed from the rural districts of Japan, attempted to overthrow the government. The eighty-two-year-old Takahashi was among those assassinated, murdered in his sleep to shouts of "Traitor!" and "Heavenly Punishment!" The coup attempt ultimately failed, but the political consequences of the incident and the practical and symbolic implications of the murder of Takahashi were profound—civilian authority would no longer check the ambitions of the military.[70]

Civilians still served as cabinet ministers and in the Diet, but the military (and the militants) was now firmly in the driver's seat. A hand-picked yes-man was installed at the Ministry of Finance, and military spending suddenly tripled in one year (to ¥3,299 million in 1937—it would double again from there within two years). Macroeconomic policies would become so reckless that it was necessary to increasingly enforce draconian regulations and controls that detached Japan's economy from the pressures of international market forces. A final prospect that the military might be checked in its ambitions occurred in April 1937, the last competitive elections in Japan until after the Pacific war. The political parties drew strong support in the election, suggesting that alternatives to military rule were still plausible. But again the military would take matters into its own hands. The army's further expansion of the China war with the attack at the Marco Polo Bridge on July 7, 1937, effectively ended whatever remained of the ability of civilian politicians to circumscribe the ambitions of Japan's military leaders.[71] Japan's brutal and barbaric attempt to conquer all of China (the blood-soaked Nanking massacre would take place before the year was out), and its affinities and ultimate alliance with Nazi Germany, would necessarily place it on a collision course with the western European powers and the clinging-to-neutrality United States.[72]

It need not have been. Japan's road to the Pacific war was paved by bitter domestic contestation, the misguided dedication to economic orthodoxy which polarized and radicalized its society, and the exogenous shocks of the Great Depression and the global financial crisis. Other visions of Japanese grand strategy and competing definitions of its national interest were articulated and advocated, and had considerable political support—and would have served Japan better. Ultimately the choice to embrace dreams of vast militarized conquest which led to the country's ruinous wars was determined not by a trap set by changing power dynamics (given the power of the United States at the time, that case very poorly fit Allison's model), nor was it the inevitable result of the imperatives of security seeking (contra the insistence of the theory of offensive realism, it was surely not fear for Japan's own security that led Japanese militarists to zealously aspire to conquer all of China)—but by dysfunctional domestic politics and a harrowingly disfiguring international economic disaster.

Classical Realism: In Search of the Least Bad Option

A key theme of this chapter has been that although a classical realist analysis of the emergence of China as a great power must be even more pessimistic than structural realist perspectives, it is nevertheless considerably more measured in its implied policy advice than that which is commonly associated with approaches labeled "realist." Offensive realism anticipates an inevitable, militarized drive for regional hegemony by China, which will necessarily be vigorously countered by the United States. A deterministic model, it nevertheless also forcefully advocates both for China's aggressive bid and for an assertive American response. Shallow structuralist readings of Thucydides see a great risk that changing power dynamics will lead states to sleepwalk into an unnecessary war, yielding policy advice that essentially amounts to "do better than others did in the past" and "avoid foolish mistakes." Both of these approaches see a possible war between the United States and China as the result of a tragedy—from the latter perspective, it would be the result of (largely the United States) clumsily stumbling into an avoidable trap; in former case, due to nothing more than the desire of each side (but especially China) to survive with their sovereignty and autonomy intact and secure in an anarchic world.

A classical analysis roots the problem not in tragedy but in hubris and fear: that it is very likely a rising China will become increasingly arrogant and throw its weight around, and that the United States, accustomed to being the superpower in a one-superpower world, will be first too arrogant and then too anxious to take the measures necessary to address the realities of the changes to the international balance of power. Nevertheless, with regard to policy prescriptions, given its emphasis on uncertainty, contingency, and the notion that politics and policy choices matter in shaping behavior and incentives, classical realism reaches for its traditional policy tool of accommodation. In particular, it flatly rejects the propositions of offensive realism that it is in China's interest to embark on a militarized bid for hegemony, and its urgent admonition that the United States do everything it can to "make sure that China does not become a peer competitor"—advice that, as discussed, is suspect (at best) in its logic and, ironically, rooted in utopianism, an attempt to reshape the world as one would like to see it, rather than respecting the realities of power.[73]

Calls for prudence, of course, are easier said than done. In the first decade of the twenty-first century, a weighing of the evidence regarding and prospects for various options yielded classical realist policy advice that was not all that far from the suggestions of liberal internationalism.[74] Aggressive measures designed to derail China's economic growth (the underlying engine of its emerging power) would damage the global economy and thus be narrowly self-harming, politically self-defeating more generally (by angering the many countries whose economies would suffer "collateral damage" from that effort), and, even if successful (not a sure thing), a self-fulfilling prophecy, assuring that China would become a wounded, hostile, dangerous, implacable adversary.[75] The much wiser strategy—the best bet available—would be to craft policies that might incentivize China to emerge as a great power within the existing American-led international order, with the additional hope that such a trajectory would empower actors and interests within the country that saw China's interests as best served by foreign policies that leaned toward cooperation and engagement.

The second decade of the century, however, was not kind to this perspective. Domestic politics matter, and they have been most unforgiving. Internally, China has taken a hard, personalist-authoritarian turn, which must be seen as concerning for the trajectory of its foreign policy posture. In the United States, tectonic shifts within its polity embarrass the notion of integrating China into an internationally oriented, liberal international order—if anything, the Americans themselves have renounced their interest in leading or even participating in that order.[76] The robustness of this rejectionist turn should not be underestimated, as it is manifested not in the (arguably fluke) outcome of the U.S. general election of 2016 but as seen in the watershed nominating processes of each of America's two predominant political parties in that fateful year. Fighting two long, losing wars, decades of widening income inequality and stagnant middle-class incomes, and, finally, the consequences of the great recession that followed the global financial crisis of 2008 collectively shattered the internationalist consensus that had for generations been embraced by the mainstream elites of both parties.[77]

Where do these changes leave classical realism on China and accommodation? In essentially the same moody place, if perhaps gloomier still. Rising powers are likely to be obtuse, self-righteous and dangerous (such are the luxuries of having too much security), but China remains unlikely to be as foolish and irrational as to try to achieve regional hegemony by serially invading its regional adversaries. The greater danger—following the analytical lead of Morgenthau and Kennan—is that China might come to *politically* dominate all of East Asia, as its neighbors and would-be adversaries choose to bandwagon with the greatest power in the region. This outcome would most likely be the result of revised political calculations, not military conquest. And unlike the more distant danger of a major, shooting war for conquest, this is a real prospect that would be contrary to the interests of the United States.

Both the principal challenge to the United States and the classical realist prescription for how it should respond remain political. The military element cannot be disregarded, and given the emergence of new challenges, the United States would of course be wise to reevaluate the scope of its global commitments. (Given changes to world energy markets and global political developments, there is a strong case for ending American security commitments in the Persian Gulf region and redeploying its forces elsewhere.) In any event, with regard to the China challenge the realities of power will almost certainly require a recognition that the United States will not be able to as freely impose its will in the western Pacific Ocean to the extent that it did in the past. But despite the need to respect the changing correlates of forces and military capabilities, the outcome of any competing clash of interests between the United States and China will largely be determined by politics. The primary American regional priority, then, should be to try to prevent widespread regional bandwagoning with China. This requires not joining a contest for regional military supremacy (which the realities of economics and geography suggest would be an expensive and unlikely prospect) but sustaining sufficient regional capabilities and engagement to provide local actors with the confidence to resist China's efforts at political domination.

This would involve maintaining and nurturing its regional security alliances with Japan and South Korea, and increasingly (if often implicitly) coordinating with other regional actors including Vietnam and India. From a classical realist perspective it is in the U.S. national interest for Asia not to fall under the political domination of any single power, but that does not (and should not) require an aggressive policy of active confrontation or vigorous containment to make that unwelcome prospect less likely. It will, however, require embracing a foreign policy guided by the far-sighted pursuit of Wolfers's milieu goals, rather than a shortsighted, transactionalist approach to foreign policy and alliance relations. Given the changes in its domestic political disposition—and again, as Morgenthau and Kennan routinely bemoaned during what now seem like much less dysfunctional times—it is not clear that the United States retains the capacity to chart such a sophisticated course of action. And if the Americans are out, then all bets are off.

CHAPTER SEVEN

Power, Politics, and Prospect

THE CRAFT OF CLASSICAL REALISM

IT WILL NEVER be a science. And wishing that it was will not make it so. And trying to act like it is one will be bound to fail and, worse, misdirect inquiry into unproductive directions and lead to basic analytical errors. A fundamental point of departure for realism is that world politics can be unforgiving. To this classical realism adds: the same is true of its study. The effort to describe, understand, explain, and anticipate behavior in world politics is, to invoke a cliché, more of a journey than a destination. And one in which chasing the horizon of certainty will prove more exhausting than enlightening. The limits of what we can know are often discouraging—but they are also disciplining, and suggest productive paths forward for essential inquiries.

International relations takes place in an environment of uncertainty, and students of world politics, striving, appropriately, to understand patterns of behavior and to reach, to the extent that it is possible, generalizable conclusions, are nevertheless confronted with vexing problems. Those challenges include the instability of behavioral relationships between variables over time and the fact that the unpredictable choices made by states—choices that are surely influenced by material constraints, but which are fundamentally shaped by their understood domestic political-social context and filtered through perceived lessons of history—in turn influence and elicit a range of plausible responses from others. And then finally and always there are the inescapable consequences of the ketchup allegory: actors will respond differently—even with regard to the most basic behavioral choices—when presented with the same stimuli, because they will have different tastes, preferences, and values. Nor will those choices and reactions be obvious in advance. As Hans Morgenthau put it, definitively, "since man is largely ignorant of his own future reactions, how can he know more about the reactions of his fellow-men?" Similarly, interpretations of historical events, which, as seen in the examples throughout this book, will have a formative influence on behavior, will also vary. Following Raymond Aron, it is "incontestable" that there are many different possible interpretations of history, and as such, specific knowledge of the distinct attributes of the actor is necessary to grasp the "intelligibility of a historical act." In sum, most questions of international politics, most of the time—and invariably the most important ones—are concerned with the particular behavior of a specific actor at a critical time, not the average reaction of an imagined median actor under everyday circumstances. For students of world politics, there is little value in being able to make an informed guess about the color of a ball drawn randomly from a vast urn of known contents.[1]

Parsimony is a welcome attribute for any scholarly endeavor, especially one that hopes to speak to the real world and communicate ideas to non-specialists. To the extent that more can be explained with less, that is something to be embraced—enthusiastically, and without inhibition. For example, even though classical realist analysis expects the clash of interests between states to be inevitable and unending, with events and outcomes buffeted by innumerable factors, many unknown and unknowable, students of international politics are wise indeed to see any such conflict through the powerful lens of the security dilemma, and understand how geography and technology will inform its intensity. The security dilemma is a simple and handy tool, one that will commonly and in general application offer basic insights into the nature of a given contestation between actors and the likelihood that such a dispute will spill over into war. For example, the fortunes of geography and presence of robust nuclear deterrence explain why the security dilemma between the United States and China in the twenty-first century is less intense than the one between Britain and Germany before World War I (although in the former case, should an international crisis erupt in the western Pacific, the prospect of a perceived tactical advantage to striking first has potentially alarming implications).

However, it must always be understood that parsimony is about "*explaining more* with less." All too often, especially since the rise and dominance of structuralism and hyper-rationalism, scholarship has chased the big brass ring of "with less"—turning a blind eye to whether or not the analysis is, in fact, "explaining more." It has been the contention of this book that structural realism—looking exclusively at states in the system as like actors distinguished only by their relative capabilities—is utterly and irretrievably incapable, on its own, of explaining behavior in world politics; and, additionally, that models based on the assumption of hyper-rationality (rooted in the deductively dubious and empirically embarrassed theory of Rational Expectations) will routinely fail to understand choices made by states, and more generally is an approach singularly unsuited to apply in moments of international crisis and war (that is, at exactly those moments when IR theory is most needed). It can also be observed that other popular varieties of inquiry in contemporary IR scholarship often reach for quick and easy devices—techniques that are nifty, clever, elegant, and available at one's fingertips and ready for quick application to any problem that might cross the mind, or the front page of today's newspaper. But understanding and explaining world politics does not come that easily.[2]

This is not intellectual nihilism—it is analytical modesty.[3] And the enterprise of classical realism is ambitious, and the need for productive scholarship in IR remains essential—lives are actually at stake in getting the best answers to the questions that it faces. The paths to follow for the study of world politics have been forged by Alfred Marshall, with his emphasis on "partial equilibrium" analysis (which, it has been argued here, in the inescapable absence of a fundamental, general equilibrium theory of politics and war, students of IR must adopt), and Charles Kindleberger, with his appeal to a "tool kit" of trusty instruments, a metaphor that classical realism eagerly seeks to embrace and deploy. The introduction of these reliable, well-honed tools can help us understand problems and puzzles in world politics that are distinct in context and setting but nevertheless can be recognized as variations on phenomena that in one form or another have attributes that are generally recurring. Deploying these tools judiciously to better describe, understand, explain, and anticipate events in international relations is the craft of classical realism—a practice tempered, always, by Kennan's admonition that we are gardeners, not mechanics. Gardeners can tell you lots of important technical and easily measurable things about sunlight and soil and rainfall and infestations and blights—but they also rely heavily on experience, wisdom, judgment, and situationally specific understandings and improvisation.

This approach involves dirty hands and common frustrations, as intelligibility often slips through the fingers, with confident conclusions routinely receding from reach as circumstances unexpectedly change (or new evidence about historical episodes comes to light, requiring reassessments). And these challenges are only compounded further by the constant struggle for the analysist to be on guard against the skewing bias of their own ingrained, implicit dispositions, assumptions, and values. As Aron described of his experiences in Germany, as the Weimar Republic disintegrated, his goal was "to understand or know my time as honestly as possible, without ever losing awareness of the limits of my knowledge." This is a challenge "modern" approaches too easily elide but to which classical realism is notably alert; it fundamentally suffuses the perspectives of Niebuhr, Carr, and the foundational thinkers of the paradigm more generally.[4] One again, much of this roots back to the unbridgeable gap, emphasized especially by Morgenthau, between the natural and the social sciences: "the analogy between the natural and social world is mistaken." Newtonian physics can tell us why and how the apple will fall from the tree. "The social sciences," in contrast, "are in doubt as to the occurrence not only of the causes but also of the effects, once a cause has taken place."[5] In sum, it is certainly the case that natural scientists tend to be very smart, and they have accomplished great things. But in many ways, they have it easy: the clarity, the finality, the airtight proofs—these are attributes to be envied but not misappropriated by social scientists toiling in very different pastures.

With some final elaboration of the distinct insights that can be provided by a classical realist approach, this concluding chapter also ties together some of the strands that have woven throughout this book. Revising the implications of anarchy, the discussion here also engages not just how the absence of a singular global authority defines the space in which actors must pursue their security and their interests but also how the presence of ungoverned spaces and power vacuums informs realist wariness about the dangers of the world. The prospects of pitiless anarchy and the very strong tendency for power vacuums to invite their exploitation also inform debates about realist "prudence" in theory and the twenty-first-century arguments about "restraint" and American grand strategy in particular. In evaluating such choices, it must be understood that power withdrawn will create opportunities for other political actors to extend their influence, factors that must be weighted in assessing the costs and benefits of any overarching foreign policy disposition. And perhaps most pointedly, from a classical realist perspective, to even contemplate the practice of "grand strategy" returns to the notion that both power and purpose matter—and that an understanding of power is not possible without attending to the distinction between underlying or even apparent material power and the ability to actualize that power; and that both power and purpose are essentially informed by variables such as domestic social cohesion (and its unraveling). In particular and illustratively, the comprehensive and catastrophic collapse of French power in the 1930s cannot be understood without an appreciation of the central role played by the hollowing out of French society in the years leading up to that fateful moment—a conclusion that is suggestive of deeply concerning implications for the United States ninety years later. Neither the formation of the American order nor its unraveling after three-quarters of a century can be understood in purely material terms.

Bringing It All Back Home: Anarchy, Power, and Purpose

Realism tends to emphasize the consequences of anarchy not simply because, with most perspectives on international politics, it is attentive to the implication that a self-help system must shape the behavior of states but also because, following Hobbes, realism tends to view anarchic spaces with enormous apprehension. Anarchy between states is a fundamentally different thing than anarchy between individuals (most importantly, because the weakest state is much more secure than the strongest person), and a failure to understand this basic difference can lead to exaggerated notions of the dire consequences of anarchy for relations between states. But anarchy in this second conception—most likely to arise from the collapse of authority—can indeed be quite nasty and brutish, and also informs realist understandings of world politics.

Much of this derives from a wariness regarding what humans are capable of. Even if individuals, perhaps, are commonly guided by some sense of decency, it is important to understand, as Niebuhr emphasized, "the brutal character of the behavior of all human collectives."[6] And it may be that even individual humans are actually not so decent (not surprisingly, a realist disposition would err on the side of caution, and reserve judgment on the issue). One need not embrace Susan Sontag's perspective, when asked what she had learned from the Holocaust, "that 10 percent of any population is cruel, no matter what, and that 10 percent is merciful, no matter what, and that the remaining 80 percent could be moved in either direction," although there are famously chilling findings in social psychology that seem to support such a contention. Nevertheless, realists tend to hold the view that humans are dangerous, have an enormous capacity for savagery, and will voluntarily participate in orchestrated acts of barbarism—especially if that behavior seems to be what is more generally accepted by the society or group with which they identify. As Tolstoy warned, "there are no conditions to which a man may not become accustomed, particularly if he sees that they are accepted by those around him."[7]

Because ungoverned, or at least unchecked, humans are capable of descending into barbarism, realist perspectives often favor the presence of power and authority, both within political entities and between them. With regard to the former, even in apparently ordered societies, the prospect of collapse—especially under situations of stress—is not to be disregarded. "Men will not always die quietly," Keynes warned in his much-misunderstood polemic, *The Economic Consequences of the Peace*, and "in their distress may overturn the remnants of organization, and submerge civilization itself." Moreover, when societies do fail—or when, more generally, for whatever reason power is withdrawn or recedes from a region or a political space—other actors, often ruthless, will rush to fill that political void. As emphasized repeatedly, classical realism avoids adopting the mechanisms of the natural sciences, but if there is one analogous metaphor it finds suggestive, it is that of equilibrium. Recall classical realism's expectation that actors are ambitious and opportunistic, and will seek to expand their power and authority—until checked by countervailing power. Once again Morgenthau is instructive: "The disenchanted sentimentalist and utopian cannot understand the elemental truth of international politics; that no nation can be so good as not to take advantage of a power vacuum."[8]

In international politics this informs the realist instinct that a "balance of power" is, in at least one important way, productive—by providing a check on the ambitions of others. Edmund Burke, illustratively, thought it was necessary that a defeated France be restored and recognized as a great power. (And as the convulsive Napoleonic Wars came to a close, ending, finally, in the decisive defeat of France, Metternich acted on similar instincts, proposing, as Kissinger lauded, "terms . . . more moderate than the military situation warranted, because Metternich was above all concerned that France remain a powerful weight in the European balance.") Checked power—even one's own—is power often exercised more responsibly, a quality not to be underestimated given the classical realist anticipation of ruinous hubris. During the early Cold War, when both Soviet power and ideology were taken seriously as each side jockeyed to showcase a model to be emulated by others, that competition had some salutary effects on American behavior. Concerns for the perception of its national image abroad, for example, created incentives to avoid practices that made capitalism seem like the Dickensian dystopia described by its critics and contributed an impetus to the federal government's receptivity to the civil rights movement.[9]

The shadow of the unknown, an acute sense that civilization is more fragile than might be thought, and the salience of the darker corners of anarchy all contribute to the realist instinct for prudence (a caution informed by an aversion to squander resources on foreign policy "luxuries"). They can also find expression in a certain type of conservatism—which is not necessarily an attractive characteristic, but nevertheless as always let us stare such unpleasant things in the face—one that places a value on order for order's sake, even at the expense of justice. It is important to emphasize that this is *not* a disposition necessarily inherent to classical realism—and certainly not as a method of inquiry, the primary concern throughout this book—nevertheless, especially in the spirit of chapter 4, this connection should be acknowledged and unpacked. The underlying logic derives from the agreeable notion that disorder is unwelcome, because people need to be able to get on with their lives with some confidence of safety and routine. This means the ability to conduct business at home, for example, with the expectation of some personal security and economic integrity—from roving bands of thugs, white-collar criminals, and ultimately from the armed agents of the state itself. The exposure to the former in particular often evokes a visceral reaction, as, when sufficiently frightened, most people will put up with a considerable extension of state authority in exchange for security (again, to some extent, this brings us all the way back to Hobbes and the unbearable misery of the state of nature). This sensibility has a parallel attribute with regard to foreign relations. In the name of their own security, countries looking abroad may be inclined to tolerate thuggish regimes (or worse), presuming that such governments will provide a level of order within their societies and predictability regarding their foreign policy behaviors, attributes that are preferable to disordered societies or failed states, which will be more susceptible to wild unpredictability in their external behavior and possibly present dangers. Thuggish states are also preferable to failed states in that, in theory, they can be deterred, because they can be held accountable for their actions (and even nefarious elites and cabals can be presumed to have a desire to retain their hold on power), whereas subgroups operating as freelance agents within ungoverned spaces can be harder to pin down. These unheroic, at times even shameful instincts to endure and even consort with evil are in some cases understandable from the imperative of state survival. But recall from chapter 4 that in practice, such concerns are very commonly used, especially by great powers, as disingenuous fig leaves to provide cover for utterly reprehensible foreign policy behaviors.

Nevertheless, civilizational frailty is not to be underestimated as a source of anxiety in an anarchic world. As the Soviet Union compellingly illustrated, even the greatest of powers can simply collapse, and in that disconcerting way that Hemingway described individuals can go bankrupt—gradually and then suddenly.[10] This requires and indeed demands an interrogation of how power is assessed and purpose is anticipated. Power as the measurement of the raw correlates of forces may lend itself to reasonably objective metrics. But the power that matters: the mobilization of power, the application of power, the ability to dedicate and apply that power to articulated ends—and to do so with patience and endurance—that is much more difficult to measure, and a function of things that material capabilities can't tell us. As suggested in chapter 5 (and, again, as the collapse of the Soviet Union should chastise), it can be a very leaky bucket from the gathering of raw power to the ability to bring that power to application, a process that will be shaped by domestic politics and domestic social forces.

And these factors of course will inform purpose, which is not reducible to power (and which can be skewed by civilizational decay). In international politics purpose without power is irrelevant, but understanding the implications of power without assessing purpose—and on a case-by-case basis—is not possible. Simple examples render this obvious: A man walks by carrying a gun. Is he a police officer, or an armed robber (or, in some instances, both)? A person in command of a fire hose can save children from a burning building, or unleash terrible force on peaceful protestors marching against racial injustice. As this book has stressed, material capability in and of itself is indeterminate. In a major contribution, Stephen Walt, trying to escape from the intellectual dead end of structural realism, revised the (underdetermining and empirically suspect) notion that states simply balance (when feasible) against the material power of others regardless of the return address, with the innovation that states balance against threats, not power.[11] But what is threatening? This is a thread that once tugged unravels the entire tapestry of analyses limited solely to material considerations. Purpose matters.

The Limits to Material Power: Interwar France

Ultimately, both power and purpose are informed by the robustness of a country's social structures, which can be more—or less—functional or thriving. A society in turmoil or distress may plausibly rally in defense against a common threat, but in general polarized or fragmenting or broadly dysfunctional societies will likely be less capable actors on the world stage, at least with regard to what might be expected of them based on their apparent underlying measurable power—in terms of both the choices selected and achievements attained. In extreme cases these divergences can be catastrophic. Interwar France, a civilization arguably in existential crisis, ultimately failed to rally even to its own defense against a mortally dangerous, plainly visible, and clearly understood enemy. The causes of France's stunning collapse on the battlefield are still debated, but there is little doubt that deep domestic social distress made that failure much more likely (both in the moment and with the astonishingly inadequate preparation in the years prior); and the effortlessness with which France so easily slipped into humiliating, blood-stained collaboration defies easy material explanation.[12] The experience of interwar France is rich with timeless relevance, illustrates the pressing need to appeal to classical realist tools for assessing power and politics, and is suggestive of deeply troubling implications for the United States a century later.

As was the case with Britain, and detailed in chapter 3, it is impossible to understand France in the interwar years without attending to the trauma of the Great War and its profound economic and social consequences. And France's immediate postwar years were difficult ones, as, essentially alone and largely unsuccessfully, it attempted to enforce the terms of the Versailles Treaty, efforts which included its disastrous, thirty-two-month occupation of the Ruhr region of Germany from January 1923. In the second half of the 1920s, however, France's position, assessed in material terms, was exceptionally secure, and its economic growth extraordinary (with boom years that rivaled the unprecedented, heady prosperity of the 1960s). Nevertheless, even those glory days masked growing and profound societal discontent and dysfunction, with deep divisions further exacerbated by the Great Depression, which, although less severe in France than elsewhere, was still difficult and bitter, and lingered much longer due to its misguided fetish for economic orthodoxy. Ideological support for the catastrophic, asphyxiating medicine of meeting depression with austerity was widespread in the country—but in addition, when necessary it was ultimately enforced by France's moneyed classes, which controlled the Bank of France and, when displeased, could bring down governments by withholding financial support or unleashing irresistible cascades of capital flight. And throughout these years, political polarization was such that bringing down left-leaning governments was perhaps the singular focus of the country's conservative actors, even if at the expense of what a disinterested outsider might describe as the country's national interest.

It was not a story that ended well. France's failure to meet the German challenge—a challenge to France's very existence—was a function of its internal disorder and atrophy.[13] Accounts that do not consider domestic factors simply cannot explain the often bizarre and self-defeating strategic, defense-related, and foreign policy choices made by France in the 1930s, rooted as they were in competing social visions, specious economic ideologies, and deep-seated domestic political conflicts.[14] For Raymond Aron, it was a deeply troubling time; he recalls "a country in decadence" as well as dysfunction. "Basically, France didn't exist any longer," he recalled. "It existed only in the hatred of the French for each other"—a jarring but common characterization of subsequent analytical accounts as well. The result, especially after 1934, was a "vicious circle" of economic distress, an "exacerbation of social conflicts, strengthening of revolutionary parties of right and left," and "paralysis of government."[15] Interwar France was indeed a deeply and profoundly troubled society—one account aptly described the nation in that era as characterized by "the embrace of unreason." The right was reactionary and in many quarters frankly anti-democratic; the left offered a bold if vaguely specified vision of a new and different France. Both sides saw the world through the lens of this basic domestic conflict, but as a practical matter, throughout the 1930s the reactionary right more than the impractical left drove the choices that led the country to disaster. The Republican Federation, composed of conservative parliamentarians affiliated with anti-Republican organizations and paramilitary groups, longed for a return to something akin to the royalist/authoritarian mid-nineteenth-century order. It was convinced that domestic social change was a grave threat to the essence of the nation, and that war would be an accelerant to unwelcome social upheaval.[16]

Retrospective analyses have the advantage of sober detachment and access to information unavailable to participants in the moment, but to really capture the "mood" of a nation—here this returns the analysis to an imprecise variable only accessible to approaches that leave room for "passions" in addition to interests in explaining behavior—reliable eyewitness accounts are of enormous value. Consider the perspective of renowned foreign correspondent William Shirer. In his view, in 1925 France was "the greatest power on the continent." Yet in the years that followed he "watched with increasing apprehension" as the Third Republic saw "its strength gradually sapped by dissention and division, by an incomprehensible blindness in foreign, domestic and military policy, by the ineptness of its leaders, the corruption of its press, and a feeling of growing confusion, hopelessness, and cynicism . . . of its people." Raymond Aron well captured this ambiance in a paper he presented in June 1939, in which he observed the extreme polarization and radicalization of politics in France, and concluded despairingly "a large part of public opinion in this country desires another form of government." Edmond Taylor, the head of the Paris bureau for the *Chicago Tribune* from 1933 to 1940, saw things similarly. When war finally came, he observed, "The vast majority answered the call to arms like somnambulists"; France responded to the German invasion stricken by symptoms of a "political malady" characterized by "apathy, absence of enthusiasm, uncertainty of aim," in a period that witnessed the "ideological collapse" of French democracy. Midway in the six-week period that marked the space between the German attack and the French surrender, France's interior minister told a visiting British general "there is no will to fight. . . . There has been a collapse of the whole French nation." As Paris fell, Shirer wrote in his diary, "What we're seeing here is the complete breakdown of French society—a collapse of the army, of government, of the morale of the people. It is almost too tremendous to believe." These sentiments were commonly shared by savvy political observers at the time.[17] It would be a mistake to disregard these essential insights simply because they are hard to measure.

And the fall of France was at the very least six years, not six weeks, in the making. Long-simmering tensions exploded on the streets of Paris in early 1934. From 1932, a series of centrist cabinets, intermittently with some minority socialist participation, struggled to guide the country through the early years of the depression, efforts that were ruthlessly undercut at almost every turn by the Bank of France, which preferred a conservative administration. The government's reach was further constrained by the fact that the nation's top generals viewed France's civilian leadership with utter contempt, a posture which was not lost on the country's anti-democratic forces.[18] These tensions came to a head with the eruption of a financial scandal that implicated some prominent political figures, and an inflamed animosity toward the government more generally soon found expression in protests and increasingly large street riots on January 22, 23, and 27.[19] A reshuffling of the cabinet (including changes at the very top) did little to stem the uprising, which was led by hundreds of young men associated with the right-wing leagues and paramilitary organizations, who fought pitched battles with the police on the streets of the capital. On February 6, the riots reached a frenzied peak in Paris when

40,000 rioters armed with improvised weapons fought with authorities in battles that left seventeen dead and over 2,000 wounded. The government considered imposing a state of siege, but fearing for the preservation of the Republic, chose instead to resign, and a new conservative-led government was formed. The broader significance of these events is still debated, but as one study concluded, the riots "unseated a government and reversed an electoral mandate," and demonstrated the strength and breadth of "right wing authoritarian nationalism" in France. This did not pass unnoticed by the left, which responded with modest countermobilizations, such as the formation of the "vigilance committee of anti-fascist intellectuals," which led a march in Paris the following month.[20]

A new conservative government still had the depression on its hands, and (with the applause and support of the Bank of France) sought to impose even more orthodox medicine. In late 1935 a government led by Pierre Laval took a stab at something called "superdeflation"—which featured draconian across-the-board spending cuts, including to defense. Laval would later spend two years leading the country's vassal Vichy government after the fall of France, and it was no coincidence that his mid-1930s austerity measures went hand in hand with a foreign policy aimed at warmer relations with Nazi Germany. For the balance of the decade, budgetary pressures and capital flight would restrain defense spending and encourage timidity at moments of international crisis, such as over the remilitarization of the Rhineland and at Munich.[21]

Superdeflation did not, of course, cure France's economic woes, but it managed to inflict enough general misery that in 1936 the Popular Front, led by Leon Blum, was swept into office, giving France the first socialist prime minister in its history. But Blum's ascension to power did not usher in a period of stability (cabinets would again come and go, and he would only last a year in office, followed by a brief echo in 1938)—and it underscored, rather than resolved, the bitter divisions that gripped the country. In one terrifying moment during the election campaign of 1936, then candidate Blum was dragged from his car and brutally beaten in the streets; a shocking photo of the bruised and bandaged soon to be prime minister held the cover of *Time* magazine. And once Blum was in office, capital flight continuously undermined expansionist economic policies (and more robust rearmament), as capital holders "repeatedly put their own interests above those of the nation." Or perhaps they had a different vision of the national interest—by late 1937 the phrase "better Hitler than Blum" was so common among the upper classes that it "became almost a chant."[22] France, hollowed out and virtually at war with itself, was in little position (and in many quarters, only modestly disposed) to resist the German onslaught. It was a civilizational failure.

Civilizational Fragility and Its Implications

Episodes of civilizational distress, decay, and crisis are by no means limited to interwar France. Attentiveness to this prospect is a characteristic of classical realism. "It stands to reason and is borne out by historic experience that societies, like individuals, have a breaking point," Morgenthau warned. "Nobody can say beforehand with precision where that point is; it is sufficient to know that it exists. A society can take so much and no more."[23] Once again, Thucydides is instructive, and reminds us that societies under stress—even robust, long-standing democracies with proud traditions—can, when pressed, become brittle, fragile, and in what amounts to moments of social panic can quickly set aside generations of revered traditions. In the latter stages of the Peloponnesian War (in the years following the Sicilian catastrophe), conspiracies and conspirators increasingly ran rife through the Athenian community, which, shaken by decades of war, was vulnerable to sedition. Eventually, although the democratic assembly continued to meet and nominally debate, governance devolved into a sham, little more than Kabuki theater, adorned by the trappings, but not the substances, of deliberative democracy. In practice "nothing was discussed that was not approved by the conspirators" (8.66.1), and those few who did speak out were "routinely put to death in some convenient way" (8.66.2), which was sufficient to cow others into a frightened silence. These were dispiriting times, as the people were "uncertain about each other" with each unwilling "to speak his mind to his neighbor" to coordinate a resistance against what was clearly an emerging tyranny. Instead men "approached each other with suspicion, each thinking his neighbor involved in what was going on, the conspirators having in their ranks persons whom no one could ever have believed capable of joining an oligarchy" (8.66.4–5). Thus although after "almost a hundred years" of democracy "it was no light matter to deprive the Athenian people of its freedom" (8.68.4), that is exactly what happened, and with barely a whimper: "The assembly ratified the proposed constitution, without a single opposing voice, and then it was dissolved" (8.69.1).[24]

Everything ends, and anything is possible—and civilization (and its grand achievements) is more fragile than we might like to think. And such catastrophes are not limited to the distant experiences of the ancient past. The Qing dynasty in China ruled for 250 years; at its peak it was among the greatest empires the world ever saw. That ended too, in 1912, and it was followed by a period of domestic implosion known as the warlord era, which lasted until 1928, when national authority was again consolidated at the center (followed soon by foreign invasion and civil war).[25] The political instability of the warlord years had all the features of a post-apocalyptic movie, if with fewer motorcycle gangs—in particular, "unpredictable and common" violence, as authority devolved from the center to scores of regional potentates, each pursuing their own narrowly defined interests and brutally clinging to power in command of often disheveled armies that seized taxes, pillaged towns, and made war on one another. Some of these battles could be quite fierce, terrorizing civilian populations, with military discipline at times literally enforced at the point of a gun (in one struggle for control over Shanghai, a city dominated by opium, prostitution, criminal gangs, and foreign intrigue, both sides in the conflict deployed machine guns to mow down any of their own troops that might retreat without orders). As one account described, "For the mass of the population, the terror, oppression, tax demands, bloodshed, intrigue, and pillaging of the warlord era made those dozen years a nightmare."[26]

Certainly, civilizational collapse does not come about every day. But for realism—or it should be said for classical realism, which focuses on what goes on within states and societies (whereas structural realism, of course, tends to "black box" such things)—its prospect, however apparently distant, informs the context for what the analyst observes, looking out the window and assessing the world. What does the world look like? In 1910 France and Germany (or at least Paris and Berlin, to which could be added what Tony Judt described as "the unrepresentative urban triangle of Prague-Budapest-Vienna") were suggestive of the heights of civilizational possibility. Stefan Zweig described that setting as a "golden age of security," one in which "everything in our almost thousand-year-old Austrian monarchy seemed based in permanency, and the state itself was the chief guarantor of this stability." Yet within eight years that monarchy was gone, and Zweig later died by his own hand in Brazil, a refugee from European fascism.[27]

Fascism emerged from disorder, and the promise of order was attractive to many, especially in interwar Europe for "certain conservative forces" which saw in fascism "a tool for their fight against socialism and unrest" and which, naively, hoped "to control fascism once they had helped it into power." Of course it must be stressed that the breakdown of civilization is not inevitable—nor is fascism the inevitable outcome of domestic disarray. (And if things do tumble out of control, in visiting horrors on humanity, history repeatedly teaches that any form of messianic fanaticism will suffice.)[28] But to emphasize, as classical realism must, the prospect of multiple plausible paths, and that no outcome is inevitable, nevertheless carries with it the admonition that this also means more appealing outcomes are also in no way assured. "Even in Italy and Germany the coming of Fascism was in no way inevitable," Hans Kohn insisted, accurately and hopefully. Less comfortingly, he also warned: "No nation is necessarily Fascist; no nation is entirely immune against Fascism. It grows faster in a soil where intellectual and social conditions or a more advanced moral disintegration facilitate its ascension to power."[29]

It is important not to let concerns for civilizational fragility take too much ownership of classical realist analysis. Again, complete social collapse is a relatively rare occurrence, and, as noted in chapter 5, it is unwise for any theory of politics to lean heavily on Nazi Germany as an exemplar.[30] Rather, more routinely relevant is that a heightened awareness of such a prospect informs the range of possibilities that are to be anticipated. And as a practical matter, sensitivity to civilizational prospects underscores the classical perceptive that the relative robustness of a country's domestic social order, for better or worse, will fundamentally shape both its power and its purpose, each of which will only be intelligible by attending to that variable. This includes the broad trajectory of the modern American experience.

American Power and American Purpose

It is an oversimplification, but a productive one, to describe the contours of world politics in the seventy-five years from 1945 to 2020 as shaped and characterized by "an American order."[31] Surprisingly, even though International Relations scholars spilled not simply barrels but hogsheads of ink vigorously debating the logic and implications of "hegemonic stability theory," as they focused on and fretted about the implications of perceived changes in U.S. power, no one anticipated the nature of how that order finally came to a close. Despite countless hypotheses about how hegemons decline, relatively—that is, overtaken by emerging, ambitious, and revisionist rivals—there simply was no theory of hegemonic suicide.

Perhaps that surprise is unwarranted. After all, the origins of the American order were a function of purpose more than power (although, of course and always, power was an essential precondition for the possibility). In the contribution that would be associated with the initial articulation of hegemonic stability theory, Charles Kindleberger argued that the Great Depression "was so deep and so long because the international economic system was rendered instable by British inability and United States unwillingness to stabilize it." Note the crucial and consequential agency here: stability is not a function of structural imperatives. Rather than resulting from a concentration of power, system-supporting leadership was possible when a state with a capacity to lead *chose to do so*. During the depression, Kindleberger argued, the United States had the power but lacked the purpose, and the former without the latter was irrelevant.[32] Similarly, as the curtain came down on the U.S. order, to an even greater extent it was a story of changing purpose, not shifting power, which led the Americans to abdicate the seat of global leadership.

The passing of the American order, despite the ease with which a laundry list of its flaws and even horrors could be constructed, is to be regretted.[33] Once again with Aron, assessments of choices made and of state behavior in world politics should be assessed not against an idealized vision of what could possibly be imagined but in comparison with plausible counterfactual worlds—what came before, what might emerge in the future, and, more than anything, what might likely otherwise have been.[34] By this final metric, the U.S. grand strategy that emerged after World War II was breathtakingly successful. Instead of returning to a shortsighted, transactionalist, "America First" style foreign policy, the United States chose a more far-sighted approach of enlightened self-interest and the pursuit of milieu goals, bearing a disproportionate share of the startup costs for a plethora of institutions and organizations, including the International Monetary Fund, the World Bank, the United Nations, and, notably, with its unprecedented alliance commitment, the North Atlantic Treaty Organization (NATO) as well as the Mutual Security Treaty with Japan. The results that followed over the ensuing years were surely beyond the most optimistic hopes of that order's founders: peace and stability in Europe; Germany and Japan rehabilitated as thriving democratic states and political and military allies; no great power wars; and decades of unprecedented global economic growth. Not bad for the architects of an order confronted with a world shattered and exhausted by years of apocalyptic world war, fearful that the postwar U.S. economy might slip back into depression, and all too easily imagining the prospects for World War III.

A classical realist analysis of the origins of the American order emphasizes two observations. First, once again, history matters. The United States chose a different path after World War II because it was trying to learn the lessons of the past and avoid the catastrophic blunders of the interwar years. The intervention of the Americans had decisively brought the mass slaughter of the Great War to a conclusion, but after flirting with internationalism, the United States chose not to join the League of Nations, and then to pursue shortsighted economic policies, and finally to hide behind isolation and timid neutrality as the fascist powers embarked on their to bids to conquer Europe and Asia. The economic face of America First ought not to be underestimated in contributing to the disasters that followed. The catastrophic Smoot-Hawley tariff and the ensuing cycles of self-defeating protectionism in the 1930s get the lion's share of attention in historical memory, but obtuse American myopia in the form of its insistence on the repayment of its war debts started much sooner and was perhaps even more consequential. A young John Foster Dulles in 1922 urged the United States to cancel those obligations, in terms that well articulated the notion of enlightened self-interest. America could go on insisting on its narrow interest—and demanding those payments. But this was not only foolish, and unrealistic, it would also not serve the broader U.S. national interest. "For the big objective, political and financial stability, will be jeopardized if one great creditor nation holds aloof and asserts the intention of repeating the experiments in collection which have, for four years past, disturbed the economic peace of the world."[35]

Those policies, of course, contributed to and exacerbated the Great Depression, abetted the successes of the fascist powers, and invited World War II. After witnessing (and contributing to) those disasters, America was keen not to make the same mistakes a second time. As President Roosevelt observed in his 1945 State of the Union Address, although the war was approaching its successful completion, military victory alone would not achieve the vital political objectives for which the war had been fought. "In our disillusionment after the last war we preferred international anarchy to international cooperation with nations which did not see and think exactly as we did," he reminded the public. "We gave up the hope of gradually achieving a better peace because we had not the courage to fulfill our responsibilities in an admittedly imperfect world. We must not let that happen again, or we shall follow the same tragic road again." Senator Tom Connolly, in urging his Senate colleagues to ratify the United Nations charter, was more blunt in his assessment of the failures of shortsighted American interwar grand strategy: "can you not still see the blood on the floor?"[36]

The second observation is that not everybody did. There was nothing inevitable about the forging of the American order—it was contested and improvised from its origins, and other plausible paths were advocated.

What followed need not have been. A crucial five-year period from 1947 to 1952 was marked by the steps that led to a sustained American commitment to internationalism. In 1947, the Truman Doctrine and the Marshall Plan heralded the pursuit of a far-sighted grand strategy. In retrospect, however, it is easy to underestimate the enduring strength of isolationist forces within the United States. To take one notable example, despite revisionist accounts that stress postwar U.S. policies as the inevitable outcome of the insatiable and expansionist demands of American capitalism, it needs to be remembered that the trade regime that was established—the General Agreement on Tariffs and Trade (GATT)—only came about as a fallback position after the U.S. Senate rejected the (American-made) International Trade Organization (ITO). And it was not just Robert Taft and the congressional isolationists that opposed the creation of the International Monetary Fund (IMF) and the Marshall Plan. The American Bankers Association (ABA), the powerful Federal Reserve Bank of New York, and the *Wall Street Journal* all opposed the creation of the IMF. The ABA thought the Marshall Plan would likely fail, and to the extent it was successful would do little more than coddle European socialism. From the perspective of American capital, "sound money and hard work"—not American handouts—were all that was needed to solve Western Europe's economic troubles.[37]

Even with all those hurdles overcome, the emergence of the Cold War was still almost undoubtedly necessary to provide domestic support for the ad hoc, piecemeal construction of an American order. And perhaps not just any Cold War but one that was accelerated and exacerbated by particular events that need not have occurred—once again, uncertainty and contingency loom large. Robert Jervis and others, for example, have argued that the Korean War, a conflict of curious origin rooted in miscalculations and complex and idiosyncratic alliance politics, played a crucial and perhaps irreplaceable role in this regard.[38] And with all that still, the matter was not fully settled until Dwight Eisenhower was chosen as the nominee for president by the Republican Party in 1952. In that close and bitterly fought contest for the nomination—which was not resolved by the first ballot of voting—Robert Taft, a long-standing and leading isolationist, who had strongly opposed the formation of NATO, ran a close second. It required the nomination (and probably the election) of someone like Eisenhower to make it clear that internationalism would win out over isolationism as a sustained and bipartisan commitment, establishing clarity and continuity in U.S. foreign policy. Only at that point was American international order, built, in its initial incarnation, on the ideological foundations of what John Ruggie would later call "the compromise of embedded liberalism"—the Keynesian-influenced understanding that "multilateralism would be predicated upon domestic interventionism"—firmly and clearly in place.[39]

All Things Must Pass

The Cold War was necessary for the American order, and with the sudden end of that confrontation cracks in the U.S. internationalist consensus—fissures which emerged in the wake of the ruinous Vietnam War and the difficult decade of the 1970s—quickly deepened and became more apparent. The Soviet Union ceased to exist in 1991. In the following year in the United States, the disenchantment of the working-class left with free trade reached a fever pitch over the North American Free Trade Agreement; on the right, nativist-nationalist voices reemerged as a force in presidential politics. (Missed in all this at the time was that the failure of public policy was at the domestic level—the insouciant and self-satisfied indifference of elites to the losers of globalization—not with the trade agreements themselves.)[40] It would take decades of disenchantments for these seeds to fully flower, but they would plainly emerge in the second decade of the next century, and the end of that decade the transformation was complete. The United States increasingly regarded the world (and, perhaps just as important, was in turn also so regarded) from a "what have you done for me lately," much more narrowly self-interested point of view.

Nativist-nationalism will poorly serve the interests of the American republic, just as surely as it did in the past, and for essentially the same reasons. Milieu goals matter, enormously; power vacuums will be quickly filled by the nefarious; and a host of pressing issues that spill across borders can only be addressed with some measure of mutual international goodwill.

Having said that, it is nevertheless the case that after three-quarters of a century, it is more than appropriate for any great power to reassess the nature of its global commitments. As discussed in chapter 4, there is no singular or unambiguously realist foreign policy or grand strategy (nor should there be). Even prudence, that realist touchstone, only gets you so far—which is to say, not very. What counts as "prudent" will ultimately be a judgment call, and in addition there are times when timidity in the name of prudence will produce suboptimal underresponsiveness, from the perspective of the long-term national interest. Nevertheless, prudence does demand a judicious and continuing assessment of the long-run costs and benefits of various commitments, and also attentiveness to the changing relationship between capabilities, obligations, and priorities over time. In that context it is hard to look at, to take a fairly straightforward example, the U.S. commitment to the Persian Gulf as anything but anachronistic, and politically unsustainable—from the perspective of both sides. It is not surprising that in the 1970s, when Gulf oil ran the world and the advanced industrial economies were dependent on it, that the United States would want to ensure that no single hostile power would come to dominate the region (what would become known as the Carter Doctrine) and, more narrowly, to prevent the closure of the Strait of Hormuz. In the 1970s, the United States went so far as to reach secret arrangements with Saudi Arabia, apparently cementing a relationship that linked American regional security guarantees to a commitment by the Gulf states to support the international role of the U.S. dollar, about which at the time there was much (ultimately unfounded) anxiety.[41]

But regarding the Gulf, by any dispassionate account the United States is now in the position once described by Bob Dylan: "I used to care/but things have changed." Compared to the 1970s, the local balance of power seems robust, the broader international political context more complex, and the natural gas and oil shale revolutions have fundamentally transformed world energy markets. In particular, the United States is now the world's largest producer of oil and natural gas, and China is currently the biggest export market for Saudi Arabia, Iraq, and Kuwait. (And if anything, given climate change, the United States should be looking to discourage, not subsidize, the burning of fossil fuels.) In sum, starting from scratch today, it would be quite difficult to explain what logic might underpin an American security commitment in the Gulf region. Moreover, local actors, concerned necessarily for their own security, must question the credibility of the U.S. security guarantee.[42] In evaluating the likelihood that the American cavalry might again come racing to the rescue, yet once again historical legacies are essential in anticipating and explaining the choices made by states. Is the United States likely to participate in a large-scale war to defend, say, Saudi Arabia in the 2020s? There are very strong reasons to doubt this. In 1991, with its war to liberate Kuwait, the United States, unrivaled militarily, embarked on an effort that was supported almost universally, and undertaken in the headiest days of its post–Cold War triumphalism. Whereas more recently, the region has been the locus for two long, unsuccessful U.S. wars that contributed to a deep domestic disenchantment with such adventures. Like the European states in the 1920s and 1930s (that is, with the impossibility of understanding their disposition toward questions of war and peace without reference to World War I), for the United States, decisions about the prospect of a new Middle Eastern war will only be comprehensible through the lens of the failed wars that came before.[43] The foreign policy choices its domestic politics will permit are more circumscribed than they once were. And at a bare minimum, the Gulf states must assess this real possibility, and recalibrate their own assessments and political relationships accordingly.

The realist case for the status quo (that is, for maintaining the security commitment) is twofold. First is the default setting of prudence—change is to leap into the unknown, which is generally unwelcome. Second is the consequences of power vacuums—if U.S. power is withdrawn, other actors, perhaps and even likely, malevolent ones, will pour in to fill that void. But although weighing costs and benefits is ultimately a judgment call, the argument in favor of a continued U.S. military commitment to the Gulf, especially in the context of other priorities, is a very hard one to make. And as for what might replace U.S. power, such concerns must be tempered by the chastising fact that it is not at all obvious that seventy-five years of active engagement in the region have actually created a political environment or outcomes conducive to American interests more generally. A bit more of a "first, do no harm" philosophy might have better served U.S. interests, to the extent that they existed, in this particular region.

But the recession of American power elsewhere in the world is more likely to have deleterious consequences along those two lines more generally—most notably, were it to occur, in Europe and East Asia. Will NATO endure past 2025? It is hard to say, again, given the rise of nativist/nationalism in the United States and greater support there for a more shortsighted, "America First," transactionalist foreign policy—and the fact that U.S. allies must be attentive to these changes. But should, from a realist perceptive, NATO endure? Here once again the divide between structural and classical realism is pivotal. Kenneth Waltz predicted in 1993 that "NATO's days are not numbered, but its years are," a forecast that turned out to be wrong in all but the most narrowly semantic sense (everything ends eventually)—in both its general expectation and underlying logic.[44] From a structuralist perspective, NATO was defined solely by its role as an anti-Soviet alliance and thus could not live long beyond the dissolution of that common, urgent, military threat. Indeed, many thoughtful scholars of international relations now hold a similar "mission accomplished" perspective and find the alliance obsolete.

From a classical point of view, however, NATO was always more than a narrow military alliance; it was also an intimate affiliation of like-minded states and a stabilizing force on a historically war-prone continent. As such, and at very little cost, the alliance was (and remains) a classic example of a policy that advances far-sighted milieu goals. Certainly it provided a sense of greater geopolitical security, stability, and confidence for its members, but it also helped shape the international environment in ways that allowed shared national values to thrive and political allies to feel secure and content in their shared affinities.

This is not to anticipate that the alliance will necessarily long endure. Indeed, by 2020 it faced two existential threats: the evident U.S. temptation to pick up its marbles and go home, and, not to be underestimated, authoritarian backsliding Europe, especially in Hungary, Poland, and Turkey (which can be contrasted with the ascension of Spain to the alliance in 1982, coterminous with its emergence as a democracy). A NATO with authoritarian members will rot from within. But the analytical question remains, is it in the U.S. interest for the alliance to endure? From a classical realist perspective the answer is an unambiguous yes. In assessing the costs, benefits, and international political consequences of an American withdrawal from Europe, the calculations are almost the opposite of those seen in the Gulf. The alliance offers large benefits for modest costs.[45] Withdrawal is neither urgently needed nor would it be prudent—again it would be a leap into the unknown that would invite the assertion of power and influence by others. There is little benefit (but terrible potential cost) to testing the theory that NATO was a force for comity and stability on the continent; more generally, such a measure would gesture at (and even perhaps invite) a post-American world that is darker, more authoritarian, and less able to address collective challenges. On what grounds are these risks worth taking?

Along similar lines, as discussed in chapter 6, a very robust case can be made for maintaining U.S. alliances in (and deep engagement with) partners in East Asia. As noted, such engagement is less about military confrontations with China or aspiring to regional primacy (an ambition, it bears repeating, of uncertain logic and prospect) and more about giving affiliated states the confidence to retain their international political independence from China. From the perspective of national security, even relatively narrowly defined—to say nothing of coveted milieu goals, broadly defined—East Asia is so big and so important that it is very much indeed a national interest of the United States for the region not to entirely fall under the spell of the People's Republic—especially one sporting a hard authoritarian edge. No American grand strategy can be indifferent to the political fate of East Asia.

Social Cohesion and the End of the American Order

Of course, it only makes sense to talk about U.S. grand strategy if in fact America is capable of pursuing a grand strategy. This may no longer be the case. Once again, to understand the likely trajectory of U.S. foreign policy behavior, a structuralist approach limited to the assessment of material power will not be just incomplete but almost certainly misleading. The country undoubtedly boasts a resilient, sophisticated, colossal economy, and the world's most impressive military machine. But that power will be circumscribed in practice by its domestic social-political disarray. Like France in the 1930s, the United States in the 2020s is characterized by radical polarization and the widespread embrace of unreason, factors that will also undermine the coherence of its purpose (and the confidence of others in the stability of that purpose and the robustness of its commitments). Everything ends, and it may be that the United States is simply taking on water. In any event, a country consumed by domestic social conflict is not one that will likely be capable of practicing a productive, predictable, or trustworthy foreign policy.

What went wrong? Not very long before these domestic problems became too salient to ignore, American global predominance appeared so great that terms like "hegemon" and "superpower" seemed inadequate to properly describe it, and the phrase "hyperpower" was invented. In 1999 the *Economist* assessed that "the United States bestrides the globe like a colossus"; not long after that, leading IR theorists forcefully and cogently argued "the unprecedented concentration in power resources in the United States generally renders inoperative the constraining effects of the systemic properties long central to research in international relations." Yet in retrospect, at the same time, America was quietly cultivating the conditions that would contribute to its social desiccation. Thus although in the two decades following the general assessment of the United States as an unprecedented hyperpower the measurable erosion of its relative material capabilities was ultimately modest; nevertheless, few in 2020 would describe American power, by the only metric that matters—the ability to achieve its desired objectives in world politics—with the same type of awe-struck terms so commonly articulated at the turn of the last millennium.[46]

As Samuel Huntington presciently observed in that same heady moment, a state in command of such immense power "is normally able to maintain its dominance over minor states for a long time until it is weakened by internal decay or by forces from outside the system, both of which happened to fifth-century Rome and nineteenth-century China."[47] And as is often the case in retrospect, it can be seen clearly that American internal decay was already well underway at the very moment commentators were genuflecting before its vaunted hyperpower. Aggregate economic growth in the United States was impressive in the 1990s, but compared to other decades of high growth, such as in the 1960s, the gains were less evenly distributed, and skewed toward the already wealthy—a trend that would only continue in the following years. The rich were getting much richer while median household income stagnated. (Thus the answer to the question of how well the economy was performing, as with so many purportedly objective assessments, depended entirely on which metric one chose to measure.)[48] Moreover, the differences in the nature of economic growth, and its implications, were attributable to domestic politics. In 1992 the Democratic Party, losers of five of the six previous presidential elections—most by landslide, the one win a post-Watergate squeaker—lurched to the center on economic issues, embracing Wall Street and an economic philosophy better described by a ruthless, Darwinian commitment to "shareholder value" than the Keynesian-inflected compromise of embedded liberalism. America was increasingly a winner-take-all society, with those already well placed and well advantaged in the best position to win.[49]

And then of course came hubris, which, from the perspective of classical realism, is a most common traveling companion of hyperpower. As has been discussed, one expression of that hubris was the reckless Iraq war, an ambitious adventure embarked upon at a time when the United States was still fighting in Afghanistan, and as the objectives for which that war was fought were still far from accomplished—and in fact it would never be accomplished, an outcome made more likely by the rush to invade Iraq. (On the "debate" over Iraq, one can hear the clear echoes of Sicily, with the duplicitous Alcibiades assuring the crowd that the war would be a cakewalk, as "the cities of Sicily are peopled by motley rabbles, and easily change their instructions and adopt new ones in their stead" [6.17.2]; whereas Nicias, speaking for Thucydides, warned against adventures in "difficult to conquer" far-off cities populated by "strangers and enemies," where an Athenian might "find everything hostile to him" [6.23.1–2].)

Hubris had an economic component as well, with the great (and misguided) American project of financial deregulation mentioned in chapter 5. That agenda (buttressed by the shaky logic of rational expectations theory), which unleashed vast riches for those in the financial community, was rooted in the arrogant (and erroneous and historically common) presumption that the new wizards of Wall Street had taken much of the risk out of high finance, permitting the good times to roll without end or inhibition. As Federal Reserve Chair Alan Greenspan explained on the eve of the global financial crisis, "increasingly complex financial instruments have contributed to the development of a far more flexible, efficient, and hence resilient financial system than the one that existed just a quarter-century ago."[50]

By the second decade of the twenty-first century, the price for all this hubris came due, in the form of failed wars and the global financial crisis. But to whom were these bills presented? The financial system was necessarily saved (and the bankers, less necessarily, spared), while mainstream America, which bore the disproportionate human costs of the ongoing wars and already under stress from international competition and the embrace of Dickensian capitalism at home, was served austerity and the great recession. Coterminous with all these imposing pressures was the rise of the internet and social media culture, which did not bring out the best in America, a society once characterized by what Richard Hofstadter called a "paranoid style" of politics, wherein resentments against a "hostile and conspiratorial world" are directed against "a culture, a way of life," and which elicit "political passions" fueled by a sense of "righteousness" and "moral indignation." Although parallels to aspects of this could be seen in interwar France, where readers took their cues by selecting, from a vast array of newspapers, the ones that confirmed their preexisting views, the contemporary hyper-media environment (characterized by low costs of entry, incentives for attention-getting extremist posturing, limited accountability, and relentless subversion of truth claims) could not have been more well designed to reinforce both polarization and a paranoid style to an even much greater extent.[51] It may or may not be, pace Morgenthau, that American society has reached its breaking point. But the prospect that the United States is unlikely capable of pursuing a productive and far-sighted grand strategy must be taken seriously—and it is not a prospect that can be understood through the lens of aggregate material power. It is one thing to embrace restraint as wise public policy; it is quite another to have it imposed by domestic political disarray and paralysis.[52]

In sum, consider some basic phenomena that any student of international relations would wish to grasp: the end of the American order, as well as its role world politics, its capacity to exercise power, the reach of its political influence, and, more generally, its ability to get what it wants, and to find security and an environment to its general liking. All of these prospects and outcomes will prove less attributable to its raw power, and more a function of its purpose, which will be formatively determined, defined, and delimited by domestic social and political factors. The choices made by great powers, and, in turn, the consequences of those choices (the responses they elicit from others, and so on), are only intelligible through these lenses.

Nobody said this was going to be easy. The study of world politics will never be a science, at least as the way that term is conventionally used. To understand, explain, and anticipate events in international relations, it is necessary to have an instinct for and attentiveness to politics, a facility with rudimentary economic theory, and a grasp of the relevant history—in all cases tempered by self-consciousness about what simply cannot be known and the inescapable limits to the objectivity of the analyst. Or what might be thought of in another setting as approaching the task at hand armed with three chords and (a constant striving for) the truth.

ACKNOWLEDGMENTS

OVER THE COURSE of the development of this project I have accumulated more intellectual debts than I can possibly hope to properly recognize: feedback at numerous talks I delivered, conversations with participants at several workshops, voluminous and often spirited correspondence on particular queries, and reactions to various drafts of parts of the manuscript-in-progress. For especially valuable comments and suggestions I thank Rawi Abdelal, James Davis, Mike Desch, Burt Diamond, Michael Doyle, David Edelstein, Frank Gavin, Randall Germain, Eric Helleiner, Sarah Kreps, Ulrich Krotz, Paul MacDonald, Alison McQueen, Jeanne Morefield, Joseph Parent, Patrick Porter, Barry Posen, Adam Quinn, Hunter Rawlings, Jeffrey Rusten, Randall Schweller (with whom I remain in vehement disagreement), Adam Segal, Silvana Toska, Stephen Walt, David Welch, Michael Williams, and William Wohlforth. Andrew Moravcsik, largely in dissent, generously participated in what diplomats call "a frank exchange of views" that was helpful for clarifying what I was trying to say. And I have benefited enormously from the insights and advice of Tom Christensen, John Ikenberry, and Robert Jervis. Throughout this process it has been a pleasure working with Princeton University Press, where I thank Eric Crahan, Bridget Flannery-McCoy, and Alena Chekanov, as well as three anonymous reviewers, each of whom offered smart, savvy, and detailed constructive criticisms. It was also a pleasure and a privilege to work with copy editor Jenn Backer. Finally, words fall short of my appreciation for the friends and colleagues who provided extensive commentaries after reading the penultimate draft of the book in your hands—Fred Logevall, Robert Ross, Jennifer Erickson, Karl Mueller, Matt Evangelista, and Peter Katzenstein.

My personal debts are of course, if anything, even greater. This book was written in what Van Morrison once called "a period of transition," one that was made much easier by the welcoming presence, support, and friendship of John, Jennifer, and Gustav, Fred and Danyel, Livia and Chris, and by the unexpected pleasure of having Elie and Carolyn and Ari nearby—unscheduled extra innings that I cherished. And what can I say about Esty, other than that I know how lucky I am to have a traveling companion who grabs your arm at the New York Film Festival at exactly the moment you are reaching for theirs.

NOTES

Introduction and Overview

1. Typically, however, the dismissal of those older approaches is hand-waving, and lacking in serious engagement with earlier contributions.

2. In contrast, abstract models tend to assume that actors have "independent and identically distributed" tastes.

3. The protagonist in Christopher Nolan's film (2000) suffers from anterograde amnesia (the inability to form new memories).

4. The crucial distinction between risk and uncertainty will be elaborated in chapter 2. In settings of risk, the underlying probability of all possible outcomes is known in advance to all (like the odds of rolling a seven with two dice); in uncertainty, underlying probabilities are unknowable, and subject to contrasting guesses.

5. Regarding structural realism, which took the discipline of international relations by storm, an old adage applies: "what's new isn't true, what's true isn't new."

6. Carveth Read, *Logic: Deductive and Inductive*, 2nd ed. (London: Grant Richards, 1901), 320.

7. Hans Morgenthau, "The Limitations of Science and the Problem of Social Planning," *Ethics* 54:3 (1944): 174–85; see also Raymond Aron, *Introduction to the Philosophy of History: An Essay on the Limits of Historical Objectivity* (London: Weidenfeld and Nicholson, 1948/1938).

8. Crucially, rational expectations theory assumes that all actors share the same underlying model of how the world works.

9. Such as, for example, the claim that interdependence is irrelevant under bipolarity, which was true for the superpowers during the Cold War but is in no way an inherent consequence of a bipolar order.

10. It is not even probabilistic, assigning specific odds to distinct outcomes. According to the model, there is only one possible outcome, and this unsuitable and misguided determinism is necessary to hold the theory together.

11. Raymond Aron, *Memoirs: Fifty Years of Political Reflection* (New York: Holmes & Meier, 1990/1983), 64.

Chapter One: What Is Classical Realism?

1. Robert Gilpin, "The Richness of the Tradition of Political Realism," in *Neorealism and Its Critics*, ed. Robert O. Keohane (New York: Columbia University Press, 1986), 304; see also Robert Gilpin, "No One Loves a Political Realist," *Security Studies* 5:3 (1996): 6.

2. One can argue, building from realist assumptions, that bipolarity is more likely to lead to war than multipolarity, or vice versa; that a preponderance of power is stabilizing, or destabilizing; that the decision to introduce force in a particular situation is wise, or reckless.

3. Structural Realists, of course, renounce purpose, but it is a stubborn fact that content matters. It might make theory less "elegant" but to wish away reality is utopianism, which realists of all stripes abhor.

4. Thomas Hobbes, *Leviathan* (New York: Penguin Classics, 1985/1651), 186.

5. John Maynard Keynes, "My Early Beliefs," in *Two Memoirs* (London: Rupert Hart Davis, 1949), reprinted in *The Collected Writings of John Maynard Keynes*, ed. Elizabeth Johnson and Donald Moggridge (London: Macmillan, 1971–89) (hereafter *CW*), 10:447, 450.

6. George F. Kennan, *Around the Cragged Hill: A Personal and Political Philosophy* (New York: Norton, 1993). As Niebuhr observes, "Man, being more than a natural creature, is not interested merely in physical survival but in prestige and social approval." Reinhold Niebuhr, *The Children of Light and the Children of Darkness* (1944), in Reinhold Niebuhr, *Major Works on Religion and Politics*, ed. Elisabeth Sifton (New York: Library of America, 2015), 367.

7. For the definitive statement, see Robert Jervis, "Cooperation under the Security Dilemma," *World Politics* 30:2 (1978): 167–214; note also John Herz, *Political Realism and Political Idealism: A Study in Theories and Realities* (Chicago: University of Chicago Press, 1951), 3–4.

8. Of course, that was Renoir speaking as the character Octave. Renoir, as writer/director, crafted a film with a witheringly condemning moral subtext that was easily recognized by audiences—and the movie was booed, banned, and for some time lost to history.

9. John Maynard Keynes, "The General Theory of Employment," *Quarterly Journal of Economics* 51:2 (1937), *CW*, 14:122; Friedrich von Hayek, "The Use of Knowledge in Society," *American Economic Review* 35:4 (1945): 519–30; see also Hayek, "The Pretence of Knowledge" (Nobel Memorial Lecture, December 11, 1974); Frank Knight, *Risk, Uncertainty and Profit* (Chicago: University of Chicago Press, 1971/1921), 241, 311.

10. Consider the power of "market sentiment" (what individuals think) in macroeconomics. If, from a hypothetical menu of five policy choices, each of which was plausible from the perspective of economic theory, three of the choices were *perceived* to be unsustainable, those untethered beliefs (that is, market sentiment) would trigger responses that would cause those policies to be unsustainable, solely for that reason. Contrast that with air travel—the beliefs of a critical mass of nervous passengers will have no effect on whether or not a plane will crash.

11. For the text, I have followed Robert B. Strassler, ed., *The Landmark Thucydides: A Comprehensive Guide to the Peloponnesian War* (New York: Touchstone, 1998), which is a modest refinement of the translation by Richard Crawley, first published in 1874. It has been helpful to read and cross-reference some difficult or controversial passages with a more recent translation, Jeremy Mynott, ed., *Thucydides: The War of the Peloponnesians and the Athenians* (Cambridge: Cambridge University Press, 2013). The magisterial three-volume Simon Hornblower, *A Commentary on Thucydides* (Oxford: Oxford University Press, 1991, 1996, 2008) has been an invaluable resource. The secondary literature is, of course, enormous. I have been especially influenced by five well-known contributions: John H. Finley Jr., *Thucydides* (Ann Arbor: University of Michigan Press, 1963/1942); Jacqueline de Romilly, *Thucydides*

and Athenian Imperialism, trans. Philip Thody (Oxford: Basil Blackwell, 1963/1947); Hunter R. Rawlings, *The Structure of Thucydides' History* (Princeton: Princeton University Press, 1981); W. Robert Connor, *Thucydides* (Princeton: Princeton University Press, 1984); Jeffrey S. Rusten, ed., *Oxford Readings in Classical Studies: Thucydides* (Oxford: Oxford University Press, 2009).

12. See, for example, Peter Hunt, "Thucydides on the First Ten Years of the War (Archidamian War)," in *The Oxford Handbook of Thucydides*, ed. Ryan K. Balot, Sara Forsdyke, and Edith Foster (Oxford: Oxford University Press, 2017), and many of the contributions to that volume.

13. Donald Kagan, *The Outbreak of the Peloponnesian War* (Ithaca: Cornell University Press, 1969).

14. Kagan, *Outbreak*, 269 (quote), 285, 287, 306–7.

15. G. E. M. de Ste. Croix, *The Origins of the Peloponnesian War* (Ithaca: Cornell University Press, 1972), 65 (quote), 67–68, 70, 101, 290. The Corinthians do seem essential to the origins of the war. As Hans Van Wees notes, from 460, Athens's principal enemy was Corinth, not Sparta. "Thucydides on Early Greek History," in *Oxford Handbook*, ed. Balot, Forsdyke, and Foster, 53.

16. W. Robert Connor, "Scale Matters: Compression, Expansion and Vividness in Thucydides," in *Oxford Handbook*, ed. Balot, Forsdyke, and Foster, 215; Here, notably, Kagan and de Ste. Croix are in full agreement—Thucydides downplayed the decree—though Kagan sees this as an error on Thucydides' part, while de Ste. Croix finds the lack of emphasis appropriate. Kagan, *Outbreak of the Peloponnesian War*, 251, 267, 269, 374; de Ste. Croix, *Origins of the Peloponnesian War*, 213–14, 251–52, 256. See also S. N. Jaffe, *Thucydides on the Outbreak of War: Character and Contest* (Oxford: Oxford University Press, 2017), 8. Thucydides tended to downplay the role of economic factors in general (see, for example, De Romilly, *Thucydides and Athenian Imperialism*, 72–73). Lisa Kallet argues against this conventional wisdom in studies that attempt to draw out the sinews of finance latent in the work, but of course she nevertheless shares the hard-to-refute consensus that Thucydides marginalized the Megarian Decree. Lisa Kallet-Marx, *Money, Expense and Naval Power in Thucydides' History 1–5.24* (Berkeley: University of California Press, 1993); Lisa Kallet, *Money and the Corrosion of Power in Thucydides: The Sicilian Expedition and Its Aftermath* (Berkeley: University of California Press, 2001).

17. For IR scholars, then, Thucydides' argument and presentation are what matter, not the details of this ancient conflict or dissenting perspectives from his position. For example, we can't know with certainty the trajectory of Athenian power in mid- to late fifth century BC, but we do know for sure that Thucydides believed it was on the rise and was the underlying cause of the war.

18. Jacqueline de Romilly, *The Mind of Thucydides*, trans. Elizabeth Rawlings, ed. Hunter Rawlings and Jeffrey Rusten (Ithaca: Cornell University Press, 2012/1967), 3, see also 2, 4, 47–48; Thomas Hobbes, *The English Works of Thomas Hobbes, Volume VIII*, ed. Sir William Molesworth (London: John Born, 1843), vii, xii.

19. On the central role of such Thucydidean choices, see, for example, Tim Rood, *Thucydides: Narrative and Explanation* (Oxford: Clarendon Press, 1998); David Gribble, "Narrator Interventions in Thucydides," *Journal of Hellenic Studies* 118 (1998): 41–67; and Rawlings, *Structure*, 50–51. The relative omniscience of the

narrator cannot but inform the way in which events are described in retrospect; not surprisingly, "Thucydides draws on hindsight, his knowledge of the outcome, to interpret and shape the history that produced this outcome." Kurt A. Raaflaub, "*Ktema es aiei*: Thucydides' Concept of 'Learning through History' and Its Realization in His Work," in *Thucydides between History and Literature*, ed. Antonis Tsakmakis and Melina Tamiolaki (Boston/Berlin: De Gruyter, 2013), 12; see also Jonas Grethelein, "The Presence of the Past in Thucydides," also in *Thucydides between History and Literature*, ed. Tsakmakis and Tamiolaki, 91.

20. Tobias Joho, "Thucydides, Epic, and Tragedy," in *Oxford Handbook*, ed. Balot, Forsdyke, and Foster, 591.

21. Compare Thucydides: "With references to the speeches . . . some I heard myself, others I got from various quarters; it was in all cases difficult to carry them word for word in one's memory, so my habit has been to make the speakers say what was in my opinion demanded of them by various occasions, of course adhering as closely as possible to the general sense of what they really said" (1.22.2), with Tolstoy: "I remembered an old story for the Caucasus, part of which I saw, part of which I heard from witnesses, and part of which I imagined to myself." Leo Tolstoy, *Hadji Murat*, trans. Richard Pevear and Larissa Volokhonsky (New York: Vintage, 2009/1904), 4.

22. As de Romilly describes: "Thucydides provided the two main speeches of Nicias and Alcibiades. . . . These are of course not the exact words of the actual speeches, but even so, one feels that the speakers are present, not only from the arguments that each would advance, but also from the two personalities, from their tones, their temperaments, and their aspirations." Jacqueline de Romilly, *The Life of Alcibiades: Dangerous Ambition and the Betrayal of Athens*, trans. Elizabeth Trapnell Rawlings (Ithaca: Cornell University Press, 2019/1995), 62.

23. A documentary, even one committed to truth and objectivity (and there is every reason to believe Thucydides was), makes foundational narrative and stylistic choices, conforms to the structure of storytelling, and necessarily and inescapably imposes a point of view. Consider two documentaries made about a strike, each with every frame of film honest and true. One might dwell on individual workers and their impoverishment, their sickly children, and diminishing life prospects, and show the factory's board of directors at a distance, arriving in a fleet of limousines to discuss strategy. The other might dwell on the distress of the company's founder and his kind, supportive spouse as they struggle to keep the factory in business, anguished at layoffs made necessary by the competitive pressures and technological change that have squeezed the firm to the breaking point, and linger on the faceless crowds of angry mobs throwing rocks at the windows of their homes. Each documentary would be equally "true"; but each would offer radically different perspectives on the same events.

24. Finley, *Thucydides*, 139, 142 (quote).

25. In this context, it is wise to recall the firm admonition above that exploring classical realism, not canonizing specific thinkers, is and remains the focus of this study. Thucydides is not realism; Realism is not Thucydides. It is nevertheless breathtaking the range of insights that this one ancient text has to offer students of Classical Realism.

26. As Mynott notes, the massacre at Hysiac is "one of the many brief references to acts of brutality in war" (*War of the Peloponnesians*, 77).

27. This despite the fact that Athens, with impressive modulation, offered Corcyra only a defensive alliance, a measure designed to contain Corinthian power without unnecessarily provoking Sparta. On this point, see Jaffe, *The Outbreak of War*, 52.

28. See, for example, Robert Gilpin, *War and Change in World Politics* (Cambridge: Cambridge University Press, 1981); as well as G. John Ikenberry, ed., *Power, Order and Change in World Politics* (Cambridge: Cambridge University Press, 2014) and the literature cited in note 1 of chapter 6, and the second half of chapter 3 more generally.

29. For more on this critique, see James Lee, "Did Thucydides Believe in Thucydides' Trap? The *History of the Peloponnesian War* and Its Relevance to U.S.-China Relations," *Journal of Chinese Political Science* 24:1 (2019): 67–86.

30. Hornblower argues that the "clear echo" at 1.33.3 is "decisive against attempts" to dispute this conclusion. *Commentary*, 1:78; see also pp. 65, 133.

31. On shifting alliances and endless political combinations, especially as described in Books V and VIII, see Geoffrey Hawthorn, *Thucydides on Politics: Back to the Present* (Cambridge: Cambridge University Press, 2014); Robin Seager, "After the Peace of Nicias: Diplomacy and Policy, 421–416 B.C.," *Classical Quarterly* 26:2 (1976): 249–69; and Cinzia Bearzot, "Mantenia, Decelia, and the Inter-war Years (421–413 BCE)," in *Oxford Handbook*, ed. Balot, Forsdyke, and Foster. On the fluid and complex jockeying in Book VIII, see, for example, de Romilly, *Life of Alcibiades*, chap. 7.

32. This is the central thesis of Jaffe, *The Outbreak of War* ("the national characters of Athens and Sparta are essential for understanding the war's outbreak," p. 11; "Thucydides' Peloponnesian War is ultimately a contest between the rival characters of Athens and Sparta," p. 159). Mark Fisher and Kinch Hoekstra remind readers how the theme of national character weaves its way throughout the entire narrative, and how these differences across communities "influenced how their members interpreted and pursued their interests" ("Thucydides and the Politics of Necessity," in *Oxford Handbook*, ed. Balot, Forsdyke, and Foster, 378); see also Ellen G. Millender, "Sparta and the Crisis of the Peloponnesian League in Thucydides' *History*," also in *Oxford Handbook*: "Through the four speeches delivered at the meetings of the Spartan Assembly and the Peloponnesian League, Thucydides explored the national character of Athens and Sparta," illustrating the clash between "two vastly different types of society" (81).

33. Jeffrey S. Rusten, ed., *Thucydides: The Peloponnesian War, Book II* (Cambridge: Cambridge University Press, 1989), 212.

34. As noted above, the concept of uncertainty (as distinct from actuarial risk) is central to Classical Realism, and one that has received greater attention more generally in the wake of the global financial crisis. The crucial differences between these two concepts for understanding (or failing to understand) world politics is elaborated in chapter 2. For an important illustration of some of the analytical stakes in play with this distinction, see Frank H. Knight, "'What Is Truth' in Economics?" *Journal of Political Economy* 48:1 (1940): 1–32.

35. Emily Greenwood, "Thucydides on the Sicilian Expedition," in *Oxford Handbook*, ed. Balot, Forsdyke, and Foster, 168.

36. Hornblower, *Commentary*, 1:478; see also Rusten, *Peloponnesian War*, 191, and Gregory Crane, *Thucydides and the Ancient Simplicity: The Limits of Political Realism* (Berkeley: University of California Press, 1998), 53.

37. The Thracians "sacked the houses and the temples and butchered the inhabitants, sparing neither youth nor age but killing all they fell in with, one after the other, children and women, and even beasts of burden, and whatever living creatures they saw" (7.29.4). "Everywhere confusion reigned and death in all its shapes; and in particular they attacked a boy's school, the largest that there was in the place, into which the children had just gone, and massacred them all" (7.29.5). See also Connor, "Scale Matters," 219 (quote).

38. As Connor notes, "since Melos was not of great strategic significance, something else must account for the attention it receives" ("Scale Matters," 213).

39. Mynott, *War of the Peloponnesians*, 47.

40. The Melians were annihilated—all the men were executed, the women and children sold into slavery, and the island repopulated. In the earlier episode a large group of those deemed responsible faced summary execution but the broader population was largely spared. For Hornblower, "it is important that the Melians, unlike the Mytilenians, are not reprieved" (*Commentary*, 3:225); see also W. Liebeschuetz, "The Structure and Function of the Melian Dialogue," *Journal of Hellenic Studies* 88 (1968): 73, 74, and Bearzot, "The Interwar Years," 155.

41. "The correctness of his foresight concerning the war became better known after his death" (2.65.6).

42. In contrast, Thucydides lauds Pericles for his ability "to have rightly gauged the power of his country" (2.65.5).

43. This was a mistake they would make more than once. The tide at Pylos turned again in Athens's favor, and Sparta sent emissaries to negotiate, but again the Athenians "kept grasping at more, and dismissed envoy after envoy" (4.41.4). On the importance of this episode, and Thucydides' emphasis on this point, see De Romilly, *Thucydides and Athenian Imperialism*, 172–76, 322, 327; Rawlings, *Structure*, 229–30.

44. As Felix Wasserman argued, "It is particularly important to keep in mind that the Melian Dialogue was written by an author and for a public who could read it as a prelude to the Sicilian Expedition, and, indirectly, to the final catastrophe." In their despair amid the ruins of a blood-soaked, shattering retreat at the end of the Sicilian campaign, the Athenians even come to echo the ill-fated Melians, appealing to the gods for salvation. Felix Martin Wasserman, "The Melian Dialogue," *Transactions and Proceedings of the American Philological Association* 78 (1947): 30, 35 (quote); Rawlings, *Structure*, 245–46; Hornblower, *Commentary*, 3:217. As Liebeschuetz notes, at Melos, the Athenians were "bullying and arrogant . . . boundlessly self-confident, lacking humility even towards the gods." The parallels are inescapable: "An Athenian reader could hardly fail to diagnose a case of *hybris* and therefore to recognize in the following account of the Sicilian expedition and of subsequent events, the unfolding of inevitable retribution" ("The Structure and Function of the Melian Dialogue," 76).

45. The reader "quickly realizes that Thucydides himself favors the views of Nicias." Hans-Peter Stahl, "Speeches and the Course of Events in Books Six and Seven of Thucydides," in *Oxford Readings*, ed. Rusten, 346 (quote), 352; see also John H. Finley Jr., *Three Essays on Thucydides* (Cambridge, MA: Harvard University Press, 1967), 147.

46. Hunter R. Rawlings III, "Writing History Implicitly through Refined Structuring," in *Oxford Handbook*, ed. Balot, Forsdyke, and Foster, 206.

47. Hobbes, *Leviathan*, 185; see also, for example, Theodore Christov, *Before Anarchy: Hobbes and His Critics in Modern International Thought* (Cambridge: Cambridge University Press, 2015), 123.

48. Niccolò Machiavelli, *The Prince*, trans. Harvey Mansfield (Chicago: University of Chicago Press, 1998/1531); Niccolò Machiavelli, *Discourses on Livy*, trans. Harvey Mansfield and Nathan Taco (Chicago: University of Chicago Press, 1996/1532). For the challenges of interpreting Machiavelli, see Corrado Vivanti, *Niccolò Machiavelli: An Intellectual Biography* (Princeton: Princeton University Press, 2013), 83, 149; Herbert Butterfield, *The Statecraft of Machiavelli* (Lindon: G. Bell & Sons, 1940), 15, 53; Erica Brenner, *Be Like the Fox: Machiavelli in His World* (New York: Norton, 2017), xvi–xix, 246, 249–51; Isaiah Berlin, "The Originality of Machiavelli" (1972), reprinted in Berlin, *Against the Current: Essays in the History of Ideas* (Princeton: Princeton University Press, 2013), 33–100.

49. Machiavelli, *The Prince*, 97.

50. Good starting points for the applications of Machiavelli and Hobbes to International Relations theory include Michael W. Doyle, *Ways of War and Peace* (New York: Norton, 1996), chaps. 2 and 3, and David Boucher, *Political Theories of International Relations* (Oxford: Oxford University Press, 1998), chaps. 5–7.

51. Hobbes, *Leviathan*, 161, 225, 226 (quotes), see also p. 184 on inevitable conflicts of interest; Machiavelli, *Discourses*, 5, 123, 125 (quotes).

52. Machiavelli offers a similar observation (if not the same enthusiastic endorsement): "it does not appear to men that they possess securely what a man has unless he acquires something else new" (*Discourses*, 4).

53. Keynes lauds Burke for "emphasizing a principle that is often in need of such emphasis. Our power of Prediction is so slight, our knowledge of remote consequences so uncertain, that it is seldom wise to sacrifice a present benefit for a doubtful advantage in the future." John Maynard Keynes, "The Political Doctrines of Edmund Burke" (undergraduate essay, Archives Centre, Kings College, Cambridge, 1904), 14.

54. That is why, Clausewitz lectures, "guesswork and luck come to play a great part in war." Carl von Clausewitz, *On War*, ed. and trans. Michael Howard and Peter Paret, with essays by Paret, Howard, and Brodie, and commentary by Brodie (Princeton: Princeton University Press, 1976), 85. Leo Tolstoy, *War and Peace*, trans. Constance Garnett (New York: Modern Library, 2004), 1138.

55. Clausewitz, *On War*, 69, 81, 87, 579 (quotes). Politics rules, as Clausewitz notes repeatedly. "War cannot be divorced from political life" (605). War is part of policy, and so "policy will determine its character" (606). In war "the result is never final" (80), as politics always continues; moreover, gesturing at the limits to the utility of force, he observes that there will be cases where "the political object will not provide a suitable military objective" (81), which is a rather tidy summary of the American military experiences in Vietnam and Iraq, about which more in chapter 3.

56. Edmund Burke, "Remarks on the Policy of the Allies" (1793), in *Empire and Community: Edmund Burke's Writings and Speeches on International Relations*, ed. David P. Fidler and Jennifer M. Welsch (Boulder: Westview Press, 1999), 281; Edmund Burke, "Speech on the Petition of the Unitarian Society," May 11, 1792, in Edmund Burke, *Reflections on the Revolution in France and Other Writing*,

ed. Jessie Norman (New York: Knopf, 2015), 794. See also Isaac Kramnick, *The Rage of Edmund Burke: Portrait of an Ambivalent Conservative* (New York: Basic Books, 1977), 12, 146.

57. As noted in the introduction, it was just called "realism" back then, of course—just as the legendary bands in the 1960s and 1970s did not call their music "classic rock," the founders of modern realism simply saw themselves as Realists. The distinction between various schools of realist thought would only become important in the closing decades of the century, when "structural realism" emerged as the preponderant school of realist thought.

58. On Carr's naiveté, see, for example, Edward Hallett Carr, *The Soviet Impact on the Western World* (New York: Macmillan, 1947), and his rather dismal *Conditions of Peace* (New York: Macmillan, 1943), a book that Carr himself would later accurately describe as "highly utopian" and "pretty feeble"; E. H. Carr, "An Autobiography," in *E. H. Carr: A Critical Appraisal*, ed. Michael Cox (New York: Palgrave, 2000), xix; see also Jonathan Haslam, *The Vices of Integrity: E. H. Carr, 1892–1982* (London: Verso, 1999). Kennan's *Democracy and the Student Left* (New York: Bantam, 1968) is an embarrassment; his cold comfort with authoritarianism in *From Prague after Munich: Diplomatic Papers, 1938–1940* (Princeton: Princeton University Press, 1968) is chilling. John Lewis Gaddis, *George F. Kennan: An American Life* (New York: Penguin, 2011) is a generous but nevertheless disheartening read; more dispiriting still is George F. Kennan, *The Kennan Diaries*, ed. Frank Costigliola (New York: Norton, 2014). See also John Lukacs, *George Kennan: A Study of Character* (New Haven: Yale University Press, 2007). On Aron, see Stanley Hoffman, "Raymond Aron (1905–1983)," *New York Review of Books*, December 8, 1983. Finally, as noted, some thinkers are not just flawed but odious. To the extent that Henry Kissinger can be taken seriously as an IR theorist—and his book, *A World Restored: Metternich, Castlereagh and the Problems of Peace, 1812–22* (Boston: Houghton Mifflin, 1957), is a notable contribution to Classical Realism—the balance of his writings need to be understood as shaped by a singular craving for proximity to power. He was also, as a practitioner, a despicable man with gratuitously bloodstained hands, whom Thucydides would surely have assessed with the revulsion he reserved for unprincipled opportunists. On Kissinger and realism, see Jonathan Kirshner, "Machinations of Wicked Men," *Boston Review* 42:2 (March/April 2016): 49–55.

59. E. H. Carr, *The Twenty Years' Crisis, 1919–1939*, 2nd ed. (New York: St. Martin's Press, 1946 [1939]), 50, 51, 53, 60 (quotes); Arnold Wolfers, "Statesmanship and Moral Choice" (1962), in his *Discord and Collaboration* (Baltimore: Johns Hopkins University Press, 1962), 63; Reinhold Niebuhr, *Moral Man and Immoral Society* (New York: Scribner, 1932), xxxi (quote), see also, e.g., pp. 4, 233.

60. Carr, *Twenty Years' Crisis*, 179 (quote), 180, 207.

61. George F. Kennan, "The Sources of Soviet Conduct," *Foreign Affairs* 25 (1947); see also Kennan, "Russia—Seven Years Later" (1944), reprinted in Kennan, *Memoirs, 1925–1950* (Boston: Little, Brown, 1967), 503–31.

62. George F. Kennan, *American Diplomacy, 1900–1950* (New York: Mentor Books, 1951); Kennan, *Realities of American Foreign Policy* (New York: Norton, 1966/1954). In the preface to *Realities*, Kennan described the book as "the most comprehensive statement I have ever made of my outlook."

63. George F. Kennan, *Memoirs, 1925–1950* (Boston: Little, Brown, 1967), 495–96; Kennan, *Realities of American Foreign Policy*, 35–36. Niebuhr speaks similarly of the status quo: *Moral Man and Immoral Society*, 234.

64. Part of this was surely attributable to Kennan's elitism as well.

65. Kennan, *Realities of American Foreign Policy*, 35; Kennan, *American Diplomacy*, 88. Kennan elaborates this key point, on the need to understand and evaluate the use of force in its political context: "We will continue to harm our interests . . . if we continue to employ the instruments of coercion in the international field without a better understanding of their significance and possibilities" (88).

66. Kennan, *American Diplomacy*, 88; see also Kennan *Memoirs, 1925–1950*, 495; Machiavelli, *The Prince*, 12; Kennan, *Realities of American Foreign Policy*, 93.

67. Hans Morgenthau, *Scientific Man vs. Power Politics* (Chicago: University of Chicago Press, 1946); Hans Morgenthau, *In Defense of the National Interest: A Critical Examination of American Foreign Policy* (New York: Knopf, 1951); Hans Morgenthau, *Politics among Nations: The Struggle for Power and Peace*, 3rd ed. (New York: Knopf, 1960/1948). Morgenthau quote is from Christoph Frei, *Hans J. Morgenthau: An Intellectual Biography* (Baton Rouge: Louisiana State University Press, 2001), 206. Morgenthau's preference for *Scientific Man* is notable. *Politics among Nations* is a valuable book, rich with insights. But ultimately, as a textbook at times it oversimplifies and can appear mechanistic. Morgenthau is right to see *Scientific Man* as his greatest achievement and enduring statement.

68. Morgenthau, *Scientific Man*; see, for example, pp. 121, 122, 139, 150, 204. Morgenthau stresses the "interminable chains of causes and effects" and the linkages between them resulting in an enmeshed, cascading series of reactions, creating "junctions and crossing-points of many other chains, supporting or counteracting each other" (129); Reinhold Niebuhr, *The Self and the Dramas of History* (New York: Scribner, 1955), 49.

69. Morgenthau, *Scientific Man*, 168; Hans Morgenthau, *Science: Servant or Master?* (New York: New American Library, 1972), 31.

70. Hans Morgenthau, "The Evil of Politics and the Politics of Evil," *Ethics* 56:1 (October 1945): 1, 13, 16–17; Martin Wight, *Power Politics* (New York: Holmes & Meier, 1978/1946), 144; Nicholas Spykman, *America's Strategy in World Politics: The United States and the Balance of Power* (New York: Harcourt, Brace, 1942), 20. Similarly from E. H. Carr: "the exercise of power always appears to beget the appetite for more power" (*Twenty Years' Crisis*, 112). Again Niebuhr adds his voice to this chorus: "In man the impulses of self-preservation are transmuted very easily into desires for aggrandizement" (*Moral Man and Immoral Society*, 41); see also *The Children of Light and the Children of Darkness*, 367, 268, 451.

71. Hans Morgenthau, "International Affairs: The Resurrection of Neutrality in Europe," *American Political Science Review* 33:3 (June 1939): 479; Morgenthau, *Scientific Man*, 75, 84, 90, 105 (quote), 121. (See also pp. 80–83 for a similarly skeptical view of the idea of the pacifying effects of international commerce.)

72. "It is the very essence of historic experience that whenever you have disposed of one danger in foreign policy another is going to raise its head." Hans Morgenthau, "Realism in International Politics," *Naval War College Review* 10:5 (1958): 4; Morgenthau, *In Defense of the National Interest*, 33 (quote).

73. Hans J. Morgenthau, "The Limitations of Science and the Problem of Social Planning," *Ethics* 54:3 (1944): 174–85, see esp. pp. 182–83 on chance in war; Morgenthau, *Scientific Man*, 219 (statesman vs. engineer). Kennan returns the favor, noting that "the greatest law of human history is its unpredictability" (*Realities of American Foreign Policy*, 92).

74. Morgenthau, *Politics among Nations*, 20–21. "The first lesson the student of international politics must learn and never forget," Morgenthau lectures, "is that the complexities of international affairs make simple solutions and trustworthy prophecies impossible" (20).

75. Raymond Aron, *Peace and War: A Theory of International Relations* (New Brunswick, NJ: Transaction Publishers, 2003/1966), 23, 85, 92, 107, 140, 585; Raymond Aron, *Clausewitz: Philosopher of War*, trans. Norman Stone and Christine Booker (London: Routledge, 1983). See also Stanley Hoffmann, "Raymond Aron and the Theory of International Relations," *International Studies Quarterly* 29:1 (1985): 14–15.

76. Raymond Aron, *Memoirs: Fifty Years of Political Reflection* (New York: Holmes & Meier, 1990/1983), 39; Raymond Aron, *The Committed Observer* (Chicago: Regnery Gateway, 1983), 48, 50; Raymond Aron, *The Dawn of Universal History: Selected Essays from a Witness to the Twentieth Century*, ed. Yair Reiner with an introduction by Tony Judt (New York: Basic Books, 2002), ix, xi. See also Raymond Aron, *Introduction to the Philosophy of History: An Essay on the Limits of Historical Objectivity* (London: Weidenfeld and Nicholson, 1948/1938), and Tony Judt, *The Burden of Responsibility: Blum, Camus, Aron and the French Twentieth Century* (Chicago: University of Chicago Press, 1998), esp. 141–42.

77. Aron, *Memoirs*, 100. We would add, nevertheless, some days it does—a challenge for realism that we consider in chapter 4.

78. Niebuhr, *Moral Man and Immoral Society*, xxvii; Aron, *The Committed Observer*, 261. Morgenthau, not surprisingly, shares this position: "we tend to overlook the fact that in the sphere of political action there is no such thing as one and the same truth for everybody" (*In Defense of the National Interest*, 216).

79. Gilpin, *War and Change*. It should be noted that *War and Change* does build an abstract, structural framework; it is nevertheless deeply enmeshed in Classical traditions and disposition. See Jonathan Kirshner, "Gilpin Approaches *War and Change*: A Classical Realist in Structural Drag," in *Power, Order and Change in World Politics*, ed. G. John Ikenberry (Cambridge: Cambridge University Press, 2014), 131–61.

80. Gilpin, *War and Change*, 4, 6, 13–14, 88–90, 93 (quote), 96 (note that the title of Gilpin's book suggests pessimism regarding this prospect; see esp. pp 206–8); Kennan, *Realities of American Foreign Policy*, 32; Robert Gilpin, "The Theory of Hegemonic War," *Journal of Interdisciplinary History* 18:4 (1988): 15, 19, 25–26 (Thucydides); Gilpin, "The Richness of the Tradition of Political Realism," 306, 309 (Carr). Gilpin also cites the influence of Morgenthau's *Scientific Man*, "Conversations in *International Relations*: Interview with Robert Gilpin," *International Relations* 19:3 (2005): 363.

81. Gilpin, *War and Change*, 7 (quote), 16, 18, 24, 211, 227 (quote); Gilpin, "Theory of Hegemonic War," 17–18, 35–36. Raymond Aron is critical of "the illusion of the orientation of history in a constant direction, of evolution towards a state of affairs in

harmony with an ideal." Raymond Aron, *The Opium of the Intellectuals* (New Brunswick, NJ: Transaction Publishers, 2007/1955), xx.

82. Gilpin, *War and Change*, 63, 96ff. (domestic factors), 106 (ambition), 152–54 (decay). See also his emphasis on "the decay of bourgeois middle class work ethic": Robert Gilpin, "Economic Interdependence and National Security in Historical Perspective," in *Economic Issues and National Security*, ed. Klaus Knorr and Frank Traeger (Lawrence: University Press of Kansas, 1977), 59.

83. Gilpin, *War and Change*, 8, 37–38, 51 (quotes). The ideological character of the superpowers, Gilpin held, was "a greatly underappreciated factor in the preservation of world peace" during the Cold War (240). Morgenthau, *Politics among Nations*, 9; Robert Gilpin, "The Politics of Transnational Economic Relations," *International Organization* 25:3 (1971): 401, 403 (sentiment and values); Wight, *Power Politics*, 81; on ideas, see also "Interview with Robert Gilpin," 361.

84. As noted in the introduction, the inquests into the nuts-and-bolts of these approaches, necessarily, are closely detailed, and general readers can skip ahead to the last few pages of the discussion that situate "the craft of classical realism."

Chapter Two: Reclaiming Realism

1. Readers disinclined to dig into the more technical arguments of this chapter can skip ahead to the section titled "The Craft of Classical Realism."

2. Sections of this chapter draw on Jonathan Kirshner, "The Economic Sins of Modern IR Theory and the Classical Realist Alternative," *World Politics* 67:1 (2015): 155–83.

3. It is notable that much of economics (and especially those aspects of economic theory embraced by IR theorists) suffers from what has been described as "physics envy." See Philip Miroski, *More Heat than Light: Economics as Social Physics, Physics as Nature's Economics* (Cambridge: Cambridge University Press, 1991).

4. Kathleen McNamara, "Of Intellectual Monocultures and the Study of IPE," *Review of International Political Economy* 16:1 (2009): 72–84; Jonathan Kirshner, "The Second Crisis in IPE Theory," in *International Political Economy: Debating the Past, Present and Future*, ed. Nicola Phillips and Catherine Weaver (London: Routledge, 2011).

5. Robert Gilpin, *U.S. Power and the Multinational Corporation* (New York: Basic Books, 1975), 27.

6. As discussed in chapter 1, another distinction between Classical and Structural Realism as it is commonly practiced is that, even when operating at the systemic level, classical realists tend to place much more emphasis on dynamics (that is, changes to the balance of power) rather than statics (such as whether the system is multipolar or bipolar).

7. Kenneth Waltz, *Theory of International Politics* (New York: Addison Wesley, 1979), 65, 68.

8. On this point, see Robert Jervis, *Perception and Misperception in International Politics* (Princeton: Princeton University Press, 1977), 19–21.

9. For a good discussion of some of these issues, see Joseph Nye, "Neorealism and Neoliberalism," *World Politics* 40:2 (1988): 235, 242, 245.

10. Robert L. Bishop, "Duopoly: Collusion or Warfare?" *American Economic Review* 50:5 (1960): 933, 960; George Stigler, "A Theory of Oligopoly," *Journal of Political Economy* 72:1 (1964): 44. "Only by making special assumptions about the oligopolistic environment . . . can we expect to wind up with a specific prediction regarding oligopoly behavior," that is, "predictions regarding the extent of competition or collusion." Carl Shapiro, "Theories of Oligopoly Behavior," in *Handbook of Industrial Organization*, ed. Richard Schmalensee and Robert Willig (Amsterdam: North Holland, 1989), 332.

11. Waltz, *Theory of International Politics*, 73. Note that another prominent structural realist theory, John Mearsheimer's *The Tragedy of Great Power Politics* (New York: Norton, 2001), is also explicitly focused on the great powers, with yields the same analytical pathologies. In fact the fundamental flaws of the arguments articulated in *Tragedy* run even deeper, as elaborated in chapter 6.

12. An important difference of course (in practical experience if not necessarily analytical consequence) is that although firms' survival is almost constantly at stake, and they are commonly driven out of existence by their rivals, they are not visited with violent annihilation. Thus states in anarchy have an additional incentive to balance rather than collude (though great power condominiums can occur and have their appeal). The point is that we knew this long before *Theory of International Politics* was published—this is realism 101 if not IR 101—and the conclusion does not flow from the logic of the would-be innovation of "Theory" of International Politics via its appeal to a microeconomic analogy, which is poorly applied at best and tells us nothing new.

13. To be clear, from a classical realist perspective, the choices of great powers shape, but do not determine, the nature of systemic forces that influence other states (and themselves). Here the microeconomic analogy holds; oligopolistic firms are not price takers, but neither are they free from the constraints of and incentives created by the market. (Aron quote is from Robert Gilpin, *War and Change in World Politics* [Cambridge: Cambridge University Press, 1981], 29.)

14. Arnold Wolfers, "The Goals of Foreign Policy," in Wolfers, *Discord and Collaboration* (Baltimore: Johns Hopkins University Press, 1962).

15. Just as states are more robust than men, making Hobbes's state of nature a very different experience for each, states are in general less fragile than firms, and thus enjoy much broader discretion with regard to the range of choices they will make—even unwise choices. As Adam Smith once observed, "there is a great deal of ruin in a nation." Ian Simpson Ross, *The Life of Adam Smith* (Oxford: Oxford University Press, 1995), 32.

16. Norrin Ripsman, "Neoclassical Realism," in *The International Studies Compendium Project*, ed. Robert Denemark et al. (Oxford: Wiley-Blackwell, 2011).

17. The term "Neoclassical Realism" was originally coined by Gideon Rose, "Neoclassical Realism and Theories of Foreign Policy," *World Politics* 51:1 (1998): 144–72, and exemplary work in this tradition includes Thomas J. Christensen and Jack Snyder, "Chain Gangs and Passed Bucks: Predicting Alliance Patterns in Multipolarity," *International Organization* 44:2 (1990): 137–68. For the state of the art, see Norrin Ripsman, Jeffrey Taliaferro, and Steven Lobell, *Neoclassical Realist Theory of International Politics* (Oxford: Oxford University Press, 2016). James Tobin, interviewed

in Brian Snowdon, Howard Vane, and Peter Wynarczyk, *A Modern Guide to Macroeconomics: An Introduction to Competing Schools of Thought* (Aldershot: Edward Elgar, 1994), 132.

18. Gilpin, *War and Change*, 51; Robert Gilpin, "The Politics of Transnational Economic Relations," *International Organization* 25:3 (1971): 401, 403. Note the affinity here with Keynes, whose approach to economic theory, as discussed below, is also consistent with classical realism. In the memoir that summarized much of his own personal philosophy, Keynes even more pointedly critiqued "an over-valuation of the economic criterion," which he saw as the source of "the final *reductio ad absurdum* of Benthamism known as Marxism." John Maynard Keynes, "My Early Beliefs," *CW*, 10:446. See Jonathan Kirshner, "Keynes, Legacies, and Inquiry," *Theory and Society* 38:4 (2009): 527–41, and especially Kirshner, "Keynes's Early Beliefs and Why They Still Matter," *Challenge* 58:5 (2015): 398–412.

19. Recall, for example, Thucydides' assessment that Syracuse was an especially formidable adversary because of its distinct political character (8.96.5), and the way that some of Sparta's allies modulated their commitments to others on the basis of their domestic political affinities (5.31.5); for some additional representative examples among the many such claims that characterize Thucydides' *History*, see, e.g., 1.21 (on the role of national myths), 5.56, 5.81 (domestic politics leading to a shift in alliance choices), 8.1 (distinct behavior of democratic societies); see also E. H. Carr, *The Twenty Years' Crisis, 1919–1939*, 2nd ed. (New York: St. Martin's Press, 1946 [1939]), 108, 132, 138; 145 (quote); Hans Morgenthau, *In Defense of the National Interest: A Critical Examination of American Foreign Policy* (New York: Knopf, 1951), 4, 13, 115–16, 208, 223, 229, 234, 237. As noted in chapter 1, Kennan's most famous and influential work stressed the importance of historical experience, internal politics, and national character. George F. Kennan, "The Sources of Soviet Conduct," *Foreign Affairs* 25 (1947): 566–82.

20. Henry Kissinger, *A World Restored: Metternich, Castlereagh and the Problems of Peace, 1812–22* (Boston: Houghton Mifflin, 1957), 331. Unfortunately, every other book by Kissinger (and the academic ones are a mixed bag at best) must be read through the lens of either his aspiration to get closer to power or the desire to burnish his historical legacy, and thus should be approached with great caution.

21. Carr, *Twenty Years' Crisis*, 69 (quote), 92, 97, 98, 101, 108, 143, 152, 220–22; Kissinger, *A World Restored*, 331.

22. Reinhold Niebuhr, *Christian Realism and Political Problems* (New York: Scribner's, 1953), 91. To take a prominent and important example of efforts to bend social science toward natural science, Paul Samuelson, one of the most influential figures in the formation of the postwar academic discipline of economics, made his reputation with a contribution based on mathematical models of economics that derived directly from Newtonian physics. Paul Samuelson, *Foundations of Economic Analysis* (Cambridge, MA: Harvard University Press, 1946).

23. Waltz, *Theory of International Politics*, 91; Mearsheimer, *Tragedy of Great Power Politics*, 30.

24. Wolfers, "The Goals of Foreign Policy."

25. See chapter 6 for more on this essential issue.

26. Milton Friedman's essay "The Methodology of Positive Economics," in his *Essays in Positive Economics* (Chicago: University of Chicago Press, 1953), remains

an excellent articulation and defense of this perspective. For an argument that the goal of science is explanation, not prediction, see Stephen Toulmin, *Foresight and Understanding: An Enquiry into the Aims of Science* (Bloomington: Indiana University Press, 1961).

27. John Lewis Gaddis, "International Relations Theory and the End of the Cold War," *International Security* 17:3 (1992–93): 53. This argument is consistent with the related, complementary critique that contemporary IR theory has converged around an orientation that privileges narrow, instrumentalist hypothesis testing and devalues (or even dismisses) exploring causal processes (that is, explanation and understanding). See John Mearsheimer and Stephen Walt, "Leaving Theory Behind: Why Simplistic Hypothesis Testing Is Bad for International Relations," *European Journal of International Relations* 19:3 (2013): 427–57.

28. In a setting of actuarial risk, such as rolling dice, or flipping a coin, it is impossible to accurately "predict" a heads (that prediction would be right about half the time) or that a roll of two dice will sum to four. But it is possible to (very successfully) predict that there is a 50 percent chance of "heads" and an 8.33 percent chance of rolling a four.

29. Carr, *Twenty Years' Crisis*, 3–4.

30. This is one reason why it is so important to establish criteria of evaluation in advance of looking at the data.

31. These critiques are to be taken seriously. With Raymond Aron in chapter 1, "objectivity" should be understood as "striving for objectivity," with an ever present attentiveness to the limitations of that prospect and how an awareness of those limitations should temper one's analysis. For Aron on seeing the world as it is, see Robert F. Colquhoun, *Raymond Aron—Volume 1: The Philosopher in History, 1905–1955* (Beverly Hills, CA: SAGE Publications, 1986), 78.

32. Carr, *Twenty Years' Crisis*, 91.

33. Hans Morgenthau, *Scientific Man vs. Power Politics* (Chicago: University of Chicago Press, 1946), 121, 139 (quote), 150; see also Robert Gilpin, "The Richness of the Tradition of Political Realism," in *Neorealism and Its Critics*, ed. Robert O. Keohane (New York: Columbia University Press, 1986), 307.

34. Frank Knight, *Risk, Uncertainty and Profit* (Chicago: University of Chicago Press, 1971/1921), 241, 311; Friedrich von Hayek, "The Pretence of Knowledge" (Nobel Memorial Lecture, December 11, 1974), 267, 271–2. On these themes, see also Emanuel Derman, *Models. Behaving. Badly.: Why Confusing Illusion with Reality Can Lead to Disaster, on Wall Street and in Life* (New York: Free Press, 2011).

35. Reinhold Niebuhr, *The Self and the Dramas of History* (New York: Scribner, 1955), 47; George F. Kennan, *Realities of American Foreign Policy* (New York: Norton, 1966/1954), 92; Robert Gilpin, "No One Loves a Political Realist," *Security Studies* 5:3 (1996): 4. Similarly, Morton Kaplan insisted "we must give up the hope that a theory of international politics can have either the explanatory or the predictive power of a 'hard' science." Morton A. Kaplan, "Problems of Theory Building and Theory Confirmation in International Politics," *World Politics* 14:1 (1961): 6, 8, 11, 20 (quote), 21, 23–24; Morton A. Kaplan, "The New Great Debate: Traditionalism vs. Science in International Relations," *World Politics* 19:1 (October 1966): 1, 3, 12, 16, 19–20.

36. John Maynard Keynes to Roy Harrod, July 16, 1938, *CW*, 14:299, 300. Keynes repeatedly returned to this point. "Economics is essentially a moral science and not

a natural science. That is to say it employs introspection and judgments of value." Keynes to Harrod, July 4, 1938, *CW*, 14:297.

37. See, for example, D. Scott Bennett and Allan C. Stam, *The Behavioral Origins of War* (Ann Arbor: University of Michigan Press, 2004), and Stephen Van Evera, *Causes of War: Power and the Roots of Conflict* (Ithaca: Cornell University Press, 1999). Bennett and Stam are very much in the business of prediction (see, for example, p. 157), although they are attentive to the challenges and pitfalls of such an enterprise (see esp. chapter 2, "Comparative Hypothesis Testing and Some Limits to Knowledge" and pp. 165–66 on the challenge of generalizability). Van Evera, near the other end of the methodological spectrum in the discipline, nevertheless explores five principal hypotheses, in order to "apply them to explain history, infer policy predictions, and predict the future" (3). Both studies, it should be emphasized, are appropriately cautious; Bennett and Stam conclude "there is no single story of war," and "In many ways we are as uncertain about the causes and likely timing of any individual war today as we were in 1942" (201). Van Evera's strongest predictive claim is a negative one; in the "total absence" of his five factors, "war rarely occurs" (255).

38. Thus robust and steady estimations of crucial factors such as elasticities of income and demand and the market sensitivity to compliments and substitutes can be confidently proffered. Whereas it should seem manifest that the behavioral relationships between variables that contribute to the causes of war change over time (that is, the same factors that led to war in one historical setting might not lead to war in another). But the problem is even more fundamental than that. Even from a very narrow, rationalist perspective, were a comprehensive "theory of war" to somehow emerge, actors would immediately integrate those findings and expectations into their own strategies and behavior. This would require an updating of the comprehensive theory, which would again lead states to alter their behavior, and so on, recursively. On this point, see, for example, Erik Gartzke, "War Is the Error Term," *International Organization* 53:3 (1999): 575. (Gartzke also observes "explaining war in individual cases becomes tantamount to accounting for the advent of 'heads' in the toss of a coin" [568].)

39. On the challenge of complexity in International Relations, and in particular with reference to the challenges of predicting the behavior of individual states, see Charles P. Kindleberger, "A Monetary Economist on Power Politics," *World Politics* 6:4 (1954): 509–10, and Kindleberger, "Scientific International Politics," *World Politics* 11:1 (1958): 86.

40. Alfred Marshall, "Fragments," in *Memorials of Alfred Marshall*, ed. A. C. Pigou (London: Macmillan, 1925), 360 (quote); Alfred Marshall, *Principles of Economics*, 8th ed. (London: McMillan, 1920), esp. book I, chapter iii, "Economic Generalizations or Laws," 30–33; Morgenthau, *Scientific Man*, 129. On the limits to prediction in economics, see also Frank H. Knight, "'What Is Truth' in Economics?" *Journal of Political Economy* 48:1 (1940): 29–31, and Andrew Rutten, "But It Will Never Be Science, Either," *Journal of Economic History* 40:1 (1980): 139, 141–42. This problem is not to be underestimated: "The kind of precise conclusions that are so highly valued in contemporary economics can be rigorously derived only when very special assumptions are made. But the very special assumptions do not fit very much of the economy around us." Nancy Cartwright, *The Dappled World: A Study of the Boundaries of*

Science (Cambridge: Cambridge University Press, 1999), 28, 143–44, 149 (quote), 151. Ironically, Marshall has a decent eye for predicting war (at least in the most general sense); in 1915 he wrote (quite accurately) to Keynes: "I shall not live to see our next war with Germany; but you will, I expect." Alfred Marshall to John Maynard Keynes, February 21, 1915, reprinted in *Memorials*, 482.

41. Jonathan Kirshner, *Appeasing Bankers: Financial Caution on the Road to War* (Princeton: Princeton University Press, 2007), chap. 6. In my view *none* of the possible alternatives to Thatcher, from either within the Conservative party or the head of any Labour government, would have tried to use force to retake the Islands. Similarly, if a hypothetical President Gore would not have fought the Iraq war—and Gore could have easily won that election, as he captured the popular vote and was arguably defeated by mistaken votes poked on confusing butterfly-ballots—it would be very hard for a general abstract theory to account for that war (and all that followed as a consequence of its persecution).

42. Consider, for example, the (very distinct) motivations and goals associated with the U.S. invasion of Panama in 1989, China's attack on Vietnam in 1979, Great Britain's declaration of war on Germany in 1939, and Chile's decision to take on Bolivia and Peru in 1879.

43. Hans Morgenthau, *Politics among Nations: The Struggle for Power and Peace*, 3rd ed. (New York: Knopf, 1960/1948), 20 (quote), 21; Raymond Aron, *Peace and War: A Theory of International Relations* (New Brunswick, NJ: Transaction Publishers, 2003/1966), 93.

44. George F. Kennan, *American Diplomacy, 1900–1950* (New York: Mentor Books, 1951), 69, 70; Morgenthau, *Scientific Man*, 150.

45. Morgenthau, *Scientific Man*, 150; also 129, 139, 146–48, 220, 221.

46. James Fearon, "Rationalist Explanations for War," *International Organization* 49:3 (1995): 392.

47. Jonathan Kirshner, "Rationalist Explanations for War?" *Security Studies* 10:1 (2000): 143–50.

48. A good introduction to this literature remains Preston Miller, ed., *The Rational Expectations Revolution* (Cambridge, MA: MIT Press, 1994).

49. Karl Brunner and Allan H. Meltzer, *Money in the Economy: Issues in Monetary Analysis* (Cambridge: Cambridge University Press, 1993), 42; Michael C. Lovell, "Tests of the Rational Expectations Hypothesis," *American Economic Review* 76:1 (1986): 122; Benjamin Friedman, "Optimal Expectations and the Extreme Information Assumptions of 'Rational Expectations' Macromodels," *Journal of Monetary Economics* 5 (1979): 26–27; Roman Frydman and Michael D. Goldberg, *Imperfect Knowledge Economics: Exchange Rates and Risk* (Princeton: Princeton University Press, 2007), 54 (quote), see also 29, 106, 113–14, 126, 132, 138, 140, 151, 203.

50. With variations representing random errors distributed around the correct underlying model.

51. John Muth, "Rational Expectations and the Theory of Price Movements," *Econometrica* 29:3 (1961): 316; George Evans and Seppo Honkapohja, "An Interview with Thomas J. Sargent," *Macroeconomic Dynamics* 9 (2005): 566.

52. Thus, variations in prediction, and variations in the accuracy of those predictions, should be distributed randomly around the correct outcomes.

53. See, for example, John Maynard Keynes, *The General Theory of Employment, Interest, and Money* (London: Macmillan, 1936), *CW*, 8:148–49, 151–52; John Maynard Keynes, "The General Theory of Employment," *Quarterly Journal of Economics* 51:2 (1937), *CW*, 14:113–14. Again, Keynes is not arguing that people are irrational; rather, with reference to "our rational selves" Keynes is "merely reminding ourselves that human decisions affecting the future, whether personal or political or economic, cannot depend on strict mathematical expectation, since the basis for making such calculations does not exist" (*The General Theory*, 162–63). As Skidelsky observes, "the centerpiece of Keynes' theory is the existence of inescapable uncertainty about the future." Robert Skidelsky, *Keynes: Return of the Master* (New York: Public Affairs, 2009), xv.

54. Hayek, "The Pretence of Knowledge," 271–72, 275; see also Friedrich von Hayek, "The Use of Knowledge in Society," *American Economic Review* 35:4 (1945): 519–30; Knight, *Risk, Uncertainty and Profit*, 19, 20, 198, 232–33, 268, 287–88, 293. See also Frydman and Goldberg, *Imperfect Knowledge Economics*, 3, 15.

55. Thomas Sargent, *The Conquest of American Inflation* (Princeton: Princeton University Press, 1999), 133; Roman Frydman and Michael D. Goldberg, *Beyond Mechanical Markets: Asset Price Swings, Risk, and the Role of the State* (Princeton: Princeton University Press, 2011), 52 (quote), 102, 139, 196.

56. Knight, *Risk, Uncertainty and Profit*, 19, 242; see also 231, 233, 241. See also Kirshner, "Rationalist Explanations"; Robert Jervis, "Signaling and Perception: Drawing Inferences and Projecting Images," in *Political Psychology*, ed. Kristin Monroe (Mahwah, NJ: Lawrence Erlbaum, 2002), 297–98.

57. David Colander et al., "The Financial Crisis and the Systemic Failure of the Economics Profession," *Critical Review* 21:2–3 (2009): 256. As one early critic observed, rational expectations assumes "that economic agents not only know the relevant current and past observations, plus the future values of selected time series, but also have whatever additional knowledge is required to transform this information into *objectively* unbiased conditional expectations of the time series to be predicted." Friedman, "Optimal Expectations," 26–27, 38. Recent critics have continued to hammer away at the utter implausibility of these assumptions, noting that they imply "all market participants would have discovered an overarching causal mechanism that characterizes aggregate outcomes, as well as how the causal factors evolve over time." Frydman and Goldberg, *Imperfect Knowledge Economics*, 52, also 4, 6, 8, 28; see also Frydman and Goldberg, *Beyond Mechanical Markets*, 56, 64, 65.

58. Colander et al., "The Financial Crisis," 256; Mervyn King, "Monetary Policy—Practice Ahead of Theory" (Mais Lecture, Cass Business School, City, University of London, May 17, 2005), 4.

59. Again, as noted above, differences across experts could still occur, but they would be randomly distributed around the mean implied by a shared underlying model. Again, in the real life of the social sciences, this rarely, if ever, occurs. Consider, for example, that minority cohort of economists who warned (quite mistakenly, it should be added) that emergency measures taken in the wake of the global financial crisis would lead to a surge of ruinous inflation. The point is not that they were embarrassingly wrong but that they were clearly drawing with confidence on very different economic models than other professional economists.

60. It is beyond the scope of the discussion here, but the global financial crisis settled the question of the "efficient markets hypothesis," a virtual Siamese twin of Rational Expectations Theory. As Eugene Fama, the intellectual father of the hypothesis, notes, "rational expectations stuff is basically efficient markets." Douglas Clement, "Interview with Eugene Fama," *The Region* (Federal Reserve Bank of Minneapolis, December 1, 2007).

61. It should nevertheless be observed that the assumptions of the approach should raise considerable skepticism as to its real-world applicability. The elimination of all political motives for conflict (which is understood only in terms of material gains and losses) does not seem to capture the motivations of conflicts throughout history; similarly, the "unitary actor" assumption assumes away the notion that domestic politics might influence foreign policy. Nevertheless, analytically it is more important to demonstrate that the REW perspective fails due to its *internal* logic—the criteria of evaluation that it would establish for itself. In a sentence: If Rational Expectations Theory is wrong (or does not properly apply to questions of war and peace), then REW and applications of the bargaining model that build on REW are, simply, wrong.

62. Ernest May, *Strange Victory: Hitler's Conquest of France* (New York: Hill and Wang, 2000) looks at the evidence and reaches conclusions that are the opposite of Marc Bloch, *Strange Defeat* (New York: Norton, 1999 [1940]). Tony Judt, in *Reappraisals: Reflections on the Forgotten Twentieth Century* (New York: Penguin, 2008), looks at the evidence and reaches conclusions that are the opposite of May's.

63. On the eve of any war, for example, both sides will be making guesses (again, drawing on different implicit models) about crucial variables that are unknown, and unknowable, to *both* sides, and will only become apparent when the war is underway.

64. A. J. P. Taylor, *The First World War: An Illustrated History* (New York: Penguin, 1967), 104.

65. For a discussion of the central role of uncertainty and chance in World War I, see Roger L. Ransom, *Gambling on War: Confidence, Fear and the Tragedy of the First World War* (Cambridge: Cambridge University Press, 2018), e.g., 83, 228–31; on the general point, see also Martha C. Nussbaum, *The Fragility of Goodness: Luck and Ethics in Greek Tragedy and Philosophy* (Cambridge: Cambridge University Press, 2001), 89, 91, 105.

66. Recall, for example, the radically differing assessments and expectations of members of the elite "Executive Committee" during the Cuban Missile Crisis.

67. Carl von Clausewitz, *On War*, ed. and trans. Michael Howard and Peter Paret (Princeton: Princeton University Press, 1976), 85, 86, 91, 136; Sidney Low, "Germanism and Prussianism," *Edinburgh Review* 220:450 (1914): 276 (Bismarck); Gilpin, *War and Change*, 74, 202.

68. Leo Tolstoy, *War and Peace*, trans. Constance Garnett (New York: Modern Library, 2004), 729.

69. Clausewitz, *On War*, 120, 593.

70. Clement, "Interview with Eugene Fama."

71. See, for example, Michael Woodford, "Convergence in Macroeconomics: Elements of the New Synthesis," *American Economic Journal: Macroeconomics* 1:1 (2009): 267–79, and Olivier Blanchard, "The State of Macro," *Annual Review of Economics* 1:1 (2009): 209–28.

72. An excellent discussion of these issues can be found in a Senate hearing tasked with evaluating the state of macroeconomic theory in the wake of the crisis. Those providing testimony included Nobel Laureate Robert Solow and one minority witness, V. V. Chari, who acknowledged that "this class of models failed to see the crisis coming" and "tended to deemphasize these kinds of financial crises," but nevertheless offered a spirited (if unconvincing) defense of the approach. "Building a Science of Economics for the Real World," Hearing Before the Subcommittee on Investigations and Oversight, Committee on Science and Technology, House of Representatives, 111/2, July 20, 2012. See also "Agents of Change," *Economist*, July 22, 2010; Willem Buiter, "The Unfortunate Uselessness of Most 'State of the Art' Academic Monetary Economics," *FT.Com*, March 3, 2009 (Buiter quotes Charles Goodhart on DSGE); Colander et al., "The Financial Crisis," 249–67.

73. Riccardo Rebonato, *Plight of the Fortune Tellers: Why We Need to Manage Financial Risk Differently* (Princeton: Princeton University Press, 2007), ix–x, 5–7, 137 (quote), 141, 145–46, 178; Derman, *Models. Behaving. Badly.*, 153, 185 (quote).

74. On this point, see Joshua Foa Dienstag, "Pessimistic Realism and Realistic Pessimism," in *Political Thought and International Relations: Variations on a Realist Theme*, ed. Duncan Bell (Oxford: Oxford University Press, 2009). "The most important events . . . cannot be predicted. Nor is this a matter which will be remedied by further developments within social science" (170).

75. Stanley Hoffmann, "An American Social Science: International Relations," *Daedalus* 106:3 (1977): 51, 57; see also Stanley Hoffmann, "Raymond Aron and the Theory of International Relations," *International Studies Quarterly* 29:1 (1985): 16, 21, 25.

76. Morgenthau, *Scientific Man*, 138–40; Morgenthau, *Politics among Nations*, 16, 21; Thucydides, *The Peloponnesian War*, 1.78.1–2, 1.79.2, 2.11.4; recall as well Thucydides' high praise for the Spartan king Archidamus, who in counseling caution expressed similar sentiments—that in wartime, "freaks of chance are not determinable by calculation" (1.84.3). See also Gilpin, *War and Change*, 3, 74, 202–3.

77. Keynes, "The General Theory of Employment," 122 (quote); see also 113–14 for a discussion of the importance of uncertainty, such as "the prospect of a European war" or "the rate of interest twenty years hence" or "the obsolescence of a new invention," matters where "there is no scientific basis on which to form any calculable probability whatsoever."

78. Kenneth Waltz, "A Response to My Critics," in *Neorealism and Its Critics*, ed. Robert O. Keohane (New York: Columbia University Press, 1986), 329. To this reader, at least, *Theory of International Politics* has four "big and important" things to say—two of which were already standard to Realism, and two of which, more novel, are not shown. The first two: (1) states that fail to attend to their security in the context of anarchy do so at great peril to their survival; (2) states tend to balance against other powerful states when that option is plausible. The second two regard bipolarity, and although they are presented as deductive arguments, they are backwardly induced from the specific circumstances of the Cold War and need not hold in general. Bipolarity is not necessarily less prone to great power war than multipolarity (consider the "hundred years' peace" from 1815 to 1914), nor is it necessarily durable (the Soviet Union vanished ten years after *Theory of International Politics* was published).

Nor is bipolarity more stable because interdependence between the superpowers is irrelevant; that the superpowers had little economic discourse between them was another particular consequence of the Cold War, and is not inherent to bipolarity (as contemporary U.S.-China relations might suggest). And noted above, we cannot even conclude—following the pristine, deductive, content-free microeconomic logic used to forge Waltz's theory—that the superpowers will even balance against each other. So what is the purchase of this parsimonious model?

79. The medical analogy, commonly invoked by Machiavelli (see, for example, *The Prince*, trans. Harvey Mansfield [Chicago: University of Chicago Press, 1998/1531], 8, 12), on political challenges that are "diseases" which must be diagnosed and cured remains a productive one for Classical Realism. Note also Myron Weiner, "The Macedonian Syndrome: An Historical Model of International Relations and Political," *World Politics* 23:4 (1971): "no matter how precise the model, no matter how often it has been tested against accumulated case histories, no individual case need fit the model of the disease in every detail. Patients are in different conditions and have different susceptibilities to the same ailment" (667). See also Alfred Marshall, "Distribution and Exchange," *Economic Journal* 8:29 (1898), who held that in economics "better analogies are to be got from biology than from physics" (39; see also pp. 43, 44).

80. Kindleberger, "Scientific International Politics," 86.

81. Charles P. Kindleberger, *Economic Laws and Economic History* (Cambridge: Cambridge University Press, 1989), ix (quote), x, 127, 193; Charles P. Kindleberger, *Historical Economics: Art or Science* (Berkeley: University of California Press, 1990), 4 ("patterns of uniformity"), 7, 9 ("toolbox"); Charles P. Kindleberger, *The Life of an Economist: An Autobiography* (Cambridge: Basil Blackwell, 1991), 194 (quote). The "tool kit" approach also has affinities with Alfred Marshall, and his emphasis on "partial equilibrium"—understanding the behavior of a particular variable in isolation, as opposed to a "general equilibrium approach [explaining everything all at once]." Marshall, "Distribution and Exchange," 37–38, 40, 47–48; Marshall, *Principles*, e.g., 36, 131, 366, 369; Alfred Marshall, "The Present Position of Economics (1895)," reprinted in *Memorials*, 168; George Stigler, "The Place of Marshall's *Principles* in the Development of Economics," in *Centenary Essays on Alfred Marshall*, ed. John K. Whitaker (Cambridge: Cambridge University Press, 1990), 5.

82. Susan Strange, "1995 Presidential Address: ISA as a Microcosm," *International Studies Quarterly* 39:3 (1995): 291. Unfortunately, in the decades that followed, graduate students in International Politics have increasingly done the opposite, with those pursuing specializations in "political economy" increasingly taking courses in economic methods and learning considerably less economic theory.

83. Kindleberger, "A Monetary Economist on Power Politics," 509.

84. Aron, *Peace and War*, 22.

85. In trade theory, of course, we can observe a wealth transfer: consumer surplus falls and is redistributed in the form of producer surplus, government revenue, and some "dead weight" efficiency losses.

86. This crucial (and often underappreciated) distinction between the average and the particular actor comes up routinely in international relations. Consider economic sanctions, for example. It is not possible to gauge the likelihood that a given sanction might compel the target to change its behavior by looking solely at the weight of the

sanction itself (say, for example, by assessing the reduction in the target's GDP). It is also necessary to understand the value the target places on *noncompliance*, which will be situationally specific and context dependent.

87. See Michael W. Doyle, *Ways of War and Peace* (New York: Norton, 1997), for an overview of the varieties of liberalism, including discussions of individualism, interdependence, institutions, law, the democratic peace, and more (205–12), and on the contrast between liberalism and realism (301–11). The definitive articulation of contemporary liberalism remains Andrew Moravcsik, "Taking Preferences Seriously: A Liberal Theory of International Politics," *International Organization* 51:4 (1997): 513–53.

88. Even the position of Norman Angell, a favorite object of scorn by some realists, is much more sophisticated (and anticipatory of war) than as usually caricatured. See his *The Great Illusion: A Study of the Relation of Military Power in Nations to Their Economic and Social Advantage* (London: Putnam, 1911); the issue of realism and interdependence will be discussed in chapter 5.

89. Jeffrey Checkel, "The Constructivist Turn in International Relations Theory," *World Politics* 50:2 (1998): 325; see also Martha Finnemore and Kathryn Sikkink, "Taking Stock: The Constructivist Research Program in International Relations and Comparative Politics," *Annual Review of Political Science* 4 (2001): 391–416. The literature on constructivism is of course enormous and evolving.

90. John Maynard Keynes, *The End of Laissez-Faire* (London: Hogarth Press, 1926), reprinted in *Essays in Persuasion*, *CW*, 9:293.

91. Alexander Wendt, "Anarchy Is What States Make of It: The Social Construction of Power Politics," *International Organization* 46:2 (1992): 391–425; Martha Finnemore, *National Interests and International Society* (Ithaca: Cornell University Press, 1996); Peter Katzenstein, ed., *The Culture of National Security: Norms and Identity in World Politics* (New York: Columbia University Press, 1996); Ted Hopf, *Social Construction of International Politics: Identities and Foreign Policies, Moscow, 1955 and 1999* (Ithaca: Cornell University Press, 2002).

92. Keynes, *The General Theory*, esp. 156–58, 161–62. For discussions of the essential and inescapable role of uncertainty in international politics, see Stephen Nelson and Peter Katzenstein, "Uncertainty, Risk, and the Financial Crisis of 2008," *International Organization* 68:2 (2014): 361–92, and Peter Katzenstein and Lucia Sylbert, "Uncertainty, Risk, Power and the Limits of International Relations Theory," in *Protean Power: Exploring the Uncertain and Unexpected in World Politics*, ed. Peter Katzenstein and Lucia Sylbert (Cambridge: Cambridge University Press, 2018), 27–55.

93. Raymond Aron, *Memoirs: Fifty Years of Political Reflection* (New York: Holmes & Meier, 1990/1983), 78–79; Waltz, *Theory of International Politics*, 118.

94. Albert Hirschman, *The Passions and the Interests: Political Arguments for Capitalism before Its Triumph* (Princeton: Princeton University Press, 1977); see also Martha C. Nussbaum, *Upheavals of Thought: The Intelligence of Emotions* (Cambridge: Cambridge University Press, 2001).

95. Keynes, "My Early Beliefs," *CW*, 10:447, 448, 449. See also Jonathan Mercer, "Feeling like a State: Social Emotion and Identity," *International Theory* 6:3 (2014): 515–35.

96. Once again there is a vast literature on this issue. But for present purposes (situating classical realism in comparison with structural realism and hyper-rationalism),

an abstract simplification of the basic notion is sufficient. At the extreme, if everything is subjective and constructed, then appeals to "fact statements" are impossible, and there can be no agreed-upon criteria of evaluation upon which to assess any action as "rational" or "irrational." Classical realism falls here clearly on the rationalist side, if with analytical caution. Recall Aron's crucial distinction between achieving objectivity (elusive) and striving for it (essential).

97. Albert Hirschman, "Rival Views of Market Society," in Hirschman, *Rival Views of Market Society* (Cambridge, MA: Harvard University Press, 1986), 139. For an incisive illustration of the distinction between passions and interests, consider, for example, Abdelal's observation: "the social fact of unfairness is more important than the material fact of income and wealth distribution." Rawi Abdelal, "Of Learning and Forgetting: Centrism, Populism, and the Legitimacy Crisis of Globalization," in *The Downfall of the American Order?*, ed. Peter Katzenstein and Jonathan Kirshner (Ithaca: Cornell University Press, 2022).

Chapter Three: Why We Need Classical Realism

1. John Lukacs, *Five Days in London, May 1940* (New Haven: Yale University Press, 1999), 5.

2. For an overview of the historiography of appeasement, see Stephen G. Walker, "Solving the Appeasement Puzzle: Contending Historical Interpretations of British Diplomacy during the 1930s," *British Journal of International Studies* 6:3 (1980): 219–46. For a summary of Britain's strategic challenges in this period, see Charles Kupchan, *The Vulnerability of Empire* (Ithaca: Cornell University Press, 1994), chap. 3.

3. Mark Potle, ed., *Champion Redoubtable: The Diaries and Letters of Violet Bonham Carter, 1914–1945* (London: Orion Books, 1998), 181 (May 18), 182 (September 16), 183 (December 6). "I can truthfully say that nothing within my political memory has ever moved me more deeply to horror and indignation than recent events in Germany," Carter stated in her December comments. "I suppose if this were Germany most of us would be behind barbed wire. I can only say, for myself that I should be ashamed to be anywhere else."

4. Abraham Ascher, *Was Hitler a Riddle? Western Democracies and National Socialism* (Stanford: Stanford University Press, 2012), 25–26, 29, 31, 33.

5. As Germany swiftly rearmed, in the first half of the 1930s military spending in France declined steadily; its expenditures would not surpass the amount spent in 1930 until 1937; British military spending was largely flat from 1930 to 1935. Anthony Adamthwaite, *France and the Coming of the Second World War, 1936–1939* (London: Frank Cass, 1977), 164.

6. Ernest Hemingway, "Notes on the Next War," *Esquire*, September 1, 1935.

7. John Maynard Keynes, *The Economic Consequences of the Peace* (London: Macmillan, 1919), 143; Keynes, "The Treatment of Inter-Ally Debt Arising Out of the War" (Treasury Memo, March 1919), *CW*, 16:420–28. As Patricia Clavin has argued, "Although often understood as a vituperative condemnation of the reparations imposed on Germany, the argument that Keynes was advancing was a much wider one about the need to put economic stability before territorial security." Patricia

Clavin, *Securing the World Economy: The Reinvention of the League of Nations, 1920–1946* (Oxford: Oxford University Press, 2013), 12–13.

8. Raymond Aron, *The Dawn of Universal History: Selected Essays from a Witness to the Twentieth Century*, ed. Yair Reiner with an introduction by Tony Judt (New York: Basic Books, 2002), 94 (first quote); Raymond Aron, *The Committed Observer* (Chicago: Regnery Gateway, 1983), 31, 46 (second quote). See also R. A. C. Parker, "The First Capitulation: France and the Rhineland Crisis of 1936," *World Politics* 8:3 (1956): 367, and Piotr Wandycz, *The Twilight of French Eastern Alliances, 1926–1936: French-Czechoslovak-Polish Relations from Locarno to the Remilitarization of the Rhineland* (Princeton: Princeton University Press, 1988).

9. George W. Baer, *Test Case: Italy, Ethiopia and the League of Nations* (Stanford: Hoover Institution Press, 1976).

10. Orwell was shot through the throat, an episode recounted in his *Homage to Catalonia* (London: Harvill Secker, 1938); see also Ernest Hemingway's novel *For Whom the Bell Tolls* (New York: Scribner, 1940).

11. For the Munich narratives, see David Faber, *Munich, 1938: Appeasement and World War II* (New York: Simon and Schuster, 2008), and Tim Bouverie, *Appeasement: Chamberlain, Hitler, Churchill and the Road to War* (New York: Tim Duggan Books, 2019), 310 (quote).

12. Bouverie, *Appeasement*, 415, 416.

13. Thomas J. Christensen and Jack Snyder, "Chain Gangs and Passed Bucks: Predicting Alliance Patterns in Multipolarity," *International Organization* 44:2 (1990): esp. 147, 162; see also the elaboration of this framework in Thomas J. Christensen, "Perceptions and Alliances in Europe, 1865–1940," *International Organization* 51:1 (1997): 65–97. On offensive dominance and the intensification of the security dilemma, see Robert Jervis, "Cooperation under the Security Dilemma," *World Politics* 30:2 (1978): 167–214; on the cult of the offensive before World War I, see Stephen Van Evera, "The Cult of the Offensive and the Origins of the First World War," *International Security* 9:1 (1984): 58–107.

14. For more on this, see "Interwar France: Your Money or Your Life," chapter 4 in Jonathan Kirshner, *Appeasing Bankers: Financial Caution on the Road to War* (Princeton: Princeton University Press, 2007).

15. Robert Shay, *British Rearmament in the Thirties: Politics and Profits* (Princeton: Princeton University Press, 1977), 3–4, 23–26, 46–47, 75–78, 136–47, 159–62, 282–83, 288 (quote). See also G. C. Peden, *The Treasury and British Public Policy, 1906–1959* (New York: Oxford University Press, 2000), 286, 288, 291, 298; Gustav Schmidt, *The Politics and Economics of Appeasement: British Foreign Policy in the 1930s* (New York: Berg, 1986), 32, 347–56, 383–84; R. A. C. Parker, "Economics, Rearmament and Foreign Policy: The United Kingdom before 1939—A Preliminary Study," *Journal of Contemporary History* 10:4 (1975): 637–39, 645; Bernd-Jurgen Wendt, "Economic Appeasement—A Crisis Strategy," in *The Fascist Challenge and the Policy of Appeasement*, ed. Wolfgang Mommsen and Lothar Kettenacker (London: George Allen and Unwin, 1983), 161, 169.

16. British defense spending did not really surge until March 1939, six months after Munich, following the fall of Prague. Mark Harrison, "Resource Mobilization for World War II: The U.S.A., U.K., U.S.S.R., and Germany, 1938–1945," *Economic*

History Review 41:2 (1988): 171–92. See also H. C. Hillman, "Comparative Strength of the Great Powers," in *The World in March 1939*, ed. Arnold Toynbee and Frank T. Ashton-Gwatkin (London: Oxford University Press, 1952), 366–507.

17. Williamson Murray, *The Change in the European Balance of Power, 1938–1939: The Path to Ruin* (Princeton: Princeton University Press, 1984), 19, 51, 54, 87; R. A. C. Parker, *Chamberlain and Appeasement: British Policy and the Coming of the Second World War* (New York: Palgrave, 1993), 272, 273, 282–83.

18. Robert Shepherd, *A Class Divided: Appeasement and the Road to Munich 1938* (London: Macmillan, 1988), 19, 21, 106 (quote), 107, 115, 158; Ian Colvin, *The Chamberlain Cabinet* (London: Victor Gollancz, 1971), 47, 71, 75, 95–96, 116, 118–20, 126, 266; Parker, *Chamberlain and Appeasement*, 274; Murray, *Change in the European Balance of Power*, 53, 58 (quote), 72; Murray argues that even Chamberlain's oft-lauded emphasis on building fighters had its roots in finance, not strategy—fighters were much cheaper to build (393).

19. On France's failure to adequately rearm despite the growing German threat, see Barry Posen, *The Sources of Military Doctrine: France, Britain and Germany between the World Wars* (Ithaca: Cornell University Press, 1984), e.g., 20, 126, 178.

20. Norrin M. Ripsman and Jack S. Levy, "Wishful Thinking or Buying Time? The Logic of British Appeasement in the 1930s," *International Security* 33:2 (2008): 150, 151.

21. Ripsman and Levy, "Wishful Thinking or Buying Time," 179; Murray, *Change in the European Balance of Power*, 120, 150, 156, 261, 263, 271 (quote), 273, 282, 291, 293, 363 (quote), 364–65; Bouverie, *Appeasement*, 193, 258, 293 ("The fact was—as both British and French intelligence were well aware—the Germans were not ready for a major war in 1938"), 294, 413, 417, 419; see also Christensen and Snyder, "Chain Gangs and Passed Bucks," which assesses the balance of power and notes the puzzle of "France's refusal to fight on extremely favorable terms in September 1938" (159–60). It was also emphasized at the time by opponents of the accord that defanging Czechoslovakia also permitted Germany to redeploy the twenty-five divisions that had been dedicated to the Czech front. Shepherd, *A Class Divided*, 192, 242.

22. Robert Self, "Introduction: Neville Chamberlain, 1934–1940: The Downing Street Years," in *The Neville Chamberlain Diary Letters, Volume IV: The Downing Street Years*, ed. Robert Self (Aldershot: Ashgate, 2005), 24; Martin Gilbert, "Horace Wilson; Man of Munich?" *History Today* 32 (1982): 6 (Wilson quote).

23. Self, "Introduction: Neville Chamberlain, 1934–1940," 12; Neville Chamberlain to Ida Chamberlain, September 9, 1938, in Self, *Neville Chamberlain Diary Letters*, 348. See also Frank McDonough, "When Instinct Clouds Judgment: Neville Chamberlain and the Pursuit of Appeasement with Nazi Germany," in *The Origins of the Second World War: An International Perspective*, ed. Frank McDonough (New York: Continuum, 2011), 186–204.

24. Colvin, *The Chamberlain Cabinet*, 168 (Swinton), 170, 172, 173 (foreign policy), 193; G. C. Peden, "Sir Horace Wilson and Appeasement," *Historical Journal* 53:4 (2010): 989, 1003; see also Murray, *Change in the European Balance of Power*, 271, 282, 365; Bouverie, *Appeasement*, 304–5; Faber, *Munich*, 7, 45, 325, 437.

25. Gabriel Gorodetsky, ed., *The Maisky Diaries: Red Ambassador to the Court of St. James's, 1932–1943* (New Haven: Yale University Press, 2015), 159; see also the

entry of October 25, 1938, in which the sluggishness of British rearmament is attributed to the fact that Chamberlain "considers Munich a Victory," and still more efforts at appeasement will prevent war (146).

26. Halifax succeeded Anthony Eden in February 1938, whose growing doubts about appeasement led him to resign. As noted above (see note 16), British rearmament only picked up in earnest at this time, while Germany raced ahead after Munich. Thus for about half of the period in which Chamberlain was purportedly "buying time" to rearm in order to be better prepared for war, the growth of British defense spending remained inhibited, and outpaced.

27. Parker, *Chamberlain and Appeasement*, 187, 200, 203, 347; Murray, *Change in the European Balance of Power*, 283, 285, 294, 295; Shepherd, *A Class Divided*, 277–78; Margaret George, *The Warped Vision: British Foreign Policy, 1933–1939* (Pittsburgh: University of Pittsburgh Press, 1965), 196, 198 (Chamberlain quotes), see also 172, 201. Halifax's dairies are quoted in Faber, *Munich*, 42–43.

28. Self, *Neville Chamberlain Diary Letters*, 418 (May 28, to Hilda), 428 (July 15, to Ida), 431 (July 23, to Ida). On the Polish loan, see Colvin, *The Chamberlain Cabinet*, 231.

29. Parker, *Chamberlain and Appeasement*, 338, 339, 342; Colvin, *The Chamberlain Cabinet*, 250–51; Bouverie, *Appeasement*, 3–4, 5, 374.

30. Self, *Neville Chamberlain Diary Letters*, 443, 444 (quotes), 445 (September 10, to Ida); Guy Nicholas Esnouf, "British Government War Aims and Attitudes towards a Negotiated Peace, September 1939 to July 1940" (PhD diss., King's College London, July 1988), 2, 29, 35, 227–28, 323; Shepherd, *A Class Divided*, 289 (quotes). In a disconcerting coda to these efforts, Chamberlain and Halifax favored exploring Germany's terms after the fall of France; fortunately for humanity Churchill prevailed in these vital debates. See Lukacs, *Five Days in London*.

31. Ripsman and Levy, "Wishful Thinking or Buying Time," 180; Chamberlain, remarks before the House of Commons, U.K. Parliamentary Papers, 20th Century House of Commons Hansard Sessional Papers, Commons Sitting of Sunday, 3rd September, 1939, https://parlipapers.proquest.com/parlipapers/docview/t71.d76.cds5cv0351p0-0005?accountid=10267.

32. Lynne Olson, *Troublesome Young Men: The Rebels Who Brought Churchill to Power and Helped Save England* (New York: Farrar, Straus, and Giroux, 2007), 38–39 (Macmillan).

33. Shepherd, *A Class Divided*, 14, 16, 67, 138 (Woolf quote; see also p. 34 for Woolf appalled by the Nazis in 1934); Aron, "From Sarajevo to Hiroshima" (1951), reprinted in Aron, *Dawn of Universal History*, 89, 92 (quotes). Moreover, in his assessment, "the French felt, rightly, that war, whatever its issue, would be a catastrophe for France. Drained of its life-blood in World War I, France could not stand a second such experience even if it ended in victory." Aron, *The Committed Observer*, 40, 51 (quote).

34. Shepherd, *A Class Divided*, 4, 223 (Berlin), 225.

35. It is worth noting that favoring an encouraging policy toward the Weimar Republic in the 1920s does not in any way imply appeasement of Nazi Germany in the 1930s. Violet Bonham Carter illustrates this point. The visionary anti-Nazi had a decade earlier sent a copy of *The Economic Consequences of the Peace* to a friend,

referring to "Keynes's book which I think *quite* brilliant—an unanswerable indictment." Potle, ed., *Diaries and Letters of Violet Bonham Carter*, 107.

36. Keynes to Kingsley Martin, November 10, 1937, *CW*, 28:93; Keynes, "A Positive Peace Programme," *New Statesman and Nation*, March 25, 1938, reprinted in *CW*, 28:28, 99, 100.

37. Keynes to Kingsley Martin, August 26, 1938, October 1, 1938, *CW*, 28:117, 134; John Maynard Keynes, "Mr. Chamberlain's Foreign Policy," *New Statesman and Nation*, October 8, 1938, *CW*, 28:126–27. Robert Skidelsky notes Keynes's vehement opposition to Chamberlain's appeasement policies (see especially the bitter letter Keynes wrote to Virginia Woolf in February 1938) and his understanding (contra Chamberlain) that the brigand powers were dangerous and unreasonable. Robert Skidelsky, *John Maynard Keynes: Fighting for Freedom, 1937–1946* (New York: Viking, 2001), 14, 30, 37.

38. See, for example, Paul Kennedy, "The Tradition of Appeasement in British Foreign Policy, 1865–1939," *British Journal of International Studies* 2:3 (1976): 195–215.

39. Leonard Woolf, in a rather lacerating critique, pointedly characterized Carr's embrace of appeasement as "utopian." Woolf, "Utopia and Reality," *Political Quarterly* 11:2 (1940): 174, see also p. 176.

40. E. H. Carr, *The Twenty Years' Crisis, 1919–1939*, 1st ed. (London: Macmillan, 1939), 106, 107 ("attitude"), 274, 275, 278 ("power relations"), 282 ("negotiations"). Throughout the key remains—and this wisdom endures—a rejection of claims to the moral superiority (or inherent correctness) of the status quo, and the realist need to address the consequences of "changed relations of power" (e.g., 106, 288 [quote]). See also the similar sentiments expressed in E. H. Carr, *Britain: A Study of Foreign Policy from the Versailles Treaty to the Outbreak of War* (London: Longmans, Green, 1939), 175. It should be noted that following similar logic, Kennan also supported the Munich accords; the American diplomat in Prague, who had authoritarian instincts, was tripped up by the same error, in his case shamefully unable to see Nazi Germany as a malevolent entity. See George F. Kennan, *From Prague after Munich: Diplomatic Papers, 1938–1940* (Princeton: Princeton University Press, 1968), 5; John Lewis Gaddis, *George F. Kennan: An American Life* (New York: Penguin, 2011), 124–25.

41. Hans Kohn, "The Totalitarian Crisis," in his *Revolutions and Dictatorships: Essays in Contemporary History* (Cambridge, MA: Harvard University Press, 1939), 354. An opponent of the Munich accords, he added this bitter postscript to his book dated March 19, 1939: "The events of the last week have probably opened the eyes of some people." Munich and "the benign trust in the words of Chancellor Hitler, have been revealed in their whole hollowness to all those who do not refuse to see" (417). Aron, *The Committed Observer*, 26, 37 (quotes); see also Raymond Aron, *Memoirs: Fifty Years of Political Reflection* (New York: Holmes & Meier, 1990/1983), 39, 48–49, 53; Hans Morgenthau, "International Affairs: The Resurrection of Neutrality in Europe," *American Political Science Review* 33:3 (June 1939), esp. his approving citation of Aurel Kolnai's *The War against the West* (1938), 484. See also Hans Morgenthau, *Scientific Man vs. Power Politics* (Chicago: University of Chicago Press, 1946), 112, 115, and Morgenthau, *In Defense of the National Interest: A Critical Examination of American Foreign Policy* (New York: Knopf, 1951), 137, 138.

42. Ascher, *Was Hitler a Riddle?*, 10, 48, 74, 77–78 (Goebbels); George, *The Warped Vision*, 115, 138–39, 175, 222–23 (*Manchester Guardian*); Faber, *Munich, 1938*, 9 (toast), 21–22, 24, 173 (Chamberlain quotes); Bouverie, *Appeasement*, 138–39, 140 (fears and suspicions), 147, 248; see also Aaron L. Goldman, "Two Views of Germany: Neville Henderson vs. Vansittart and the Foreign Office, 1937–1939," *British Journal of International Studies* 6:3 (1980): 247–77.

43. Aron, *The Committed Observer*, 59; Paul Kennedy, *The Rise of the Anglo-German Antagonism, 1860–1914* (Boston: Allen and Unwin, 1980), 47–48, 302 (quote). Eyre Crowe of the Foreign Office wrote of "panic in the city" in a memo sent to Foreign Secretary Grey on July 31, reprinted in G. D. Gooch and H. Temperley, eds., *British Documents on the Origins of the War, 1898–1914* (London: HMSO, 1926–38), vol. 11, *The Outbreak of War*, 228; see also the similar assessment of Chancellor of the Exchequer Lloyd George, *War Memoirs of David Lloyd George, Volume 1: 1914–1915* (Boston: Little, Brown, 1933), 68, and the sense of the City in "The Great Crisis," *Bankers' Magazine* (London) 98 (September 1914): 318 ("disastrous"), 321–22, 331, 337 ("catastrophe"); John Maynard Keynes, "War and the Financial System, August 1914," *Economic Journal* 24 (September 1914): 461, 464, 471–73, 484 (quotes); and more generally Kirshner, *Appeasing Bankers*.

44. David Blaazer, "Finance and the End of Appeasement: The Bank of England, the National Government and the Czech Gold," *Journal of Contemporary History* 40:1 (2005): 25, 26, 35; Scott Newton, *Profits of Peace: The Political Economy of Anglo-German Appeasement* (Oxford: Clarendon Press, 1996), 58, 62, 65–66, 91, 93; Neil Forbes, "London Banks, the German Standstill Agreements, and 'Economic Appeasement' in the 1930s," *Economic History Review*, 2nd ser., 40:4 (1987): 573, 583–84, 585, 586 (quote), 6; C. A. MacDonald, "Economic Appeasement and the German 'Moderates,' 1937–1939," *Past and Present* 56 (August 1972): 105–8, 115, 121, 128; David Kynaston, *The City of London: Vol. III—Illusions of Gold, 1914–1945* (London: Chatto and Windus, 1999), 441–46, 450–53; Paul Einzig, *Appeasement Before, During, and After the War* (London: Macmillan, 1942), 9–10, 15, 22, 76–77, 83.

45. Michael Jabara Carley, *1939: The Alliance That Never Was and the Coming of World War II* (Chicago: Ivan R. Dee, 1999), 84 (quote); Mark L. Haas, *The Ideological Origins of Great Power Politics* (Ithaca: Cornell University Press, 2005), esp. 122–23, 128–29; Shepherd, *A Class Divided*, 245–46 (rearmament).

46. Carley, *1939: The Alliance That Never Was*, 5, 15 (quote), 37, 43, 88; Bouverie, *Appeasement*, 90 (Baldwin); Shepherd, *A Class Divided*, 61, 79; Haas, *Ideological Origins*, 124–25; Ascher, *Was Hitler a Riddle?*, 52.

47. Self, *The Neville Chamberlain Diary Letters*, 412 (letter to Hilda, April 29, 1939, quotes), 416 (letter to Hilda, May 14), 417 (letter to Ida, May 21), 418 (letter to Hilda, May 28); Parker, *Chamberlain and Appeasement*, 219, 246; Neville Chamberlain to Ida Chamberlain, September 9, 1938, in Self, *Neville Chamberlain Diary Letters*, 348 (Hitler comment).

48. Self, *The Neville Chamberlain Diary Letters*, 425 (letter to Hilda, July 2), 428 (letter to Hilda, July 15); Carley, *1939: The Alliance That Never Was*, xvii, 4, 120, 142, 144, 147 (Maisky, journal entry of May 18, 1939), 163–64, 184, 210 , 213, 256; Murray, *Change in the European Balance of Power*, 300, 306–7 (British-German negotiations in July); George, *The Warped Vision*, 189, 205; Parker, *Chamberlain and*

Appeasement, 233, 245; see also Gorodetsky, *The Maisky Diaries*, 103, 163, 166, 186, 207; on August 4, Maisky assessed that Chamberlain remained more interested in "cutting a deal with Hitler" (212).

49. *The National Security Strategy of the United States of America* (The White House, Washington, DC, September 2002). A personal anecdote illustrates this nicely. In early 2003 I hosted a dinner; the guests included a legendary hawk and a well-known dove. Looking to stimulate conversation, I asked the hawk, "So, where are you on this upcoming war?" Without hesitating, and to my surprise, he said, "I'm against it." With a surprised smile I said, "You disappoint me. On what basis do you oppose the war?" "There is no casus belli," he said plainly. That is, there was no justification for the United States to attack Iraq.

50. See the prescient dissents from "declinism" in Susan Strange, "The Persistent Myth of Lost Hegemony," *International Organization* 41:4 (1987): 551–74; and Samuel P. Huntington, "The U.S.: Decline or Renewal," *Foreign Affairs* 67:2 (1988): 76–96.

51. Robert Gilpin, *War and Change in World Politics* (Cambridge: Cambridge University Press, 1981).

52. Gilpin, *War and Change*, 1, 241. The book's incongruous epilogue reflects this tension. Gilpin throughout the volume emphasizes continuity over change ("it has always been thus and always will be" [210]), and he argues forcefully that neither nuclear weapons nor economic interdependence has altered the basic nature of world politics, yet *War and Change* concludes on a "cautiously optimistic note" that despite the compelling and pessimistic logic of the preceding chapters, such factors might forestall "real danger" of hegemonic war (243).

53. Gilpin, *War and Change*, x–xiii.

54. Gilpin, *War and Change*, 51 (historical experience, lessons), 54 (nature of society), 63, 87 (primary determinants), 96ff. (domestic politics), 152–54 (moral decay). See also Gilpin's emphasis on "the decay of bourgeois middle class work ethic" in explaining state behavior in Gilpin, "Economic Interdependence and National Security in Historical Perspective," in *Economic Issues and National Security*, ed. Klaus Knorr and Frank Traeger (Lawrence: University Press of Kansas, 1977), 59.

55. Gilpin, *War and Change*, 3 (unique), 8, 30–31, 37–38, 51 (decision-making), 74, 202–3, 205 (in truth), 215, 228 (Thucydides), 240 (underappreciated factor). Thucydides' influence on Gilpin is profound; he is invoked sixteen times in *War and Change*, more than any other thinker; see also Robert Gilpin, "The Richness of the Tradition of Political Realism," in *Neorealism and Its Critics*, ed. Robert O. Keohane (New York: Columbia University Press, 1986), 306, 309.

56. Gilpin, *War and Change*, 10–11.

57. One cannot typically extend a commitment (say, for example, a security guarantee) by ten miles; an additional country is either protected or left out in the cold.

58. For a modestly formalized model of why great powers will tend to err (and disagree with others) on the trajectory of their relative power, see Charles Doran, "War and Power Dynamics: Economic Underpinnings," *International Studies Quarterly* 27:4 (1983): 419–41.

59. Or, at least, to be systematically biased toward such a predisposition.

60. *Citizen Kane* (RKO, Orson Welles, 1941), written by Herman Mankiewicz and Orson Welles.

61. For a thoughtful attempt to address this paradox, see Kupchan, *The Vulnerability of Empire*. See also David Edelstein, *Over the Horizon: Time, Uncertainty, and the Rise of Great Powers* (Ithaca: Cornell University Press, 2017).

62. Gilpin, *War and Change*, 152–54, 162–63, 165, 167.

63. Gilpin, *War and Change*, 138 (emphasis added), 142, 177, 178. On hegemonic expectations of relative gains from openness, see Stephen Krasner, "State Power and the Structure of International Trade," *World Politics* 28:3 (1976): esp. p. 320.

64. On the difficulty of retrenchment, note the dissent of Paul MacDonald and Joseph Parent, *Twilight of the Titans: Great Power Decline and Retrenchment* (Ithaca: Cornell University Press, 2018).

65. Carr, *Twenty Years' Crisis*, 169, 222 (quote); Gilpin, *War and Change*, 206 (quote).

66. Gilpin, *War and Change*, 192 (politically difficult, emphasis added), 194 (seldom), 207 (appetite). On the wisdom of hegemonic restraint, see G. John Ikenberry, *After Victory: Institutions, Strategic Restraint, and the Rebuilding of Order after Major Wars* (Princeton: Princeton University Press, 2001).

67. Thucydides, *The Peloponnesian War*, 2.11.5 (apprehension), 4.65.4 (extraordinary success).

68. The Vietnam War literature is enormous; the narrative here relies heavily on Fredrik Logevall, *Choosing War: The Lost Chance for Peace and the Escalation of War in Vietnam* (Berkeley: University of California Press, 1999); George McT. Kahin, *Intervention: How America Became Involved in Vietnam* (New York: Anchor Books, 1987); Herbert Y. Schandler, *Lyndon Johnson and Vietnam: The Unmaking of a President* (Princeton: Princeton University Press, 1977); George C. Herring, *America's Longest War: The United States and Vietnam, 1950–1975*, 2nd ed. (New York: Knopf, 1986); Jeffrey Kimball, *Nixon's Vietnam War* (Lawrence: University Press of Kansas, 1998); and Larry Berman, *No Peace, No Honor: Nixon, Kissinger and Betrayal in Vietnam* (New York: Free Press, 2001).

69. Kahin, *Intervention*, 3, 27 (State Department), 30, 66, 87–89; Fred Logevall, *Embers of War: The Fall of an Empire and the Making of America's Vietnam* (New York: Random House, 2012), xiv (Kennedy).

70. Eisenhower thought that in 1954, Ho would have carried 80 percent of the vote; the CIA estimated that it was a "virtual certainty" that Ho would win an all-Vietnam election. Dwight Eisenhower, *The White House Years: Mandate for Change* (New York: Doubleday, 1963), 372; Lloyd C. Gardner, *Approaching Vietnam: From World War II through Dienbienphu* (New York: Norton, 1988), 316–17, 318 (quote).

71. Fred Greenstein and Richard Immerman, "What Did Eisenhower Tell Kennedy about Indochina?" *Journal of American History* 79:2 (September 1992): 579 (quote), 581; Kahin, *Intervention*, 93, 101, 126, 129; Herring, *America's Longest War*, 29, 55, 65, 75; Logevall, *Choosing War*, xviii–xix, 51–52, 69.

72. Logevall, *Choosing War*, 73–74, 78, 145, 298, 314, 388, 393; Kahin, *Intervention*, 260, 262, 286, 306, 366, 393, 399, 423, 426, 432; Herring, *America's Longest War*, 144–45, 146, 151, 161.

73. Hans Morgenthau, "Another Korea?" *Commentary* (1962); Hans Morgenthau, "The Case against Further Involvement," *Washington Post*, March 15, 1964; Hans Morgenthau, "The Realities of Containment," *New Leader*, June 8, 1964; see also his long

essay, "We Are Deluding Ourselves," *New York Times*, April 18, 1965, all reprinted in Hans J. Morgenthau, *Vietnam and the United States* (Washington, DC: Public Affairs Press, 1965), 36, 38, 48, 49 (quotes). See also Robert F. Colquhoun, *Raymond Aron—Volume 1: The Philosopher in History, 1905–1955* (Beverly Hills, CA: SAGE Publications, 1986), 442–43; Hans Morgenthau, "Truth and Power: The Intellectuals and the Johnson Administration," *New Republic*, November 26, 1966, esp. 1337, 1339, 1351, as well as Jennifer W. See, "A Prophet without Honor: Hans Morgenthau and the War in Vietnam, 1955-1965," *Pacific Historical Review* 70:3 (2001): 419–48, and Lorenzo Zamberernardi, "The Impotence of Power: Morgenthau's Critique of American Intervention in Vietnam," *Review of International Studies* 37:3 (2011): 1335–56.

74. George F. Kennan, U.S. Senate Testimony, February 10, 1966, pp. 331, 335, 337; see also John Lukacs, *George Kennan: A Study of Character* (New Haven: Yale University Press, 2007), 148; Reinhold Niebuhr, "Vietnam: Study in Ironies," *New Republic*, July 24, 1967, reprinted in Reinhold Niebuhr, *Major Works on Religion and Politics*, ed. Elisabeth Sifton (New York: Library of America, 2015), 689, 692, 693. Aron would echo these sentiments, observing that the American war "did not arise from an imperialist impulse" but from the arrogant inability to understand the limits of its own power and what it might be capable of accomplishing. He also noted that the enterprise "was all the more dubious because the leaders in Washington themselves had no clear idea of why they were fighting." Raymond Aron, *Memoirs: Fifty Years of Political Reflection* (New York: Holmes & Meier, 1990/1983), 391. See also the forceful opposition in Kenneth Waltz, "The Politics of Peace," *International Studies Quarterly* 11:3 (1967), "The perils of weakness are matched by the temptations of power" (206); the United States should "not gear [its] actions to wayward political movements in states of minor consequence" (211). In March only 26 percent of the public thought sending troops to Vietnam was a mistake, the figure would not reach 50 percent until after the Tet Offensive.

75. Like German generals after World War I, Vietnam War revisionists often stress that the United States never "lost" the war on the battlefield. Once again, this is irrelevant; following proper Clausewitzian logic, the use of force can only be evaluated by the extent that it achieves its political objectives. And not only would the war effort fail to achieve those objectives—the creation of an independent, legitimate, self-sustaining South Vietnam to hold the line against communism after the United States left—fighting the war was actually undermining broader U.S. political goals. Even if (and this was unlikely) further escalation might have improved the military situation in Vietnam, it would not have brought the United States closer to achieving its political goals in Vietnam or globally.

76. Clark Clifford, "A Vietnam Reappraisal," *Foreign Affairs* 47:4 (1969): 601–22; Schandler, *Lyndon Johnson and Vietnam*, 98, 109, 119–20, 129, 140–41, 197–98, 258, 263–64.

77. Richard Nixon, "Asia after Vietnam," *Foreign Affairs* 46:1 (1967): 111, 114–15, 121; Stephen E. Ambrose, *Nixon: Volume Two—The Triumph of a Politician, 1962-1972* (New York: Simon and Schuster, 1989), 43–44, 61, 64, 68, 81, 142–44, 147, 260; Richard Nixon, *RN: The Memoirs of Richard Nixon* (New York: Grosset and Dunlap, 1978), 269–71; Logevall, *Choosing War*, 135; Berman, *No Peace No Honor*, 45.

78. Henry Kissinger, "The Vietnam Negotiations," *Foreign Affairs* 47:2 (1969): 213–14, 216–17; Ambrose, *Nixon: Volume Two*, 167; Kimball, *Nixon's Vietnam War*, 29–31, 39–40, 101. On Kissinger's duplicity and craving for power, see Jonathan Kirshner, "Machinations of Wicked Men," *Boston Review* 42:2 (March/April 2016): 49–55.

79. Kimball, *Nixon's Vietnam War*, 125, 131, 135, 137, 193; Berman, *No Peace, No Honor*, 108, 111; Herring, *America's Longest War*, 151, 225, 240; Kahin, *Intervention*, 404; Ambrose, *Nixon: Volume Two*, 224; Nixon, *RN*, 382; Richard Reeves, *President Nixon: Alone in the White House* (New York: Simon and Schuster, 2001), 177–78, 303.

80. Kimball, *Nixon's Vietnam War*, 240, 260, 272, 341–42; Berman, *No Peace, No Honor*, 50, 142, 158, 161, 180; Jeffrey Kimball, *The Vietnam War Files* (Lawrence: University Press of Kansas, 2004), 163, 165 (quotes). Kissinger wrote "We want a decent interval" in the margin of his notes for his trip to China in July 1971 (Kimball, *War Files*, 187). Mark Clodfelter, *The Limits of Air Power: The American Bombing of North Vietnam* (Lincoln: University of Nebraska Press, 2006), 156, 167–68, 173–74, 175; Nixon, *RN*, 693; Berman, *No Peace, No Honor*, 123, 126, 132 (quote); Herring, *America's Longest War*, 253–54.

81. Clodfelter, *The Limits of Air Power*, 186, 188, 194, 196; Kimball, *Nixon's Vietnam War*, 363–64.

82. Robert F. Colquhoun, *Raymond Aron—Volume 2: The Sociologist in Society, 1955–1983* (Beverly Hills, CA: SAGE Publications, 1986), 421, 423; Aron, *Memoirs*, 391.

83. The cover of Paul Kennedy's hugely popular *The Rise and Fall of the Great Powers: Economic Change and Military Conflict from 1500–2000* (New York: Random House, 1987) featured an arresting image of Japan poised to replace the United States, portrayed as following in the footsteps of Great Britain in decline. On American unipolarity, see, for example, G. John Ikenberry, ed., *America Unrivaled: The Future of the Balance of Power* (Ithaca: Cornell University Press, 2002).

84. Jane Cramer and Trevor Thrall, eds., *Why Did the United States Invade Iraq?* (New York: Routledge, 2012), offers a good representative overview of some of the principal hypotheses; see also Ahsan Butt, "Why Did the United States Invade Iraq in 2003?" *Security Studies* 28:2 (2019): 250–85.

85. On the Iraq war (and the 9/11 context), see, for example, Thomas Ricks, *Fiasco: The American Military Adventure in Iraq* (New York: Penguin, 2006); Robert Draper, *To Start a War: How the Bush Administration Took America into Iraq* (New York: Penguin, 2020).

86. Recall as well the unresolved anthrax attacks in the United States, which occurred just a week after 9/11 and remained front-page news for months. See, for example, Todd S. Purdum and Alison Mitchell, "A Nation Challenged: The Anthrax Threat; Tests Show Anthrax Exposure in at Least 30 Capital Workers," *New York Times*, October 18, 2001.

87. *The National Security Strategy of the United States of America*.

88. See Richard Betts, in his blistering critique of the approaching war, "Suicide from Fear of Death?" *Foreign Affairs* 82:1 (January/February 2003): 35 (quote); for an elaborate postmortem, see Michael J. Mazarr, *Leap of Faith: Hubris, Negligence and America's Greatest Foreign Policy Tragedy* (New York: Public Affairs, 2019). On

the perils of asymmetric conflict in general, see Andrew Mack, "Why Big Nations Lose Small Wars: The Politics of Asymmetric Conflict," *World Politics* 27:2 (1975): 175–200.

89. Jonathan Kirshner, "U.S. Must Maintain Postwar Goals," *Ithaca Journal*, April 18, 2003, p. A8. On these points more generally, see also Jonathan Kirshner, "Prevent Defense: Why the Bush Doctrine Will Hurt U.S. Interests," in *Iraq and Beyond: The New U.S. National Security Strategy*, ed. Matthew Evangelista (Ithaca: Cornell University Peace Studies Program Occasional Paper #27, January 2003), 2, 6, 7, 9, 10; Jonathan Kirshner, "Winning the Peace Is No Easy Task," *Ithaca Journal*, March 20, 2003, p. A8. ("After the U.S. wins the war in Iraq" [the United States] "might easily find itself at the center of an unpopular and intractable occupation of Iraq.")

90. For a representative overview and critique of the (lack of) plans after military victory had been achieved, see Michael O'Hanlon, "Iraq without a Plan," *Brookings*, January 1, 2005.

91. Albert Eisele, "George Kennan Speaks Out about Iraq," *History News Network*, September 26, 2002, https://historynewsnetwork.org/article/997; see also George F. Kennan, *The Kennan Diaries*, ed. Frank Costigliola (New York: Norton, 2014), 677; Robert Gilpin, "War Is Too Important to Be Left to Ideological Amateurs," *International Relations* 19:1 (2005): 5.

Chapter Four: The Limits of Classical Realism

1. One false controversy that will not be explored here is the hand-waving dismissal by some critics of classical realism—commonly caricaturing the work of Hans Morgenthau in particular—as "human nature" realism, which, it is claimed, purportedly attributes international conflict to the aggressive nature of mankind. Since human nature is constant but outcomes vary widely (we observe both war and peace, for example), "human nature" realism, such disingenuous critics aver, is hopelessly underdefined. But no classical realist has ever looked at a war and explained it by saying, "yes, this war occurred because humans are war-like." Assumptions about the nature of the actor are simply that, building blocks of a larger analytical framework. All approaches to International Relations make implicit or explicit assumptions about the nature of the actor, which inform their analyses but do not preclude variation in outcomes.

2. Raymond Aron, *Memoirs: Fifty Years of Political Reflection* (New York: Holmes and Meier, 1990/1983), 100. See also Aron on the "real danger" that the social scientist will see "only what he wanted to see and [fail] to recognize his own bias." Quoted in Robert F. Colquhoun, *Raymond Aron—Volume 2: The Sociologist in Society, 1955–1983* (Beverly Hills, CA: SAGE Publications, 1986), 91.

3. Hans Morgenthau, *Politics among Nations: The Struggle for Power and Peace*, 3rd ed. (New York: Knopf, 1960/1948), 11; Hans Morgenthau, *In Defense of the National Interest: A Critical Examination of American Foreign Policy* (New York: Knopf, 1951), 241.

4. Reinhold Niebuhr, *Moral Man and Immoral Society* (Louisville: John Know Press, 2001/1932), xxv, xxx; see also pp. 268–69 on the limits to pacifism in a dangerous world, which derives from "the moral obtuseness of human collectives" (272).

Morgenthau, with most realists, also sees this distinction and sings a similar tune: "The individual as such is moral by nature; political society is amoral, also by nature." Hans Morgenthau, *Scientific Man vs. Power Politics* (Chicago: University of Chicago Press, 1946), 176, see also pp. 195, 197.

5. Niccolò Machiavelli, *The Prince*, trans. Harvey Mansfield (Chicago: University of Chicago Press, 1998/1531), 77; Niccolò Machiavelli, *Discourses on Livy*, trans. Harvey Mansfield and Nathan Taco (Chicago: University of Chicago Press, 1996/1532), 301, emphasis added.

6. Machiavelli, *The Prince*, 61. As Raymond Aron observed, "Unfortunately, foreign policy is a game for gangsters." Raymond Aron, *The Committed Observer* (Chicago: Regnery Gateway, 1983), 240. On the moral imperative of self-preservation, see also Hans Morgenthau, "The Mainsprings of American Foreign Policy: The National Interest vs. Moral Abstractions," *American Political Science Review* 44:4 (1950): 854: "For the individual nations to take care of their own national interests is, then, a political necessity. There can be no moral duty to neglect them; for as the international society is at present constituted, the consistent neglect of the national interest can only lead to national suicide."

7. Aron, *The Committed Observer*, 246 (first quote), see also p. 248; Morgenthau, *Scientific Man*, 201 (there is "no escape from the evil of power, regardless of what one does"), see also p. 202. This perspective, generally shared by classical realists, is a key theme throughout Aron's writings. More generally, he held that "the worst form of utopian thought consists in a failure to recognize the relationships between those things which are good and those things which are evil, or the incompatibilities between equally precious values." Quoted in Robert F. Colquhoun, *Raymond Aron—Volume 1: The Philosopher in History, 1905–1955* (Beverly Hills, CA: SAGE Publications, 1986), 472 (present realities), 283 (equally precious values). See also Michael Walzer, "Political Action: The Problem of Dirty Hands," *Philosophy & Public Affairs* 2:2 (1973): 160–80.

8. This is a point of great emphasis for Morgenthau: "no nation's power is without limits, and hence that its policies must respect the power and interests of others" (*In Defense of the National Interest*, 242). A classic illustration of this is the recognition of spheres of influence during the Cold War, which George F. Kennan acknowledged even before the end of World War II. "We must reconcile ourselves to the fact that the Russians will insist on having . . . a certain sphere of influence along their western border." *The Kennan Diaries*, ed. Frank Costigliola (New York: Norton, 2014), 173 (September 18, 1944).

9. Alan J. Kuperman, "Obama's Libya Debacle: How a Well-Meaning Intervention Ended in Failure," *Foreign Affairs* 94:2 (2015): 66–77. On this point more generally, see Stephen Walt, *The Hell of Good Intentions: America's Foreign Policy Elite and the Decline of U.S. Primacy* (New York: Farrar, Straus and Giroux, 2018).

10. Morgenthau, "The Mainsprings of American Foreign Policy," 840; George F. Kennan, *American Diplomacy, 1900–1950* (New York: Mentor Books, 1951), 50. Morgenthau and Aron—more troubled by the suggestion of amorality than Kennan—go so far as to take solace in "the morality of prudence" given that, by ignoring the realities of power, all too often "he who attempts to play the angel plays the beast." Raymond Aron, *Peace and War: A Theory of International Relations* (New Brunswick, NJ: Transaction Publishers, 2003/1966), 609 (quotes). Morgenthau is eager to claim

that realism is not immoral but a set of moral principles derived from reality, which he further defends with reference to the "moral dignity of the national interest." Morgenthau, *In Defense of the National Interest*, 33; see also Morgenthau, *Politics among Nations*, 10; Morgenthau, "The Mainsprings of American Foreign Policy," 854.

11. Arnold Wolfers, "Statesmanship and Moral Choice," *World Politics* 1:2 (1949): 189 (quote), 190 (quote), 191, 193–94 (quote), 195. See also Alison McQueen, "Political Realism and Moral Corruption," *European Journal of Political Theory* 19:2 (2020): 141–61. On Nixon and Kissinger, see William Shawcross, *Sideshow: Kissinger, Nixon, and the Destruction of Cambodia* (New York: Simon and Schuster, 1987); Gary Bass, *The Blood Telegram: Nixon, Kissinger and a Forgotten Genocide* (New York: Knopf, 2013); and Robert Dallek, *Nixon and Kissinger: Partners in Power* (New York: Harper Collins, 2007).

12. Robert Frank, Thomas Gilovich, and Dennis Regan, "Does Studying Economics Inhibit Cooperation?" *Journal of Economic Perspectives* 7:2 (spring 1993): 159–71.

13. E. H. Carr, *The Twenty Years' Crisis, 1919–1939*, 2nd ed. (New York: St. Martin's Press, 1946 [1939]), 92 concedes this point; Morgenthau goes further: "A discussion of international ethics must guard against the two extremes either of overrating the influence of ethics upon international politics or else of denying that statesmen and diplomats are moved by anything else but considerations of material power." Hans Morgenthau, "The Twilight of International Morality," *Ethics* 58:2 (1948): 79.

14. Hans Morgenthau, "The Political Science of E. H. Carr," *World Politics* 1:1 (1948): 133, 134. Although there are inescapable and often agonizing trade-offs, and the imperatives of anarchy impose clear limits on the desire to help others in distress, nevertheless Morgenthau stresses "the crucial role for morality in politics." Robert Jervis, "Hans Morgenthau, Realism, and the Scientific Study of International Politics," *Social Research* 61:4 (winter 1994): esp. 867–69 (quote at 869); for a critique of the caricature of realism as void of moral content and purpose, with specific reference to Morgenthau and Aron, see also Murielle Cozette, "What Lies Ahead: Classical Realism on the Future of International Relations," *International Studies Review* 10 (2008): esp. 678.

15. On the centrality of the national interest for the realist tradition, see, for example, Morgenthau, *In Defense of the National Interest*; Kennan, *American Diplomacy*; Stephen Krasner, *Defending the National Interest: Raw Materials Investments and U.S. Foreign Policy* (Princeton: Princeton University Press, 1978).

16. Robert Gilpin, *War and Change in World Politics* (Cambridge: Cambridge University Press, 1981), esp. 40–41, 43, 62. Gilpin attributes the early modern "triumph of the nation-state over other political forms" to changes in the nature and cost of war.

17. Aron, *Peace and War*, 92 (quote); Raymond Aron, "Thucydides and the Historical Narrative," in *Politics and History: Selected Essays of Raymond Aron*, ed. and trans. Miriam Bernheim Conan (New York: The Free Press, 1978), 43 (second quote). Krasner plainly echoes these sentiments: "the objectives sought by the state cannot be reduced to some summation of private desires" (*Defending the National Interest*, 30).

18. Imagine a libertarian seeking to "privatize" traffic lights by charging for a subscription to a device, without which drivers would be unable to tell whether the light was red or green.

19. Esme Howard, "British Policy and the Balance of Power," *American Political Science Review* 19:2 (1925): 261–67; Nicholas J. Spykman, *The Geography of the Peace* (New York: Harcourt Brace, 1944), e.g., 43; Giles D. Harlow and George C. Maerz, eds., *Measures Short of War: The George F. Kennan Lectures at the National War College, 1946–47* (Washington, DC: National Defense University Press, 1991).

20. Rather, Huntington argues, a number of context-specific factors "pervasively influence how states define their interests," including "domestic values." Samuel P. Huntington, *The Clash of Civilizations and the Remaking of World Order* (New York: Simon and Schuster, 1996), 34.

21. Gilpin, *War and Change*, 13, see also p. 54; Robert Gilpin, "Conversations in *International Relations*: Interview with Robert Gilpin," *International Relations* 19:3 (2005): 361–72. "I think many realists believe that there is an objective national interest and they know what it is. I think somewhat differently. Looking at the United States, I think crises and great debates lead to a definition of national interests any particular time" (363). On these themes, see also Peter Trubowitz, *Defining the National Interest: Conflict and Change in American Foreign Policy* (Chicago: University of Chicago Press, 1998), and Richard Bensel, *Sectionalism and American Political Development, 1880–1980* (Madison: University of Wisconsin Press, 1984).

22. Arnold Wolfers, "'National Security' as an Ambiguous Symbol," *Political Science Quarterly* 67:4 (1952): 481 (quote), 488–89, 502 (quote).

23. David Hume, *Treatise of Human Nature* (1739); Max Weber, "The National State and Economic Policy (1885)," reprinted in *Economy and Society* 9:4 (1980): 428–49; see also Philip S. Gorski, "Beyond the Fact/Value Distinction: Ethical Naturalism and the Social Sciences," *Society* 50:6 (2013): 544–46.

24. Consider the reification of gross domestic product as the broadly agreed upon metric of economic progress. There are a number of alternative measures—median household income, for example—that are different (and arguably better) measures of a society's overall social welfare. But the choice of which metric to focus on and reify will imply different assessments of success, and thus favor distinct policy measures—which, presented as "scientific findings," will nevertheless have inevitable distributive and normative implications. For a recent rehearsal of these arguments, see Joseph E. Stiglitz, "GDP Is the Wrong Tool for Measuring What Matters," *Scientific American* 323:2 (2020): 21–34.

25. To take one illustration of this, many have noted the tension between the generally understood daring nature of the Athenian character and Pericles' advocacy of a cautious war strategy.

26. John Mearsheimer, *The Tragedy of Great Power Politics* (New York: Norton, 2001), 11–12.

27. Many scholars hope that their work will "make the world a better place"—and there is certainly nothing wrong with that aspiration. But as Niebuhr notes, in history, the observer "is to a certain degree engaged in its ideological conflicts." And because in the social world, ambiguous evidence all too commonly *can* be interpreted as conforming with a theorist's prior expectations (or values)—as well as with opposing theories—relentless self-discipline is necessary to avoid undermining the intellectual integrity of the effort. The grave but subtle threat here comes not from the obvious academic crimes of falsifying data or suppressing evidence but by too easily seeing

what one had hoped to see, or by reaching for post hoc rationalizations of new events that to disinterested eyes might appear disconfirming. Reinhold Niebuhr, *Christian Realism and Political Problems* (New York: Scribner's, 1953), 91.

28. I retain the view that, as a practical matter, positive and normative analysis can (and most urgently should) be distinguished and that scholars must be vigilant against the temptation to root for their theories, and not permit scholarly work (as opposed to opinion essays, of which I have written many) to become a vehicle to advance their normative preferences. Following the realist credo—seeing the world as it is, as opposed to seeing it as we wish it might be—requires acknowledging unpleasant facts. For example, I have a visceral opposition to torture. I would argue that, for a variety of reasons, it is in the U.S. National Interest to stand firmly opposed to its practice. Nevertheless, it is almost certainly the case that there are times when torture can "work"—that is, it can extract information from humans (although "ticking time bomb" scenarios are vanishingly rare). Moreover, it is important for me to entertain the theoretical claim that the embrace of torture could be productive for the United States. If this turned out to be the case (exceedingly unlikely, for reasons I have argued elsewhere), my obligation would be to acknowledge this unpleasant fact—yet I would still be steadfastly against the practice. (Just as one could still oppose the death penalty even if it turned out to be the case that it did act as a deterrent to crime.) For an elaboration of these issues, see Jonathan Kirshner, "ISSF Forum on the SSCI and U.S Post-9/11 Policy on Torture," *H-Diplo/ISSF Forum* 5 (February 2015): 4–9.

29. Thucydides, *The Peloponnesian War*, 3.82.4, 3.83.3, translations as always follow Robert Strassler, *The Landmark Thucydides: A Comprehensive Guide to The Peloponnesian War* (New York: Simon and Schuster, 1996). On Thucydides' visceral distaste of demagogues, see, e.g., John H. Finley Jr., *Three Essays on Thucydides* (Cambridge, MA: Harvard University Press, 1967), 52, 155; H. D. Westlake, *Individuals in Thucydides* (Cambridge: Cambridge University Press, 1968), 75, 86; Mathieu de Bakker, "Character Judgements in the Histories: Their Function and Distribution," in *Thucydides between History and Literature*, ed. Antonis Tsakmakis and Melina Tamiolaki (Boston/Berlin: De Gruyter, 2013), 26; Jeremy Mynott, ed., *Thucydides: The War of the Peloponnesians and the Athenians* (Cambridge: Cambridge University Press, 2013), 552; Simon Hornblower, *A Commentary of Thucydides* (Oxford: Clarendon Press, 1991), 1:478, 481.

30. Isaac Kramnick, ed., *The Federalist Papers* (New York: Penguin, 1987), *The Federalist 1* 1787, p. 89 (Hamilton); *The Federalist 55*, 1788, p. 336 (Madison); Reinhold Niebuhr, *The Irony of American History*, reprinted in Reinhold Niebuhr, *Major Works on Religion and Politics*, ed. Elisabeth Sifton (New York: Library of America, 2015/1952). Kennan gave a major anti-McCarthy address in the senator's home state of Wisconsin as early as May 1950. Within a year, the characteristically morose Kennan wrote in his diary, "The fact of the matter is that in this country McCarthyism has already won in the sense of making impossible the conduct of an intelligent foreign policy. The result is there is no place in public life for an honest and moderate man" (*Kennan Diaries*, April 17, 1951, p. 284); also George F. Kennan, *Memoirs, 1950–1963* (New York: Pantheon, 1972), 221, 223, 224. See also Hans Morgenthau, "The Impact of the Loyalty-Security Measures on the State Department," *Bulletin of the Atomic Scientists* 11:4 (1955): 134–40.

31. Thucydides, *The Peloponnesian War*, 2.21.2, 2.21.3, 2.22.1, 2.65.8–9, 2.65.10. See also John H. Finley Jr., *Thucydides* (Ann Arbor: University of Michigan Press, 1963/1942). Thucydides saw the "greatness of Athens" as "dependent on her being a democracy," but "he was not blind, however, to the weaknesses which could develop in a democracy through popular pressure and under the strain of war" (92).

32. Kennan, *American Diplomacy*, 56, 81. Kennan's anti-democratic proclivities are aback-taking, and must be part of any assessment of his thought; in the words John Lukacs, "a problem his biographers must not ignore." *George Kennan: A Study of Character* (New Haven: Yale University Press, 2007) 33, 34, 38 (quote), 39. See also John Lewis Gaddis, *George F. Kennan: An American Life* (New York: Penguin, 2011), 114–16, and various passages in George F. Kennan, *From Prague after Munich: Diplomatic Papers, 1938–1940* (Princeton: Princeton University Press, 1968), which reveal a coldness and a comfort with authoritarianism not easy to read—or to dismiss. On Morgenthau and U.S. foreign policy, see Hans Morgenthau, "What Is the National Interest of the United States," *Annals of the American Academy of Political and Social Science* 282:1 (1952): 6 (quote); elsewhere he bemoans an American foreign policy process that "border[s] on chaos" ("The Impact of Loyalty-Security Measures," 134); on realism and democracy more generally, see Morgenthau, *Politics among Nations*, 25 (quote). Note the elitist streak even in Niebuhr, e.g., *Moral Man and Immoral Society*, 21, 87, 93.

33. Kennan, *American Diplomacy*, 82; John Lewis Gaddis, *Strategies of Containment: A Critical Appraisal of American National Security Policy during the Cold War*, rev. ed. (Oxford: Oxford University Press, 2005), 106 (Acheson); Thomas Christensen, *Useful Adversaries: Grand Strategy, Domestic Mobilization, and Sino-American Conflict, 1947–1958* (Princeton: Princeton University Press, 1996), 50 (Vandenberg); Reinhold Niebuhr, "The Moral World of Foster Dulles," *New Republic* December 1, 1958 (reprinted in Niebuhr, *Major Works*, 680). See also Christensen's "domestic mobilization model," which illustrates how leaders in both democracies and non-democracies can face domestic political barriers to the implementation of ideal foreign policy postures that can necessitate "over-active" security strategies (*Useful Adversaries*, 13).

34. Many realists, theorists of grand strategy, and structural realists in particular explicitly or implicitly assume that there is an "optimal" foreign policy posture; one that best advances the national interest and is thus a-political and far-sighted. (Recall from chapter 2 Neoclassical Realism's observation that "states occasionally respond inconsistently with systemic imperatives," which implies divergence from such a Platonic ideal.) But in practice, even among experts, "optimal" foreign policy practices will prove debatable, and, more important, no choices will escape domestic political implications. Consider for comparison the attributes of independent central banks with an imagined insulated foreign policy establishment. Both would insulate policy choices from the passions of the political process (and the machinations of devious demagogues). But note that for monetary policy, although independent central banks can guard against the pathology of "political business cycles," they do *not* remove politics more generally from monetary policy choices. In addition, there is also a greater degree of expert consensus on causal relationships in monetary policy than foreign policy (though, again, the choice of metric—and value judgments about trade-offs—matters enormously, and politically). Thus although one can appeal to the

broad "National Interest" in the conduct of monetary policy and wise foreign policy, the issue of *whose* interest is being advanced will invariably linger; and with regard to foreign policy measures there is much more room for dispassionate/disinterested experts to still disagree on optimal policy. Philosophically this is further complicated by the fact that questions of foreign policy often involve decisions about war and peace and thus sending people off to war—it would be a dramatic move indeed to remove or further insulate such decisions from the democratic process.

35. Jonathan Kirshner, "When the Wise Men Failed," *New York Times*, October 31, 2017.

36. Carr, *Twenty Years' Crisis*, 89; Martin Wight, *Power Politics* (New York: Holmes & Meier, 1978/1946), 81; Reinhold Niebuhr, "Plans for World Reorganization," *Christianity and Crisis* 2 (October 19 1942): 3. That people crave motivation and purpose is not to be underestimated. Keynes, in abject horror of the totalitarian movements of both the left and the right, nevertheless feared that they might have an advantage in comparison with the empty materialism of liberal capitalism by offering philosophies that appeared to speak to larger social purposes. John Maynard Keynes, "A Short View of Russia" (1925), *CW*, 9:266–67.

37. Carr, *Twenty Years' Crisis*, 92; Morgenthau, "The Political Science of E. H. Carr," 129; Hans Morgenthau, "Foreign Policy: The Conservative School," *World Politics* 7:2 (1955): 285. Morgenthau continues, irresistibly: "The author attacks a problem very much as a cat attacks a mouse. He tosses it around, takes hold of it, lets it go, and catches it again; but, in contrast to the cat, he never consumes and digests more than part of it. For the reader the subtlety, suppleness, and elegance of the play will always be enjoyable. . . . Yet from time to time he cannot help asking himself in confusion what happened to the mouse" (285–86).

38. As discussed in chapter 1, realism is not a "theory" but a perspective from which a range of theories can be derived. Such theories will share common analytical roots but can and will generate divergent expectations. Moreover, as demonstrated in chapter 2, the extreme unlikelihood—and almost certain practical impossibility—that international relations scholars (and, even more consequentially, policymakers) will ever converge around the same, shared implicit or explicit model of world politics means that expectations and thus policy advice will differ across actors—even, it should be stressed, among those sharing the same policy objectives and general paradigmatic disposition.

39. Choosing the "optimal" exchange rate regime, for example, would depend essentially on normative trade-offs between competing goals, such as stability of rates versus domestic macroeconomic policy autonomy. Similar to disagreeing realists, however, our dueling international macroeconomists will often disagree on what policies *should* be pursued but are likely to agree that certain choices would be disastrous.

40. Compare, for example, Michael Beckley, "The Power of Nations: Measuring What Matters," *International Security* 43:2 (fall 2018): 7–44, and Jonathan Kirshner, *American Power after the Financial Crisis* (Ithaca: Cornell University Press, 2014).

41. Morgenthau, *Politics among Nations*, 9; Arnold Wolfers, "The Goals of Foreign Policy," in Wolfers, *Discord and Collaboration* (Baltimore: Johns Hopkins University Press, 1962), see esp. p. 72 ("the foreign policy of all nation-states are not uniform in scope or character and must, therefore, be treated as significant variables.

Governments conceive of these cherished values in more or less moderate and in more or less ambitious and exacting terms") and p. 73 (on milieu goals and efforts at "shaping conditions beyond their national boundaries").

42. The locus classicus on this issue remains Robert Jervis, *Perception and Misperception in International Politics* (Princeton: Princeton University Press, 1976), chap. 3.

43. Hans Morgenthau, "International Affairs: The Resurrection of Neutrality in Europe," *American Political Science Review* 33:3 (June 1939): 483–84; Hans Morgenthau, *In Defense of the National Interest* (New York: Knopf, 1951), 137, 138.

44. George F. Kennan, *Realities of American Foreign Policy* (New York: Norton, 1966/1954), 93.

45. Machiavelli, *The Prince*, 101. (Here Machiavelli compares fortune to a woman—it was the sixteenth century out there—and "like a woman, she is a friend of the young, because they are less cautious, more ferocious, and command her with more audacity.") Machiavelli, *Discourses on Livy*, 117 (quote), 118–120, 121 (quote). On these issues, see also Corrado Vivanti, *Niccolò Machiavelli: An Intellectual Biography* (Princeton: Princeton University Press), 40, 85, and Peter Katzenstein and Lucia Sylbert, "Power Complexities and Political Theory," in *Protean Power: Exploring the Uncertain and Unexpected in World Politics*, ed. Peter Katzenstein and Lucia Sylbert (Cambridge: Cambridge University Press, 2018), 288.

46. Morgenthau, *Politics among Nations*, 10; Thomas Hobbes, *Leviathan* (New York: Penguin Classics, 1985/1651): "Reputation of prudence in the conduct of Peace or War, is power" (151). Niebuhr situates prudence in the context of the classical realist emphasis on uncertainty: "A wise statesmanship naturally rests upon a modest disinclination to penetrate, or seem to penetrate, the veil of the future any further than immediate foresight makes necessary." Reinhold Niebuhr, *The Self and the Dramas of History* (New York: Scribner, 1955), 213; Kennan, e.g., *American Diplomacy*, 50.

47. Carl von Clausewitz, *On War*, ed. and trans. Michael Howard and Peter Paret (Princeton: Princeton University Press, 1976), 69, 80, 81.

48. On the egregious misuse of the notion of a "Thucydides Trap," see Jonathan Kirshner, "Handle Him with Care: The Importance of Getting Thucydides Right," *Security Studies* 28:1 (2019): 1–24. On grasping for more in general, and Sicily in particular, see Thucydides, *The Peloponnesian War*, 4.21.2, 4.27.2, 4.41.4, 6.10.1–5, 6.11.1, 6.13.1, as well as Jacqueline de Romilly, *Thucydides and Athenian Imperialism*, trans. Philip Thody (Oxford: Basil Blackwell, 1963/1947), 172–76, 322, 327; Hunter R. Rawlings, *The Structure of Thucydides' History* (Princeton: Princeton University Press, 1981), 229–30; Hans-Peter Stahl, "Speeches and the Course of Events in Books Six and Seven of Thucydides," in *Oxford Readings in Classical Studies: Thucydides*, ed. Jeffrey S. Rusten (Oxford: Oxford University Press, 2009), 346, 352; Finley, *Three Essays on Thucydides*, 147; Hunter R. Rawlings, "Writing History Implicitly through Refined Structuring," in *The Oxford Handbook of Thucydides*, ed. Ryan K. Balot, Sara Forsdyke, and Edith Foster (Oxford: Oxford University Press, 2017), 206.

49. See, for example, Hans Morgenthau, *Vietnam and the United States* (Washington, DC: Public Affairs Press, 1965); George F. Kennan, U.S. Senate Testimony, February 10, 1966, pp. 331–38; Kenneth Waltz, "The Politics of Peace," *International Studies Quarterly* 11:3 (1967): 199–211.

50. See, for example, the statement placed as an advertisement in the *New York Times*, "War with Iraq Is Not in America's National Interest," September 26, 2002, and Jonathan Kirshner, "Prevent Defense: Why the Bush Doctrine Will Hurt U.S. Interests," in *Iraq and Beyond: The New U.S. National Security Strategy* (Ithaca: Cornell University, Peace Studies Program Occasional Paper #27, January 2003).

51. For an illustrative example, see Stephen Walt, "The Worst Case for War with Iran," *Foreign Policy*, November 16, 2011.

52. Thucydides, *The Peloponnesian War*, 1.144.3, 1.114.5. On Pericles' war advocacy see also, among others, Mark Fisher and Kinch Hoekstra, "Thucydides and the Politics of Necessity," and Mary P. Nichols, "Leaders and Leadership in Thucydides' History," both in *Oxford Handbook*, ed. Balot, Forsdyke, and Foster, 373, 461.

53. Even Keynes, inspired by and full of lavish praise for the prudence of Edmund Burke, nevertheless opined that "Burke's timidity was often extreme to the point of absurdity." John Maynard Keynes, "The Political Doctrines of Edmund Burke" (undergraduate essay, Archives Centre, Kings College, Cambridge, 1904), 42.

54. Machiavelli, *The Prince*, 91; George F. Kennan, *Memoirs, 1925–1950* (Boston: Little, Brown, 1967), 408, 463; Kennan, *Memoirs, 1950–1963*, 23, 50. Kennan's support for the initial U.S. intervention in the Korean War, an uncertain adventure undertaken in a distant country that had been deemed outside of the essential U.S. defense perimeter, can be seen as proof of Machiavelli's point about the limits to "safe choices." See *Kennan Diaries*, 250–51; Gaddis, *George F. Kennan*, 396–98.

55. Niebuhr, *Christian Realism and Political Problems*, 54 (adventurism); Niebuhr, "Plans for World Reorganization," 3 (new political achievements); Reinhold Niebuhr, "Our Moral and Spiritual Resources for International Cooperation," *Social Action* 22 (February 1956): 18 (self-defeating); see also Niebuhr, *The Irony of American History*, 570.

56. For the representative articulation of a strategy of "restraint" for the United States, see Barry Posen, *Restraint: A New Foundation for U.S. Grand Strategy* (Ithaca: Cornell University Press, 2015).

57. Looking at American commitments in 2020, a strong case can be made for a withdrawal of its forces from the Persian Gulf region. The notion that it is a vital U.S. interest that no single hostile power dominate the Gulf's oil fields was a plausible one in the 1970s but is much less compelling in 2020; ceding that space to others seems worth the risk. It is much harder to make a similar case for withdrawing from NATO or abandoning most other U.S. long-standing alliances, in assessing the costs, benefits, and international political consequences of such actions. We will return to these questions in chapter 7.

58. Edmund Burke, "Speech on the Petition of the Unitarian Society," May 11, 1792, in Edmund Burke, *Reflections on the Revolution in France and Other Writing*, ed. Jessie Norman (New York: Knopf, 2015), 794.

Chapter Five: Realism, Economics, and Politics

1. On this last issue, see Jonathan Kirshner, *American Power after the Financial Crisis* (Ithaca: Cornell University Press, 2014).

2. E. H. Carr, *The Twenty Years' Crisis, 1919–1939*, 2nd ed. (London: Macmillan, 1946 [1939]), 117. Jonathan Haslam, "E. H. Carr's Search for Meaning, 1892–1982,"

in *E. H. Carr: A Critical Appraisal*, ed. Michael Cox (New York: Palgrave, 2000), 27 (quote), and more generally for the evolution of Carr's economic philosophy.

3. Carr, *Twenty Years' Crisis*, 50, 60; see also 54–55, 114–15.

4. Donald Kagan, *The Outbreak of the Peloponnesian War* (Ithaca: Cornell University Press, 1969), 269, 374; see also W. Robert Connor, "Scale Matters: Compression, Expansion and Vividness in Thucydides," in *The Oxford Handbook of Thucydides*, ed. Ryan K. Balot, Sara Forsdyke, and Edith Foster (Oxford: Oxford University Press, 2017), 215; Richard Ned Lebow and Robert Kelly, "Thucydides and Hegemony: Athens and the United States," *Review of International Studies* 27:4 (2001): 598. On Thucydides' general blind spot for economics, see, for example, Jacqueline de Romilly, *Thucydides and Athenian Imperialism*, trans. Philip Thody (Oxford: Basil Blackwell, 1963/1947), 72–73. Lisa Kallet has attempted to draw together the strands of economic arguments in Thucydides' work, but this remains a very hard case to make systematically, and she of course acknowledges his slim treatment of the Megarian Decree. See Lisa Kallet-Marx, *Money, Expense and Naval Power in Thucydides' History 1–5.24* (Berkeley: University of California Press, 1993); Lisa Kallet, *Money and the Corrosion of Power in Thucydides: The Sicilian Expedition and Its Aftermath* (Berkeley: University of California Press, 2001).

5. Early examples of work in "economics and national security" include Jacob Viner, "International Finance and Balance of Power Diplomacy, 1880–1914," *Political and Social Science Quarterly* 9:4 (1929): 408–51, and Herbert Feis, *Europe, the World's Banker, 1870–1914* (New Haven: Yale University Press, 1930); for an overview of this literature see Michael Mastanduno, "Economics and Security in Statecraft and Scholarship," *International Organization* 52:4 (1998): 825–54.

6. Recall Aron's admonition from chapter 4 (a principle this chapter will again elaborate as essential to realism) that although the pursuit of power and wealth is not easily disentangled, "politics is never reducible to economics even through the struggle for the possession of sovereign power may in many ways be linked to the mode of production and the distribution of wealth." Raymond Aron, "Thucydides and the Historical Narrative," in *Politics and History: Selected Essays of Raymond Aron*, ed. and trans. Miriam Bernheim Conant (New York: The Free Press, 1978), 43 (quote); see also Raymond Aron, *In Defense of Decadent Europe* (New Brunswick, NJ: Transaction Publishers, 1977/1996), 193.

7. Liberal theories of international political economy initially tended to focus on the consequences of interdependence, which was more about how international economics affected international relations and foreign policy choices. See, for example, Richard N. Cooper, *The Economics of Interdependence: Economic Policy in the Atlantic Community* (New York: McGraw-Hill, 1968), and the special issue of *International Organization* 25:3 (1971), "Transnational Relations and World Politics," edited by Robert Keohane and Joseph Nye. Realists, not surprisingly, tended to point the arrows in the opposite direction. See Robert Gilpin, "The Politics of Transnational Relations," in the special issue of *International Origination*; Klaus Knorr, *The Power of Nations: The Political Economy of International Relations* (New York: Basic Books, 1975); Susan Strange, "International Relations and International Economics: A Case of Mutual Neglect," *International Affairs* 46:2 (1970): 304–15; Susan Strange, *Sterling and British Policy: A Political Study of an International Currency in Decline* (Oxford: Oxford University Press, 1971); Charles Kindleberger, *Power and Money: The*

Economics of International Politics and the Politics of International Economics (New York: Basic Books, 1970); Charles Kindleberger, *The World in Depression, 1929–1939* (Berkeley: University of California Press, 1973). It should be noted that Kindleberger would be horrified to be characterized as a realist.

8. Robert Gilpin, "The Richness of the Tradition of Political Realism," in *Neorealism and Its Critics*, ed. Robert O. Keohane (New York: Columbia University Press, 1986), 309 (Carr); Gilpin, "The Politics of Transnational Economic Relations," 403–4, 409, 410 (quotes); Robert Gilpin, "Three Models of the Future," *International Organization* 29:1 (1975): 37–60; Robert Gilpin, *U.S. Power and the Multinational Corporation* (New York: Basic Books, 1975); Robert Gilpin, "Economic Interdependence and National Security in Historical Perspective," in *Economic Issues and National Security*, ed. Klaus Knorr and Frank Trager (Lawrence: University Press of Kansas, 1977), 59; Robert Gilpin, *War and Change in World Politics* (Cambridge: Cambridge University Press, 1981). See also the discussion of *War and Change* in chapter 3 of this book; Robert Gilpin, *The Political Economy of International Relations* (Princeton: Princeton University Press, 1987), 119 (political order).

9. There has been notable work in realist political economy; see, for example, Michael Mastanduno, *Economic Containment: Cocom and the Politics of East-West Trade* (Ithaca: Cornell University Press, 1992); Jonathan Kirshner, *Currency and Coercion: The Political Economy of International Monetary Power* (Princeton: Princeton University Press, 1995); Stefano Guzzini, *Realism in International Relations and International Political Economy: The Continuing Story of a Death Foretold* (London: Routledge, 1998); David E. Spiro, *The Hidden Hand of American Hegemony: Petrodollar Recycling and International Markets* (Ithaca: Cornell University Press, 1999). On the hyper-rationalist hijacking of liberal IPE and its unfortunate consequences, see Jonathan Kirshner, "The Second Crisis in IPE Theory," in *International Political Economy: Debating the Past, Present and Future*, ed. Nicola Phillips and Catherine Weaver (New York: Routledge, 2011), 203–9.

10. Kenneth Waltz, *Theory of International Politics* (New York: Addison Wesley, 1979), 151–52; Robert Keohane, *After Hegemony: Cooperation and Discord in the World Political Economy* (Princeton: Princeton University Press, 1984), 137. There were, of course, exceptions to this trend. Notable among these is Stephen Krasner, *Structural Conflict: The Third World against Global Liberalism* (Berkeley: University of California Press, 1985). Krasner offered a well-argued realist take on "North-South" relations. His expectations turned out to be well off-base.

11. An exemplary illustration of non-hyper-rationalist liberal international political economy is Charles Kindleberger, "The Rise of Free Trade in Western Europe, 1820–1875," *Journal of Economic History* 35:1 (1975): 20–55. For shattering critiques of "open economy politics" (by scholars whose analytical instincts have affinities with the approach), see Sungmin Rho and Michael Tomz, "Why Don't Trade Preferences Reflect Economic Self Interest?" *International Organization* 71:S1 (2017): S85–S108, and Thomas Oatley, "Open Economy Politics and Trade Policy," *Review of International Political Economy* 24:4 (2017): 699–717.

12. Hans Morgenthau, *Politics among Nations: The Struggle for Power and Peace*, 3rd ed. (New York: Knopf, 1960/1948), 5, 12, 14; Gilpin, *U.S. Power and the Multinational Corporation*, 27; Paul Samuelson, "Economists and the History of Ideas,"

American Economic Review 52:1 (1962): 12; John Maynard Keynes, "My Early Beliefs," (1949), *CW*, 10:445; see also the sharp anti-economism in Keynes, "Economic Possibilities for Our Grandchildren" (1930), *CW*, vol. 6, e.g., p. 328.

13. Gilpin, *War and Change*, 67 (quote). As noted, on the centrality of the national interest for the realist tradition, see chapter 4, and the discussion of "Hirschman effects" below.

14. An excellent overview of the breadth of classical mercantilist thought remains Eli F. Heckscher, *Mercantilism*, 2 vols. (London: George Allen and Unwin, 1935).

15. James Stewart, *An Inquiry into the Principles of Political Oeconomy* (Chicago: University of Chicago Press, 1966 (1767), 283 (quote), see also 363; Thomas Mun, *England's Treasure by Forraign Trade: Or, the Ballance of our Forraign Trade is the Rule of our Treasure* (Oxford: Basil Blackwell, 1949 [1664]), see esp. 83–86. English mercantilist Roger Coke, author of *England's Improvement by Foreign Trade* (1675), is quoted in Heckscher, as is Philipp von Hörnigk, who assessed in 1684 that the wealth and might of a nation depend "principally on whether its neighbors possess more or less of it. For power and riches have become a relative matter" (Heckscher, *Mercantilism*, 2:22 [quotes], see also 26, 239). On the conception of trade as zero sum, Heckscher stated: "Scarcely any other element in mercantilist philosophy contributed more to the shaping of economic policy, and even of foreign policy as a whole" (*Mercantilism*, 2:24). From the perspective of Richard Cantillion (whose contributions to monetary economists, it should be noted, remain important), "above all . . . care must be taken to maintain the balance against the foreigner" (*Essay on the Nature of Trade in General* [New York: Augustus M. Kelley, 1964/1755], 243), echoing sentiments expressed a century before that in Germany by Johann Joachim Becher, as quoted by Heckscher: "it is always better to sell goods to others than to buy goods from others, for the former brings a certain advantage and the latter inevitable damage." Heckscher argues that "this attitude became crystallized in a demand for an export surplus, a demand which was expressed in every possible way" (*Mercantilism*, 2:116).

16. Adam Smith, *An Inquiry into the Nature and Causes of The Wealth of Nations* (Chicago: University of Chicago Press, 1976 [1776]), esp. book 1, pp. 450–73, 496–502, 513–24; book 2, pp. 3–10, 103–57.

17. Jacob Viner, "Adam Smith and Laissez Faire," *Journal of Political Economy* 35:2 (1927): 232. Note, for example, Smith favored government regulation of interest rates—left to its own devices, he thought, the free market would skew investment toward suboptimally risky enterprises. David Levy, "Adam Smith's Case for Usury Laws," *History of Political Economy* 19:3 (1987): 18–27. Heckscher notes affinities between the perspectives, *Mercantilism*, e.g., 1:26, 456, 2:13–14, 271, 285, 316, 328. Similarly, according to Schumpeter, "We have seen that, as far at least as economic analysis is concerned, there need not have been any spectacular break between 'mercantilists' and 'liberals.'" Joseph Schumpeter, *History of Economic Analysis* (New York: Oxford University Press, 1954), 376. See also William D. Grampp, "The Liberal Elements in English Mercantilism," *Quarterly Journal of Economics* 66:4 (1952): 465–501. The classic statement of the mercantilist conception of harmony between economic and political goals remains Jacob Viner, "Power versus Plenty as Objectives of Statecraft in the Seventeenth and Eighteenth Centuries," *World Politics* 1:1 (1948):

1–29; for representative passages in Smith, see *Wealth of Nations*, book 1, pp. 484–85, book 2, p. 28.

18. Alexander Hamilton, "Report on the Subject of Manufactures" (1791), in *Industrial and Commercial Correspondence of Alexander Hamilton*, ed. Arthur Cole (Chicago: A. W. Shaw, 1928); Friedrich List, *The National System of Political Economy* (London: Longmans, Green, 1885); Gustav Schmoller, *The Mercantile System and Its Historical Significance* (New York: Macmillan, 1897).

19. Hamilton, "Report on the Subject of Manufactures," see, e.g., p. 248. On the profound influence of Smith on Hamilton, see Edward G. Bourne, "Alexander Hamilton and Adam Smith," *Quarterly Journal of Economics* 8:3 (1894): 329–48; note, however, that Hamilton's mercantilist proclivities predate Smith. See his pamphlet "The Farmer Refuted" (New York: James Rivington, 1775). More generally, see also Edward Meade Earle, "Adam Smith, Alexander Hamilton, Friedrich List: The Economic Foundations of Military Power," in *Makers of Modern Strategy*, ed. Peter Paret (Princeton: Princeton University Press, 1986), esp. 230–44; and Edward C. Lunt, "Hamilton as a Political Economist," *Journal of Political Economy* 3:3 (1895): 289–310.

20. List, *National System*, 133 (quote), 308–14; 351 (quote). *National System* brought to full flower ideas List had been developing for some time. See his *The Natural System of Political Economy*, trans. and ed. W. O. Henderson (London: Frank Cass, 1983/1837), and "Outlines of American Political Economy" (Philadelphia: Samuel Parker, 1827), reprinted in Margaret E. Hirst, *Life of Friedrich List and Selections from His Writings* (London: Smith Elder, 1909). For more on List, see W. O. Henderson, *Friedrich List: Economist and Visionary, 1789–1846* (London: Frank Cass, 1983); Earle, "Adam Smith, Alexander Hamilton, Friedrich List," 243–58; and William Notz, "Frederick List in America," *American Economic Review* 16:1 (1926): 249–65.

21. See, for example, Gilpin, *Political Economy of International Relations*, e.g., 328–36.

22. List, *National System*, 347, 316. These sentiments are stressed throughout the work. On p. 120, for example, List, in reference to Smith, states: "Although here and there he speaks of wars, this occurs only incidentally. The idea of a perpetual state of peace forms the foundation of all his arguments."

23. Carr, *Twenty Years' Crisis*, 67, 80; Schmoller, *Mercantile System*, 80. Well illustrating Carr's expectations regarding "the relativity of thought to the interests of the thinker," new dissenting voices against free trade argued that particular circumstances, not universal laws, were the best guide to policy, and they urged Britain to introduce protectionist measures that were necessary "to ward off the dangers which threaten her very existence." William Cunningham, *The Rise and Decline of the Free Trade Movement* (London: C. J. Clay and Sons, 1904), 45 (quote), see also 86, 108–9; William Cunningham, *The Growth of English Industry and Commerce in Modern Times*, 5th ed. (Cambridge: Cambridge University Press, 1912), 740, 869, 870 (quote).

24. List, *National System*, 316; Hamilton, "Report on the Subject of Manufacturers," 265, 266. Note that this is an area in which contrasting perspectives on political economy can converge. The heterodox economist Joan Robinson, revisiting Ricardo's own famous example, argued that "the imposition of free trade on Portugal killed off a promising textile industry and left her with a slow-growing export market for wine, while for England, exports of cotton cloth led to accumulation, mechanization, and the whole spiraling of the industrial revolution." And the leading classical economist

of the mid-nineteenth century, John Stuart Mill, accepted the infant industry argument as the "only case" where "protecting duties can be defensible." Joan Robinson, *Aspects of Development and Underdevelopment* (Cambridge: Cambridge University Press, 1979), 103; John Stuart Mill, *Principles of Political Economy*, rev. ed. (New York: Colonial Press, 1899), 2:423.

25. Sun also argued that "in international trade an industrial nation has an advantage over an agricultural nation." On non-Western articulations of neomercantilist thought, see Eric Helleiner, *The Neomercantilists: A Global Intellectual History* (Ithaca: Cornell University Press, 2021); Sun quotes are from pp. 254 and 250.

26. See, for example, Peter Liberman, "Trading with the Enemy: Security and Relative Economic Gains," *International Security* 21:1 (1996): 147–75.

27. J. B. Condliffe, *The Commerce of Nations* (New York: W. W. Norton, 1950), 278 (quote).

28. Heckscher, *Mercantilism*, 1:21 (quote) see also 273, and part 1, "Mercantilism as a Unifying System." It should be remembered that this emphasis on statism took place in the context of transition from (and opposition to) medieval political economy, and as such is somewhat less "illiberal" than might be assumed by contemporary readers. See, for example, Grampp, "Liberal Elements in English Mercantilism." Heckscher repeatedly emphasizes how from the perspective of internal commerce, the options of individuals increased during this period, as the formation of nation-states eliminated "internal" barriers to trade. *Mercantilism*, 2:273–74, 282–83.

29. Schmoller, *The Mercantile System*, 49, 50 (emphasis in original); see also F. W. Taussig, "Schmoller on Protection and Free Trade," *Quarterly Journal of Economics* 19:3 (1905): 501–11, and Thorsten Veblen, "Gustav Schmoller's Economics," *Quarterly Journal of Economics* 16:1 (1901): 69–93.

30. On the divergence between private and public interests, see, for example, Mun, *England's Treasure*, 25, 26; Viner "Power versus Plenty," 19; Heckscher, *Mercantilism*, 2:317; List, *National System*, 269.

31. Edmund Silberner, *The Problem of War in Nineteenth Century Economic Thought* (Princeton: Princeton University Press, 1946), 278 (List quote).

32. That is a lot to keep track of; here thus, a quick summary/overview of what follows:

> *Points of Departure*: anarchy; the purposeful state
>
> *Basic Assumptions*: the liberal-realist synthesis (power derives from an economic base); economic change is to be expected and is destabilizing; states have a preference for autonomy
>
> *Expectations*: international politics formatively shape the patterns of global economic activity; the interests of states and actors within states will commonly diverge; cooperation will often be difficult to establish and maintain

33. Liberal theories of hegemonic stability hold that cooperation is easier when there is one great power because the hegemon will recognize the overlap between their own interests and those of the system as a whole, and thus be willing to provide the "public goods" necessary to keep the system thriving. In such a setting, all participants gain, but the leader gains relatively less. Realist theories stress the anticipation of the dominant power that it will gain relatively more than others in an open (that is, cooperative) economic system. For this contrast, see Stephen Krasner, "State Power

and the Structure of International Trade," *World Politics* 28:3 (1976): 317–47, and Charles Kindleberger, "Dominance and Leadership in the International Economy," *International Studies Quarterly* 25:2 (1981): 242–54.

34. See, for example, Viner, "Power versus Plenty," esp. 10; Gilpin, "The Politics of Transnational Relations," 403–4, 409–10; Mastanduno, "Economics and Security," 827, 842–43, 848.

35. Heckscher, *Mercantilism*, 1:273 (quote).

36. As beautifully expressed by Adam Smith, "It is not from the benevolence of the butcher, the brewer, or the baker that we expect our dinner, but from their regard to their own self-interest" (*Wealth of Nations*, 10); see also Douglass North, *Structure and Change in Economic History* (New York: Norton, 1981), on the crucial role of the institutional and legal infrastructure necessary for market societies to function. Stephen Krasner, *Defending the National Interest: Raw Materials Investments and U.S. Foreign Policy* (Princeton: Princeton University Press, 1978), 300 (quote).

37. Condliffe, *The Commerce of Nations*, 800 (quotes). See also Gilpin, *War and Change* ("the distribution of power itself ultimately rests on an economic base" [67]). On the essential economic components of power, see, for example, Paul Kennedy, "The First World War and the International Power System," *International Security* 9:1 (1984): 7–40; on their complementarity, Paul Kennedy, *The Rise and Fall of British Naval Mastery* (London: Ashfield Press, 1976). For illustrations of the central role of finance in determining the outcomes of wars, see, for example, Karen Rasler and William Thompson, "Global Wars, Public Debts, and the Long Cycle," *World Politics* 35:4 (1983): 489–516; John Brewer, *The Sinews of Power: War, Money and the English State* (London: Hutchinson, 1988); and Douglas Ball, *Financial Failure and Confederate Defeat* (Urbana: University of Illinois Press, 1991).

38. In general, realist analyses have overstated the extent to which states will make economic sacrifices to retain their autonomy—North Koreas are, ultimately, rare. As indicated in note 10, Krasner, in his book *Structural Conflict*, was very much wrong in his expectation that developing nations would reject economic liberalization for these reasons (as anticipated in his subtitle, *The Third World against Global Liberalism*). See also Robert W. Tucker, *The Inequality of Nations* (New York: Basic Books, 1977). On the divergence of the national interest and the interests of finance, see, for example, John Maynard Keynes, "The Economic Consequences of Mr. Churchill" (1925), *CW*, 9:207–30; Paul Kennedy, "Strategy versus Finance in Twentieth-Century Britain," *International History Review* 3:1 (1981): 44–61, and Kirshner, *American Power after the Financial Crisis*.

39. John McCallum, "National Borders Matter: Canada-U.S. Regional Trade Patterns," *American Economic Review* 85:3 (1995): 615–23; Benjamin Cohen, *The Geography of Money* (Ithaca: Cornell University Press, 1998); Eric Helleiner, *The Making of National Money: Territorial Currencies in Historical Perspective* (Ithaca: Cornell University Press, 2002).

40. Mun, *England's Treasure*, 25, 26; List, *National System*, 269.

41. On these issues, see Keohane, *After Hegemony*, and Kenneth Oye, *Economic Discrimination and Political Exchange* (Princeton: Princeton University Press, 1992).

42. For Secretary of the Treasury Henry Morgenthau, the agreement reflected his "growing determination to use monetary policy to build a united, democratic front to

resist Hitler." J. M. Blum, *From the Morgenthau Diaries* (Boston: Houghton Mifflin, 1959), 1:140; see also Ian M. Drummond, *London, Washington, and the Management of the Franc*, Princeton Studies in International Finance 45 (November 1979), 3–4, 32, 53. On the American system, see Robert Pollard, *Economic Security and the Origins of the Cold War, 1945–1950* (New York: Columbia University Press, 1985), and chapter 7 in this book.

43. Keohane, *After Hegemony*, e.g., 7–9, 29; in the preface to the 2005 edition Keohane states, "on this realist foundation I build an institutionalist edifice" (ix). Joseph Grieco, *Cooperation among Nations: Europe, America, and Non-Tariff Barriers to Trade* (Ithaca: Cornell University Press, 1990), 217.

44. Lawrence Summers, "Relative Wages, Efficiency Wages, and Keynesian Unemployment," *American Economic Review* 78:2 (1988): 383–88; John Maynard Keynes, *The General Theory of Employment, Interest, and Money* (London: Macmillan, 1936), *CW*, 8:14.

45. Similarly, the voice actors on the television show *The Simpsons* went on strike despite being paid extraordinarily high salaries. As one cast member explained, although their current compensation was "ridiculous by any normal standard," those salaries "nevertheless pale in comparison to what the show's profit participants have been taking home," which was the relevant referent. Harry Shearer, "Why *The Simpsons* Cast Deserves a Profit Share," *Daily Beast*, October 7, 2011.

46. On the difficulties in distinguishing underlying motives, see Michael Mastanduno, "Do Relative Gains Matter?" *International Security* 16:1 (1991): 73–113. Liberman, "Trading with the Enemy," features fine examples of how difficult it is to distinguish these behaviors in settings where security concerns should be highly salient. For an introduction to and overview of this enormous literature, see David Baldwin, ed., *Neorealism and Neoliberalism: The Contemporary Debate* (New York: Columbia University Press, 1993).

47. Richard Cobden, *Speeches on Questions of Public Policy* (New York: Klaus Reprint Co., 1970), speech of January 27, 1848, pp. 233–41.

48. Raymond Vernon, *Sovereignty at Bay: The Multinational Spread of U.S. Enterprise* (New York: Basic Books, 1971); Robert Keohane and Joseph Nye, *Power and Interdependence: World Politics in Transition* (Boston: Little, Brown, 1977).

49. See Kenneth Waltz, "The Myth of National Interdependence," in *The International Corporation*, ed. Charles Kindleberger (Cambridge, MA: MIT Press, 1970); Kindleberger, *Power and Money*, 104.

50. Waltz, *Theory of International Politics*, 140–41.

51. Norman Angell, *The Great Illusion: A Study of the Relation of Military Power in Nations to Their Economic and Social Advantage* (New York: G. P. Putnam and Sons, 1910), see esp. chap. 3, "The Great Illusion," also pp. vi, 52 (on the consequences of "complex financial interdependence" for the costs and benefits of war), 54–56, 59–61, 372; Ivan S. Bloch, *Is War Now Impossible?* (Aldershot: Gregg Revivals, 1991 [1899]), xlv, lxxix, 114, 347; see also Howard Weinrith, "Norman Angell and the Great Illusion: An Episode in Pre-1914 Pacifism," *Historical Journal* 17:3 (1974): 551, 556–57, 564, 568–69, and "Prophet of Trench Deadlock Vindicated: Ivan S. Bloch, Who Wrote Seventeen Years Ago, Foresaw 'Stalemate' Like That on Western Front Today, and Other Excellent Guesses," *New York Times Magazine*, January 23, 1916.

52. See, for example, Kenneth Waltz, "Globalization and Governance," *PS: Political Science and Politics* 32:4 (1999): 693–700; John Mearsheimer, *The Tragedy of Great Power Politics* (New York: Norton, 2001), 370–72.

53. For these reasons (and others, such as his emphasis on continuity over change in the nature of world politics), even Gilpin, who was much more sensitive than most realists to the significance of economic factors in international relations, underestimated the significance of globalization. He specifically anticipated instead somewhat greater closure, along political lines, and the emergence of "loose regional blocs." This may yet emerge, but did not in the third of a century that followed his first expression of that claim—and at some point it must be acknowledged that events diverged considerably from Gilpin's expectations. Gilpin, *Political Economy of International Economic Relations*, 395, 397 (quote); see also Robert Gilpin, *Global Political Economy: Understanding the International Economic Order* (Princeton: Princeton University Press, 2001), esp. 362–76.

54. As then U.S. Treasury undersecretary (soon to be secretary) Lawrence Summers put it at the time, "Financial liberalization, both domestically and internationally, is a critical part of the U.S. agenda." Lawrence Summers, "Financial Services Negotiations," Congressional Economic Leadership Institute Luncheon, August 12, 1997.

55. See the similar distinction between "internationalization" and "globalization" in Peter Katzenstein, *A World of Regions: Asia and Europe in the American Imperium* (Ithaca: Cornell University Press, 2005), 15–19. On system-wide pressures, see, for example, David Andrews, "Capital Mobility and State Autonomy: Toward a Structural Theory of International Monetary Relations," *International Studies Quarterly* 38:2 (1994): 193–218.

56. And, as emphasized, political relationships will typically have foundational consequences for the pattern of economic activity.

57. Albert Hirschman, *National Power and the Structure of Foreign Trade* (Berkeley: University of California Press, 1980 [1945]); see also Allan G. Fisher, "The German Trade Drive in South-Eastern Europe," *International Affairs* 18:2 (1939): 143–70, and Antonín Basch, *The Danube Basin and the German Economic Sphere* (New York: Columbia University Press, 1943), esp. 178. Krasner applies this logic, arguing that the United States established international openness because it would have the least to lose from closure, in "State Power and the Structure of International Trade," 320.

58. Fernando Henrique Cardoso and Enzo Faletto, *Dependency and Development in Latin America* (Berkeley: University of California Press, 1979).

59. Hirschman, *National Power*, 18, 28, 29 (quote), 34, 37. On Latin America, see H. Gerald Smith, "German Trade Competition in Latin America," *Commercial Pan America* 53 (1936); "The Aski Mark," *Economist*, August 12, 1939, p. 322; and Herbert M. Bratter, "Foreign Exchange Control in Latin America," *Foreign Policy Reports* 14:23 (1939). For illustrations of this phenomenon more generally, see Rawi Abdelal and Jonathan Kirshner, "Strategy, Economic Relations, and the Definition of National Interests," *Security Studies* 9:1–2 (1999–2000): 119–56.

60. Joseph Nye, *Bound to Lead: The Changing Nature of American Power* (New York: Basic Books, 1990). For a brilliant if understated and ultimately ambivalent illustration of this phenomenon, see the representations of America, real and imagined, in Wim Wenders, *Alice in the Cities* (1974).

61. On domestic wrangling between interest groups and contestations about the national interest, see, for example, Charles Kindleberger, "Group Behavior and International Trade," *Journal of Political Economy* 59:1 (1959): 30–47; Peter Gourevitch, *Politics in Hard Times: Comparative Responses to International Economic Crises* (Ithaca: Cornell University Press, 1986); Rawi Abdelal, *National Purpose in the World Economy* (Ithaca: Cornell University Press, 2001); Peter Trubowitz, *Defining the National Interest: Conflict and Change in American Foreign Policy* (Chicago: University of Chicago Press, 1998); Benjamin Cohen, *In Whose Interest? International Banking and American Foreign Policy* (New Haven: Yale University Press, 1986).

62. On arguments for the definitive role of hard power, see Robert S. Ross, "Balance of Power Politics and the Rise of China: Accommodation and Balancing in East Asia," *Security Studies* 15:3 (2006): 355–95. On inhibitions against the overt exercise of coercive power that derives from asymmetric relations, see Scott Cooper, "The Limits of Monetary Power: Statecraft within Currency Areas," in *International Monetary Power*, ed. David Andrews (Ithaca: Cornell University Press, 2006). For an attempt to measure Hirschman effects, see Gustavo Flores-Macías and Sarah E. Kreps, "The Foreign Policy Consequences of Trade: China's Commercial Relations with Africa and Latin America, 1992–2006," *Journal of Politics* 75:2 (2013): 357–71.

63. "The Aski Mark," 321–22. (Even during the war, the United States was worried about the loyalty of its hemispheric neighbors. Among other efforts to shore up relations, Nelson Rockefeller, then President Roosevelt's coordinator of Inter-American Affairs, sent Orson Welles to Brazil on a goodwill tour.)

64. Seymour E. Harris, "Cost of the Marshall Plan to the United States," *Journal of Finance* 3:1 (1948): 1–15. In carefully enumerating the costs and evaluating various economic consequences of the effort, Harris, an economist, also noted, "The political aspects are even more important" (7).

65. Note of course the absence of military coercion or an environment of economic closure (along both dimensions in fact the opposite conditions held) with regard to the Hirschmanesque effort that was the American Marshall Plan. Michael Hogan, *The Marshall Plan: America, Britain, and the Reconstruction of Western Europe* (Cambridge: Cambridge University Press, 1987), esp. 443–44; Melvyn Leffler, *A Preponderance of Power: National Security, the Truman Administration, and the Cold War* (Stanford: Stanford University Press, 1992), 187; Pollard, *Economic Security and the Origins of the Cold War*, 281; George F. Kennan, *Memoirs, 1925–1950* (Boston: Little, Brown, 1967), 333–38.

66. For the monetary side of Germany's efforts, see Allen Thomas Bonnell, "German Control over International Economic Relations," *Illinois Studies in the Social Sciences* 13:1 (1940); Howard S. Ellis, *Exchange Control in Central Europe* (Cambridge, MA: Harvard University Press, 1941); and Frank C. Child, *The Theory and Practice of Exchange Control in Germany* (The Hague: Martinus Nijhoff, 1958). On the theory and practice of monetary dependence more generally, see Kirshner, *Currency and Coercion*, chap. 4.

67. Marcello DeCecco, *The International Gold Standard* (New York: St. Martin's Press, 1984), 44 (quote); Henry Parker Willis, *A History of the Latin Monetary Union* (Chicago: University of Chicago Press, 1901); Emily Rosenberg, "Foundations of United States International Financial Power: Gold Standard Diplomacy, 1900–1905,"

Business History Review 59 (1985): 169–202; Frank Costigliola, "Anglo-American Financial Rivalry in the 1920s," *Journal of Economic History* 37:4 (1977): 911–34. On Nixon shocks of 1971, see John S. Odell, *U.S. International Monetary Policy: Markets, Power, and Ideas as Sources of Change* (Princeton: Princeton University Press, 1982). On the Asian Monetary Fund, and the fierce U.S. reaction to it, see Phillip Lipscy, "Japan's Asian Monetary Fund Proposal," *Stanford Journal of East Asian Affairs* 3:1 (2003): esp. 95–96.

68. Susan Strange, "Finance, Information and Power," *Review of International Studies* 16:3 (1990): 259–74; Susan Strange, "The Persistent Myth of Lost Hegemony," *International Organization* 41:4 (1987): 569.

69. Odell, *U.S. International Monetary Policy*, 263; Harold James, *International Monetary Cooperation since Bretton Woods* (Oxford: Oxford University Press, 1996), 210 (quote); Henry M. Paulson Jr., *On the Brink: Inside the Race to Stop the Collapse of the International Monetary System* (New York: Business Plus, 2010), 161 (Russia). How long dollar dominance will endure is an open question, as is the extent to which China is now motivated to advance a greater role for its own currency. But this would take us far afield from the argument here, which is that international monetary arrangements are routinely shaped by the pursuit of political influence.

70. World Trade Organization, *International Trade Statistics, 2019* (WTO, 2019); International Monetary Fund, *Direction of Trade Statistics, Yearbook 2019* (IMF, 2019); World Bank, *World Integrated Trade Solution*, https://wits.worldbank.org/countrystats.aspx.

71. On the increasing political weight of China's economy, see Ja Ian Chong, "Shifting Winds in Southeast Asia: Chinese Prominence and the Future of the Regional Order," in *Strategic Asia 2019: China's Expanding Economic Ambitions*, ed. Ashley Tellis, Alison Szalwinski, and Michael Willis (Seattle: National Bureau of Asian Research, 2019); Robert Ross, "On the Fungibility of Economic Power: China's Economic Rise and the East Asian Security Order," *European Journal of International Politics* 25:1 (2019): 302–27, and Jacques de Lisle and Avery Goldstein, eds., *China's Global Engagement: Cooperation, Competition, and Influence in the 21st Century* (Washington, DC: Brookings Institution Press, 2017). On the AIIB, Larry Summers was hyperbolic: "This past month may be remembered as the moment the United States lost its role as the underwriter of the global economic system." Lawrence Summers, "A Global Wake Up Call for the U.S.?" *Washington Post*, April 5, 2015. For a general, qualified overview of the Belt and Road Initiative, see Jonathan Hillman, *The Emperor's New Road: China and the Project of the Century* (New Haven: Yale University Press, 2020).

72. Thomas Wright, *All Measures Short of War: The Contest for the 21st Century and the Future of American Power* (New Haven: Yale University Press, 2017), 95; Scott A. Snyder, *South Korea at the Crossroads: Autonomy and Alliance in an Era of Rival Powers* (New York: Columbia University Press, 2018), 3 ("debate" and "pathways") quotes, 212, 214 ("China lobby"), 220, 227 ("a debate for the first time in Korea's modern history" over basic strategic choices), 263. Ellen Kim and Victor Cha, "Between a Rock and a Hard Place: South Korea's Strategic Dilemmas with China and the United States," *Asia Policy* 21 (January 2016): 107 (quote), 108. On the Hirschmanesque issues at play more generally, see Masanori Hasegawa, "Close

Economic Exchange with a Threatening State: An Awkward Dilemma over China," *Asian Security* 14:2 (2018): 155–71. On China-South Korea trade, see World Bank, *World Integrated Trade Solution*, https://wits.worldbank.org/CountryProfile/en/Country/KOR/Year/LTST/Summary.

73. Stanley Hoffmann, "Clash of Globalizations," *Foreign Affairs* 81:4 (2002): 111; Henry Farrell and Abraham Newman, "Weaponized Interdependence: How Global Economic Networks Shape State Coercion," *International Security* 44:1 (2019): 42–79.

74. Albert O. Hirschman, "The Changing Tolerance for Income Inequality in the Course of Economic Development," *Quarterly Journal of Economics* 87:4 (1973): 544–66. See also Mary Kaldor, *New and Old Wars: Organized Violence in a Global Era* (Stanford: Stanford University Press, 2001); Audrey Kurth Cronin, "Behind the Curve: Globalization and International Terrorism," *International Security* 27:3 (2002/2003): 30–58; Siniša Malešević, *The Rise of Organised Brutality: A Historical Sociology of Violence* (Cambridge: Cambridge University Press, 2017).

75. Peter Beinart, "An Illusion for Our Time: The False Promise of Globalization," *New Republic*, October 20, 1997, p. 20.

76. On earlier episodes of financial globalization, see Larry Neal, *A Concise History of International Finance: From Babylon to Bernanke* (Cambridge: Cambridge University Press, 2015); on the reversibility of globalization, see Harold James, *The Creation and Destruction of Value: The Globalization Cycle* (Cambridge, MA: Harvard University Press, 2009).

77. World Bank, *World Development Indicators, 2006*; UNCTAD, *Statistical Handbook, 2006*; World Trade Organization, "World Merchandise Exports, Production, and Gross Domestic Production, 1950–2005," *International Trade Statistics 2006*, table 6.1; World Trade Organization, *World Trade Statistical Review* 2019, https://www.wto.org/english/res_e/statis_e/wts2019_e/wts19_toc_e.htm; World Bank, *World Integrated Trade Solution*, https://wits.worldbank.org/Default.aspx?lang=en. The novelty of the fragmentation of production, and its political significance, is emphasized by Stephen Brooks, *Producing Security: Multinational Corporations, Globalization, and the Changing Calculus of Conflict* (Princeton: Princeton University Press, 2005). For investment figures, see UNCTAD, *World Investment Report 2006* (New York and Geneva, 2006); UNCTAD 2019 *Handbook of Statistics*: https://stats.unctad.org/handbook/EconomicTrends/Fdi.html.

78. Bank for International Settlements, *Triennial Central Bank Survey: Foreign Exchange and Derivatives Market Activity in 2004* (Basle: BIS, 2005), 5; Bank for International Settlements, *Triennial Central Bank Survey Foreign Exchange Turnover in April 2019*, Monetary and Economic Department, September 16, 2019, https://www.bis.org/statistics/rpfx19_fx.htm; World Bank, *World Development Report*, 2006, table 6.8.

79. Harold Innis, *Empire and Communications* (Oxford: Oxford University Press, 1950); Peter J. Hugill, *Global Communications since 1844: Geopolitics and Technology* (Baltimore: Johns Hopkins University Press, 1999); Ronald J. Deibert, *Parchment, Printing and Hypermedia: Communication in World Order Transformation* (New York: Columbia University Press, 1997), see esp. 2, 67, 137, 142. Note, for example, in 2020 six billion people operated eight billion distinct telephone

numbers. On authoritarian empowerment, see, for example, Paul Mozur, Jonah M. Kessel, and Melissa Chan, "Made in China, Exported to the World: The Surveillance State," *New York Times*, April 24, 2019, and note 84.

80. This consequence of the fragmentation of production is a key theme of Brooks, *Producing Security*. See Peter Liberman, "The Spoils of Conquest," *International Security* 18:2 (1993): 125–53, for the opposing (if now somewhat dated) perspective. On the aversion of finance to war, see Jonathan Kirshner, *Appeasing Bankers: Financial Caution on the Road to War* (Princeton: Princeton University Press, 2007). As always, changing incentive structures do not in any way render war impossible, just less likely.

81. Matthew Evangelista, "Globalization and International Conflict: An Introduction," and Fabio Armao, "Militarism and Hegemonic (In)stability in the Age of Private Wars," *Annals of the Fondazione Luigi Einaudi* 53:1 (2019): 3–8, 63–80; Peter Andreas, "Illicit Globalization: Myths, Misconceptions, and Historical Lessons," *Political Science Quarterly* 126:3 (2011): 403–25. Note that Andreas emphasizes the non-novelty of these phenomena, and the need not to oversell claims (423). On the need for leaders of weak states to focus on internal threats, see Steven David, "Explaining Third World Alignment," *World Politics* 43:2 (1991): 233–56.

82. Kennan, *Memoirs, 1925–1950*, 359; see also Halford Mackinder, "The Geographical Pivot of History," *Geographical Journal* 23:4 (1904): 421–37, and Nicholas Spykman, *America's Strategy in World Politics: The United States and the Balance of Power* (New York: Harcourt, Brace, 1942). On the geopolitical consequences of globalization, see, for example, Robert Keohane, "The Globalization of Informal Violence, Theories of World Politics, and the 'Liberalism of Fear,'" in *Power and Governance in a Partially Globalized World*, ed. Keohane (London: Routledge, 2002).

83. David Sanger, *The Perfect Weapon: War, Sabotage, and Fear in the Cyber Age* (New York: Crown, 2018); Adam Segal, *The Hacked World Order: How Nations Fight, Trade, Maneuver, and Manipulate in the Digital Age* (New York: Public Affairs, 2016).

84. On these issues in general and the relative vulnerabilities of democracies in particular, see Sarah Kreps, *Social Media and International Relations* (Cambridge: Cambridge University Press, 2020); see also Deibert, *Parchment, Printing and Hypermedia* on modes of communication and elements of collective mentality, or the "web of beliefs" (see, e.g., 36, 38, 95, 177ff.), and Ronald J. Deibert, *Reset: Reclaiming the Internet for Civil Society* (CBC, House of Anansi Press, 2020). On the broader social-political implications of the hypermedia environment, see Shoshana Zuboff, *The Age of Surveillance Capitalism: The Fight for a Human Future at the New Frontier of Power* (New York: Public Affairs, 2018).

85. Fredrik Logevall, *Embers of War: The Fall of an Empire and the Making of America's Vietnam* (New York: Random House, 2012); Andrew Mack, "Why Big Nations Lose Small Wars: The Politics of Asymmetric Conflict," *World Politics* 27:2 (1975): 175–200.

86. For an insightful discussion of this debate, see Tony Judt, "The Catastrophe: The Fall of France, 1940," in *Reappraisals: Reflections on the Forgotten Twentieth Century* (New York: Penguin, 2008).

87. Eugen Weber, *The Hollow Years: France in the 1930s* (New York: Norton, 1994); Frederick Brown, *The Embrace of Unreason: France, 1914–1940* (New York: Knopf, 2014).

88. Jonathan Kirshner, "Political Economy in Security Studies after the Cold War," *Review of International Political Economy* 5:1 (1998): 81.

89. Salman Ahmed et al. "Reckoning with the Link between Middle-Class Anxieties and U.S. Foreign Policy" (Washington, DC: Carnegie Endowment for International Peace, 2020). See also Rawi Abdelal, "Of Learning and Forgetting: Centrism, Populism, and the Legitimacy Crisis of Globalization," in *The Downfall of the American Order?*, ed. Peter Katzenstein and Jonathan Kirshner (Ithaca: Cornell University Press, 2022). For an important, underappreciated engagement with some of the underlying economic issues and their social consequences, see Stephan Klasen, "Growth and Well-being: Introducing Distribution-Weighted Growth Rates to Reevaluate US Postwar Economic Performance," *Review of Income and Wealth* 40:3 (1994): 251–72.

90. Florian Hoffmann, David S. Lee, and Thomas Lemieux, "Growing Income Inequality in the United States and Other Advanced Economies," *Journal of Economic Perspectives* 34:4 (2020): 52–78; David H. Autor, David Dorn, and Gordon H. Hanson, "The China Syndrome: Local Labor Market Effects of Import Competition in the United States," *American Economic Review* 103:6 (2013): 2121–68.

91. This was seen most visibly in the nominating processes of both political parties, each of which was upended by insurgent candidates who forced the mainstream of each party to renounce once-prized internationalist measures such as the Trans Pacific Partnership. Adam Tooze, *Crashed: How a Decade of Financial Crises Changed the World* (New York: Viking, 2018), 566.

Chapter Six: Classical Realism and the Rise of China

1. The literature on this issue, not surprisingly, is enormous. As discussed in chapter 3, the locus classicus remains Robert Gilpin, *War and Change in World Politics* (Cambridge: Cambridge University Press, 1981). Some other notable and recent contributions include A. F. K. Organski, *World Politics* (New York: Knopf, 1968); Charles Doran and Wes Parsons, "War and the Cycle of Relative Power," *American Political Science Review* 74:4 (1980): 947–65; T. V. Paul, Deborah Larson, and William Wohlforth, eds., *Status in World Politics* (Cambridge: Cambridge University Press, 2014); Steven Ward, *Status and the Challenge of Rising Powers* (Cambridge: Cambridge University Press, 2017); Joshua Shifrinson, *Rising Titans, Falling Giants: How Great Powers Exploit Power Shifts* (Ithaca: Cornell University Press, 2018). There is also a large literature on the British experience with relative decline and its international political consequences, which is often looked to as an analogous referent for contemporary issues. See, for example, Corelli Barnett, *The Collapse of British Power* (New York: Morrow, 1972); Paul Kennedy, *The Rise of the Anglo-German Antagonism, 1860–1914* (Boston: Allen and Unwin, 1980); Aaron Friedberg, *The Weary Titan: Britain and the Experience of Relative Decline, 1985–1905* (Princeton: Princeton University Press, 1988).

2. Kenneth Waltz, *Theory of International Politics* (New York: Addison Wesley, 1979), esp. chaps. 6 and 8; see also Kenneth Waltz, "The Stability of a Bipolar World," *Daedalus* 93:3 (1964): 881–909. For a compelling and empirically well-informed illustration of why polarity is indeterminate in explaining stability, see Ted Hopf, "Polarity: The Offense Defense Balance and War," *American Political Science Review*

85:2 (1991): 475–93. On the large number of factors overdetermining Cold War stability, see John Lewis Gaddis, "The Long Peace: Elements of Stability on the Postwar International System," *International Security* 10:4 (1986): 99–142; Gilpin, *War and Change*, 93 (quote).

3. As one would expect, there is a vast and still burgeoning literature on this issue. See, for example, Thomas J. Christensen, *The China Challenge: Shaping the Choices of a Rising Power* (New York: Norton, 2015); Asle Toje, ed., *Will China's Rise Be Peaceful?: Security, Stability, and Legitimacy* (Oxford: Oxford University Press, 2018); Robert Ross and Øystein Tunsjø, eds., *Strategic Adjustment and the Rise of China: Power and Politics in East Asia* (Ithaca: Cornell University Press, 2017); Yan Xuetong, *Leadership and the Rise of Great Powers* (Princeton: Princeton University Press, 2019); Ashley Tellis, Alison Szalwinski, and Michael Wills, eds., *Strategic Asia 2019:China's Expanding Strategic Ambitions* (Seattle: National Bureau of Asian Research, 2019).

4. John Mearsheimer, *The Tragedy of Great Power Politics* (New York: Norton, 2001); Graham Allison, *Destined for War: Can America and China Escape Thucydides's Trap?* (Boston: Houghton Mifflin Harcourt, 2017).

5. "If the United States just keeps doing what it has been doing, future historians will compare American 'strategy' to illusions that British, German and Russian leaders held as they sleepwalked into 1914." Allison, *Destined for War*, 214. Allison here and elsewhere is invoking the perspective of Christopher Clark, *The Sleepwalkers: How Europe Went to War in 1914* (New York: Penguin, 2012).

6. As discussed in chapter 4, there is no singular "realist foreign policy."

7. Actually, in many settings modern physics embraces indeterminacy, with fascinating implications for anticipating outcomes. On these issues, and their implications for the social sciences, see Peter Katzenstein, ed., *Uncertainty and Its Discontents: Worldviews in World Politics* (Cambridge: Cambridge University Press, 2022), especially chaps. 1 and 10.

8. Mearsheimer, *Tragedy of Great Power Politics*, 401–2; see also John Mearsheimer, "Clash of the Titans," *Foreign Policy* 146 (2005): 46–50.

9. The normative prescriptions could not be plainer: "if states want to survive, they should always act like good offensive realists." Mearsheimer, *Tragedy of Great Power Politics*, 11–12.

10. As should now be familiar, classical realism expects states to want more than survival, especially great powers, which typically want much more; classical realism, while assuming baseline rationality, also permits a role for factors such as arrogance and hubris, which are not narrowly rational.

11. Mearsheimer, *Tragedy of Great Power Politics*, 30 (emphasis added to assumption four).

12. John Lukacs, *George Kennan: A Study of Character* (New Haven: Yale University Press, 2007), 48.

13. Mearsheimer, *Tragedy of Great Power Politics*, 2, 3, 33, 35.

14. Mearsheimer, *Tragedy of Great Power Politics*, 34, 46. This critique of offensive realism develops arguments first presented in Jonathan Kirshner, "The Tragedy of Offensive Realism: Classical Realism and the Rise of China," *European Journal of International Relations* 18:1 (2012): 53–75.

15. Raymond Aron, *Peace and War: A Theory of International Relations* (New York: Doubleday, 1966), 72; Thucydides, *The Peloponnesian War*, 2.8.4, 2.8.5.

16. That the war initiator lost nearly half the time is remarkable, and raises still more doubts about the potential utility of hyper-rationalist theories of state behavior. Losing a war of choice is no small error.

17. "The United States is the only regional hegemon in modern history, although other states have fought major wars in pursuit of regional hegemony: imperial Japan in Northeast Asia, Napoleonic France, Wilhelmine Germany, and Nazi Germany in Europe. But none succeeded." (Again, not only did they not "succeed," they brought about their own destruction.) Mearsheimer, *Tragedy of Great Power Politics*, 41; see also 143, 212.

18. One could add German victories in Denmark, Norway, Belgium, and elsewhere, racking up the "success" rate for the offensive even higher.

19. Mearsheimer, *Tragedy of Great Power Politics*, 39, 209, 211 (quote).

20. Mearsheimer, *Tragedy of Great Power Politics*, 212, 213.

21. Mearsheimer, *Tragedy of Great Power Politics*, 44, 129, 146. (MAD refers to "mutually assured destruction," that is, a situation where both sides have a robust nuclear deterrent.)

22. China's nuclear weapons might possibly be vulnerable to a sudden, massive surprise attack from the United States, but that far-fetched scenario would be true regardless of whether it achieved regional hegemony, and certainly its nuclear capabilities would enhance its prospects for survival against the (hard to imagine in any event) prospect that regional actors might embark on a war of conquest against it. On the implications of the nuclear revolution, see, for example, Robert Gilpin, "The Theory of Hegemonic War," *Journal of Interdisciplinary History* 18:4 (1988): 611, and Robert Jervis, *The Meaning of the Nuclear Revolution* (Ithaca: Cornell University Press, 1989).

23. Russia is weak enough, especially in its east, that it might arguably bandwagon with China rather than balance against it. See Robert Ross, "Sino-Russian Relations: The False Promise of Russian Balancing," *International Politics* 57:5 (2020): 834–54. But to some extent, this is the point—a highly aggressive China might elicit balancing from states otherwise disposed to accede to its political preferences were it not to engage in overtly bullying and obtuse behavior.

24. Mearsheimer, *Tragedy of Great Power Politics*, 375, 381–82, 393, 396.

25. Mearsheimer, *Tragedy of Great Power Politics*, 40, 41, 114–19, 126, 141.

26. Thomas Christensen, "Fostering Stability or Creating a Monster? The Rise of China and U.S. Policy toward East Asia," *International Security* 31:1 (summer 2006): 83, 125.

27. Exceptional modern engagements with Thucydides by international relations scholars include Michael W. Doyle, *Ways of War and Peace* (New York: Norton, 1997); Richard Ned Lebow, *The Tragic Vision of Politics: Ethics, Interests and Orders* (Cambridge: Cambridge University Press, 2003); Paul A. Rahe, "Thucydides' Critique of Realpolitik," *Security Studies* 5:2 (1995): 105–41; and Mark V. Kauppi, "Thucydides: Character and Capabilities," *Security Studies* 5:2 (1995): 142–68. Other noteworthy contributions include Daniel Garst, "Thucydides and NeoRealism," *International Studies Quarterly* 33:1 (1989): 3–27; Laurie M. Johnson Bagby, "The Use and Abuse

of Thucydides in International Relations," *International Organization* 48:1 (1994): 131–53; Steven Forde, "International Realism and the Science of Politics: Thucydides, Machiavelli, and Neorealism," *International Studies Quarterly* 39:2 (1995): 141–60; and David Welch, "Why International Relations Theorists Should Stop Reading Thucydides," *Review of International Studies* 29 (2003): 301–19.

28. Thucydides, *The Peloponnesian War*, 1.23.6; see also "The Spartans out of fear of you want war," 1.33.3, and the Spartans chose war "because they feared the growth of the power of the Athenians," 1.88.1. As always, Thucydides translations here follow Robert B. Strassler, ed., *The Landmark Thucydides: A Comprehensive Guide to the Peloponnesian War* (New York: Touchstone, 1998), cross-referenced with the translation of Jeremy Mynott, ed., *Thucydides: The War of the Peloponnesians and the Athenians* (Cambridge: Cambridge University Press, 2013) and the invaluable three-volume Simon Hornblower, *A Commentary on Thucydides* (Oxford: Oxford University Press, 1991, 1996, 2008). Classical scholars even debate whether "inevitable" is the proper term of translation, which it may or may not be. But Hornblower argues convincingly that Thucydides' decision to repeatedly drive home the general point (especially at 1.33.3) makes claims that he did not see this as a primary cause of the war untenable (1:78, see also 65, 133).

29. Allison's litany of errors regarding *The Peloponnesian War* is vast. Two egregious if perhaps superficial examples include his announcement that Thucydides "did not live to see" the end of the war—this contrasts with Thucydides' recollection: "I lived through the whole of it, being of an age to comprehend events, and giving my attention to them" (5.25.5); Allison also declares, "Every one of the six hundred pages in the *History of the Peloponnesian War* offers compelling details about the twists and turns along the path" to the war, although in fact the overwhelming majority of the book details events that take place after the war has started. Allison, *Destined for War*, xv, 29. On these basic points, see Jeffrey S. Rusten, "Thucydides and His Readers," in *Oxford Readings in Classical Studies: Thucydides*, ed. Jeffrey S. Rusten (Oxford: Oxford University Press, 2009). And these gaffes are the tip of an iceberg of error. For review of many of Allison's basic blunders, see Jonathan Kirshner, "Handle Him with Care: The Importance of Getting Thucydides Right," *Security Studies* 28:1 (2019): 1–24.

30. This language may sound unduly harsh, but the influence of this book—world leaders and high-profile commentators routinely bandy about the phrase "Thucydides Trap"—is such that it is essential to be very clear about the extent to which this is deeply flawed scholarship.

31. For a discussion of the central role of distinct "national character" in explaining behavior and outcomes, see S. N. Jaffe, *Thucydides on the Outbreak of War: Character and Contest* (Oxford: Oxford University Press, 2017).

32. See, for example, Clarke, *The Sleepwalkers: How Europe Went to War in 1914* and Barbara Tuchman, *The Guns of August* (New York: Macmillan, 1962). President Kennedy was famously influenced by his reading of Tuchman's Pulitzer Prize–winning book in his efforts to prevent the Cuban Missile Crisis from tragically spiraling out of control.

33. Allison, *Destined for War*, xv, 30, 32, 37, 40.

34. Thucydides, *The Peloponnesian War*, 1.114.3, 1.144.5. 2.63.2. On Pericles' war advocacy and his efforts to persuade the public of its necessity, see, for example, Mark

Fisher and Kinch Hoekstra, "Thucydides and the Politics of Necessity," and Mary P. Nichols, "Leaders and Leadership in Thucydides' History," both in *The Oxford Handbook of Thucydides*, ed. Ryan K. Balot, Sara Forsdyke, and Edith Foster (Oxford: Oxford University Press, 2017), 373, 461.

35. Thucydides, *The Peloponnesian War*, 7.18.2. On the Spartan acknowledgment of their culpability, see Hornblower, *Commentary*, 3:373, 574; Mynott, *War of the Peloponnesians*, 462. On Athenian belligerence and Spartan intransigence, see, for example, Lisa Kallet, "The Pentecontaetia," in *Oxford Handbook*, ed. Balot, Forsdyke, and Foster, 64.

36. On the routine resort to arms in ancient Greece, see Arthur M. Eckstein, "Thucydides, International Law and International Anarchy," in *Oxford Handbook*, ed. Balot, Forsdyke, and Foster, esp. 498–99, 502. For a bold statement on reduced likelihood of great power conflict in the contemporary era, see John Mueller, *Retreat from Doomsday: The Obsolescence of Major War* (New York: Basic Books, 1989). Note as always that the perceived "illegitimacy" of naked aggression does not *prevent* such actions from taking place, but it does change the political costs and benefits of the calculation.

37. Allison, *Destined for War*, ix, 41.

38. Paul Schroeder, "Historical Reality vs. Neo-Realist Theory," *International Security* 19:1 (1994): 148.

39. It is not even obvious that the U.S.-Japan case fits the "model" of the "Thucydides Trap," as the United States at that time was not a power in relative decline but a rising superpower. Moreover, in considering the U.S.-Japan confrontation, Allison puzzlingly focuses on the late, proximate issue of American sanctions against Japan and ignores what Thucydides would surely have emphasized, the long-term underlying power dynamics between the two states. Allison's focus on economic sanctions in this case also exposes yet another misreading of Thucydides in *Destined for War* (as noted, Thucydides generally tended to overlook economic factors in his analyses). In placing the emphasis on the American sanctions, Allison suggests that U.S. diplomats were shocked by the reaction in Japan and "had no one to blame but themselves." If only, he laments, they had "taken an afternoon to read the consequences of Athens's Megarian Decree . . . they could have better anticipated Japan's initiative." This is, once again, exactly wrong. Aside from reflecting a radical oversimplification of the political conflict between the two states, as reviewed in chapter 5, it is widely understood, even by Thucydidean scholars who disagree on much else, that Thucydides *downplayed* the significance of the decree. See, for example, Donald Kagan, *The Outbreak of the Peloponnesian War* (Ithaca: Cornell University Press, 1969), 251, 267, 269, 374, and G. E. M. de Ste. Croix, *The Origins of the Peloponnesian War* (Ithaca: Cornell University Press, 1972), 213–14, 251–52, 256.

40. Allison, *Destined for War*, 206, italics in original.

41. Kauppi, "Thucydides: Character and Capabilities," 142 (quote); see also Richard Ned Lebow and Barry Strauss, eds., *Hegemonic Rivalry: From Thucydides to the Nuclear Age* (Boulder: Westview Press, 1991). For an especially strong critique of attempts to distill simple structuralist lessons from Thucydides, see James Lee, "Did Thucydides Believe in Thucydides' Trap? The *History of the Peloponnesian War* and Its Relevance to U.S.-China Relations," *Journal of Chinese Political Science* 24:1 (2019): 67–86.

42. Athens, to Thucydides' repeated disapproval, constantly "grasped at something further" (4.21.2) and "kept grasping at more" (4.41.4). See also Hunter R. Rawlings, "Writing History Implicitly through Refined Structuring," in *Oxford Handbook*, ed. Balot, Forsdyke, and Foster, 195–209.

43. Mearsheimer, *Tragedy of Great Power Politics*, 30.

44. On these themes, see Robert Gilpin, "The Richness of the Tradition of Political Realism," in *Neorealism and Its Critics*, ed. Robert Keohane (New York: Columbia University Press, 1986), 304, 305; Hans Morgenthau, *Scientific Man vs. Power Politics* (Chicago: University of Chicago Press, 1946), 5, 42, 168, 195; Hans Morgenthau, "The Evil of Politics and the Politics of Evil," *Ethics* 56:1 (1945): 1, 13, 16–17; E. H. Carr, *The Twenty Years' Crisis, 1919–1939*, 2nd ed. (New York: St. Martin's Press, 1946 [1939]), 75, 80, 108, 111, 213, 215.

45. Gilpin, *War and Change*, 106; Raymond Aron, *The Committed Observer* (Chicago: Regnery Gateway, 1983), 240. In John Huston's film *Key Largo* (1948), mob boss Johnny Rocco, boasting that he wants "more," is asked if he will ever get enough. "Well, I never have," he responds, "I guess I won't." On such instincts, see also Nicholas Spykman, *America's Strategy in World Politics: The United States and the Balance of Power* (New York: Harcourt, Brace, 1942), 20, 24; Carr, *Twenty Years' Crisis*, 112; Hans Morgenthau, *In Defense of the National Interest: A Critical Examination of American Foreign Policy* (New York: Knopf, 1951), 33, 135; Reinhold Niebuhr, *Moral Man and Immoral Society* (Louisville: John Know Press, 2001/1932), 42; Niccolò Machiavelli, *Discourses on Livy*, trans. Harvey Mansfield and Nathan Taco (Chicago: University of Chicago Press, 1996/1532), 4.

46. See, for example, Zheng Wang, *Never Forget National Humiliation: Historical Memory in Chinese Politics and Foreign Relations* (New York: Columbia University Press, 2012); Suisheng Zhao, *A Nation-State by Construction: Dynamics of Modern Chinese Nationalism* (Stanford: Stanford University Press, 2004); and Peter Gries, *China's New Nationalism: Pride, Politics, and Diplomacy* (Berkeley: University of California Press, 2004), esp. chap. 3.

47. Morgenthau, *In Defense of the National Interest*, 70, 88, 136, 150, 242; George F. Kennan, *American Diplomacy, 1900–1950* (New York: Mentor Books, 1951), 88; George F. Kennan, *Memoirs, 1925–1950* (Boston: Little, Brown, 1967), 256, 491, 493, 495–96.

48. Carr, *Twenty Years' Crisis*, 91, 169.

49. John Mearsheimer, "Roundtable: The Battle Rages On," *International Relations* 19:3 (2005): 355; John Mearsheimer, "E. H. Carr vs. Idealism: The Battle Rages On," *International Relations* 19:2 (2005): 141, 143.

50. Carr, *Twenty Years' Crisis*, 169, 222.

51. George F. Kennan, *From Prague after Munich: Diplomatic Papers, 1938–1940* (Princeton: Princeton University Press, 1968), 5, 107; see also Kennan, *Memoirs, 1925–1950*, 97; Lukacs, *George Kennan*, 41, 42, 44; E. H. Carr, *The Twenty Years' Crisis, 1919–1939*, 1st ed. (London: Macmillan, 1939), 107, 274, 278, 282. See also Carr's defense of appeasement in E. H. Carr, *Britain: A Study of Foreign Policy from the Versailles Treaty to the Outbreak of War* (London: Longmans, Green, 1939), 175.

52. Actually, as noted in chapter 3, given the military capabilities of Czechoslovakia and the European balance of power in 1938, even by the more narrow metrics of

power politics Munich was a foolish act of geopolitical self-sabotage, which required a belief in the wishful thinking that it might bring about "peace in our time."

53. Hans Morgenthau, "International Affairs: The Resurrection of Neutrality in Europe," *American Political Science Review* 33:3 (1939): 483–84; Morgenthau, *In Defense of the National Interest*, 133, 136, 137, 138, 150; Winston Churchill, *The History of the Second World War, Volume I: The Gathering Storm* (New York: Houghton Mifflin, 1948); John Mearsheimer, "The Gathering Storm: China's Challenge to U.S. Power in Asia," *Chinese Journal of International Politics* 3 (2010): 382.

54. Gilpin, *War and Change*, 192, 194, 206, 207; note the dissent (that strategic retrenchment is more common than Gilpin suggests) in Paul MacDonald and Joseph Parent, *Twilight of the Titans: Great Power Decline and Retrenchment* (Ithaca: Cornell University Press, 2018).

55. Recall Keynes's observation from chapter 2 that the study of economics (and the social sciences in general) was a distinct enterprise from investigations in the natural sciences, in that the former necessarily had to take account of "motives, expectations [and] psychological uncertainties," which meant that a diverse range of outcomes in any given setting was possible, due to the varied motives and beliefs of the actors involved. John Maynard Keynes to Roy Harrod, July 16, 1938, in *CW*, 14:299–300; Friedrich von Hayek, "The Use of Knowledge in Society," *American Economic Review* 35:4 (1945): 519–30; Frank Knight, *Risk, Uncertainty and Profit* (Chicago: University of Chicago Press, 1971/1921); Morgenthau, *Scientific Man*; Raymond Aron, *Introduction to the Philosophy of History: An Essay on the Limits of Historical Objectivity* (London: Weidenfeld and Nicholson, 1948/1938).

56. W. G. Beasley, *Japanese Imperialism, 1894–1945* (Oxford: Oxford University Press, 1987); Frederick R. Dickenson, *World War I and the Triumph of a New Japan, 1919–1930* (Cambridge: Cambridge University Press, 2013), see esp. 6–7, 12 on the fundamental difference between the 1920s and 1930s.

57. Simon James Bytheway and Mark Metzler, *Central Banks and Gold: How Tokyo, London and New York Shaped the Modern World* (Ithaca: Cornell University Press, 2016), 80; Edward M. Lamont, *The Ambassador from Wall Street: The Story of Thomas W. Lamont, J. P. Morgan's Chief Executive* (Lanham, MD: Madison Books, 1994), esp. 157, 195–96, 236–37, 311.

58. Mark Metzler, *Lever of Empire: The International Gold Standard and the Crisis of Liberalism in Prewar Japan* (Berkeley: University of California Press, 2006); Richard J. Smethurst, *From Foot Soldier to Finance Minister: Takahashi Korekiyo, Japan's Keynes* (Cambridge, MA: Harvard University Press, 2007).

59. Peter Duus, *Party Rivalry and Political Change in Taisho Japan* (Cambridge, MA: Harvard University Press, 1968); Robert A. Scalapino, *Democracy and the Party Movement in Prewar Japan* (Berkeley: University of California Press, 1953).

60. Yamamira Katsuro, "The Role of the Finance Ministry," in Dorothy Borg and Shumpei Okamoto, *Pearl Harbor as History: Japanese-American Relations, 1931–1941* (New York: Columbia University Press, 1973); Kato Shuichi, "Taisho Democracy as the Pre-Stage for Japanese Militarism," in *Japan in Crisis: Essays on Taisho Democracy*, ed. Bernard S. Silberman and H. D. Harootunian (Ann Arbor: University of Michigan Press, 1999); Leonard A. Humphreys, *The Way of the Heavenly Sword: The Japanese Army in the 1920s* (Stanford: Stanford University Press, 1995); Shin'ichi

Kitaoka, "The Army as a Bureaucracy: Japanese Militarism Revisited," *Journal of Military History* 57:5 (1993): 67–86.

61. Bytheway and Metzler, *Central Banks and Gold*; Lamont, *Ambassador from Wall Street*; Ian Nish, *Japanese Foreign Policy in the Interwar Period* (Westport CT: Praeger, 2002); Michael A. Barnhart, *Japan Prepares for Total War: The Search for Economic Security, 1919–1941* (Ithaca: Cornell University Press, 1987); Robert Scalapino, *Democracy and the Party Movement in Prewar Japan* (Berkeley: University of California Press, 1975).

62. Junnosuke Inouye, *Problems of the Japanese Exchange, 1914–1926*, trans. E. H. de Bunsen (Glasgow: Robert Maclehose, 1931), 153; Sobun Yamamuro, "Economic Depression and the Gold Embargo," *Contemporary Japan* 1:1 (1932): 53 (quote), 58, 61; Kozo Yamamura, "Then Came the Great Depression: Japan's Interwar Years," in *The Great Depression Revisited: Essays on the Economics of the Thirties*, ed. Herman van der Wee (The Hague: Nijhoff, 1972), 183, see also 312–16, 319; Nakamura Takafusa, *Lectures on Modern Japanese Economic History, 1926–1994* (Tokyo: LTCB International Library Foundation, 1994), 35.

63. Nakamura, *Japanese Economic History*, 12 (quote), 13–14, 27–28, 142, 227; Hugh T. Patrick, "The Economic Muddle of the 1920s," in James William Morley, *The Dilemmas of Growth in Prewar Japan* (Princeton: Princeton University Press, 1971), 215–17, 220, 226, 232, 234; Kozo Yamamura, "The Japanese Economy, 1911–1930: Concentration, Conflicts, and Crises," in *Japan in Crisis: Essays on Taisho Democracy*, ed. Bernard S. Silberman and H. D. Harootunian (Princeton: Princeton University Press, 1974), 312–16, 319.

64. R. P. Dore and Tsutomu Ouchi, "Rural Origins of Japanese Fascism," in Morley, *Dilemmas of Growth*, 197, 203; Tsutomu Ouchi, "Agricultural Depression and Japanese Villages," *Developing Economies* 5:4 (1967): 618, 620; Humphreys, *Heavenly Sword*, 98, 176; Richard Smethurst, *A Social Basis for Prewar Japanese Militarism: The Army and the Rural Community* (Berkeley: University of California Press, 1974), esp. xxi–xxix, 69–76; Mark Metzler, "Woman's Place in Japan's Great Depression: Reflections on the Moral Economy of Deflation," *Journal of Japanese Studies* 30:2 (2004): 326, 332.

65. G. C. Allen, "The Political and Economic Position of Japan," *International Affairs* 13:4 (1934): 547–48; Nakamura, *Japanese Economic History*, 38, 41; Yamamura, "Then Came the Great Depression," 198.

66. Paul Einzig, *Behind the Scenes of International Finance* (London: Macmillan, 1932), 145; Zara Steiner, *The Lights That Failed: European International History, 1919–1933* (Oxford: Oxford University Press, 2007), 800, see also p. 809, "the effects of the depression created the conditions under which Weimar ultimately collapsed" (note that Steiner stresses the entire 1929–33 period as the "hinge years" between the hopes of the 1920s and the horrors of the 1930s); John Maynard Keynes, "The Consequences to the Banks of the Collapse of Money Values" (August 1931), *CW*, 9:150. See also Patricia Clavin, *Securing the World Economy: The Reinvention of the League of Nations, 1920–1946* (Oxford: Oxford University Press, 2013), 80 ("the financial crisis of 1931 acted as a powerful accelerant on the already energetic flames of nationalism burning around the world"), and Tobias Straumann, *1931: Debt, Crisis, and the Rise of Hitler* (Oxford: Oxford University Press, 2019).

67. Nakamura, *Japanese Economic History*, 39, 49; Chu Yukio, "From the Showa Economic Crisis to Military Economy: With Special Reference to the Inoue and Takahashi Financial Policies," *Developing Economies* 5:4 (1967): 580; Shinobu Seizaburo, "From Party Politics to Military Dictatorship," *Developing Economies* 5:4 (1967): 672.

68. James B. Crowley, *Japan's Quest for Autonomy: National Security and Foreign Policy, 1930–1938* (Princeton: Princeton University Press, 1966); Barnhart, *Japan Prepares for Total War*; Louise B. Young, *Japan's Total Empire: Manchuria and the Culture of Wartime Imperialism* (Berkeley: University of California Press, 1998); Stephen S. Large, "Nationalist Extremism in Early Showa Japan: Inoue Nissho and the Blood-Pledge Corps Incident, 1932," *Modern Asia Studies* 35:3 (2001): 533, 547–48, 552–53, 555; Metzler, *Lever of Empire*.

69. Smethurst, *From Foot Soldier to Finance Minister*; Ippei Fukuda, "Korekiyo Takahashi—Japan's Sage of Finance," *Contemporary Japan* 1:4 (1933): 610–18; Dick K. Nanto and Shinji Takagi, "Korekiyo Takahashi and Japan's Recovery from the Great Depression," *American Economic Review* 75:2 (1985): 369–74; Nakamura Takafusa, *Economic Growth in Prewar Japan* (New Haven: Yale University Press, 1983), 236–37.

70. Smethurst, *From Foot Soldier to Finance Minister*; Ben-Ami Shillony, *Revolt in Japan: The Young Officers and the February 26, 1936 Incident* (Princeton: Princeton University Press, 1973), ix, 3, 7, 11, 135, 137; Patrick, "The Economic Muddle," 249; Gordon M. Berger, "Politics and Mobilization in Japan, 1931–1945," in *The Cambridge History of Japan, Volume 6: The Twentieth Century*, ed. Peter Duus (Cambridge: Cambridge University Press, 1988), 116–17, 119–20.

71. Scalapino, *Democracy and the Party Movement in Prewar Japan*, 220, 281, 385–87; Shillony, *Revolt in Japan*, 210–12. See also Kurt Bloch, "Far Eastern War Inflation," *Pacific Affairs* 13:3 (1940): 331–32, 335; and Frank M. Tamagna, "The Financial Position of China and Japan," *American Economic Review* 36:2 (1946): 619–20.

72. All of this—in particular the path chosen by Japan from 1937—underscores the severely circumscribed vision of attempts to explain the origins of the Pacific war that focus on events which took place in 1940 or 1941.

73. Mearsheimer, *Tragedy of Great Power Politics*, 400.

74. For the representative statement of this perspective, see G. John Ikenberry, "The Rise of China and the Future of the West: Can the Liberal System Survive?" *Foreign Affairs* 87:1 (2008): 23–37. This again illustrates the limits of insisting that contrasting paradigmatic perspectives are invariably at odds with one another.

75. Thomas Christensen, "Fostering Stability or Creating a Monster? The Rise of China and U.S. Policy toward East Asia," *International Security* 31:1 (summer 2006): 125. "Full-spectrum containment . . . would be counter-productive," Christensen argued, "The United States would likely gain no new allies in such an effort and would lose some, if not all of its current regional allies." See also David Shambaugh, "China Engages Asia: Reshaping the Regional Order," *International Security* 29:3 (2004–5): 85.

76. Susan Shirk, "China in Xi's 'New Era': The Return to Personalistic Rule," *Journal of Democracy* 29:2 (2018): 22–36; Ian Buruma, "The End of the Anglo-American Order," *New York Times Magazine*, November 29, 2016; Adam Posen, "The Post-American World Economy: Globalization in the Trump Era," *Foreign Affairs* 97:2 (2018): 28–38; Peter Katzenstein and Jonathan Kirshner, eds., *The Downfall of the*

American Order? (Ithaca: Cornell University Press, 2022). For a thoughtful critique of these notions (regarding the U.S.-led liberal international order and the nature of the challenge that China presents), see Alastair Iain Johnston, "China in a World of Orders: Rethinking Compliance and Challenge in Beijing's International Relations," *International Security* 44:2 (2019): 9–60.

77. As Adam Tooze argues, "the presidential race of 2016 turned out to be more about the financial crisis of 2008 than 2012 had been." Adam Tooze, *Crashed: How a Decade of Financial Crises Changed the World* (New York: Viking, 2018), 566. On the political consequences of the global financial crisis, as Martin Wolf of the *Financial Times* observed, it was hard to argue with the widespread perception that it was a system in which "well-connected insiders" are "shielded from loss but impose massive costs on everybody else." Martin Wolf, *The Shifts and the Shocks: What We've Learned—and Have Still to Learn—from the Financial Crisis* (New York: Penguin, 2014), 352; see also Jonathan Kirshner, *American Power after the Financial Crisis* (Ithaca: Cornell University Press, 2014).

Chapter Seven: Power, Politics, and Prospect

1. Hans Morgenthau, "The Limitations of Science and the Problem of Social Planning," *Ethics* 54:3 (1944): 175; similarly, recall Niebuhr's admonition from chapter 1: "The radical freedom of the self and the consequent dramatic realities of history are naturally embarrassing to any scientific effort, either to understand or master history." Reinhold Niebuhr, *The Self and the Dramas of History* (New York: Scribner, 1955), 49. See also Raymond Aron, *Introduction to the Philosophy of History: An Essay on the Limits of Historical Objectivity* (London: Weidenfeld and Nicholson, 1948/1938), 131, and Raymond Aron, "Three Forms of Historical Intelligibility," in *Politics and History: Selected Essays of Raymond Aron*, ed. and trans. Miriam Bernheim Conant (New York: The Free Press, 1978), 49.

2. For a thoughtful engagement with the issue of parsimony in IR theory, see Seva Gunitsky, "Rival Visions of Parsimony," *International Studies Quarterly* 63:3 (2019): 707–16.

3. This distinction is well captured by Aron's biographer: "The principle of the plurality of interpretations did not imply, Aron argued, that all interpretations were arbitrary or that the impartiality of the truth was destroyed. Nevertheless, he warned that the social scientist should not confuse his point of view, which was one legitimate point of view among others, with a philosophy which laid claim to absolute truth on the grounds that it alone was scientific." Robert F. Colquhoun, *Raymond Aron—Volume 1: The Philosopher in History, 1905–1955* (Beverly Hills, CA: SAGE Publications, 1986), 174.

4. Raymond Aron, *Memoirs: Fifty Years of Political Reflection* (New York: Holmes and Meier, 1990/1983), 39; Reinhold Niebuhr, *Moral Man and Immoral Society* (Louisville: John Know Press, 2001/1932), xxvii. See also Niebuhr, *Christian Realism and Political Problems* (New York: Scribner's, 1953), 91. "The belief of a hard core of historical facts existing objectively and independently of the interpretation of the historian is a preposterous fallacy." E. H. Carr, *What Is History?* (New York: Vintage, 1961), 10, see also 35, 69, 116.

5. Morgenthau, "The Limitations of Science," 174, 176. "The social cause itself is an indeterminate element which can never be reproduced identical with itself," Morgenthau elaborates, and "the object upon which the social cause exerts its influence is equally a social phenomenon." Ultimately, the "exact nature" of the reactions to measures taken in the social world "at any given time [are] impossible to foresee or to determine" (175). This is not simply an abstract theoretical qualification but speaks importantly to real-world practice: "We plan a political strategy in order to achieve a certain result, but the result, more often than not, has only a very remote relation to what we intend." Hans Morgenthau, "The Influence of Reinhold Niebuhr in American Political Life and Thought," in *Reinhold Niebuhr: A Prophetic Voice in Our Time*, ed. Harold T. Landon (Greenwich: Seabury Press, 1962), 106.

6. Niebuhr, *Moral Man and Immoral Society*, xxx. In addition, there is no escape from these hard truths: "History does not move forward without catastrophe, happiness is not guaranteed by the multiplication of physical comforts, social harmony is not easily created by more intelligence, and human nature is not as good or as harmless as had been supposed." Reinhold Niebuhr, *Christianity and Power Politics* (New York: Scribner, 1940), 188.

7. See also Primo Levi, *The Drowned and the Saved* (New York: Simon and Schuster, 1986). On human capacity for evil, see Stanley Milgram, "Behavioral Study of Obedience," *Journal of Abnormal and Social Psychology* 67:4 (1963): 371–78; Craig Haney, Curtis Banks, and Phillip Zimbardo, "A Study of Prisoners and Guards in a Simulated Prison," *Naval Research Review* 30 (1973): 4–17; Leo Tolstoy, *Anna Karenina* (1878), part 7, chapter 13, line 1.

8. John Maynard Keynes, *The Economic Consequences of the Peace* (London: Macmillan, 1919), 144. (On misunderstanding *Consequences*, see chapter 3.) Hans Morgenthau, *In Defense of the National Interest: A Critical Examination of American Foreign Policy* (New York: Knopf, 1951), 135. This notion is related to the realist emphasis on the constant and endless influences of politics and power on human relations. "To understand politics is to recognize the elements of power which underlie all social structures—the play of power which may be obscured or submerged, but which cannot be eliminated" (Niebuhr, *Christianity and Power Politics*, 92).

9. Edmund Burke, "Remarks on the Policy of the Allies" (1793), in *Empire and Community: Edmund Burke's Writings and Speeches on International Relations*, ed. David P. Fidler and Jennifer M. Welsch (Boulder: Westview Press, 1999), 281; recall as well Burke's lament "I dread our *own* power and our *own* ambition" (281). Burke was also wary of the fragility of civilized order and the ease with which men can descend into barbarism; see, for example, Isaac Kramnick, *The Rage of Edmund Burke: Portrait of an Ambivalent Conservative* (New York: Basic Books, 1977), 136; Henry Kissinger, *A World Restored: Metternich, Castlereagh and the Problems of Peace, 1812–22* (Boston: Houghton Mifflin, 1957), 101; Mary Dudziak, *Cold War Civil Rights: Race and the Image of American Democracy* (Princeton: Princeton University Press, 2011).

10. Ernest Hemingway, *The Sun Also Rises* (New York: Scribner's, 1926), 127.

11. Stephen Walt, *The Origins of Alliances* (Ithaca: Cornell University Press, 1987); see also the engaging extension and application of this underlying argument in Stephen Walt, *Revolution and War* (Ithaca: Cornell University Press, 1996). "One cannot understand the international effects of a mass revolution by focusing solely

on the balance of power or the constraining effects of international anarchy," Walt argues. Once again, the key variable is changes to "perceptions of *balances of threats*" (*Revolution and War*, viii, emphasis in original).

12. It is not simply the unexpected military collapse of France that demands attention, it is the ease (and in many quarters, shameful enthusiasm) with which the country submitted to their new German masters. On these themes, see Robert O. Paxton, *Vichy France: Old Guard and New Order, 1940–1944*, rev. ed. (New York: Columbia University Press, 2001); see also Alan Riding, *And the Show Went On: Cultural Life in Nazi-Occupied Paris* (New York: Vintage Books, 2010), and the devastating, watershed film by Marcel Ophüls, *The Sorrow and the Pity* (1969).

13. For a broad overview of French society and politics from this perspective, see William L. Shirer, *The Collapse of the Third Republic: An Inquiry into the Fall of France in 1940* (New York: Simon and Schuster, 1969); see also Alexander Werth, *The Twilight of France, 1933–1940*, ed. and intro. D. W. Brogan (New York: Howard Fertig, 1966/1942), and Eugen Weber, *The Hollow Years: France in the 1930s* (New York: Norton, 1994). Works such as these are sometimes criticized as presenting an overly deterministic account of the failure of interwar France and its conquest. See, for example, Anthony Adamthwaite, *Grandeur and Misery: France, 1914–1940* (London: Arnold, 1995). Adamthwaite argues that "contingency is the theme of this book" (viii), and he insists that the collapse in 1940–41 was not inevitable—notions with which any classical realist analysis would obviously sympathize. Nevertheless, *Grandeur and Misery*, especially for a book that is pushing back against the "France in decay" argument, paints an extremely distressing picture of the Third Republic. It describes a country with toxic civil-military relations, one which, in 1938, "without proper reflection and organization . . . drifted helplessly on the tide," and where more generally "the whole complex of issues and maladies induced a mood of fatalistic resignation" (159, 160); see also the general discussions of a decadent public order and a menu of unattractive policy options. These factors did not dictate inevitable defeat, but they surely mattered greatly.

14. Barry Posen, in his landmark study of interwar grand strategy, finds it puzzling that the French failed "to insure themselves against the worst"; he notes that "French domestic politics played a role in French grand strategy that I have not even attempted to analyze." Barry Posen, *The Sources of Military Doctrine: France, Britain and Germany between the World Wars* (Ithaca: Cornell University Pres, 1984), 224, 234, 240. On some of those domestic politics left unexamined, see Elizabeth Kier, *Imagining War: French and British Military Doctrine between the Wars* (Princeton: Princeton University Press, 1997).

15. Aron, *Memoirs*, 64; Raymond Aron, *The Committed Observer* (Chicago: Regnery Gateway, 1983), 53. See also Olivier Bernier, *Fireworks at Dusk: Paris in the Thirties* (Boston: Little, Brown, 1993). "By 1935, in fact, it was becoming clear that there really was no such thing as France. Instead, the disunited French, class against class, party against party, one half of the nation loathing the other, seemed well on their way to civil war" (7; see also 156, 276).

16. Frederick Brown, *The Embrace of Unreason: France, 1914–1940* (New York: Alfred A. Knopf, 2014); William D. Irvine, *French Conservatism in Crisis: The Republican Federation of France in the 1930s* (Baton Rouge: Louisiana State University Press, 1979); Julian Jackson, *The Popular Front in France: Defending Democracy* (Cambridge: Cambridge University Press, 1988).

17. Shirer, *Collapse of the Third Republic*, 11, 12, 22; Raymond Aron, "Democratic States and Totalitarian States: An Address to the French Philosophical Society" (June 17, 1939), reprinted in Aron, *Thinking Politically* (New Brunswick, NJ: Transaction Publishers, 1997), 333 (quote); Edmond Taylor, "Democracy Demoralized: The French Collapse," *Public Opinion Quarterly* 4:4 (1940): 634, 636, see also 648–49; Taylor reports his account was based on "my familiarity with the French political milieu, my knowledge of the personal convictions of the French leaders who played a decisive role in the drama, and the general atmosphere overhanging the deliberations . . . which I covered as a journalist" (631). "No will to fight," Georges Mandell to General Edward Spears, May 26, 1940, is reported by Shirer, *Collapse of the Third Republic*, 22. As the final surrender swiftly approached, Ivan Maisky wrote in his diary, "I'm growing more and more convinced that France capitulated because of its internal disintegration." Gabriel Gorodetsky, ed., *The Maisky Diaries: Red Ambassador to the Court of St. James's, 1932–1943* (New Haven: Yale University Press, 2015), entry of June 17, 1940, p. 287. Once again, retrospective analyses reach similar conclusions; see, for example, Bernier, *Fireworks at Dusk*: "It had taken just ten years for the leading country in Europe to become a helpless victim" (9 [quote], 40; see also pp. 32, 37, 276 on morale and the will to fight).

18. Robert J. Young, *In Command of France: French Foreign Policy and Military Planning, 1933–1940* (Cambridge, MA: Harvard University Press, 1978), 37; Martin S. Alexander, *The Republic in Danger: General Maurice Gamelin and the Politics of French Defense, 1933–1940* (Cambridge: Cambridge University Press, 1992).

19. For colorful details of "the Stavisky scandal," which involved the sale of worthless municipal bonds, implicated government ministers, and a swindler who subsequently died in mysterious circumstances, see "Distraction from the Scandal," *Time*, March 12, 1934.

20. Shirer, *Collapse of the Third Republic*, 199, 204, 208–9, 219–20, 223; see his entire compelling eyewitness account of the riots, pp. 199–230; Weber, *Hollow Years*, 141, 147, 150; Adamthwaite, *Grandeur and Misery*, 164–65; Brown, *Embrace of Unreason*, 193–94, 206 (vigilance committee); Brian Jenkins, "The *Six Fevrier* 1934 and the 'Survival' of the French Republic," *French History* 20:3 (2006): 337, 345 (quotes).

21. Werth *Twilight of France*, 33, 35; Alexander, *Republic in Danger*, 56, 58–61; Julian Jackson, *The Politics of Depression in France, 1932–1936* (Cambridge: Cambridge University Press, 1985), 2, 18–19, 23, 108, 218. On Laval's affinity for fascists abroad, see also Bernier, *Fireworks at Dusk*, 27, 200.

22. Brown, *Embrace of Unreason*, 228. (One right-wing newspaper announced the 1936 election outcome with the banner headline "France under the Jew" [228].) "Better Hitler than Blum," Shirer, *Collapse of the Third Republic*, 324. Note also that Adamthwaite, for whom Shirer is an explicit foil, reports the same slogan and attributes it to similar roots: "By the autumn of 1936 opposition to communism and the Popular Front eclipsed hatred of Germany" (*Grandeur and Misery*, 171). See also Charles A. Micaud, *The French Right and Nazi Germany, 1933–1939: A Study of Public Opinion* (Durham: Duke University Press, 1943), 229. On politically motivated capital flight, see Talbot Imlay, *Facing the Second World War: Strategy, Politics and Economics in Britain and France 1938–1940* (Oxford: Oxford University Press, 2003), 256 (quote), 262, 264; see also Rene Girault, "The Impact of the Economic Situation on the Foreign Policy of France, 1936–9," in *The Fascist Challenge and the Policy of*

Appeasement, ed. Wolfgang J. Mommsen and Lothar Kettenacker (London: George Allen and Unwin, 1983). "Since many capital holders preferred to forget national priorities, and even national defense, for political reasons or out of self-interest, any government was condemned to a certain impotence" (223).

23. Hans Morgenthau, *Science: Servant or Master?* (New York: New American Library, 1972), 129.

24. It should be noted that the story of Athenian democracy did not end there; soon enough that oligarchy would be chased from power, although a new tyranny would be imposed after the war was finally lost in 404. That regime, too, was short lived; the remnants of Athenian democracy would not be fully snuffed out until later in the third century. Still, the sudden collapse of a long-standing democracy as described by Thucydides is more than sobering, and the passages regarding the conspiracies and what he describes as "the reign of terror" are linked by Hornblower as an explicit parallel to Thucydides' elaborate treatment of the horrors that accompanied the revolution in Corcyra sixteen years earlier (3.81–3.85). Simon Hornblower, *A Commentary on Thucydides* (Oxford: Oxford University Press, 2008), 3:944, 946. See also Martha C. Taylor, "Implicating the Demos: A Reading of Thucydides on the Rise of the Four Hundred," *Journal of Hellenic Studies* 122 (2002): 91–108 (as Athenian democracy collapsed, "Thucydides shows few, if any, resisting oligarchy and defending the traditional regime" [94]); and Mark Chou, *Democracy against Itself* (Edinburgh: Edinburgh University Press, 2014), who emphasizes the willingness of the citizenry in 413/411 to cede "extraordinary authority" to the oligarchs (35).

25. The warlord era is conventionally described as ending in 1928 with the reconstitution of central authority as the Nationalist Government headed by Chiang Kai-shek was able to assert control over much of the country. In fact, however, in large swaths of the country warlords, in command of formidable armies that fought bloody, large-scale battles, continued to hold sway; and until after World War II Shanghai remained dominated by organized criminal gangs, corrupt, overlapping authority structures, and ubiquitous dens of iniquity. James E. Sheridan, *China in Disintegration: The Republican Era in Chinese History, 1912–1949* (New York: The Free Press, 1975), 183–85; Frederic Wakeman, *Policing Shanghai, 1927–1937* (Berkeley: University of California Press, 1996).

26. Jonathan Spence, *The Search for Modern China* (New York: Norton, 1990), 263, 271, 276 (quote), 288, 298; Arthur Waldron, "The Warlord: Twentieth-Century Chinese Understandings of Violence, Militarism, and Imperialism," *American Historical Review* 96:4 (1991): 1076 (Shanghai); Edward A. McCord, "Warlordism in Early Republican China," in *A Military History of China*, ed. David A. Graff and Robin Higham (Lexington: University of Kentucky Press, 2012); Sheridan, *China in Disintegration*, 57–58, 85, 86, 88, 89 (quote).

27. Tony Judt, "Toni," *New York Review of Books*, April 19, 2010; Stefan Zweig, *The World of Yesterday* (New York: Viking Press, 1943), 1.

28. In 1919 Keynes feared that the failure to repair Europe's shattered economy after the Great War would lead to "bloodshed, misery and fanaticism" in any number of forms, "from the Rhine eastwards through two continents." Keynes, *Economic Consequences of the Peace*, xxi. And recall from chapter 6 Paul Einzig's warning that the 1931 global financial crisis would unleash forces that would "bring about a compete

political upheaval in Germany" and lead to "extreme nationalists or communists" seizing control of the state. Paul Einzig, *Behind the Scenes of International Finance* (London: Macmillan, 1931), 145.

29. Hans Kohn, "The Totalitarian Crisis," in his *Revolutions and Dictatorships: Essays in Contemporary History* (Cambridge, MA: Harvard University Press, 1939), 355 (quotes throughout this paragraph).

30. Though a gloomy analyst might suggest the phenomenon of Vichy France is less sui generous.

31. Among these oversimplifications is that the order, which was often disorderly and obviously not comprehensive, unfolded in two different phases, each characterized by distinct political contexts, material and ideational underpinnings, and which were interrupted by an unsteady but still U.S.-centric interlude in the dozen or so years from 1973 to 1985. On these issues and more, see Peter Katzenstein and Jonathan Kirshner, eds., *The Downfall of the American Order?* (Ithaca: Cornell University Press, 2022).

32. Charles P. Kindleberger, *The World in Depression, 1929–1939* (Berkeley: University of California Press, 1973), 292. Kindleberger's argument was, unintentionally, still another devastating indictment of structuralist augments. Once again, classical realism has this right: structure informs, purpose determines.

33. On the achievements of the American postwar order, see G. John Ikenberry, *A World Safe for Democracy: Liberal Internationalism and the Crises of Global Order* (New Haven: Yale University Press, 2020), chap. 6 ("The Rise of Liberal Hegemony"), and also G. John Ikenberry, *Liberal Leviathan: The Origins, Crisis, and Transformation of the American World Order* (Princeton: Princeton University Press, 2012), e.g., 2–3. Ikenberry is a prominent liberal scholar, which once again calls attention to the limits of forcing intellectual confrontations between contrasting paradigms. If the U.S. postwar project had an advertising campaign, its slogan might easily have been: "The American order—it's not just for liberals!"

34. Aron, *The Committed Observer*, 246; Robert F. Colquhoun, *Raymond Aron—Volume 1: The Philosopher in History 1905–1955* (Beverly Hills, CA: SAGE Publications, 1986), 283, 472.

35. John Foster Dulles, "The Allied Debts," *Foreign Affairs* (September 1922); for a brief overview of U.S. trade policy follies and failures, see Kindleberger, *World in Depression*, 131–35.

36. Franklin D. Roosevelt, State of the Union Address, January 6, 1945; U.S. Senate, Congressional Record, 79th Cong., 1st Sess. 91:6 (July 23, 1945), p. 7954 (Connolly).

37. Raymond F. Mikesell, "The Bretton Woods Debates: A Memoir," *Essays in International Finance* 192 (March 1994), International Finance Section, Princeton University, p. 43; "The Anti-Inflation Program of the American Bankers Association," *Banking* 40:8 (1948): 33 (quote); Thomas G. Paterson, *Soviet-American Confrontation: Postwar Reconstruction and the Origins of the Cold War* (Baltimore: Johns Hopkins University Press, 1973), 150; Michael Hogan, *The Marshall Plan: America, Britain, and the Reconstruction of Western Europe* (Cambridge: Cambridge University Press, 1987), esp. 443–44; Barry Eichengreen, *The European Economy since 1945* (Princeton: Princeton University Press, 2007), 45–46, 65–70; Fred I. Kent, "Are We Coddling Socialism Abroad, Too?" *Banking* 41:12 (1949): 33.

38. Robert Jervis, "The Impact of the Korean War on the Cold War," *Journal of Conflict Resolution* 24:2 (1980): 563–92; Thomas Christensen, *Worse than a Monolith: Alliance Politics and Problems of Coercive Diplomacy in Asia* (Princeton: Princeton University Press, 2011), 28ff.; also Aaron Friedberg, *In the Shadow of the Garrison State: America's Anti-Statism and Its Cold War Grand Strategy* (Princeton: Princeton University Press, 2000).

39. Taft had earlier opposed lend-lease aid to Britain and the repeal of the Neutrality Act in November 1941. Geoffrey Matthews, "Robert A. Taft, the Constitution and American Foreign Policy, 1939–53," *Journal of Contemporary History* 17 (1982): 507–22. See also Geir Lundestad, "Empire by Invitation? The United States and Western Europe, 1945–1952," *Journal of Peace Research* 23:3 (1986): 263–77, and Michael Hogan, *A Cross of Iron: Harry S. Truman and the Origins of the National Security State, 1945–1954* (Cambridge: Cambridge University Press, 1998). John Gerard Ruggie, "International Regimes, Transactions, and Change: Embedded Liberalism in the Postwar Economic Order," *International Organization* 36:2 (1982): 393; see also Jonathan Kirshner, "Keynes and the Elusive Middle Way," in *Downfall of the American Order?*, ed. Katzenstein and Kirshner.

40. International competition was going to put greater pressure on American labor with or without agreements like NAFTA, as the Springsteen doctrine, articulated in 1985, made clear: "Foreman says these jobs are going, boys, and they ain't coming back." Bruce Springsteen, "My Home Town," from *Born in the USA*.

41. In 1974, the midst of the first oil crisis, Treasury Secretary William Simon traveled to Saudi Arabia and reached a secret agreement that assured the Saudis would "recycle" their overflowing petrodollars into U.S. government securities and arranged for the Saudis to buy U.S. Treasury instruments secretly and outside of normal market channels. (Despite the economic logic of a global oil market run on dollars, American elites saw the need for politics to ensure what markets might possibly not.) In exchange the United States agreed to more intimate military cooperation with the Kingdom and, most likely, an American security guarantee. During the second oil shock, Carter Treasury Secretary W. Michael Blumenthal reached another secret deal, this time to assure that oil would continue to be priced in dollars; presumably, once again, security commitments were the quid pro quo on hand. David E. Spiro, *The Hidden Hand of American Hegemony: Petrodollar Recycling and International Markets* (Ithaca: Cornell University Press, 1999), x, 109–12, 124, 148; see also Andrea Wong, "The Untold Story behind Saudi Arabia's 41-Year U.S. Debt Secret," *Bloomberg*, May 30, 2016. It should be noted that as a result of the very high levels of secrecy associated with these agreements, demanded by both sides, which shielded even top officials within the U.S. government from knowledge of the specifics, scholars have yet to uncover a "smoking gun" document that makes reference to an explicit security guarantee in exchange for these dollar arrangements. The Simon and Blumenthal missions, however, and the pattern (and special nature of) Saudi treasury holdings are well documented.

42. As one leading international journalist reports, the Saudis "fear that the shale revolution in the United States is gradually removing the underlying rationale for an American commitment to the security of Saudi Arabia." Gideon Rachman, *Easternization: Asia's Rise and America's Decline* (New York: Other Press, 2016), 166 (quote), 167.

43. To make the counterfactual explicit, it is much less likely that the United States would come to the rescue of Kuwait in 2025 than it did in 1991 (and even then the decision to authorize war was very closely debated at the time), because the center of political gravity in the country about the wisdom of such a war will have changed, based on the perceived lessons of recent relevant experience.

44. Kenneth Waltz, "The Emerging Structure of International Politics," *International Security* 18:2 (1993): 76. Waltz anticipated that it would be the Germans that would want out: "Some hope that NATO will serve as an instrument for constraining a new Germany. But once the new Germany finds its feet, it will no more want to be constrained by the United States acting through NATO than by any other state" (76).

45. The United States could remain in NATO while slashing its military spending, and a withdrawal from the alliance would unlikely be met with commensurate reductions in American defense spending.

46. Sheryle Bagwell, "France Bridles at U.S. 'Hyperpower,'" *Financial Review*, November 11, 1999; "America's World," *Economist*, October 23, 1999; Stephen Brooks and William Wohlforth, *World Out of Balance: International Relations and the Challenge of American Primacy* (Princeton: Princeton University Press, 2008), 3.

47. Samuel Huntington, "The Lonely Superpower," *Foreign Affairs* 78:2 (1999): 36.

48. Stephan Klasen, "Growth and Well-being: Introducing Distribution-Weighted Growth Rates to Reevaluate US Postwar Economic Performance," *Review of Income and Wealth* 40:3 (1994): 251–72; see also Jonathan Kirshner, "The Political Economy of Low Inflation," *Journal of Economic Surveys* 15:1 (2001): 41–70.

49. Lynn Stout, *The Shareholder Value Myth: How Putting Shareholders First Harms Investors, Corporations, and the Public* (San Francisco: Berrett-Koehler, 2012); Robert Frank and Phillip Cook, *The Winner Take All Society* (New York: Free Press, 1995). On the politics and consequences of the shift to the center by the Democratic Party, see Jonathan Kirshner, *American Power after the Financial Crisis* (Ithaca: Cornell University Press, 2014), and Rawi Abdelal, "Of Learning and Forgetting: Centrism, Populism, and the Legitimacy Crisis of Globalization," in *Downfall of the American Order?*, ed. Katzenstein and Kirshner.

50. Alan Greenspan, "Economic Flexibility," remarks before the National Italian American Foundation, Washington, DC, October 12, 2005 (quote); see also Alan Greenspan, *Age of Turbulence* (New York: Penguin Press, 2007), 360, 367, 368, 371, 492. This was, of course, pompous, presumptive, and catastrophically wrong. See, for example, Charles P. Kindleberger, *Manias, Panics, and Crashes: A History of Financial Crises* (New York: Basic Books, 1978), and Carmen Reinhart and Kenneth Rogoff, *This Time It Is Different: Eight Centuries of Financial Folly* (Princeton: Princeton University Press, 2009).

51. Richard Hofstadter, *The Paranoid Style in American Politics, and Other Essays* (New York: Knopf, 1964), 4; Brown, *The Embrace of Unreason*, 90. The enduring social-political consequences of the aftermath of the global financial crisis in the United States are not to be underestimated; the alienation of much of the country contrasts with elites that remain tone-deaf to implications of their self-satisfaction. In their joint, self-congratulatory memoir of the crisis, Ben Bernanke, Tim Geithner, and Hank Paulson obtusely and repeatedly express frustration that regular folks don't seem to understand that the bailouts were ultimately paid back, and thus did not come at the expense of

the average taxpayer. What they seem to overlook is that those who caused the global financial crisis bore few if any costs, and soon returned to business as usual, while average American families were left to endure the long, difficult great recession. Ben S. Bernanke, Timothy Geithner, and Henry Paulson Jr., *Firefighting: The Financial Crisis and Its Lessons* (New York: Penguin, 2019). For essential correctives, see Martin Wolf, *The Shifts and the Shocks: What We've Learned—and Have Still to Learn—from the Financial Crisis* (New York: Penguin, 2014), and Adam Tooze, *Crashed: How a Decade of Financial Crises Changed the World* (New York: Viking, 2018).

52. It might be suggested that with the election of President Biden in 2020, U.S. foreign policy could "return to normal." But this fails to appreciate the extent to which the Trump presidency was epiphenomenal, and reflective of fundamental, underlying changes in American society. In addition, the rest of the world must now assess that the U.S. political system can easily produce such leadership, and must hedge their bets accordingly. See Jonathan Kirshner, "Gone but Not Forgotten: Trump's Long Shadow and the End of American Credibility," *Foreign Affairs* 100:2 (2021): 18–26.

INDEX

A NOTE ON THE TYPE

THIS BOOK has been composed in Miller, a Scotch Roman typeface designed by Matthew Carter and first released by Font Bureau in 1997. It resembles Monticello, the typeface developed for The Papers of Thomas Jefferson in the 1940s by C. H. Griffith and P. J. Conkwright and reinterpreted in digital form by Carter in 2003.

Pleasant Jefferson ("P. J.") Conkwright (1905–1986) was Typographer at Princeton University Press from 1939 to 1970. He was an acclaimed book designer and AIGA Medalist.

The ornament used throughout this book was designed by Pierre Simon Fournier (1712–1768) and was a favorite of Conkwright's, used in his design of the *Princeton University Library Chronicle*.